W9-CHP-380

KEEPING CURRENT WITH

TEXAS
REAL ESTATE MCE
2012–2013

CHARLES J. JACOBUS

DREI, CREI

•

JOSEPH E. GOETERS

HOUSTON COMMUNITY COLLEGE

CENGAGE
Learning

Australia • Brazil • Japan • Korea • Mexico • Singapore • Spain • United Kingdom • United States

Keeping Current with Texas Real Estate MCE, 11e
Charles J. Jacobus and Joseph E. Goeters

VP/Editorial Director: Dave Shaut

Acquisitions Editor: Sara Glassmeyer

Developmental Editor: Arlin Kauffman, LEAP
Publishing Services

Marketing Director: Diane Buckley Jones

Art and Cover Direction, Production Management,
and Composition: PreMediaGlobal

Rights Acquisition Specialist, Text and Image: Amber
Hosea

Senior Manufacturing Planner: Charlene Taylor

Cover Image(s):

Far left: (inside of dome): © Brandon Seidel /
Shutterstock

Center photo (capitol building): ©Suzannah Skelton/
Istockphoto

Far right (gate and building): © James W. Stoneham/
Istockphoto

© 2013, 2011 Cengage Learning

ALL RIGHTS RESERVED. No part of this work covered by the copyright
hereon may be reproduced or used in any form or by any means—graphic,
electronic, or mechanical, including photocopying, recording, taping, Web
distribution, information storage and retrieval systems, or in any other
manner—except as may be permitted by the license terms herein.

For product information and technology assistance, contact us at
Cengage Learning Customer & Sales Support, 1-800-354-9706

For permission to use material from this text or product,
submit all requests online at **www.cengage.com/permissions**
Further permissions questions can be emailed to
permissionrequest@cengage.com

Library of Congress Control Number: 2011944787

ISBN-13: 978-1-133-36472-6
ISBN-10: 1-133-36472-1

Cengage Learning
5191 Natorp Boulevard
Mason, OH 45040
USA

Cengage Learning products are represented in Canada by
Nelson Education, Ltd.

For your course and learning solutions, visit **academic.cengage.com**
Purchase any of our products at your local college store or at our preferred
online store **www.cengagebrain.com**

Printed in the United States of America
1 2 3 4 5 6 7 15 14 13 12 11

ACC LIBRARY SERVICES AUSTIN, TX

Contents

Foreword

Chapters 1 and 2 of this book contain mandatory TREC material. They consist of three hours of legal update and another three hours of ethics. All licensees are required to receive this same, up-to-date information. Instructors are required to be certified to teach the courses.

Chapter 3 is an extended discussion on legal topics by the authors. Chapter 4 focuses on finance and Chapter 5 on Environmental Issues in Real Estate (all approved to complete the full 15 hour required MCE).

Updates to this material can be found on the website for this text, www.cengage.com/real-estate/jacobus.

We cannot emphasize enough…education for professionals is ongoing; there is always more to learn; things keep changing. That's what makes this business so exciting. Thank you for participating.

Chuck Jacobus

Joe Goeters

Texas Real Estate Commission

MCE
Legal
Update

Edition 5.0

Acknowledgments

Real Estate Center Staff

Gary W. Maler, Director
David S. Jones, Communications Director
Robert P. Beals II, Art Director
Denise Whisenant, Education Coordinator

MCE Writing Group

Loretta Dehay
Tom Morgan
Charles Jacobus
Philip Schoewe
Ron Walker
Reid Wilson
Avis Wukasch

Texas Real Estate Commission

Douglas Oldmixon, Administrator
Avis Wukasch, Chair
Joanne Justice, Vice Chair
Jaime Blevins Hensley, Secretary
Troy C. Alley, Jr.
Adrian A. Arriaga
Robert C. Day
Bill Jones
Weston Martinez
Dona Scurry

Real Estate Center Advisory Committee

Joe Bob McCartt, Chairman
Mario A. Arriaga, Vice Chairman
Avis Wukasch, ex-officio
Mona R. Bailey
James M. Boyd
Russell Cain
Jacquelyn K. Hawkins
Kathleen McKenzie Owen
Kimberly A. Shambley
Ronald C. Wakefield

FOREWORD

In cooperation with the Texas Real Estate Commission, the Real Estate Center at Texas A&M University developed this real estate legal update curriculum with the assistance of an advisory committee of active licensees, attorneys and education providers. Real estate licensees are encouraged to acquire additional information and to take courses in specific, applicable topics.

This curriculum has been developed using information from publications, presentations and general research. The information is believed to be reliable, but it cannot be guaranteed insofar as it is applied to any particular individual or situation. The laws discussed in this curriculum have been excerpted, summarized or abbreviated. For a complete understanding and discussion, consult a full version of any pertinent law. This curriculum contains information that can change periodically. This curriculum is presented with the understanding that the authors and instructors are not engaged in rendering legal, accounting or other professional advice. The services of a competent professional with suitable expertise should be sought.

The authors, presenters, advisory committee, Real Estate Center and Texas Real Estate Commission disclaim any liability, loss or risk personal or otherwise, incurred as a consequence directly or indirectly from the use and application of any of the information contained in these materials or the teaching lectures and media presentations given in connection with these materials.

When using this course for three hours of Legal Update MCE credit as required by the Texas Real Estate Commission, this textbook must be reproduced and used in its entirety, without omission or alteration.

Contents _____

Chapter 1

Legislative Changes _____

SB 747: Changes to License Act

Senate Bill 747 amends the Real Estate License Act (the Act) to provide additional education, experience and accountability standards, and cleanup provisions for Texas Real Estate Commission (TREC) licensees.

Educational Requirements for Salesperson License

License education requirements for a salesperson's license changed from 210 total hours to 180 core hours (12 semester hours). The first renewal of a salesperson's license increases the related educational requirements from 60 to 90 core hours so that the total number of hours for the first renewal (2nd year following licensure) of a salesperson's license will remain at 270 hours.

Broker Experience Requirements

An applicant for a broker license would need to have at least 4 years of active experience as a license holder during the preceding 5-year period before the application's file date. Under recently adopted rules implementing SB 747, an applicant may supplement an application with experience gained after the application is filed but before a license is issued.

Broker Responsibility Course

A sponsoring broker or any other licensee who is authorized by a broker to supervise other licensees is required to take a 6-hour Mandatory Broker Responsibility course for each license renewal.

Exams

The first-time examination pass rate benchmark for pre-license education programs has been changed from 55 percent to an average percentage of examinees.

The period in which an applicant must satisfy an examination requirement is increased from 6 months to 1 year.

Educational Programs

An education program accredited by TREC is required to meet or exceed the benchmark for each license category before the program's accreditation renewal for a specific category.

TREC is authorized to deny accreditation of an education program if an applicant owns or controls, or has owned or controlled an educational program that has been revoked.

TREC may now take the same types of disciplinary action against real estate educational programs it accredits as it is authorized to take against educational programs for other types of licenses it regulates.

Broker Accountability Measures

- The exception for licensure is eliminated for a partnership or limited liability partnership acting through a partner who is a licensed broker.
- Any type of business entity that engages in real estate brokerage and that is required to be registered to do business in Texas with the Secretary of State is required to be licensed as a broker.
- The definition of "broker" is clarified to distinguish between brokers and agents who provide written price opinions routinely as part of their services and persons who provide appraisals of real property that require licensure under Occupations Code Chapter 1103.
- The definition of "broker" is amended to include a person who controls the collection or acceptance of rent from a tenant in a single family residential unit.
- An attorney licensed in a state other than Texas is no longer exempt from the requirement to hold a broker or salesperson license.

Housekeeping Measures

- TREC is authorized to solicit and accept gifts, grants and donations.

- Applicants and licensees are now required to provide TREC their current mailing address, telephone number, and email address, if available, and to notify TREC of any changes.
- The maximum period of time in which a person may late renew a license with monetary penalties is decreased from 1 year to 6 months.
- Fingerprinting and background checks are required for an application for or renewal of an easement or right-of-way certificate.

Business Entities

Any business entity (LLC, corporation, partnership) is required to obtain a license if the entity is to receive commissions. The business entity must designate a broker to take responsibility for the conduct of that business entity. If the designated broker of the business entity owns less than 10 percent of the entity, the entity would then be required to obtain errors and omissions insurance of at least $1 million.

SB 1000: Self-Directed, Semi-Independent (SDSI) Agency

SB 1000 establishes TREC and Texas Appraiser Licensing and Certification Board (TALCB) as the state's newest Self-Directed, Semi-Independent (SDSI) agency. TALCB will remain as an independent subdivision of TREC. Their respective enabling acts are not affected, except to effectuate SDSI status, and both will still be subject to the state's open meetings, public information, administrative procedure and other applicable laws. The governor of Texas will continue to appoint commission and board members.

Each agency will adopt an annual budget, set salaries and expenditures, and control the amounts of the fees that they are required or permitted to collect. In short, they will be responsible for all of the direct and indirect costs of their existence and will be prohibited from incurring any costs to be borne by the Texas General Revenue Fund.

SB 1000 also requires the agencies to keep specific statistical and financial records and submit periodic reports to the state legislature and governor disclosing their financial condition, revenue and expense budgets, salaries, regulatory jurisdiction, rules, and other information. The state benefits and retirement system status of agency employees will not be affected.

Some of the other operative features of SB 1000 include:

- continued representation by the Texas Attorney General and payment of an annual minimum $75,000 retainer, plus additional incurred attorneys fees,
- payment of an annual minimum $75,000 retainer to the State Office of Administrative Hearings plus additional incurred hearing fees,
- continued audits by the Texas State Auditor and an annual minimum $10,000 payment for that purpose,
- authority to enter into contracts, acquire, use and dispose of or sell real and personal property, use and operate facilities, and borrow money.

In addition to the minimum retainers and audit payments, TREC will be required to deposit $750,000 annually to the Texas General Revenue Fund. To facilitate the transition to SDSI status, TREC will receive appropriations for fiscal years 2012 and 2013 amounting to 50 percent of its 2011 appropriation. TREC must, however, repay those amounts. TREC is also required to relocate to state-owned offices, which occurred in July of 2011, and pay aggregate rents of not less than $550,000 in fiscal year 2012 and 2013 and $425,000 in fiscal years 2014–2016. The rent for the first 2 years is higher to fulfill state cost recovery requirements for new modular furnishings at the newly redesigned office space.

HB 1146: Regulation of Appraisal Management Companies

HB 1146 requires appraisal management companies to report separately the various fees charged for an appraisal. Compensation to appraisers must be reasonable and customary and be paid not later than 60 days after completion of the appraisal assignment. The appraisal management company will verify that each appraiser receiving an assignment satisfies the USPAP competency rule. To remove an appraiser from the appraisal management company's appraiser panel, it must notify the appraiser of the reason for removal and provide opportunity for the appraiser to respond in writing.

HB 1887, HB 2203: State Office of Administrative Hearings

Effective June 17, 2011, HB 2203 expands the State Office of Administrative Hearings (SOAH) pilot program to allow property owners to resolve property tax disputes through the SOAH. Effective September 1, 2011, CSHB 1887 amends several procedural items relating to property tax protests and makes the protest and appeal process under the Tax Code fairer, more efficient and more effective.

SB 710, HB 3389, HB3391: Seller's Disclosure

Both bills are effective September 2, 2011. SB 710 adds "single blockable main drain in pool or hot tub" to the notice. These drains can trap a person and have been linked to deaths. HB 3389 adds more disclosure detail regarding the gas source of a property fueled by liquid propane gas. HB 3391 amends the notice to require disclosure of any rainwater harvesting system connected to the property's public water supply that can be used for indoor potable purposes

HB 1111, HB 1162, HB 1168, HB 1862: Property Management

Certificate of Occupancy

Effective September 1, 2011, HB 1862 provides remedies to a tenant against a landlord if a municipality or county revokes a certificate of occupancy because of a landlord's failure to maintain the premises.

Pauper's Affidavit

HB 1111 requires the justice court, on request, to issue immediately and without hearing, a writ of possession if a tenant fails to pay the initial rent deposit into the justice court registry within 5 days of the date the tenant filed the pauper's affidavit.

Smoke Alarms and Fire Extinguishers

HB 1168 applies to a home, mobile home, duplex unit, apartment unit, condominium unit, or any dwelling unit in a multi-unit residential structure that is being leased to a tenant. HB 1168 makes state law consistent with model codes by requiring at least 1 smoke alarm to be placed in each bedroom (including efficiency units). In addition, if multiple bedrooms are served by the same hallway, there must be a smoke alarm in the hallway in the immediate vicinity of the bedrooms. If the unit has multiple levels, there must be a smoke alarm on each level. For properties occupied as a residence before September 1, 2011, a smoke alarm may be battery operated and is not required to be interconnected with other smoke alarms. Owners will have until January 1, 2013, to comply. For properties built after September 1, 2011, local ordinances may impose stricter requirements. This legislation does not affect the alternative compliance method for a 1-family or 2-family dwelling unit, which may be satisfied by complying with the local code.

If a landlord has installed a 1A10BC residential fire extinguisher or other non-rechargeable fire extinguisher required by a local ordinance, the landlord must inspect the fire extinguisher at the beginning of the tenant's possession and within a reasonable time after receiving a written request from the tenant. The inspection must determine if the extinguisher is present and the pressure indicator shows that it is filled according to the manufacturer's requirements. A landlord, at the landlord's expense, is required to repair or replace a nonfunctioning fire extinguisher, one that does not have the correct pressure as recommended by the manufacturer, or one the tenant has used for a legitimate purpose.

SB1353: Deceptive Trade Practices Act

The Deceptive Trade Practices Act (DTPA) protects consumers against false, misleading and deceptive business practices. In 1995, the Legislature amended the DTPA by enacting an exemption for the rendering of a professional service. However, no Texas trial court has applied the exemption to real estate licensees. Because DTPA cases carry the threat of triple damages, many licensees have settled out of court.

This bill adds real estate brokerage as a specific exemption to the Deceptive Trade Practices Act in most circumstances. Licensees can still be held liable if they

- committed an unconscionable act,
- misrepresented a material fact, or
- failed to disclose information with the intention of inducing a consumer into a transaction.

HB 2408: Title Insurance Companies and Mandatory Continuing Education (MCE)

Title companies are strictly prohibited from certain marketing activities. HB 2408 amended the Texas Insurance Code §2502.055(a) to provide that title companies are *not* prohibited from

- engaging in promotional and educational activities that are not conditioned on the referral of title insurance business, or
- providing MCE courses at market rates, regardless of whether participants receive credit hours.

Groundwater Ownership

The legislature amended the Water Code to clarify that groundwater below the surface of the owner's land is real property. The landowner may drill for groundwater provided he or she does not cause waste or malicious drainage to other property or negligently cause subsidence. The amended code does not, however, entitle an owner to capture a specific amount of groundwater below the surface. If the property is located in a water district, the landowner has to comply with all the rules of that district (Texas Water Code, §36.002).

Chapter 2

Hot Topics

Choice of Title Company

Section 9 of the Real Estate Settlement and Procedures Act (RESPA), provides that no seller of property that will be purchased with the assistance of a federally related mortgage shall require directly or indirectly, as a condition to selling the property, that title insurance be purchased by the buyer from any particular title company. Buyers may sue a seller who violates this provision for an amount equal to 3 times all charges made for the title insurance. While a licensee might have a preferred title company or closer, the choice of the title company must be made by the buyer.

Residential Real Property Affidavit T-47

Under the Texas Real Estate Commission's promulgated contract forms, the survey contingency [Paragraph 6.C.(1)] has a provision for the seller to provide the seller's existing survey to the potential buyer for review. The contingency, however, provides that the survey must be acceptable to the title company and the buyer's lender.

The seller is also obliged to provide an Affidavit Form T-47, which is promulgated by the Texas Department of Insurance. This affidavit requires that the seller, under oath, swear that no easements have been granted on the property and that no material change exists in the structures, fence, structures on adjoining properties, conveyances, or replats.

The TREC One-to-Four Family Contract form [Paragraph 6.A.(8)] provides that the buyer, at buyer's expense, may have the exception for encroachments amended to read "shortages in area" only. The buyer may require that the title company delete the exception for encroachment and overlapping improvements under Schedule B.2 of the title commitment. This deletion provides the buyer title coverage for any discrepancies or encroachments on the property.

Paragraph 6.C.(1) of the contract form provides that within the specified time, the seller is to deliver both a copy of the existing survey and the notarized affidavit to the buyer. To comply fully with the paragraph, the seller must timely deliver both items.

Homeowner Associations

HOA Form 36-6 Changes in 2010

The amendments to Form No. 36-6, Addendum for Property Subject to Mandatory Membership in a Property Owners Association are as follows: Subparagraph A.2 is revised to add a reference to providing an updated resale certificate; new paragraph C is added regarding deposits for reserves. However, additional changes are expected in light of legislative changes discussed below.

Notice of Membership in a Property Owners Association

This statute was expanded by the 2011 legislature to change the format of the notice of mandatory HOA membership under Section 5.012 of the Property Code. The notice must contain language that informs the owner that he or she is entitled to receive copies of any documents that govern the establishment, maintenance and operation of the subdivision. This includes restrictions, by-laws, rules and regulations, and resale certificates. That portion of the disclosure must be in bold print and underlined. TREC's Form 36-6 should soon be amended to reflect these changes.

Fee Payments

An HOA governing over 14 lots must adopt reasonable guidelines for an alternative payment schedule with partial payments owed without penalties with a minimum term of 3 months and not more than 18 months.

HOA Foreclosures

Members of Military

If the HOA intends to foreclose on a member in the active military service, the HOA must also provide a special notice, in conspicuous and in bold face or underlined type, notifying the owner he or she may exercise his or her rights under the Soldiers and Sailors Relief Act [§51.002(i)].

Assessment Lien

A HOA may not foreclose a lien against a property for an association assessment unless the association first obtains a court order in an application for expedited foreclosure under the rules adopted by the Texas Supreme Court. The expedited foreclosure is not required if the owner of the property agrees in writing at the time the foreclosure is sought to waive the expedited foreclosure. The waiver may not be required as a condition of the transfer of title to the property (§209.0092).

Removal from Dedicatory Instrument

A provision granting the right to foreclosure a lien on real property for unpaid amounts due to an HOA may be removed from a dedicatory instrument if it is approved by at least 67 percent of the total votes of property owners.

Opportunity to Cure for Lienholders

An HOA may not foreclose an assessment lien by an out-of-court foreclosure proceeding unless the HOA has provided written notice of the total amount of the delinquency to any recorded, subordinate deed of trust holder and given 60 days to cure.

Open Records

Records

HOA books and records must be reasonably available for examination and copying. The HOA board must adopt and record a records production and copying policy.

If the HOA governs over 14 lots, it must adopt a document retention policy with specified requirements.

Meetings

HOA meetings must be open to owners. Executive sessions (closed to owners) are permissible only for issues relating to personnel, litigation, contract negotiations, enforcement actions, or confidential communications. Notice of HOA board meetings to all members is required at least 72 hours before the meeting.

Votes must be in writing and signed by the member but may also be electronic. All owners may vote and run for the HOA board, notwithstanding dedicatory instruments that purport to prohibit or limit their rights.

Website Access

Any HOA website must contain all recorded dedicatory instruments.

Prohibited Restrictions

Flags

Flags of the USA, the State of Texas, or any branch of the United States armed forces may not be prohibited, but they may be reasonably regulated (Property Code §202.011).

Roof Solar Panels

A solar energy device may not be prohibited unless it threatens the public health or safety or violates a federal or state law, but it may be reasonably regulated.

Religious Symbols

A religious symbol display may not be prohibited, but it may be reasonably regulated.

Speed Feedback Signs

An HOA may install a speed feedback sign as long as the HOA receives the consent of the local subdivision's governing body and the HOA pays for the sign's installation.

Private Transfer Fees

In the past, some developers have charged a "transfer fee," usually about 1 percent of the sales price of the property, which is paid every time a property is transferred. The issue is that there are no services performed for this fee. It is often categorized as a payment to a "foundation," which is owned and controlled by the developer, and the developer is creating an income stream in perpetuity for no services performed.

A private transfer fee is now defined by statute as an amount of money that is payable, regardless of the method used to determine the amount, on the transfer of an interest in real property or payable for a right to make or accept a transfer. A private transfer fee created after September 1, 2011, is not binding or enforceable against a subsequent owner or subsequent purchase of the property. The restriction does not prohibit payment by the purchaser to the seller for real property or mineral interests, commissions to real estate brokers, fees charged by lenders, fees charged by HOAs, and some charitable organizations.

If there is a private transfer fee created before September 1, 2011, the recipient of the fee must file a "Notice of Private Transfer Fee Obligation" to continue collecting it. The notice must be at least 14-point bold-face type and state the

- amount of the transfer fee,
- purpose for which the money from the private transfer fee obligation will be used, and
- legal description of the property subject to the private transfer fee obligation.

The notice must be re-filed every 3 years and reflect any changes that may have occurred within that 3-year period. Disclosure of the existing transfer fee is also required in the contract for sale to provide written notice to potential purchasers that the obligation may be governed by this new statutory provision (Property Code §5.01).

One-to-Four Family Contract Proposed revisions at the October 10, 2011 TREC meeting

The proposed revisions to Standard Contract Form TREC No. 20-11, One to Four Family Residential Contract (Resale) are as follows:

- paragraph 6.B. is amended to add a sentence regarding the buyer's ability to terminate the contract if the commitment and exception documents are not delivered within the time required, which was deleted from paragraph 15;
- paragraph 6.D. is amended to add the phrase "by Buyer" to the sentence regarding waiver of Buyer's right to object to defects, exceptions or encumbrances to title;
- paragraph 6.E.(2) is amended to add additional disclosures required by amendments to §207.003, Property Code;
- new subparagraph 6.E.(8) adds a new statutory disclosure regarding private transfer fee obligations;
- paragraph 7.A. is amended to require a seller to have utilities turned on and keep them on while the contract is in effect;
- paragraph 7.E. is amended to change a phrase regarding the buyer's remedies if the seller fails to complete agreed repairs and treatments prior to the closing date; the new text provides that the buyer may exercise remedies under paragraph 15 or extend the closing date up to 15 days;
- paragraph 15 is amended to delete the sentence regarding seller's failure to make non-casualty repairs or deliver the commitment or survey (the sentence was moved to paragraph 6.B.).

The amendments to TREC No. 9-10, Unimproved Property Contract are the same as those proposed for TREC Form No. 20-9, except that the transfer fee notice is new subparagraph 6.E.(9).

The amendments to TREC No. 23-12, New Home Contract (Incomplete Construction) are the same as those proposed for TREC Form No. 20-9, except that there are no amendments to paragraphs 7.A. or 7.E.

The amendments to TREC No. 24-10, New Home Contract (Completed Construction) are the same as those proposed for TREC Form No. 20-9.

The amendments to TREC No. 25-7, Farm and Ranch Contract are the same as those proposed for TREC Form No. 20-9, except that paragraph 6.E.2 is not amended.

The amendments to TREC No. 30-8, Residential Condominium Contract are the same as those proposed for TREC Form No. 20-9, except that paragraph 6.E.2 is not amended and the transfer fee notice is new subparagraph 6.D.(6).

The amendments TREC No. 37-4, Subdivision Information, Including Resale Certificate for Property Subject to Mandatory Membership in a Property Owners' Association are that Paragraphs D, H, and I are amended to more closely track recent statutory changes to Chapter 207, Property Code.

The amendment to TREC No. 39-7, Amendment to Contract - Paragraph (8) is changed to reference the correct title of the Third Party Financing Condition Addendum for Credit Approval.

Joint Tenancy

Case Study

Holmes v. Beatty,
290 S.W. 3ᵈ 852 (Tex., 2009)

Thomas and Kathryn Holmes were married in 1972. During their marriage, they amassed over $10 million in brokerage accounts and securities certificates. Kathryn died in 1999. Her will appointed Douglas Beatty, her son from a previous marriage, as independent executor of her estate. Thomas died about 9 months later. His son, Harry Holmes II, also from a previous marriage, was appointed independent executor of Thomas' estate.

All of the accounts and certificates were variously listed as "JT Ten"; "JT WROS," which indicated that all of the accounts were established as joint tenants with right of survivorship, not as tenants in common.

There was a question as to whether or not those short-hand designations were enough to pass title as joint tenant with right of survivorship.

Beatty wanted a declaratory judgment that all of the assets were community property. Holmes argued that the assets passed to Thomas through right of survivorship so that none of Kathryn's children inherited anything.

The trial court concluded that some of the assets were held jointly with right of survivorship and others were community property. The court of appeals affirmed in part and reversed in part.

The Texas Supreme court reaffirmed that the only way a couple can create survivorship rights is to partition their community property into separate property and then agreeing to hold it as joint tenants with right of survivorship. In opening the accounts, they both signed the agreement, and "JT. TEN" appeared next to both signatures on the signature lines. The court held that this was sufficient to create joint tenancy with right of survivorship. The court further held that the agreement to hold property as joint tenants can be revoked only by another agreement.

HB 10: New Registration for Mortgage Originators, Texas Secure and Fair Enforcement for Mortgage Licensing Act

HB 10 was passed to comply with the Federal Secure and Fair Enforcement of Mortgage Licensing Act (SAFE). Under SAFE, a residential mortgage loan originator who is an employee or subsidiary of a depository institution will be registered with the federal banking agency having jurisdiction over that institution and will be included in the Nationwide Mortgage Licensing System. All other residential mortgage loan originators (mortgage brokers and mortgage bankers) are subject to state licensing and regulation.

A residential mortgage loan originator is defined as an individual who, for compensation or gain or any expectation of compensation or gain, takes a residential mortgage loan application or offers or negotiates the terms of a residential mortgage loan. It does not include

- a person who performs solely administrative or clerical tasks on behalf of the residential loan originator,
- a person who performs only real estate brokerage activities (unless that person is compensated by a lender or agent of the lender), or
- a person who is involved solely in providing extensions of credit related to timeshare plans.

The statute exempts
- a registered mortgage loan originator acting for a depository institution,
- a person who offers or negotiates a residential mortgage for an immediate family member,
- a licensed attorney who negotiates the terms of a residential mortgage loan on behalf of a client, (unless the attorney takes a residential mortgage loan application and offers or negotiates the terms of the loan),
- a person who is an exclusive agent of a registered financial services company,
- a person who offers or negotiates the terms of a residential loan secured by his own residence, and
- a non-profit organization providing self-help housing that originates zero interest residential loans.

The statute also requires applicants to complete education requirements and meet surety bond requirements (or pay a recovery fund fee). A residential mortgage loan originator's unique identifier is to be shown clearly on each loan application form, solicitation, advertisement, and other documents. A mortgage loan originator must comply with reporting requirements.

The new law sets forth other specific prohibited acts and practices and gives enforcement powers to the Finance Commission including
- suspending or revoking licenses,
- ordering restitution,
- imposing an administrative penalty, and
- issuing cease and desist orders.

Executory Contracts, Contracts for Deed, & Lease-Purchase Agreements

The 2005 legislature made additional efforts to protect consumers in transactions involving executory contracts. In the statute, an executory contract is a contract involving the sale of a residence in which closing occurs later than 180 days after execution. The Property Code considers lease-purchases to be executory contracts and treats them in much the same way as contracts-for-deed. An option to buy that includes, is combined, or is executed concurrently with a residential lease is an executory contract under the law.

Under an executory contract, there are significant penalties for a seller who does not strictly comply with Subchapter D of Chapter 5 of the Property Code. Do not attempt to use TREC forms or other such standard forms to create lease-purchase or lease-option contracts. Do not attempt to write a lease-option clause into a standard residential lease agreement. TREC does not promulgate standard forms for executory contracts. Real estate licensees should advise clients and customers to seek an attorney's assistance before entering an executory contract, contract-for-deed, lease-purchase contract, or a lease-option contract.

Case Study

Schultz v. Taylor
(10th Court of Appeals, Waco, unreported)

> Seller used a lease form to create a lease-purchase contract. Buyer did not exercise option to buy and requested deposit refund, ending the lease. Seller argued deposit was a down payment on purchase and non-refundable. Trial court entered judgment for tenant that contract was a lease. Appeals court upheld trial court's judgment.

In 2005, Schultz and the Taylors signed an agreement entitled "Residential Lease." The pre-printed form contained handwritten additions and deletions. The agreement stated that Schultz would lease the Taylors a home whose monthly rent would be $1,900. Under "Security Deposit," it provided that on or before execution of the lease, Tenant would pay a $10,000 security deposit to Landlord. However, "non-refundable" was written in. The form's preprinted language states "Refund: Tenant must give Landlord at least thirty (30) days written notice of surrender before Landlord is obligated to refund or account for the security deposit."

The "Special Provisions" section of the form included the following, which was handwritten:

> This is an owner-financed property. Sold as-is for $199000.00. $10,000 down payment. $2000 at signing (2/22/2005) $8000.00 due in 90 days (5/22/2005), otherwise re-negotiated by seller & buyer by (8/22/2005).
> Buyer will obtain own financing by March 07 for a sales price of 186425.00. If for some reason buyer cannot obtain own financing, we will renegociate [sic] owner financing, at that time. Reguardless [sic] of how financing is settled, buyers are purchasing home.

Schultz testified that a "realtor friend" prepared the agreement. She told her friend that she and the Taylors were "doing a lease-to-own." The Taylors were not able to obtain financing; therefore, she had given them two years to resolve their credit issues. Schultz believed

at the time the Taylors signed the agreement, they had purchased the property from her. She testified that although the agreement provides that the Taylors were to pay $1,900 per month in rent to her, they were actually making a mortgage payment to her, which was the same amount as her own monthly mortgage payment on the property. Her friend added "non-refundable" in the "Security Deposit" section of the agreement, because Schultz was selling the property to the Taylors, and the $10,000 was a non-refundable down payment.

Schultz received the $1,900 monthly payments through August 2006. In September 2006, the Taylors advised Schultz they could not obtain financing and could no longer afford the payment and were moving out. The Taylors requested a refund of their security deposit. Schultz told the Taylors that she would not be able to refund. At the end of September, 2006, new tenants moved into the house and lived in it approximately 3 months. Schultz had no more tenants after they left, and the property eventually went into foreclosure.

The Taylors testified that the agreement they signed was a lease with an option to buy. Although they referred to the payment as a down payment, the $10,000 was just a deposit. If they decided to purchase the house, then the money would serve as a down payment; however, before the purchase, the money was a deposit.

The trial court entered a judgment in favor of the Taylors for $8,100 (not $10,000) with prejudgment interest at 4.52 percent from the date the suit was filed together with all costs of court. The defendant is entitled to an offset in the amount of $1,900 only for September rent payment. The case was appealed by Schultz, and the appeals court upheld the trial court's judgment.

Changes to the Fair Credit Reporting Act Affect Property Managers

The 2010 Dodd-Frank Wall Street Reform Act amended the Fair Credit Reporting Act (FCRA). The FCRA already requires a landlord to provide an applicant with notice of any adverse action (Adverse Action Notice) taken based on information obtained from the applicant's consumer report. The amendment goes a step further by requiring the disclosure of an applicant's credit score when the adverse action is based in whole or in part on the applicant's credit score.

What does this mean for property managers?

If adverse action is based on an applicant's credit score, the property manager must adhere to the credit score disclosure requirements. An adverse action includes any action taken that is unfavorable to the applicant, which may include denying an applicant or requiring a higher security deposit.

How to comply?

The property manager must disclose the following:
- the numerical credit score used in making the credit decision,
- the range of possible credit scores under any screening,
- the top 4 key factors that adversely affected the applicant's credit score (or the top 5 if the "number of inquiries" made with respect to that consumer report is a key factor),
- the date on which the credit score was created, and
- the name of the person or entity that provided the credit score.

When are the credit score disclosure requirements not applicable?

If a property manager uses other information in an applicant's consumer report but not the credit score on which to base the decision, he or she will not be subject to the credit score disclosure requirements. The property manager still has to provide the Adverse Action Notice that was already required under the FCRA. If the property manager uses a tenant-screening company that creates its own model that is not a credit score, he or she is not subject to the credit score disclosure requirements.

HUD Interpretive Rule on Residential Service Companies and Disclosure Form

On June 25th, HUD published an Interpretive Rule under RESPA involving services provided by real estate brokers and agents on behalf of home warranty companies. The Interpretive Rule discusses the application of Section 8(a)'s prohibition on referral fees in relation to payments made by home warranty companies to real estate brokers. The Interpretive Rule concludes that
- A payment by a home warranty company for marketing services performed by real estate brokers on behalf of the home warranty company that are directly related to particular buyers or sellers is an illegal kickback for a referral under Section 8. HUD bases this conclusion on the fact that a real estate agent is in a unique position to refer settlement service business and, as they hold a position of influence, can easily influence

a buyer's or seller's selection of a home warranty company.
- Depending on the case, a home warranty company may compensate a real estate broker for services when those services are actual, necessary, and distinct from the primary services provided by the real estate broker, and when those additional services are not nominal and are not services for which there is a duplicate charge. HUD offers some examples of such additional services, which include, among others:
  - conducting annual inspections of the items to be covered by the warranty to identify pre-existing conditions that could affect home warranty coverage, and
  - recording serial numbers of the items to be covered.

HUD also provides guidance on the types of evidence that would support a determination that compensable services have been performed by the real estate broker, such as that the services to be performed are specified in a contract between the home warranty company and the real estate broker or agent, and the home warranty company assumes responsibility for any representations made by the broker or agent about the warranty product.
- The amount of the compensation that is permitted under Section 8 for such additional services must be reasonably related to the value of those services and may not include compensation for referrals of business. The Interpretive Rule does not provide much guidance on this point, other than to cite language in Policy Statement 99-1, which covers mortgage broker compensation, regarding how HUD analyzes compensation to determine reasonableness. Brokers with "exclusive" agreements with a home warranty company should have the agreements reviewed by an attorney, especially when the fees paid to the broker are based on the number of residential service contracts purchased by the broker's clients. (TREC *Advisor* 2010)

Case Study

Busby v. JRHBW Realty, Inc.

[513 F.3d 1314 (N.D. Ala. 2009]

> The use of "administrative" or "transaction" fees by brokers in listing or buyer representation agreements may violate RESPA provision as an unearned fee.
>
> Class action against broker. Trial court refused to certify case. Court of Appeals remanded to certify class. Trial court then held administrative fee violated RESPA.

A buyer purchased a home from a broker using a federally insured loan. A fee (administrative brokerage commission, $149) was charged to the buyer at closing. The fee was in addition to the commission paid by the seller. It was the broker's practice to charge both buyers and sellers the fee.

The buyer filed a lawsuit against the broker and sought to have the lawsuit certified as a class action involving all other sellers and buyers who had been charged the fee by the broker. The buyer reasoned that the fee was a violation of the Real Estate Settlement Procedures Act (RESPA).

The trial court denied the motion for class certification. The appellate court reversed the trial court. The trial court then certified the lawsuit as a class action.

The trial court found that the broker had not identified settlement services that supported charging the fee, stating that unearned fees are when "...duplicative work is done, or the fee is in excess of the reasonable value of goods or facilities provided or the services actually performed." The court disagreed with the broker's characterization that the fee was charged to recover costs for an array of brokerage services, such as regulatory compliance costs, office facilities, and website enhancements. The court ruled that the "array" of services mentioned was not settlement related.

The court also ruled that many of the identified services were covered by the broker's commission paid at closing; the fee constituted a duplication of the commission. The court entered judgment in favor of the buyer and the class.

Case Studies

Chapter 3

Boehl v. Boley

2011 WL 238348 (Tex. App. –Amarillo, 2011)

To prevail on a case alleging the failure to disclose a known defect or a misrepresentation about a defect, the plaintiff must prove the defendant had actual knowledge of the defect. The parties and the brokers are entitled to recover attorney fees under the attorney fees provision in the TREC contract forms.

The trial court granted summary judgment for broker and seller and, after a bench trial, also awarded attorney fees for both broker and seller.

In Boehl vs. Boley, et al., the Boehls sought damages arising from misrepresentations and omissions with respect to the home they bought from Boley. The parties used a One-to-Four Family Texas TREC form. Prior to signing the contract, the seller told the buyer that everything in his home worked, the water well had 280 feet of water in it, and he had not had any problems with the well. Within a month after closing, the buyer began experiencing shortages of water. A further investigation revealed that the well was going dry and needed extensive repairs. The buyer sued for fraud, DTPA violations, fraudulent inducement, negligent and fraudulent representations, and breach of contract.

The seller responded by saying the property was an "as is" sale, and the court granted summary judgment for the seller. The court reconfirmed a long line of Texas cases stating that the TREC contract, using the language "in its present condition," has been construed to be an "as is" agreement. The court further noted that both parties were represented by real estate agents and that the buyer paid extra for an option to withdraw from the transaction (Paragraph 23). The court found no evidence illustrating that the seller knew the actual condition of the well and further noted that the buyer did not have the well inspected.

The trial court awarded attorney fees to the listing broker when it found that the broker was the prevailing party and owed no damages to the buyers, citing the TREC form "the prevailing party in any legal proceeding relating to this contract is entitled to recover reasonable attorney fees and all costs of such proceeding incurred by the prevailing party." The court held that such language permits real estate brokers to recover attorney fees as long as they are the prevailing party in a legal proceeding related to the contract. The court noted that since the contract was an "as is" contract, which was used as a defense by the sellers and the brokers, it was clearly related to the contract.

Joseph v. James

2009 WL 3682608 (Tex. App. –Austin, 2009)

> Offers and counter-offers that are communicated by brokers must be authorized by the party to be bound and comply with the statute of frauds by containing evidence of signatures or initials. Brokers are special agents and not general agents who can bind their principals.
>
> On competing motions for summary judgment, the trial court granted summary judgment for the buyer holding that no contract had been created. Appellate court affirmed.

In Joseph v. James, the seller sued the buyers and the buyers' agent for breach of contract and real estate fraud (Chapter 27, Texas Business and Commerce Code). The trial court granted a motion for summary judgment for the buyer.

The buyers, through their real estate agent, faxed an offer to purchase Joseph's home in the amount of $1.875 million. The buyers initialed the bottom of each page of the TREC form and signed the last page. The next day, the seller's agent informed the buyers' agent that the seller would not consider an offer of less than $2 million. After consulting with the buyers, the buyers' agent drew a line through the figures and changed the sales price to $2 million. The buyers did not initial these changes or re-sign the contract. Upon receipt of the modified offer, the seller made several changes, including raising the sales price to $2.195 million. The seller initialed each change and sent the form back to the buyers' agent. The buyers' agent again drew a line through the figures of the first page of the form and changed the total sales price to $2.1 million. Again, the buyers did not initial these changes. The buyers' agent emailed the form to the seller's agent saying the buyers love the home and are countering at $2.1 million with no other changes to your client's counter. The seller's agent then called the buyers' agent and communicated orally that the seller was increasing the sales price to $2.125 million and would convey some personal property in the home. Two days later, the seller, without informing the seller's agent, initialed the last written offer sent by the buyers' agent. The seller also asked the selling agent's assistant to send an email to the buyers' agent acknowledging that the seller accepted the offer of $2.1 million, which was sent. The buyers claimed that no contract had been created. The buyers' agent also stated that he did not have the buyers' permission to make the changes that were faxed to the seller's agent at a price of $2.1 million. Instead, he stated that he had mistakenly faxed that document to the seller's agent and had intended to fax it to the buyers for their consideration.

The seller sued for breach of contract and fraud. The court first looked at the issue of statute of frauds wherein the court noted that the changes were never initialed, but the seller argued that the buyers' agent had the authority to sign on behalf of the buyers and by sending the information, bound the buyers. The court relied on a long line of Texas cases confirming that a real estate agent is a special agent, not a general agent, and therefore, cannot bind a principal to a transaction. The court also noted that the seller had presented no evidence that the buyer had signed or initialed the last "counter-offer" at $2.1 million, which would bind the buyers under the Statute of Frauds. Additionally, the court noted that the seller presented no evidence that the buyers even knew that the buyers' agent was sending the seller's agent the "counter-offer" at $2.1 million with their original signatures and initials, let alone any evidence that they adopted them for purposes of a counter-offer. The seller tried to argue that even if the buyers did not sign or initial the last counter-offer, the buyers had ratified it. The court held that the seller had presented no evidence of such ratification.

Italian Cowboy Partners, Ltd. v. The Prudential Insurance Company of America

341 S.W 3d 323 (Tex., 2011)

> A standard merger clause in a commercial lease was not disclaimer of tenant's reliance on property manager's oral assurances that there had been no problems with the building and that the building was in perfect condition.
>
> Trial court entered judgment in favor of tenants alleging misrepresentation of material defect in a commercial lease transaction. The appellate court reversed and rendered take-nothing judgment, and entered judgment in favor of landlord. The Supreme Court reversed holding for tenant.

The Texas Supreme Court reversed a Court of Appeals ruling that was reported in the prior Legal Update textbook (edition 4). A restaurant tenant and its owners sued a landlord and property manager for fraud, negligent misrepresentation, breach of warranty of suitability, and other claims based on the defendant's representations regarding condition of the premises.

There was a persistent sewer gas odor on the premises that the tenant alleged made the premises unsuitable for its intended use as a restaurant. The lease was a commercial lease with a "standard" merger clause that acknowledged that neither the landlord nor its tenants made any representations regarding condition of the building and a disclaimer of reliance of the property manager's oral assurances that there had been no problems with the building. The court of appeals held that the parties were not in a disparate bargaining position, the "as is" provisions of the lease control, and all repairs were the tenant's responsibility.

The Texas Supreme Court reversed, holding that the disclaimer-of-representations language written on the lease was not a disclaimer of the tenant's reliance on the property manager's oral assurance during the negotiations of the lease. The manager of the center made very specific representations that "the building was practically new and had no problems" and "the building was in perfect condition, never a problem whatsoever" and "this is my baby and I was here from the first day… it's in perfect condition."

At trial, prior tenants who had occupied the same premises (and who also had vacated the premises because of the foul odors) testified that the manager "knew of the smell," and she herself had acknowledged to other people that it was "almost unbearable" and "ungodly."

Acknowledging the disclaimer of reliance on the merger clauses in the lease, the court held that these provisions do not control if there is a fraudulent inducement. The landlord also attempted to defend by saying expressions by the manager were mere expressions of opinion. The court specifically rejected this issue noting that whether a statement is an actionable statement as a "fact" or merely one of "opinion" often depends on the circumstances in which the statement is made. When a speaker purports to have special knowledge of the facts, or does have superior knowledge of the facts, a party may maintain a fraud action. Testimony indicated that the manager herself personally experienced the odor.

The court also upheld Texas' Implied Warranty of Suitability established in *Davidow* unless the Implied Warranty of Suitability is expressly waived. The Court upheld an award for special damages for lost investment, accounts payable and interest carried, in addition to rescission of the lease.

Williams v. Dardenne

345 S.W. 3d 118 (Tex. App. –Houston [1 Dist.], 2011)

> A failure to disclose the existence of a document that duplicated information that the buyer otherwise received or knew was not actionable as fraud or a deceptive act.
>
> After a jury trial, trial court held for buyer on claims of fraud, DTPA violation and negligent misrepresentation. Seller moved for JNOV, which was denied. Court of Appeals reversed the JNOV.

The Dardennes bought a home from the Williams in November 2007, using the TREC residential resale contract form. The buyers received a seller's disclosure notice, in which the sellers stated that they were not aware of any defects in the foundation and that the foundation had been repaired before they owned it.

In the seller's disclosure notice, the sellers identified three prior inspection reports: one in 2005 and two in 2006, two of which discussed the foundation.

The 2005 report by a registered structural engineer concluded the house did not need any additional foundation repairs above what had already been done. There was a "tilt of a floor that was plainly visible."

The 2006 report by a TREC-licensed inspector reported that the home's foundation was not functioning and needed repairs. The buyers admitted having access to the report before closing and not reviewing it. There was a document that the sellers did not list in the seller's disclosure notice, which was a 2-page letter that showed recommended repairs to the foundation. The sellers considered this letter to be a bid to perform foundation work; the buyers considered this letter to be an inspection report. Before closing, the buyers had the property inspected by their own inspector. The buyers informed the inspector of the information about the foundation in prior inspection reports they had received. The buyer's inspector reported that the foundation of the home was considered to be adequately performing the function for which it was intended.

The buyers admitted they were aware the house exhibited signs of prior foundation movement and that the sellers did not represent to them there was no damage due to foundation movement.

Approximately 6 months after closing, signs of foundation problems surfaced. The buyers hired an engineering company, which was the same engineering company that had given the sellers the bid for repairs in 2006. It was then that the buyers found out about the prior 2-page letter.

The buyers sued the sellers alleging violations of the DTPA, fraud, and negligent misrepresentation based on the sellers' failure to disclose the 2-page letter. The jury found in favor of the buyers. The sellers appealed.

The appellate court held that Paragraph 7 is an "as is" clause, and it negates the elements of causation and reliance for DTPA, fraud, or negligence claims relating to the value or condition of the property.

The buyers contended that the "as is" provision of the contract was not enforceable because it was procured by fraudulent inducement. The issue was whether the buyers presented any evidence of reliance to support the buyers' claim for fraudulent inducement. Ultimately, the court had to determine if the sellers' failure to disclose this information was concealed because it contains information that they were not otherwise conveying to the buyers about a material defect.

The court held that

- the undisclosed report was a duplicate of the information contained in the reports that were disclosed (the court made a side-by-side analysis of all 3 reports); and
- the element of reliance had not been established because there was no evidence that if they had received the letter, the buyers' decision to close would have been different.

The appellate court held that the trial court was in error in refusing to grant the buyers' motion for judgment notwithstanding the verdict. Reversed and rendered that the buyer take nothing on their claims.

Hue Nguyen vs. Chapa,

305 S.W. 3d 316 (Tex. App. –Houston [14 Dist.], 2009)

> A buyer is charged with knowledge of all facts appearing in the chain of title.
>
> The appellate court found no evidence that the buyer had knowledge of all facts or should have been put on inquiry.

Ruiz sold a 3-acre tract to Chapa. Chapa did not file the deed from Ruiz. Thirteen months later, Ruiz sold the same 3 acres to Nguyen. Nguyen immediately filed a general warranty deed with the county reflecting his interest in the property. After learning of the Ruiz-Nguyen sale, Chapa sought to establish his title by filing suit. Challenging Chapa's unrecorded interest, Nguyen claimed he was a bona fide purchaser. The bank that financed Nguyen's loan on the property intervened and asserted status as a bona fide mortgagee. A jury found in favor of Chapa on his contract claims against Ruiz and found against Nguyen's and the bank's claims of bona fide purchaser and mortgagee, respectively.

Under Texas law, an unrecorded conveyance of an interest in real property is void as to a subsequent purchaser who purchases the property for valuable consideration and without notice. However, the unrecorded instrument is binding on a subsequent purchaser who does not pay a valuable consideration or who has notice of the instrument. Thus, to receive the bona fide purchaser protection, a party must acquire the property in good faith, for value, and without notice of any third-party claim or interest. A bona fide mortgagee takes a lien in good faith, for valuable consideration, and without notice of outstanding claims.

Notice of a third-party's claim or interest can be either actual or constructive, which has been broadly defined as information concerning a fact actually communicated to a person, derived by him from a proper source, or presumed by law to have been acquired. Generally, the question of whether a party has notice is a question of fact; it becomes a question of law only when there is no room for ordinary minds to differ as to the proper conclusion to be drawn from the evidence.

A subsequent purchaser has actual notice if he has personal information or express knowledge of an adverse right. The only evidence of actual knowledge at trial was Chapa's testimony that once he and Nguyen realized Ruiz had sold each of them the same property, Nguyen asked Chapa if he had filed his interest with Harris County. Chapa answered no, and Nguyen replied "bad luck for you." Chapa contends that Nguyen's inquiry and response shows that he knew of Chapa's interest and knew Chapa did not file the interest with the county. Contrary to Chapa's argument, Nguyen's query is not evidence that he had personal or express knowledge that Chapa had a competing interest in the same property. Rather, Nguyen's statements merely reflect his knowledge of a party's duty to record interests in real estate. Nguyen's question and reply are not evidence of actual knowledge; at best, this evidence provides nothing more than basis for surmise, guess, or conjecture as to Nguyen's knowledge of Chapa's interest.

Constructive notice is notice the law imputes to a person not having personal information or knowledge. One form of constructive knowledge imputes notice where a subsequent purchaser has a duty to ascertain the rights of a party in possession. The duty to ascertain arises only if the possession is visible, open, exclusive, and unequivocal. This case, however, is not a constructive-knowledge-by-possession case.

Nevertheless, a subsequent buyer is also charged with notice of the terms in deeds that form an essential link in his chain of ownership. Although a deed outside the chain of title does not impute constructive knowledge, a person may be charged with the duty to make a diligent inquiry using the facts at hand in the recorded deed. Thus, every purchaser of land is charged with knowledge of all facts appearing in the chain of title through which he claims that would place a reasonably prudent person on inquiry as to the rights of other parties in the property conveyed. Accordingly, if Nguyen or his bank had knowledge of any fact or circumstance sufficient to put a prudent man upon inquiry which, if prosecuted with ordinary diligence, would lead to actual notice of Chapa's claim to the 3 acres, Nguyen and the bank are charged with such knowledge. The court reviewed the evidence and found nothing that would have put Nguyen or the bank on inquiry.

Neary v. Mikob Properties, Inc.

340 S.W. 3d 316 (Tex. App. –Dallas, 2011)

> To enforce a commission against a party to a transaction, the broker must clearly produce the written commission agreement signed by the party against whom it is to be enforced. An entity must be licensed to maintain a claim for payment of a commission.
>
> Trial court granted summary judgment for seller against broker, holding that there was no enforceable commission agreement in writing. Court of Appeals affirmed.

A lawsuit was filed after the parties failed to agree on the terms for payment of a commission. Neary and his company, St. John Holdings (SJH) filed suit to recover a brokerage fee in connection with the sale of 8 apartment complexes. The purchase agreement did not include a provision for a broker's fee. Neary held a valid broker license at all times; however, SJH did not hold a real estate broker license at the time of the transaction.

Neary claimed a document dated November 17, 2003, entitled "Term Sheet," combined with several email messages exchanged before and after the date of the Term Sheet, constitute a contract for a brokerage fee of 1 percent of the purchase price. The defendants claimed that the Term Sheet and other documents did not satisfy the requirements of §1101.806(c) of the Real Estate License Act. They also contended that SJH was not licensed as a broker until November 1, 2007, and could not file suit to recover a commission from the transaction.

Written in above the signature lines on the Term Sheet appeared the sentence, "This term sheet is a guideline only, and is not binding." The Term Sheet identified the "Purchaser" as a Texas limited liability company "to be formed." Although the term "Seller" was used in the Term Sheet, no seller was identified. The "Property" was defined as 8 complexes, but by name only (without addresses or legal descriptions). The Term Sheet also included a paragraph entitled "Brokerage Fee," which provided for conditions for payments to the brokers involved in the sale and commission pay-out.

The emails, which the broker argues establish a writing (along with the Term Sheet) that satisfies the Act, were exchanged before and after the date of the Term Sheet. The emails were between the brokers and set forth several proposals regarding the commission payment. The emails did not settle on an amount that the brokers were to be paid.

The trial court granted the defendants' motion for summary judgment. Neary appealed.

Section 1101.806(c) provides that a broker cannot maintain a suit for a commission unless it is based on a writing that is signed by the person against whom the broker seeks to enforce the commission. The issue in this case was whether the emails and the Term Sheet satisfy the requirement for a written commission agreement. The court noted that strict compliance with the Act is required. To comply, an agreement or memorandum must

- be in writing and must be signed by the person to be charged with the commission,
- promise that a definite commission will be paid or must refer to a written commission schedule,
- state the name of the broker to whom the commission is to be paid, and
- either itself or by reference to some other existing writing, identify with reasonable certainty the property to be conveyed.

The defendants signed no written agreement to pay a commission. The defendants contended the Term Sheet and the other communications relied upon by Neary do not constitute a written agreement to pay a commission. The court agreed.

The court also noted the Term Sheet did not identify Neary as a "broker to whom the commission was to be paid." SJH was the only broker identified in the Term Sheet. But SJH could not recover a commission from the sale, because it was not a licensed broker until several years after the transaction.

Smith Gilbard v. Perry

332 S.W. 3d 709 (Tex. App. –Dallas, 2011)

> Seller claimed a mutual mistake caused her to sell more property than intended. The court agreed the seller was entitled to reformation of the deed.
>
> The appellate court reversed and held that the parties intended to rely on the metes and bounds description in the deed.

The buyer, Smith-Gilbard, desired to build a healthcare facility in Kaufman County. The buyer was informed that Ray Raymond, a long time Kaufman resident, might be able to assist the buyer in locating a suitable parcel of land. Raymond, who was the Executive Director for the Kaufman Economic Development Corporation, agreed to help.

Raymond asked Perry if she would be interested in selling part of her property. Perry replied that she might be interested in selling the lot west of the fence line on her property. Raymond notified the buyer that Perry was interested in selling her land west of the fence line. The buyer hired a broker to handle the rest of the transaction, and the parties entered into an Unimproved Property Contract.

At the time of contract, the seller gave the buyer a copy of a 1965 deed. The seller told the buyer that she did not see any reason to incur the additional expense of having a new survey made because there had been no changes to the property described in the 1965 warranty. The 1965 deed described the land as "situated in the County of Kaufman, State of Texas, a part of the C.A. Lovejoy Survey, Abstract Number 303 (the C.A. Lovejoy Survey)." The contract described the land as "Lot 125, Block C.A. Lovejoy Addition, City of Kaufman, Kaufman County, Texas, and indicated that it measured "113 x 200" feet, adjacent to 1003 W. Grove." The property measurements in the contract were provided by Perry's son, who was not a trained surveyor. Perry's son did not testify at trial, and Perry testified that she did not know how her son ascertained the "113 x 200" foot measurement.

Closing occurred in 2002. The deed described the land as "situated in the County of Kaufman, State of Texas, a part of the C.A. Lovejoy Survey, Abstract Number 303." It then described the property by metes and bounds in terms that were identical to the 1965 warranty deed. The metes and bounds descriptions of the property included an additional 1,881 square feet of the lot that extended east beyond the fence line. At trial, it was undisputed that the "Lot 125" of the "C.A. Lovejoy Addition" referred to in the contract between the parties was the same piece of property described in both the 1965 and 2002 warranty deeds as part of the "C.A. Lovejoy Survey." The seller did not tell the buyer she did not intend to convey all of the land described in both the 1965 and 2002 deeds.

As the buyer started the process to construct a building, the buyer learned that a third of the property located on a service road at the front of the property was subject to a highway frontage easement. The buyer was reimbursed under her title policy for the loss of the property subject to the easement.

The seller sued the buyer in 2004 to reform the deed based on an alleged mutual mistake. The seller argued that the parties' intent was to sell the land up to but not including the portion of the lot that extended east beyond the fence line. Following a bench trial, the trial court concluded the seller was entitled to reformation of the deed. The buyer appealed.

A mutual mistake of fact occurs when the parties to an agreement have a common intention, but the written contract does not reflect the intention of the parties due to a mutual mistake. To prove a mutual mistake, the evidence must show that both parties were acting under the same misunderstanding of the same material fact. The mistake must be mutual rather than unilateral. The doctrine of mutual mistake is not available to avoid the result of an unhappy bargain.

The appellate court held that the parties intended to rely on the metes and bounds description in the 1965 deed that was incorporated into the 2002 deed to accurately describe the property. There is no indication in the record that the seller told the buyer she did not intend to convey all of the property described in the deeds.

The record did not reflect any representations or discussions between seller and real estate agent regarding the property line or what portion of that property was intended to be conveyed. Therefore, the appellate court concluded that the seller's sole cause of action for mutual mistake was not supported by sufficient evidence. Reversed and rendered judgment in favor of the buyer.

Sheehan v. Adams

320 S.W. 3d 890 (Tex. App. –Dallas, 2011)

> A jury returned a verdict in favor of the buyer on a claim a house had a foundation problem that was both misrepresented and not disclosed.
>
> Appellate court noted that the seller's disclosure notice is not a representation that the foundation is in good condition and the seller did not make such a representation. Overall, the evidence was not sufficient to support the jury's findings.

In 2002, Sheehan contacted a real estate agent who agreed to represent her in the purchase of her first house. Around that same time, the Adams listed their house with another real estate agent associated with the same firm. Sheehan saw the Adams' house twice and then signed a contract to buy it. The Adams delivered the seller's disclosure notice. The seller's disclosure indicated that the sellers were not aware of any defects or malfunctions in the foundation, walls, floors, ceilings, or roof. It did indicate that they were aware of "settling." Next to the box where he checked "Yes" for settling, the seller inserted a handwritten comment in which he characterized the settling as "normal."

After he filled out the seller's disclosure, but before the house was inspected, the seller called his agent and spoke about a "hairline crack" in the brick on the west side of the exterior of the house (the west-side crack). They made no changes to the disclosure notice based on that conversation.

The buyer hired an inspector who noticed some exterior cracks in the brick of the house. He did not note them on his report, because he considered them normal for a house of that age. The inspector told the buyer that he found no problems with the foundation. His report included the notation that the foundation was inspected and "[t]here were no signs of significant cracks or movement noted in the foundation at this time." He did note roof and termite issues and recommended that the buyer consult a roofer. The parties amended the contract to require the Adams to pay the roof repair cost.

The buyer, with her agent present, conducted a final walk-through the day before closing and signed the "Buyer's Walk Thru and Acceptance Form." The acceptance form included a notice that the "real estate brokers and the seller have no knowledge of any defects in the property other than what has been disclosed in the Seller's Disclosure Notice or other written information."

Two months after closing, the buyer found cracks in the interior and exterior walls of the house. She sent an email to her agent stating that she saw the cracks and wondered if the inspector should have uncovered the problem. The buyer obtained a proposal from a foundation repair company at a cost of $10,475. The proposal also recommended the implementation of a watering system to maintain consistent moisture level around the perimeter of the foundation.

The buyer hired a geotechnical engineer to assess the condition of the foundation. The engineer noted cracks in the mortar and brick, wall and ceiling sheetrock, and the foundation. He did not offer an opinion as to when the foundation failed.

The buyer sued and then settled with the inspector. She also sued the sellers and the brokerage firm for alleged violations of the Texas Deceptive Trade Practices and Consumer Protection Act, fraud, breach of contract, and breach of fiduciary duty. All allegations were premised on a claim the house had a foundation problem that was both misrepresented and not disclosed.

The jury returned a verdict in favor of the buyer, but the trial court granted motions for judgment notwithstanding the verdict (JNOV) by the sellers and the brokerage firm and rendered judgment that the buyer take nothing on her claims. The judgment also included an award of attorney fees in favor of the brokerage firm and against the buyer. The sellers and the brokerage firm appealed.

The buyer claimed the court was in error by granting the JNOV because the jury could infer that the west-side crack, coupled with interior cracks that were repaired, were symptoms of foundation problems and abnormal settling and that the sellers made false statements. She argued that the seller knew of the west-side crack for at least 4 years. She also argued that the conversation between the listing agent and the seller regarding the seller's disclosure notice was evidence that they knew of the defects, because the listing agent advised the seller that the seller did not need to amend the seller's disclosure notice, because the cracks in the house were normal for a house of that age. To prevail, the court noted that the buyer had to prove that the seller or listing agent actually knew of the foundation defect. A showing that they should have known was not sufficient.

All experts testified that a crack does not necessarily mean a foundation problem exists. The experts also affirmed that a foundation can fail within weeks. The court found that the buyer's repair persons were interior sheetrock repair persons and did not and could not tie the cracks to a foundation problem. The court reviewed the seller's disclosure notice and noted that the seller stated that he was not aware of foundation defects but was aware of normal settling. While the seller knew of settling, the appellate court held that the seller was not aware that defects or abnormal movement existed. The court noted that the seller's disclosure notice is not a representation that the foundation is in good condition and the seller did not make such a representation. The court noted that no expert was able to testify, and no evidence established, that the foundation defects were known to exist at the time of closing. Overall, the evidence was not sufficient to support the jury's findings.

Lesieur v. Fryar

325 S.W. 3d 242 (Tex. App. –San Antonio, 2010)

> Failing to provide a prior inspection report is not evidence of fraud or concealment if the buyer has the same or substantially the same information from other sources. This case disagrees with other cases on the award of attorney fees to the broker under the attorney fees paragraph of the TREC forms.
>
> Trial court awarded summary judgment for broker and seller and awarded attorney fees to broker and seller based on Paragraph 17 of TREC contract form. Appellate court affirmed but reversed the award of attorney fees.

In 2002 the Fryars bought a house and surrounding property in Medina County, Texas. They hired Adams to inspect the house. According to the report, the house showed "[s]igns of structural movement," but it was supporting the house. The inspector noted "[c]racks in walls and/or ceilings," "[d]oor frames out of square," and "[c]racks in brick/stone veneers." However, the inspector did not check the box advising the foundation was "Not Functioning or In Need of Repair." The Fryars purchased the home without making repairs.

In 2005, the Fryars decided to sell the house and property to Lesieur. No problems with the foundation, walls, floors, or ceilings were noted in the Seller's Disclosure Notice. The Fryars stated that they had not received any prior inspection reports within the last 4 years (the first inspection was received in 2002), which the listing agent had in her file from the first transaction.

Lesieur hired his own inspector in 2005. The report described problems in the structural section of the report. The report noted "[s]tress cracks" in the floor tile in the carport and inside the house. The inspector did not check the box that would have advised the foundation was "Not Functioning or In Need of Repair."

Lesieur was advised by his broker to review the inspection report. Lesieur stated he believed the problems noted were "cosmetic."

Lesieur signed a "Buyer's Walk-Through and Acceptance Form" prior to the closing. Both parties were represented at the closing by their own brokers and attorneys.

After he moved in, Lesieur noticed signs of possible foundation problems. He hired a foundation repair company to conduct another inspection. The foundation repair company claimed the foundation needed repair, and "there was an attempt to conceal signs of damage to the foundation of the home." Lesieur filed suit against the Fryars and the listing firm, alleging violations of the DTPA, common law fraud, statutory fraud, civil conspiracy, negligence, and negligent misrepresentation. Most of the claims were based on the alleged concealment of the 2002 inspection report, claiming that the Fryars and the listing broker knew of the 2002 report and concealed it.

The trial court granted the Fryars and the listing agent summary judgment and awarded the Fryars and the listing agent their attorney fees. Lesieur appealed.

The appellate court held Lesieur's pre-purchase inspection and the information he obtained from it negates the elements of causation and reliance as a matter of law, thereby precluding recovery on any of his claims.

The issue in this case was whether the Fryars and their broker knew "anything more or different" about the foundation based on the 2002 report, which was not given to Lesieur, than Lesieur did based on his own inspection report. The court conducted a side-by-side comparison of the information contained in the 2 reports. The court saw that the differences between the reports were merely a matter of word usage, not substance. Even when every reasonable inference was indulged in Lesieur's favor, he was not able to present more than a scintilla of evidence that either the Fryars or the listing broker "*knew anything more or different than [he] did about the condition of the home [,],*" specifically the foundation.

Lesieur argued that the trial court erred in granting the listing broker her attorney fees because she is not a party to the contract. The court looked at the attorney fees provision in the TREC contract forms and determined that it is broadly written and specifically includes the brokers to the sale. The court held that there is no evidence to establish Lesieur and the Fryars intended to confer a direct benefit upon the listing broker. The court noted that Paragraph 8 of the contract belies that possibility. The appellate court held that the broker did not establish that she was a party or third-party beneficiary to the contract and reversed the trial court granting the listing broker's attorney fees.

C.W.100 Louis Henna, Ltd. v. El Chico Restaurants of Texas, L.P.

295 S.W. 3d 748 (Tex. App. –Austin, 2009)

> A commercial lease defining trade fixtures can include items that may normally be considered improvements or fixtures and, under the lease, may permit the tenant to remove the trade fixture.
>
> Trial court awarded summary judgment to tenant. Court of Appeals affirmed.

Near the end of a longterm ground lease, a landlord and tenant squabbled when the HVAC units on a vacated restaurant were vandalized and the tenant refused to repair. Tenant claimed the units as their property, which they could do with as they wished (including removing them). The landlord sued alleging that the units were improvements (fixtures) which must be repaired and passed to the landlord in working order as part of the real property at lease termination.

As in most lease disputes, the court stated that the lease language would control the result, as the intent of the parties determines this issue. The lease permitted the tenant to install "trade and business fixtures" which would "remain the property of Tenant," and later in the lease permitted the tenant to remove "removable fixtures." These terms were not defined, but the court held that "trade fixtures" have an accepted definition in Texas as articles annexed to the realty by a tenant to carry on their trade, profession or enterprise, which can be removed without material or permanent injury to the premises. Although not all HVAC systems are trade fixtures, the court cites several reported Texas cases holding they can be. Looking to the lease language, the court held these units were trade fixtures and not improvements. As a result, the landlord ended up without a functioning HVAC system. In fact, the tenant could remove the HVAC system completely!

Franco v. Lopez

307 S.W. 3d 551 (Tex. App. –Dallas 2010)

> Although the effective date of the contract was later than the stated closing date, a court held an enforceable contract existed based on provisions in the contract permitting closing to occur 7 days after objections have been cured or waived.
>
> Following a trial before the court without a jury, the trial judge awarded specific performance of the contract to buyers. Appellate court upheld the trial court's judgment.

Failure to properly complete a commercial sales contract (believed to be the TAR form) resulted in litigation. The contract's closing date preceded the contract's effective date. Nonetheless, the parties muddled forward, obtaining a survey and depositing additional earnest money, until the seller refused to close. The seller asserted that no binding contract existed, and even if it did, the buyer breached by not "timely" closing on the date in the contract (which preceded the execution of the contract). After the court rejected those claims, the court considered whether the buyer was required to "tender performance" by submitting the purchase price and closing documents, which is the standard requirement in Texas for specific performance. The court applied the longstanding exception to that general rule that a seller, which "openly refused to perform," excuses the lack of a tender of performance. Normally, the buyer must prove "ready, willing and able to perform" by tendering performance. However, if there is evidence the seller refused to perform and evidence the buyer was ready, willing and able to perform, then specific performance will be awarded. Further, the buyer recovered attorney fees.

Mushtaha v. Kidd

2010 WL 5395694 (Tex. App. –Houuston [1 Dist.], 2010)

> A broker who changes an offer at the principal's instruction should not initial the change but clarify as to whether the principal desires to sign the offer or make a non-binding communication.
>
> On summary judgment for the seller, the trial court refused to award the buyer's claim for specific performance. Court of Appeals affirmed.

Using a TAR commercial form, the first buyer made a "low ball" offer. The seller directed his agent to mark through the price and substitute a higher price, which the broker did, initialed and delivered to the buyer's broker.

Then, a higher offer from a second buyer was presented. Shortly thereafter, the deadline for acceptance of the offer passed without action by either party. When the first buyer became aware of the higher offer, and the seller's position that the buyer must match it (despite the initialed change in the buyer's offer), the buyer simply signed the offer that had been sent to him with the change made by the broker (lower than the price the second buyer had offered) and sent it to the seller's broker. The seller signed a contract with the second buyer for the higher price. The first buyer filed suit to enforce his contract and filed a notice of the pending suit in the real property records, thus preventing the sale to the second buyer. The court ruled that no binding contract existed between the first buyer and the seller, citing that the special agency relationship of a broker did not include the right to bind the owner or consummate a sale. However, the court stated that there could be situation in which a broker's signature could bind the broker's principal. Finally, the court awarded the seller attorney fees, not based on the provision in the contract form that permitted attorney fees in a dispute, but for the declaratory judgment action brought by the seller seeking a determination that no contract existed. Brokers should never sign (or initial) documents on behalf of their principals!

Texas Real Estate Commission

MCE
Ethics
Update

Edition 5.0

Acknowledgments

Real Estate Center Staff

Gary W. Maler, Director
David S. Jones, Communications Director
Robert P. Beals II, Art Director
Denise Whisenant, Education Coordinator

MCE Writing Group

Loretta Dehay, Austin
Tom Morgan, Austin
Charles Jacobus, Bellaire
Philip Schoewe, Lubbock
Ron Walker, Austin
Reid Wilson, Houston
Avis Wukasch, Georgetown

Texas Real Estate Commission

Douglas Oldmixon, Administrator
Avis Wukasch, Chair
Joanne Justice, Vice Chair
Jaime Blevins Hensley, Secretary
Troy C. Alley, Jr.
Adrian A. Arriaga
Robert C. Day
Bill Jones
Weston Martinez
Dona Scurry

Real Estate Center Advisory Committee

Joe Bob McCartt, Chairman
Mario A. Arriaga, Vice Chairman
Avis Wukasch, ex-officio
Mona R. Bailey
James M. Boyd
Russell Cain
Jacquelyn K. Hawkins
Kathleen McKenzie Owen
Kimberly A. Shambley
Ronald C. Wakefield

FOREWORD

In cooperation with the Texas Real Estate Commission, the Real Estate Center at Texas A&M University developed this real estate ethics curriculum with the assistance of an advisory committee of active licensees, attorneys and education providers. Real estate licensees are encouraged to acquire additional information and to take courses in specific, applicable topics.

This curriculum has been developed using information from publications, presentations and general research. The information is believed to be reliable, but it cannot be guaranteed insofar as it is applied to any particular individual or situation. The laws discussed in this curriculum have been excerpted, summarized or abbreviated. For a complete understanding and discussion, consult a full version of any pertinent law. This curriculum contains information that can change periodically. This curriculum is presented with the understanding that the authors and instructors are not engaged in rendering legal, accounting or other professional advice. The services of a competent professional with suitable expertise should be sought.

The authors, presenters, advisory committee, Real Estate Center and Texas Real Estate Commission disclaim any liability, loss or risk personal or otherwise, incurred as a consequence directly or indirectly from the use and application of any of the information contained in these materials or the teaching lectures and media presentations given in connection with these materials.

When using this course for three hours of Ethics Update MCE credit as required by the Texas Real Estate Commission, this textbook must be reproduced and used in its entirety, without omission or alteration.

Contents

The Canons of Professional Ethics

Chapter 1

Title 22 of the Texas Administrative Code (TAC) Chapter 531 includes five canons of professional ethics and conduct. The canons apply to real estate licensees and are included in the rules of the Texas Real Estate Commission (TREC). Acting as a fiduciary, the real estate licensee must exercise a standard of duty and care when representing a client in a real estate transaction. The licensee must subordinate his or her own interest to the client's interest. The canons also support the Federal Fair Housing Act in forbidding discrimination in real estate activities. These canons are similar in content to general business ethics and common law agency principles from a variety of sources including case law, statutory law and codes of ethics of many professional and trade associations.

The Five Canons

1. Fidelity (22 TAC §531.1)

A licensee represents the interest of the agent's client. The agent, in performing duties to the client, must

- make his or her position clear to all parties concerned in a real estate transaction,
- treat other parties to a transaction fairly,
- be faithful and observant to the trust placed in the agent,
- perform his or her duties scrupulously and meticulously, and
- place no personal interest above the client's interest.

2. Integrity (22 TAC §531.2)

A licensee

- has a special obligation to perform his or her responsibilities, and
- must use caution to avoid misrepresentation by acts of commission or omission.

3. Competence (22 TAC §531.3)

A licensee

- is knowledgeable as a real estate practitioner,
- is informed on market conditions that affect the real estate business,
- continues his or her education in the intricacies involved in marketing real estate for others,
- stays informed about national, state and local issues and developments in the real estate industry, and
- exercises judgment and skill in the performance of his or her work.

A licensee might ask the following:

- What are my strengths and deficiencies?
- Do I attend classes to improve my services to my clients or customers? How often?
- What resources are available to help me maintain my competence?
- Do I keep abreast of market conditions in the area in which I practice? How?
- Am I aware of trends in real estate practices? How do I usually find out about these trends?
- Do I read Real Estate Commission and trade publications? Which ones? How do they help me maintain my competence?
- Can I identify local, state and national issues that are currently under development or consideration?

4. Consumer Information Form 1-1 (22 TAC §531.18)

Each active real estate broker or real estate inspector licensed by the Texas Real Estate Commission (TREC) must display Consumer Information Form 1-1 prominently in each place of business that the broker or inspector maintains.

5. Discriminatory Practices (22 TAC §531.19)

No real estate licensee shall inquire about, respond to or facilitate inquiries about or make a disclosure, which indicates or is intended to indicate any preference, limitation or discrimination based on protected classes. Protected classes include race, color, religion, sex, national origin, ancestry, and familial status. Protected classes also include handicap of an owner, previous or current occupant, potential purchaser, lessor or potential lessee of real property. A handicapped individual includes a person who had, may have had, has or may have AIDS, HIV-related illnesses or HIV infection as defined by the Centers for Disease Control of the U.S. Public Health Service.

TREC Complaints

A person may file a complaint with TREC against a real estate licensee if the person believes the licensee violated the Real Estate License Act (TRELA). If TREC has jurisdiction over the complaint, it will typically investigate the allegations by interviewing the parties and witnesses and gathering relevant information. After review, TREC's enforcement division will notify the licensee if it intends to initiate disciplinary proceedings. After a hearing or other settlement procedure, it will render a decision. If the evidence establishes a violation, TREC may impose a reprimand, suspension of the license, revocation of the license, a fine, probation, or any combination.

Complaint Provision

TREC is required to maintain a system to act promptly and efficiently on complaints and must maintain a file on each complaint. TREC gives priority to the investigation of complaints filed by a consumer and an enforcement case resulting from the consumer complaint. TRELA requires that TREC assign priorities and investigate complaints using a risk-based approach based on the
- degree of potential harm to the consumer,
- potential for immediate harm to the consumer,
- overall severity of the allegations and the complaint,
- number of license holders potentially involved in the complaint,
- previous complaint history of the license holder, and
- number of potential violations in the complaint [TRELA §1101.204(h)].

Refund to Consumer

TREC may order a licensee to pay a refund to a consumer as provided by an agreement resulting from an informal settlement conference or an enforcement order in addition to imposing an administrative penalty, suspension, revocation or other sanction (TRELA §1101.659).

TREC Advisory Letters

When appropriate, TREC may close a complaint file by issuing an advisory letter to a licensee. This is generally appropriate in more technical matters, when the provision that was violated is new, or when evidentiary or procedural problems exist, such as the unavailability of witnesses. An advisory letter is not formal disciplinary action. Instead, the advisory letter is a notification that there were items revealed in the investigation that do not warrant disciplinary action but, if not corrected, could lead to further complaints and, ultimately, disciplinary action.

Informal Proceedings

TREC is also required to adopt procedures governing informal disposition of contested cases. An informal disposition must provide the complainant and the license holder the opportunity to be heard. The proceeding requires the presence of a public member of TREC for a case involving a consumer complaint and at least 2 TREC staff members with experience in the regulatory area that is the subject of the proceeding (TRELA §1101.660).

Temporary Suspension

TREC's presiding officer for a case involving a consumer is required to appoint a disciplinary panel, consisting of 3 commission members, to determine whether a person's license to practice should be suspended temporarily. If the disciplinary panel determines that the licensee constitutes a threat to the public by continuing to practice, or the licensee constitutes a continuing threat to the public welfare, the panel will temporarily suspend the person's license (TRELA §1101.662).

Association Complaints

The Associations of REALTORS®, the National Association of Real Estate Brokers (NAREB®, Realtists), and other trade associations receive complaints alleging ethics violations against their members. Such complaints can be directed to the local association to which the member belongs. Typically, a grievance panel will conduct an initial review to determine if the complaint alleges a violation of the organization's code of ethics. If there is an alleged ethics violation, a hearing panel will convene to hear testimony and presentation of evidence, decide whether a violation of the association's code of ethics occurred, and order any warranted disciplinary action. Disciplinary action could include

- a reprimand,
- a fine,
- probation,
- suspension of membership,
- revocation of membership, or
- any combination of the above actions.

The panel will advise the parties of any rights to appeal the decision.

Citation Program

The Texas Association of REALTORS® (TAR) began a citation policy in January, 2011, to provide an option for faster resolution of ethics complaints. Only complaints related to certain articles (NAR Code of Ethics) qualify for the program. A model citation schedule lists conduct that is subject to citation. A grievance tribunal determines whether a complaint is subject to citation. If a citation is issued, the respondent is advised that he or she has the right to request a full due process hearing rather than pay the citation fine. Sanctions for an agreed-to citation include fines and education.

Agency Relationships

Chapter 2

Customer or Client?

It is important to keep in mind the difference between a customer and a client.

> **Customer:** a person(s) who is not represented by an agent but can receive information and assistance from a licensee. Example: a listing broker who assists an unrepresented buyer
>
> **Client:** a person(s) whom the licensee has agreed to represent

The example below shows how a seller's agent would treat a buyer — a customer, not a client.

A buyer (customer) might expect some or all of the following services:

- providing the customer information about and showing the customer available properties,
- disclosing any known property defects,
- preparing any offers for submission,
- assisting in coordination of inspections or surveys, etc.,
- assisting the customer in locating and obtaining financing, and
- working with all parties to solve problems and facilitate the closing.

The seller's agent is **unable** to provide the following to a buyer (customer):

- advising on how much to offer on a property, if less than the asking price,
- disclosing the amount the seller will take, if less than the asking price,
- informing the customer about the seller's motivation or deadline to sell,
- informing the customer about previous offers,
- advising the customer regarding positions to take during negotiations, or
- disclosing information to the customer that would be detrimental to the seller's negotiating position or that is confidential, unless required by law to disclose.

If the seller grants specific permission to disclose the foregoing information, the seller's agent may do so. Such permission should be documented!

Fiduciary Duties

A fiduciary is a person who has a high duty of care for another person, the client. The law requires the fiduciary to place the client's interest ahead of his or her own interest. When a licensee begins to provide agency services to a party, or a party believes that such services are being provided, the fiduciary relationship begins. Fiduciary relationships are common and can involve attorneys, trustees, investment brokers and real estate agents, among others. The principal, or client, is the person with whom the licensee has a fiduciary relationship. Although the licensee's duty is to act in the principal's interest, the licensee owes a duty of honesty and fairness to all parties in the transaction.

Information About Brokerage Services and Agency Disclosure

At the first substantive dialogue with a client or prospect, always provide the *Information About Brokerage Services (IABS)* statement, which contains the statutory information relating to brokerage services. The statement may appear in any format as long as it is in at least 10-point type [TRELA §1101.558(d)]. TREC publishes a form entitled *Information About Brokerage Services* that most licensees use to comply with the statute.

A substantive dialogue is a meeting or written communication that involves a substantive discussion relating to specific real property. A substantive dialogue does not include a dialogue at an open house or a meeting after the time of the contract. For example, a face-to-face meeting with a prospective client in which you are discussing properties is a substantive dialogue. Any written correspondence (including email or other electronic means) about specific properties constitutes a substantive dialogue. A telephone conversation by itself might or might not constitute a meeting that would require providing the form. If a telephone conversation constitutes a substantive dialogue, a prompt delivery of the form should follow.

The *Information About Brokerage Services* statement is not required if the licensee is meeting with a party represented by another licensee. For example, if you are the listing broker and happen to meet a represented buyer, you do not need to provide the form. The *Information About Brokerage Services* statement also is not required if the transaction is a residential lease for 1 year or less and a sale is not being considered.

The *IABS* form published by TREC provides for signatures. The signatures are not required by statute; however, it is prudent to request acknowledgment of the consumer's receipt of the form.

Disclosure of Agency Representation

The *Information About Brokerage Services* form informs parties only to potential representation and does not disclose the licensee's agency or representation. A licensee representing a party is required to disclose such representation at the first contact with another party to the transaction or another licensee who represents another party to the transaction. Agency disclosure may be oral or in writing. For example, when making an appointment with a listing agent or seller to show a property, a buyer's agent must disclose that he or she represents the buyer. Another example is when the listing agent meets a prospect at an open house or listed property.

Intermediary Brokerage Relationship Services

Intermediary status was created by statute in 1996 to acknowledge that a broker could be in the position of assisting two principals involved in the same transaction. An intermediary is a broker who is employed to negotiate a transaction between parties and acts as an agent of the parties. A broker who represents the buyer and the seller in the same transaction must act as an intermediary. For a broker to negotiate a transaction for two principals as an intermediary, the broker first must obtain written permission from the parties to act in such capacity, and the agreement must state the source of any expected compensation.

When entering into an agreement with a principal, the agreement may address whether the intermediary relationship is a possibility. To authorize the possibility of an intermediary relationship in a listing agreement or buyer representation agreement, the statute requires that the agreement be in writing and that the following be in bold print [TRELA §1101.651]:

- intermediary may not disclose that the seller will accept a price less than the asking price, unless authorized in writing to do so by the seller,
- intermediary may not disclose that the buyer will pay a price greater than the price submitted in a written offer, unless authorized in writing to do so by the buyer;

- intermediary may not disclose confidential information, unless authorized in writing to disclose the information or required to do so by the Texas Real Estate License Act, a court order, or if the information materially relates to the condition of the property;
- intermediary may not treat a party dishonestly; and
- intermediary may not violate the Real Estate License Act.

The intermediary may appoint different associated licensees to communicate with and carry out instructions of the respective parties. The appointment of associated licensees requires the written consent of the parties and written notification of appointments to the parties. The appointed licensees must still comply with the requirements listed above. Each appointed licensee may provide opinions and advice to his or her respective party. The intermediary is required to treat both parties fairly and impartially. The appointed licensees are not subject to the intermediary's duty of impartiality.

An intermediary is not required to make appointments in every transaction. There should be clear company policies regarding appointments. The issue of compensation is a matter of the brokerage's policy and is an internal concern. If appointments are made

- there must be a written authorization from both parties for the broker to act as an intermediary (this could be included in the written buyer representation agreement and the written listing agreement),
- the intermediary may not appoint himself or herself to either party,
- the intermediary cannot make appointments to one party without also making appointments to the other party,
- the intermediary must give written notice to each principal that appointments have been made and identify the respective appointees to the principals, and
- the appointees must keep confidential information confidential.

Example 1

Agent A lists a shopping center. Agent B, working for the same company, comes in with a buyer (client). In this example, the broker's policy in such a situation is to appoint Associate A to the seller and Associate B to the buyer. The intermediary (broker)

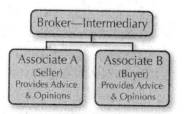

does not provide any opinions or advice to either party during negotiations. Each associate may provide opinions and advice during negotiations to the parties to whom each is appointed. The intermediary (broker) and the appointed associates remain obligated to comply with the items under TRELA §1101.651(d). *All associates in a brokerage act in the role of an intermediary except for those associates who are appointed to the parties.*

Example 2

Assume the same facts as Example 1 except now the broker's policy is not to make appointments. In this example, the associates

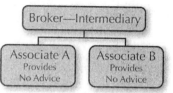

may not provide opinions or advice during negotiations to the party(s) each is serving. The associates may facilitate the transaction and assist the parties as neutral service providers.

Example 3

In a multi-agent brokerage, Associate A brings in both the buyer and seller. The Real Estate License Act permits the broker to select an appropriate course of action in this example.

Alternative 1

The intermediary may choose to make no appointments, in which case the intermediary (broker) and Associate A may not provide opinions or advice to

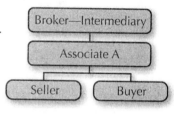

either party during negotiations and remains obligated to comply with the items under TRELA §1101.651(d). Associate A and the intermediary may process or facilitate the transaction.

Alternative 2

The intermediary may choose to reassign one or both of the parties to another agent. In the following example, the buyer is reassigned to Associate

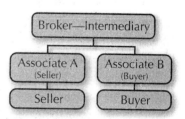

B. The intermediary (broker) does not provide any opinions or advice to either party during negotiations. Each associate may provide opinions and advice during negotiations to the parties to whom each is appointed. The intermediary (broker) and the appointed associates remain obligated to comply with the items under TRELA §1101.651(d). The broker must have written consent for appointment.

Example 4

What if the broker is a solo practitioner? May the solo practitioner act as an intermediary?

Yes, but the solo practitioner cannot make appointments of associated licensees. The intermediary (broker) does not provide any opinions or advice to either party during negotiations and remains obligated to comply with the items under §1101.651(d). No appointments are possible. The intermediary may process or facilitate the transaction.

Example 5

When a broker owns a small brokerage and actively lists and sells property, may the broker appoint himself or herself to one of the parties?

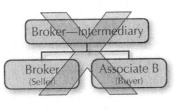

No. The broker shall not appoint himself or herself to one of the parties because the broker would be in two different roles. The broker may choose to make no appointments, and the broker and Associate B would not provide opinions or advice during negotiations. Each could process or facilitate the transaction. Alternatively, the broker could reassign the seller to another agent in the example above and make appointments.

Example 6

A broker orally agrees to represent a buyer. The buyer now wants to buy one of the broker's listings. The broker must get a written consent from both buyer and seller to act as an intermediary before proceeding, and the written consent must comply with statutory requirements (TRELA §1101.559). One practical solution is to have the broker seek a written buyer representation agreement containing the consent for the broker to act as an intermediary.

If the buyer does not agree to give written consent, the broker must advise the buyer that he or she is no longer represented and that fiduciary duties are owed to the seller under the listing agreement.

I have a listing, and an unrepresented buyer wants to make an offer. Must I act as an intermediary?

No. A broker representing one party (client) to a transaction in which the other party is unrepresented (customer) is not an intermediary. One may assist the buyer and represent the seller in this example. Agents should check with their brokers about this situation as many companies have policies addressing this and other situations.

Conflicts of Interest

When the Licensee is a Principal

When buying, selling or leasing property on his or her own behalf, on behalf of his or her spouse, parent, or child, or on behalf of a business entity in which he or she is more than a 10 percent owner, the licensee must disclose in writing that he or she is a licensee. Due to potential conflicts of interest, care should be exercised when attempting to act in this capacity. The licensee may not use his or her expertise to the disadvantage of the other party when acting in this capacity.

Receiving Fee from a Service Provider (22 TAC §535.148)

If a licensee receives a commission, rebate or fee from a service provider, he or she must obtain his or her principal's consent and must also disclose to the person being referred to the service provider that the licensee is receiving a commission, rebate or fee.

Sharing Fees with Unlicensed Persons (22 TAC §147)

Generally speaking, a licensee may not share a commission or fee with an unlicensed person. However, several exceptions have been part of the rules for many years. One exception permits a licensee to give a gift certificate worth not more than $50 to a person who is not licensed. The licensee may not give cash, and the gift certificate may not be exchangeable for cash. Another exception permits a licensee to pay a rebate to a buyer or seller in a transaction as long as the licensee obtains the consent of the party whom the licensee represents. Finally, a business entity licensed as a broker may share income with an unlicensed owner as long as the unlicensed owner does not personally engage in real estate brokerage activity. This rule acknowledges that an unlicensed person may own and share in the profits of a business entity licensed as a broker.

Residential Service Company Disclosure [22 TAC §535.148(e)]

A broker or salesperson is often paid a fee for providing advertising and other services on behalf of a residential service company. These fees are separate and apart from the typical services they provide as an agent in a real estate transaction. A new TREC rule requires a licensee to use RSC-1 to disclose such fee in writing to their client. A licensee is not required to use the form if he or she is not being paid a fee by a residential service company. However, if the licensee or the sponsoring broker is paid for advertising services unrelated to any one transaction, the licensee must disclose such payments to the client. For example, if a brokerage firm is paid $100 per month for advertising, the agent must disclose that payment in any transactions in which the licensee acted as an agent in the payment period. The disclosure form should not be attached to the contract as an addendum, but the form should be retained in the transaction records maintained by the broker as evidence that the disclosure was provided.

Conflicts Arising in Early Termination of Agency

Representation

The agency relationship is highly personal. It requires continuing consent of the principal and the agent. At any time, the agency relationship may be terminated by either party; however, an early termination without cause might expose the terminating party to liability under the representation agreement.

If an agent continues to offer the property for sale after termination, without the consent of the principal, it constitutes a violation of TRELA. Upon receipt of a notice of termination from a principal, the agent should cease acting as the principal's agent. A listing agent should cease all advertising. For example, remove signs, remove MLS listing, remove information from web site, etc.

Representing a Party Who is Subject to a Prior Agency Relationship

If a principal approaches a licensee and informs the licensee that the principal is subject to an existing exclusive agency relationship with another broker, the licensee should not provide any services until confirmation that the prior agency relationship has been terminated. The licensee should not interfere with an existing exclusive agency relationship under any circumstances [TRELA §1101.652 (b)(22)]. For example, the licensee should not suggest to the principal how the existing agency relationship should be terminated.

Compensation and Release of Contractual Obligation

Upon early termination of an agency relationship, a broker might be due compensation. At the time of termination, the broker and the principal should resolve the amount of compensation, if any, that might be due. However, the broker may not take actions that, in effect, prohibit the principal from engaging the services of another broker or otherwise buying, selling or leasing the property after termination.

Chapter 3

Contract Issues

Effective Date

The effective date is the most crucial date in the contract. It is the date from which most, if not all, performance periods are measured. One of the most significant complaints that many escrow agents make about real estate licensees is that licensees often fail to insert the effective date into the contract.

Who determines the effective date?

The promulgated contract forms instruct the broker to fill in the final date of acceptance as the effective date. The broker may be either the seller's broker or buyer's broker. It may be prudent for both brokers to confirm the effective date between themselves when communicating final acceptance.

How does a broker determine the effective date?

The final date of acceptance is the date on which the contract becomes binding between the parties. It is the date that both buyer and seller have agreed to all terms of the contract and have executed the contract. Four

elements must be satisfied for final acceptance to take place. *The effective date is the date when the last element (communication back) is made after the other 3 elements are satisfied.*

1. The final contract must be in writing (typically satisfied when negotiations are made using promulgated forms).
2. Both buyer and seller must sign the final contract (including the initialing of any handwritten changes to the initially drafted offer, if applicable).
3. Acceptance must be unequivocal.
4. The last party to accept must communicate acceptance back to the other party (or the other party's agent).

Under the following example, what is the effective date?

The buyer makes a written offer through his agent to the seller on January 1. The listing agent delivers the offer to the seller on January 2. The seller signs the offer on January 3 (making no changes) and delivers the offer back to the listing agent on January 4. The listing agent faxes the executed contract to the buyer's agent on January 5. The buyer's agent calls the buyer on January 6 and informs the buyer that the seller has accepted the offer.

The effective date is January 5, the date the listing agent communicated to the buyer's agent that the seller signed and unequivocally accepted the buyer's offer. Note that it might be prudent for the listing agent to confirm with the buyer's agent the exact effective date at the time the listing agent communicates acceptance to the buyer's agent.

Would the answer have been the same if there had been no buyer's agent and, instead, the buyer was working directly with the listing agent?

No. In this case, the effective date is the date the buyer is informed that the seller accepted the offer.

If the effective date is not filled in, does that mean that there is no contract?

No. By signing the promulgated forms, the parties have mutually instructed the broker to fill in the final date of acceptance as the effective date. He or she may be placed in the precarious position of later having to determine the effective date of the contract. The final date of acceptance must be resolved by the parties with the assistance of the brokers or, ultimately, a court of law.

When calculating the time for performance, is the effective date included as the first day?

No. Here is an example. The buyer has the right to terminate the contract within 5 days after the effective date, and the effective date is January 1. The buyer may terminate the contract at any time until 11:59 p.m. on January 6. Note that January 2 is the first day after the effective date.

Saturday or Monday?

On Saturday evening, the listing agent notifies the buyer's agent that the seller accepted the offer from the buyer. The seller accepted the offer unequivocally and signed the contract. The buyer's agent informs the listing agent that he will not be able to notify the buyer of the acceptance until Monday. Should the brokers insert Monday as the effective date?

No. Under these facts, the elements of final acceptance are satisfied on Saturday.

Proper Treatment of Option Money

When a buyer purchases an unrestricted right to terminate pursuant to Paragraph 23 (Termination Option) in any of the 6 TREC promulgated contracts, the buyer has 2 days after the execution date of the contract to tender the agreed upon option fee to the seller. The buyer's agent/broker should deliver the option fee to the listing agent/broker or seller within the 2-day period. Delivery may be by mail, courier, certified mail, or by personally delivering the option fee to the listing office. The option fee should not be delivered to any third party involved in the transaction, such as the title company or the lender. The buyer will <u>not</u> have a termination option if the option fee is delivered after the 2-day period [TRELA §1101.557(b)(3)].

Paragraph 11 — Special Provisions

The TREC contract forms and rules provide that the licensee may insert only factual statements and business details into the contract forms, including special provisions. Inserting a provision that materially affects the legal rights or duties of the parties may move the licensee into the unauthorized practice of law. In the past, licensees might typically insert statements such as *"the big screen television and round sofa in the family room is to convey to the buyer."* Recently, TREC adopted (for voluntary use) the Non-Realty Items Addendum. This form is voluntary (because of lender-related issues); however, using the addendum eliminates the need to draft a special provision dealing with personal property items.

Case Study

A broker wrote in special provisions, "Both Seller and Purchaser agree that there are items of Personal Property which will be removed from the Property and that all fixtures which are attached to the Property will remain with the Property, said fixtures including, but not limited to fences, working pens, gates, chutes, water well fixtures, and tanks." The buyer argued that the seller defaulted when the seller failed to remove <u>all</u> the personal property (having left a few items). The seller prevailed because the court noted that the seller substantially complied with the provision and the word *all* did not apply to "personal property" in the special provision [Lewis v. Foxworth, 170 S.W. 3d 900 (2005)].

Case Study

In another case, a broker inserted a provision in the Farm and Ranch Contract form, with respect to minerals, that stated, "None of the above are available to be conveyed." The seller thought he was retaining the minerals. The court concluded that the provision did not reserve the minerals and held for the buyer [Johnson v. Conner, 260 S.W. 3d 575 (2008)]. The Addendum for Oil, Gas and Other Minerals is now promulgated and licensees should provide this form to the parties who wish to negotiate mineral reservations.

As-Is Clause

Several court cases in the last few years have consistently held that the provision in Paragraph 7, which states the buyer accepts the property in its present condition, is an as-is clause. Therefore, licensees do not need to attempt to negotiate additional as-is provisions in special provisions. This type of clause should originate only with the principals' attorneys, if at all.

Brokerage Fees

Paragraph 8 of the contract forms provides that agreements to pay brokers are contained in separate written agreements. Therefore, it is prudent for the licensee to address the payment of brokerage fees outside the contract and not in special provisions.

The following clauses have been inserted into special provisions and should not have originated with licensees. These clauses are vague, incomplete, border on the unauthorized practice of law, or are addressed by other promulgated addenda.

"This contract is subject to a satisfactory appraisal report." (or inspection report)

"This contract is subject to the buyer selling buyer's existing home."

"Buyer agrees not to require seller to complete any repairs."

"Buyer may begin to move-in 3 days before closing." (or seller to stay after closing)

"If for some reason buyer cannot obtain financing, the parties will renegotiate owner financing at that time."

"Buyer requests seller to paint all exterior doors."

"Seller shall provide buyer with an allowance at closing in the amount of $1,000.00."

"Buyer has the right to do inspections and negotiate repairs, if any, through August 4, 2011 or as soon as the property is vacated. If such negotiations do not result in mutual agreement of the parties, buyer may terminate this contract and his earnest money will be refunded." (This provision was drafted because the seller did not intend to vacate until about 10 days after the option period expired. The house was full of boxes and other items that blocked many of the walls and floors. The buyer wanted the right to review and terminate after he saw the house vacant.)

A factual statement is a statement that can be verified as true. It is not a provision under which the parties agree to perform some obligations. A business detail is more of an accounting term that is used to provide more information helpful to an audit or transaction. Business details are, in essence, footnotes to help the reader to better understand a report. Similarly, the business detail in special provisions of the TREC contract forms should only provide information about the existing obligations of the parties found in other provisions of the contract form. Generally, it is not a place to insert additional provisions without the assistance of an attorney.

Matters that may be appropriate for special provisions include, but are not limited to the following:

- disclosure that the licensee is related to one of the parties;
- disclosure that one of the parties is a licensee;
- certain instructions to the title company, such as the buyer purchasing the boundary deletion; or
- provisions that cannot fit into the limited space or line of another provision (for example, if 4 persons are the sellers).

Electronic Signatures

UETA

The Uniform Electronic Transactions Act (UETA) was published by the National Conference of Commissioners on Uniform State Laws (NCCUSL) in 1999. It was adopted in Texas in 2001 (effective 1/1/2002) and is codified as Chapter 43, Business and Commerce Code.

UETA removes barriers to electronic commerce by establishing electronic records and signatures as being the legal equivalent to paper writings and manual signatures. UETA is purely a procedural law that permits electronic records and signatures without changing existing substantive laws. UETA *does not require* the use of electronic signatures. UETA defines an electronic signature as "an electronic sound, symbol, or process attached to or logically associated with a record and executed or adopted by a person with the intent to sign the record." No specific format is provided.

Both parties to a transaction must agree to conduct the transaction electronically. UETA also allows a person who has agreed to an electronic transaction to withhold his or her consent in connection with other transactions. This would apply specifically to a provision in an agreement that required a person to consent to using electronic signatures in future transactions.

E-sign

In 2000, Congress enacted the Electronic Signatures in Global and National Commerce Act (E-Sign). E-Sign overlaps with UETA, but it is not identical to UETA. E-Sign specifies the legal effect and enforceability of electronic contracts and electronic signatures, but it does not address how to establish the authenticity or validity of those signatures. Under E-Sign, if a state has adopted UETA, the state's law will preempt E-Sign and will govern electronic transactions.

Consumer's Consent

Both UETA and E-Sign require the consumer's consent to conduct the transaction electronically, and E-Sign requires that consent itself be communicated electronically. Initial consent may be given in paper or electronically. Since the definition of an electronic signature is broad, it appears that consent could be established by any reasonable means. A court might hold that "reasonable means" could include the click of a mouse, or it might require a more sophisticated means of establishing consent. Until custom and practice develop electronic transactions involving signatures, most experts are suggesting that secure platforms involving verifiable signatures be employed (for example, VeriSign or Entrust).

Under UETA, the consumer must be able to decline to use electronic means to transact. E-Sign specifically allows a consumer to withdraw his or her consent to the use of electronic records at any point in the transaction. If a consumer who initially gives consent to the use of electronic records withdraws that consent, the parties will need to complete the rest of the transaction in paper and ink format.

Brokers will need to obtain the consent of both the buyer and the seller to conduct the transaction electronically. If only one consents, the broker may continue to have an electronic relationship with him or her; however, the relationship with the other party would need to be handled in paper format. Privacy is a critical issue. Many consumers are very wary of using electronic means to conduct business.

Before relying on electronic signatures in a transaction, it seems prudent to

- obtain the necessary consents to the electronic transaction at the outset (both consent to the receipt of electronic records and consent to the use of electronic signatures),
- disclose to consumers that they have the right to withdraw their consent at any point in the transaction, and
- provide adequate means to withdraw the consent (providing notice of any ramifications, such as additional costs or a delay in the transaction because of switching to a paper system).

Technology

The law is technology neutral. The parties must agree on the method for digitally authenticating the documents of the transaction, and the consumer must consent electronically, thereby proving they can access the information that is the subject of the consent.

Records Retention

Records can be retained electronically and must be kept for a minimum of 4 years. The storage method used must ensure that the record can be accurately reproduced for later reference by all parties who are entitled to retain the record.

Short Sale Addendum

The Short Sale Addendum is to be used when a seller desires to place a contingency in the contract under which the seller will seek approval from his lender to sell the property for a price that is less than the amount owed against the property. The parties agree that if the seller cannot obtain lender approval by a certain date, the contract will terminate.

While the parties wait for the lender's approval, does the buyer need to perform under the contract?

Paragraph C of the addendum provides that the parties only need to perform as the addendum requires. The seller is obliged to apply and make every reasonable effort to obtain the lender's approval. The seller is also obliged to furnish all information and documents required by the lender. The buyer is to deposit the earnest money and pay the option fee, if any, to the seller at the time the parties execute the addendum.

What is the effective date under the Addendum?

The effective date (for purposes of depositing earnest money and paying the option fee) is the date of final acceptance (the date both parties sign the contract). The effective date for all other performance under the contract is the "amended effective date," which is the date the seller notifies the buyer that the seller has obtained the lender's consent.

If the option applies, may the buyer terminate while the parties are waiting for approval from the lender?

Yes. Paragraph F in the addendum answers this question. The buyer may terminate at any time when the parties are awaiting the lender's approval. The option period runs from the amended effective date through the number of days specified as the option period.

If the seller never obtains the lender's approval, does the buyer receive a refund of the earnest money and the option fee?

The earnest money is returned to the buyer, but the seller retains the option fee. Note that the buyer retained the right to terminate the contract at any time while awaiting the lender's approval.

Can the seller accept more than one offer when both offers have the Short Sale Addendum attached?

Yes, if used together with the back-up addendum. The seller agrees under the addendum to use every reasonable effort to obtain the lender's consent.

How does a seller notify a buyer that the contract is terminated if lender's approval is not obtained?

Notice must be in writing.

If the seller does not notify the buyer that the contract terminated by the date specified in Paragraph D of the addendum, should the buyer notify the seller that the contract is terminated?

Such notice is not required, although it is a good way of documenting the termination.

Backup Addendum

The Addendum for Backup Contract is to be used when a prospective buyer wishes to make an offer to purchase a property that the seller has already agreed to sell to another buyer. The backup buyer and seller agree that if the first contract terminates by a certain date, the seller will sell the property to the backup buyer.

While in the backup position, does the backup buyer need to perform under the contract?

The first line in Paragraph A requires the backup buyer to deposit the earnest money and pay the option fee, if any, to the seller at the time the parties execute the backup contract.

What is the effective date under the Addendum for Backup Contract?

The effective date (for purposes of depositing earnest money and paying the option fee) is the date of final acceptance (the date both parties sign the backup contract). The effective date for all other performance under the contract is the "amended effective date," which is the date the seller notifies the backup buyer that the first contract is terminated.

If the option applies, may the backup buyer terminate when in the backup position?

Yes. Paragraph E provides that the backup buyer may terminate at any time when the backup buyer is in the backup position. The option period, then, runs from the amended effective date (the date the backup contract becomes the primary contract) through the number of days specified as the option period.

If the backup contract never moves into the primary position, does the backup buyer receive a refund of the earnest money and the option fee?

The earnest money is returned to the backup buyer, but the seller retains the option fee. Note that the backp buyer retained the right to terminate the backup contract at any time the buyer remained in the backup position.

If the seller agrees to extend closing under the first contract or otherwise change the first contract, may the backup buyer claim that the first contract is terminated?

No. Paragraph D provides that an amendment to the first contract does not terminate the first contract.

May the Addendum for Backup Contract be used to negotiate a backup contract to another backup contract?

No. The addendum is not designed for this purpose.

How does a seller notify a backup buyer that the first contract is terminated?

Notice must be in writing.

If the seller does not notify the backup buyer that the first contract terminated by the date specified in Paragraph B of the addendum, should either party notify the other that the backup contract is terminated?

Such a notice is not required by the form but may be prudent.

Defect Disclosure

Chapter **4**

Seller's Disclosure of Property Condition

House Bill 3391, House Bill 3389, and Senate Bill 710, 82nd Texas Legislature, Regular Session (2011), amend §5.008 of the Texas Property Code to provide additional disclosures in the Seller's Disclosure of Property Condition Notice.

- House Bill 3391 amends the notice to require disclosure of any rainwater harvesting system connected to the property's public water supply that can be used for indoor potable purposes.
- House Bill 3389 amends the notice to require disclosure of information regarding liquid propane gas.
- Senate Bill 710 amends the disclosure notice to require disclosure of whether there is a blockable main drain in a pool, hot tub or spa.

The effective date for the changes to the disclosure notice is September 1, 2011. At a meeting on August 1, 2011, TREC approved amendments to the Seller's Disclosure of Property Condition Notice, TREC No. OP-H, to incorporate the amendments to Section 5.008.

Property Defects

What is a defect?

It is some irregularity in a surface or a structure of the property that mars its appearance or causes some aspect of the property to weaken or fail. It involves tangible aspects of the property, whether its physical appearance or its physical structure. When we call something defective, we mean it is blemished, broken, deficient or imperfect in some physical sense (Coldwell Banker Whiteside v. Ryan Equity, 181 S.W. 3d 879).

Disclosure

A seller of real property in Texas and a real estate broker must disclose to a prospective buyer any known defect in the property. The broker's duty to disclose known defects is the same regardless of whom the broker represents. This duty applies to all types of property (residential and commercial) [TRELA §1101.652(b)(4)].

The Texas Property Code (§5.008) provides that a seller of residential property consisting of not more than one dwelling unit is to complete a seller's disclosure notice and deliver it to the buyer on or before the effective date of a contract.

Defect Disclosure FAQ

What if, as a licensee, I learn that there is a defect, but the seller does not want it disclosed?

Inform the seller that you are obligated by statute to make the disclosure and that an attorney should be consulted if the seller chooses not to disclose the defect.

Exceptions to the Seller's Disclosure Form

The requirement to provide the Seller's Disclosure Form does not apply to any transfers:

- pursuant to a court order;
- by a trustee in bankruptcy;
- to a mortgagee by a mortgagor or successor in interest;
- by a mortgagee or beneficiary under a deed of trust who has acquired the real property by sale conducted to a power of sale under a deed of trust or a sale pursuant to a court-ordered foreclosure or has acquired the real property by deed in lieu of foreclosure;
- by a fiduciary in the course of the administration of a decedent's estate, guardianship, conservatorship, or trust;
- from one co-owner to one or more co-owners;
- made to a spouse or a person or persons in the initial line of consanguinity of one or more of the transferors;
- between spouses resulting from a decree of dissolution of marriage or a decree of legal separation or from a property settlement agreement incident to such a decree;
- to or from a governmental entity;
- of new residences of not more than one dwelling unit that have not previously been occupied for essential purposes; or
- of real property where the value of any dwelling does not exceed 5 percent of the value of the property.

Why do multiple variations of the seller's disclosure notice exist?

The seller's disclosure notice statute requires that the seller use the form set out in the statute or a form that is substantially similar containing all of the items in the statutory form. The TREC Seller's Disclosure of Property Condition form is identical to the statutory form. TREC publishes the form as a convenience for brokers, sellers and buyers. Some professional associations also publish seller's disclosure notice forms that comply with the statute and contain additional disclosures that those groups have determined are relevant. Whichever form the seller uses, it must contain all items in and be substantially similar to the statutory form.

Must every seller deliver the seller's disclosure notice to a prospective buyer?

The seller's disclosure notice statute contains 11 narrow exemptions that most real estate brokers typically will not encounter on a regular basis. The most common exemption is the new home exemption or builder exemption. The next two most common exemptions are the trustee or executor exemption and the foreclosure exemption. Under these exemptions, the following are not required to complete the seller's disclosure notice: a builder of a new home, a trustee or executor of an estate, and a lender after it has foreclosed on a property. Keep in mind, however, that even though these sellers are exempt under Texas Property Code §5.008, they are still required under common law and other statutes to disclose any known defect. It is the mechanism of disclosure, namely the seller's disclosure notice, which is not mandated.

Is a relocation company required to deliver a seller's disclosure notice?

If the relocation company is the seller, it must deliver the seller's disclosure notice.

Must a seller disclose a previous death at a property?

The statute provides that neither a seller nor a broker must disclose deaths that occurred by natural causes, suicide, or accidents unrelated to the condition of the property [Texas Property Code §5.008(c)].

Must a seller disclose prior water penetration in a property?

If the prior water penetration has been cured and any ensuing damage from the prior water penetration has been cured, there is no longer a defect and the seller would not be obligated to disclose the prior water penetration. However, if the prior water penetration has not been cured or the ensuing damage has not been cured, then such items would be considered defects.

Must a seller or broker disclose to a prospective buyer the fact that a registered sex offender resides in the neighborhood?

The Code of Criminal Procedures §62.056 provides that neither the owner of a single-family residential property nor real estate agents have a duty to disclose that a nearby resident is a registered sex offender. Texas Government Code §411.088 requires that DPS information about sex offender registrants be made available to the public at no cost over the Internet.

Is an off-site condition considered a defect (for example, roadways, landfills, feed lots, etc.)?

Generally, an off-site condition is not a defect with the property in question. However, the off-site condition might affect the property. If it affects the property in a physical way, it is possible that the off-site condition could be the source of a defect that has moved onto the property. For example, if a neighboring property contains underground tanks that leak, the contaminant might leak onto the property in question.

Chapter 5

Advertising ────────

TRELA §1101.652(b)(23) prohibits a licensee from publishing an advertisement that
- misleads or is likely to deceive the public,
- tends to create a misleading impression, or
- fails to identify the person causing the advertisement to be published as a licensed broker or agent.

This provision is twofold: It prohibits misleading advertising and it requires licensees to identify themselves in advertising as a broker or agent.

Definition

Revised 22 TAC §535.154 clarifies the statutory provision relating to advertisements. Several changes were made to address ambiguities and to update various subsections. The definition of "advertisement" was updated to encompass a broader variety of electronic communications including social networking websites, such as Twitter or Facebook. The rule was also amended to clarify that real estate information (including a listing), that is on a licensee's website and behind a firewall or software requiring a password or registration to access the information, is not considered an "advertisement."

Including the Broker's Name

The rule requires brokers and salespersons to clearly and conspicuously include the broker's name in all advertising and permits the use of a broker's assumed name if it has been filed with the commission. A broker must notify the commission within 30 days of starting or stopping the use of an assumed name. Although the rule does not specifically define "clear and conspicuous," TREC adopted a safe harbor policy statement that the commission considers the broker's name to be clear and conspicuous if it is no less than half the font size of the largest telephone number or other contact information in the advertisement.

Teams

What are the advertising implications when a team or group of licensees in a brokerage firm work together and wish to advertise under a team name? First, the broker must register the team name as the broker's

"assumed name" with TREC. If the team name does not include the name of a salesperson, the team can advertise using that name. The broker's name does not need to be included in the advertisement, since the assumed name belongs to the broker. In addition, the advertisement must include the additional designation of "agent," "broker," or trade association name. The "agent" designation is not required after each licensee's name if the advertisement includes more than one name. As always, the sponsoring broker remains responsible for a team's advertising.

If the team name includes the name of a salesperson, the rules against implying that the salesperson is responsible for the operations of a brokerage must be considered. TREC has determined that using names such as the "Sally Salesperson Team" or the "Sam Salesperson Group" do not imply that the salesperson is responsible for operation of a brokerage so long as the advertisement also includes the name or another assumed name of the broker. However, some names such as "Sally Salesperson and Associates" or "Sam Salesperson and Company" do imply that the salesperson is responsible for the operation of a brokerage, even when the broker's name is included in the advertising. Thus, including the broker's name in the advertising does not cure the potential for misleading the public, and so the use of such names is not allowed.

Duke is not the broker for this company.
What is missing on this website?

Assumed Names

Assumed names that have been filed with TREC are now searchable in the "Licensee Lookup" section of the TREC website. Brokers may use the Notice of DBA or Assumed Name for Broker's License form available on the Forms page of the TREC website to notify TREC of the use of assumed names.

Corporations

If the salesperson's name is part of the name of a corporation or limited liability company registered with the Secretary of State and licensed as a broker, the corporation or LLC may use the salesperson's name in advertising. The name of the designated broker must also be included because the designated broker is the person responsible for the entity's actions. An unlicensed person's name may be used in advertising only if the name is properly filed as a business, trade or assumed name of a broker with TREC. The advertisement may not suggest the unlicensed person is authorized to engage in real estate brokerage.

Trade Names

A licensee is prohibited from using a copyrighted trade name unless he or she has the authority to use the name. The best examples are when licensees use the term "Realtist" or "Realtor" in advertising. A licensee may use such terms only if he or she is a member of the trade association.

Signs

The rule requires road signs to include the designation "agent" or "broker" (or presumably trade association name if a member) in a clear and conspicuous manner. Although proposed at one time, a minimum font size for this designation was not enacted. Instead, TREC adopted a policy statement that says TREC considers the print to be clear and conspicuous if it is no less than half the font size of the largest phone number or other contact information in the road sign. The subsection regarding the designation as a broker or agent does not apply to directional signs or to signs placed in the yard of a listed property.

Other Changes

The revised rule provides clarification about the types of advertising considered deceptive and misleading. A licensee may not advertise information regarding service providers that ranks the providers unless the ranking is based on disclosed objective criteria. A licensee may not advertise that he or she offers, sponsors or conducts TREC-approved courses unless the licensee is approved to offer the courses.

Intellectual Property

Numerous lawsuits have been filed over copyright infringement against real estate licensees. Brokers and agents, often without malicious intent "cut and paste" articles from newspapers or magazines to post on their blog or website only to find themselves involved in a lawsuit over protected works. The answer a licensee might give is, "I gave credit to the newspaper for this material in my blog." This is NOT good enough for copyrighted material. The licensee must have expressed written permission from the creator of the work in order to reproduce the work. The licensee should keep these simple things in mind: any copying of work, whether from a news source, software, photos, music or print material is prohibited without the express written permission from the creator of the work.

Copyright Laws

Copyright laws apply to blogs, websites and social media postings as well as printed materials. For example, a licensee wishing to give an opinion about a newspaper article in his or her blog may simply refer to the article by date and placement. The licensee should NOT cut and paste the entire article. With regard to copying only parts of an article, there are some fair use rules in the copyright law. However, there are no specific rules about how many words constitute fair use. These rules depend on the circumstances of use. Copyright FAQs are available at http://www.copyright.gov.

Photographs and Music

Many times photographs and music are copyright protected, also. The licensee should be certain to read all the fine print on websites before downloading files regarding the guarantee that the music or photographs are not copyright protected.

Software

Be sure you are using licensed software on all your equipment. A copyright infringement lawsuit will eliminate the money saved by not purchasing a software license.

Dispute Resolution

Chapter 7

Mediation

In 1987, mediation became one of the five statutorily recognized types of Alternative Dispute Resolution (ADR). Texas statutes define a mediation resolution procedure as a forum before an impartial person (the mediator) designed to facilitate communication between parties and to promote reconciliation, settlement or understanding. Mediators do not make decisions or give awards. In a successful mediation, the parties agree on a settlement in writing, which becomes binding on both parties. Mediators follow ADR Procedures that are included in Chapter 154 of the Texas Civil Practices and Remedies Code. Researchers at the Real Estate Center at Texas A&M University surveyed practitioners and found that mediation has been used to settle a high percentage of disputes. Many Texas judges require court-ordered mediation before hearing a case.

Mediators are neither judges nor arbitrators. They are neutral facilitators in establishing dialogue among the parties to reach a settlement. Mediators do not need to be attorneys or hold special licenses or credentials. There are numerous mediation service providers, such as county supported mediation services, private mediators, university law schools, and professional and trade associations. County or district court clerks usually maintain lists of mediators for their area.

Mediators should possess some knowledge of the subject matter, the outcome of prior cases involving the controversy, recoveries for similar matters in local courts, and ADR procedures. Although mediators should remain neutral, their expertise can provide valuable guidelines for settlement. Mediators may not impose their judgment on the issues.

Arbitration

Texas statutes define arbitration as a forum where parties and counsel present their positions before an impartial third party who renders a specific award. The parties must agree in writing to arbitrate a dispute.

There are numerous arbitration providers, such as the American Arbitration Association, private attorneys, private arbitrators, and professional and trade associations. Typically, the arbitration procedure calls for a complaint or petition to be filed describing the dispute. The respondent will be given the opportunity to respond. A hearing is convened at which the parties present evidence and make arguments. The arbitrator(s) renders an award. The prevailing party may seek to enforce the award as a judgment by requesting that a court of law do so. Arbitration awards may be appealed on procedural or due process grounds.

Chapter 8

Section 535 Changes

The Texas Real Estate Commission adopted a series of rule amendments and new rules under Chapter 535 of Title 22 of the Texas Administrative Code (the Rules). Along with substantive revisions, the amendments and new rules reorganize and streamline the chapter into a more logical order. The effective date of the amendments is January 1, 2011, unless the text of the rule provides a different effective date.

The following is a list of most of the substantive changes to the rules. The TREC website has comprehensive summaries and the text of the adopted amendments and new rules (www.trec.texas.gov).

Broker Responsibility, §535.2

A broker is required to advise a sponsored salesperson of the scope of the salesperson's authorized activities under TRELA (the Act). The section clarifies that a broker is liable for the activities of the salesperson if the broker permits a salesperson to engage in activities beyond the scope originally authorized. A broker may designate *in writing* that another licensee will be responsible for day-to-day supervision of sponsored salespersons; however, the broker will have overall responsibility of the salesperson.

A broker is responsible for any property management and advertising conducted by sponsored salespersons.

A broker must maintain business records such as disclosures, commission agreements, work files, contracts and related addenda, property management contracts, appraisal related records, and sponsorship agreements for at least 4 years from the date of closing or termination of the contract.

Brokers will be required to maintain *written* policies and procedures to ensure that

- each sponsored salesperson is advised of the scope of the salesperson's authorized activities subject to the Act and is competent to conduct such activities,
- each sponsored salesperson maintains his or her license in active status while engaged in activities subject to the Act,
- any and all compensation paid to a sponsored salesperson for acts or services subject to the Act is paid by, through, or with the *written* consent of the sponsoring broker, and
- each sponsored salesperson is provided, on a timely basis prior to the effective date of the change, notice of any change to the Act, Rules, or TREC promulgated contract forms.

Brokers will ensure that

- each sponsored salesperson receives any education the broker may deem necessary to obtain and maintain on a current basis competency in the scope of the sponsored salesperson's practice subject to the Act in addition to completing statutory minimum continuing education requirements,
- each sponsored salesperson complies with TREC advertising rules,
- all trust accounts and other funds received from consumers are handled by the broker with appropriate controls, and
- records retention requirements in the rules are followed.

The amendments also specify that a broker must respond promptly to a sponsored salesperson's clients and licensees representing other parties in real estate transactions. Additionally, the sponsoring broker must also deliver to or otherwise provide correspondence on the commission to responsible salespersons.

The amendments clarify that the broker responsibility rules are not meant to create an employer/employee relationship where there is none.

Commissions for Salespersons, §535.3

Amendments to §535.3 require that a compensation agreement between a broker and sponsored salesperson must be in writing.

When a License is Required / Business Entities, §535.4, 535.5

New §535.4 is a compilation of existing rules that are put together into 1 comprehensive rule that addresses the instances in which a license is required under the Act. It clarifies that a corporation, partnership or limited liability company owned by a broker or salesperson that receives compensation on behalf of the licensee **must be licensed** as a broker under the Act. If a corporation or limited liability company is dissolved with the Secretary of State, the license becomes null and void.

Education and Experience, §535.54

Section 535.54 provides that a bachelor's degree from an accredited college or university satisfies all of the "related" education requirements for a salesperson or broker license. A bachelor's degree does not satisfy the required "core" courses.

Section 1101.362 of the Act authorizes TREC to waive some or all of the education and experience requirements for someone who has been licensed within the 4 years preceding the date the application is filed. TREC had previously waived the broker license education and experience if a broker had been licensed in the preceding 6 years and otherwise met the requirements of the section. The new rule changes the period from 6 years to 4 years, so that a person who was licensed in the preceding 4 years and otherwise meets the experience requirements of the section could apply to reinstate an expired broker license. If applying more than 2 years after a license expired, one would need to retake the examination. At its October 10, 2011 meeting, TREC made additional changes to the broker experience requirements along with other changes consistent with the requirements of SB 747 enacted by the 82nd Legislature. The text of the new rules is available on the TREC website at www.trec.texas.gov.

TREC will not grant credit to a student who has taken a core course with substantially the same content as one taken within the previous 2-year period.

Violations

License Under Suspension, §535.141

Section 535.141 now adds advertising to the list of prohibited activities that a licensee may not engage in while the license is under suspension. TREC may automatically suspend a license if the licensee violates certain types of terms or conditions of an agreed probated revocation or suspension. If an investigation reveals reasonable cause to believe the licensee may have committed other violations of the Act or Rules, no additional authorization shall be required to investigate to take action.

If a **salesperson** is subject to an order suspending the license, prior to the suspension, he or she must notify the sponsoring broker *in writing* that his or her license will be suspended. If the **salesperson** is involved in any real estate transaction, he or she must notify *in writing* all other parties, including principals and other brokers, that he or she cannot continue performing real estate brokerage services during the suspension.

If **a broker** is subject to an order suspending the license, prior to the suspension, he or she must notify *in writing* the following that his or her broker's license will be suspended:

- any salespersons he or she sponsors, and
- any corporation, limited liability company, or partnership for which the broker is engaged as an officer, manager or partner.

Licensee as Principal, §535.144

When engaging in a real estate transaction on his or her own behalf, on behalf of the business entity in which the licensee is more than a 10 percent owner, or on behalf of the licensee's spouse, parent, or child, the licensee is obligated to disclose *in writing* to any person with whom the licensee deals that he or she is a licensed real estate broker acting on his or her own behalf, or on behalf of the licensee's spouse, parent, or child.

Trust Accounts, §535.146

Amendments to §535.146 clarify existing requirements that apply to maintenance of trust accounts.

- Subsection (h) requires a broker to notify all parties in writing when a broker makes a disbursement to which all parties have not expressly agreed in writing.
- New subsection (k) clarifies that a broker may deposit and maintain additional amounts in a trust account to cover bank service fees.

Shared Commission, §535.147

- Section 535.147(a) clarifies that a licensee may not share a commission with an unlicensed person except as provided by the Act or Rules.
- New subsection (b) authorizes an unlicensed person to share in the income earned by a licensed business entity as long as the person does not engage in real estate brokerage activity.
- New subsection (c) clarifies that a broker or salesperson may not share a commission with an unlicensed corporation or limited liability company created by a licensee for the purpose of collecting a commission or fees on behalf of the licensee.

Service Providers, §535.148

- New subsection (c) prohibits a licensee from contracting with a service provider if the contract does not allow the licensee from entering into or offering similar service on behalf of a competing service provider.
- New subsection (d) prohibits fee arrangements based on a party to the real estate transaction purchasing a contract or services from a specific service provider.
- New subsection (e) adopts RSC-1, Disclosure of Relationship with Residential Service Company, which licensees are required to use as of March 1, 2011, to disclose compensation for services provided to or on behalf of a residential service company.

Miscellaneous License Provisions

Email Address, §535.96

Under §535.96, licensees are required to notify TREC of the licensee's current email address, if any, and other contact information.

Probationary License Renewal, §535.94(d)

New §535.94(d) clarifies that if a person who has a probationary license renews the license within the 6-month late renewal period, the new license is subject to the remaining probationary period from the previous probationary license.

Terminated Sponsorship, §535.121

Amended section 535.121 clarifies that a salesperson's license becomes inactive if the sponsoring broker notifies TREC in writing that the sponsorship is terminated.

Home Inspectors

Online Activity

Changes were made throughout the rules to reflect a greater emphasis on online transactions and electronic delivery of notices and license certificates.

Reports

Inspection reports must be delivered to the client within 3 days unless otherwise agreed to by the client (§535.223). Inspection reports must contain the name and license number of each inspector who participated in performing the inspection, as well as the names of the sponsoring inspector (§535.223). Signatures of sponsoring inspectors are no longer required on reports (§§535.223 and 535.224).

Inspector Continuing Education, (§535.212)

Effective September 1, 2011, every real estate inspector and professional inspector (but not apprentice) is required to take a 6-hour course in Standards of Practice/Ethics/Legal Update to renew the license.

Applicants for real estate inspector or professional inspector license will be required to take a specific number of hours in each core subject matter area (plumbing, electrical, report writing, etc.). See the TREC website for more details about this requirement.

Property Management
Chapter 9

TREC Rules Addressing Property Management

In January of 2011, TREC adopted a series of amendments to all the rules, which included revisions to rules dealing with property management including the following:

- a broker is responsible for any property management activity conducted by sponsored salespersons and for all advertising done by sponsored salespersons,
- all trust accounts, including but not limited to property management trust accounts, and other funds received from consumers are handled by the broker with appropriate controls,
- a broker must notify all parties in writing when a broker makes a disbursement to which all parties have not expressly agreed to in writing, and

- a broker may deposit and maintain additional amounts in a trust account to cover bank service fees.

Case Study

Theft From Property Management Accounts

Facts:

A broker established new trust and operating accounts for a recently purchased property management company. A sponsored salesperson ran the everyday business. Property owners were notified of the purchase of the business, but the broker and sponsored salesperson who ran the company both failed to obtain assignments of the prior property management agreements or enter into new ones.

Property management continued until April, 2008, when the broker discovered that over $18,000 was missing. The salesperson admitted to having used the property management accounts for personal purchases and justified her actions based on the money spent being equal to what she would have earned as the sponsored salesperson. Additionally, the salesperson had not sent out monthly statements to the property owners, only sending them checks for money due. The broker agreed to continue sponsoring the salesperson if the salesperson's grandmother, a former salesperson, would do the bookkeeping. Accounts would be inaccessible to the salesperson, although she would continue to run the property management company.

During May, 2008, the broker relocated her real estate business to the location of a rival real estate business, which specialized in REO and foreclosed properties for banks, maintaining them for a fee and reimbursement of their expenses. The broker, knowing this, assumed their identity by filing an assumed name adding "The" before the name, and opened a bank account in that name, collecting and cashing checks not due her ($35,000). She kept the funds despite knowing they were not for her. The broker also never notified TREC of usage of the new assumed name.

In June 2008, the broker ran into personal financial difficulties. The broker abruptly closed the property management business with no notice to the property owners. The broker terminated sponsorship of the salesperson, and discontinued contact with the owners. The broker transferred all funds in the trust and operating accounts to her attorney for distribution to the owners. However, checks outstanding to the property owners for June and July, 2008, were returned for insufficient funds.

The salesperson obtained a new sponsoring broker and resurrected the property management business under a new name. The salesperson then notified the property owners that her prior broker had stolen their money and written them insufficient funds checks. She then sent a letter to her former broker demanding return of all of the property management business funds on behalf of the owners who were now her clients. When this effort failed, the salesperson sent each owner a partially completed TREC complaint form to file complaints against her former broker. She also sent them form letters addressed to the local district attorney.

Several property owners filed complaints against the broker with the district attorney and TREC. During TREC's investigation, the salesperson was added for her role in the property management business. The broker blamed her attorney for taking the money. The attorney claimed the funds were due him for legal fees with no knowledge of the source. The attorney later relinquished his law license. No money was returned.

In July, 2009, felony charges were filed against the broker with trial pending. The broker of the rival real estate business filed a complaint with TREC in February, 2010.

Conclusions:

- The broker was negligent in overseeing the actions of her sponsored salesperson in property management, failing to properly document assumption of property management agreements with property owners and not keeping clients informed of closing of the business; the salesperson was also negligent in failing to keep clients informed of property occupancy, accounting for security deposits, and utilizing funds properly for property maintenance in violation of Texas Occupations Code §1101.652(b)(1).
- The broker failed within a reasonable time to properly account for or remit money received by her that belonged to others to be held in trust within a reasonable time in violation of Texas Occupations Code §1101.652(b)(9).
- The broker and salesperson commingled the broker's money with money belonging to others, which must be maintained in a trust account and may not be used to pay operating expenses or withdrawn for any purpose other than proper disbursement of the monies held in trust in violation of Texas Occupations Code §1101.652(b)(10).
- The broker engaged in conduct which was dishonest or done in bad faith by failing to keep clients informed of her financial difficulties or the inability to pay monies due under the

property management agreements in violation of Texas Occupations Code §1101.652(b)(2).

Orders:

- The broker's license was revoked, and the broker assessed a $60,000 administrative penalty.

- The salesperson's license was voluntarily surrendered, and she cannot renew, attempt to renew or apply for a real estate license for 6 years.

Chapter 10

TREC Cases

Dishonest Conduct and Flagrant Course of Misrepresentation

Facts:

In May, 2009, a salesperson contacted another agent stating that he needed $20,000 for a real estate investment in a condominium. The other agent had a buyer who wanted to purchase rental property. The buyer's agent told the buyer about the condominium, and she agreed to purchase it as a rental property. The buyer wired $20,000 to the buyer's agent believing it would be held in escrow by a title company. The buyer's agent, upon instruction from the salesperson, wired the $20,000 directly to the salesperson's account.

The buyer was never shown a condominium and never signed a contract or other documentation related to a real estate transaction. When the buyer questioned why she did not have to sign any documentation, she was told that the money was for an investment in real estate and not for the purchase of any particular property, she would be a partial owner of a property when the deal was closed, and she did not need to sign any documents. When the buyer repeatedly requested to see a copy of what contract was signed using her money, she was shown an unsigned contract for a house that she was told the salesperson had listed. The contract, however, showed that the salesperson was the owner of the property.

The buyer became suspicious and demanded that her agent obtain a return of her money. The buyer's agent made repeated attempts to get the money back, as evidenced by emails; however, the salesperson acted deceptively and evasively on numerous occasions, assuring the buyer's agent that his client would receive a refund or that the refund was being processed. In fact, the salesperson commingled the funds with his own money and spent the money for his own personal use. The money was never refunded to the buyer.

The buyer's agent entered into an agreed order with TREC. The salesperson requested a hearing, and TREC entered a final order against the salesperson based on the proposal for decision prepared by the administrative law judge.

Conclusions:

Buyer's Agent

The buyer's agent failed within a reasonable time to properly account for or remit money received by the buyer's agent and belonging to another person in violation of Texas Occupations Code §1101.652(b)(9).

Salesperson

- The salesperson engaged in conduct that is dishonest or in bad faith or that demonstrates untrustworthiness in violation of Texas Occupations Code §1101.652(b)(2).
- The salesperson pursued a continued and flagrant course of misrepresentation or made false promises in violation of Texas Occupations Code §1101.652(b)(6).
- The salesperson failed within a reasonable time to properly account for or remit money received by the salesperson and belonging to another person in violation of Texas Occupations Code §1101.652(b)(9).
- The salesperson commingled money another person's money with his own in violation of Texas Occupations Code §1101.652(b)(10).

Orders:

Buyer's Agent

The buyer's agent was assessed a fine of $1,500 and suspended for a period of 3 years. The 3-year suspension was probated under the following terms and conditions:

- The agent must comply with Chapter 1101 of the Texas Occupations Code and with the Rules of the Commission.
- The agent must fully cooperate with the Commission's Standards & Enforcement Services in completing its investigation of

any complaints which may be filed against the agent and testify at any SOAH hearing related to this transaction.
- The agent must complete a 30-hour agency law course as defined by Texas Occupations Code §1101.003(a)(1) from a school or provider approved by or acceptable to TREC. These hours are in addition to the Mandatory Continuing Education (MCE) hours required for the next renewal of the agent's Texas real estate license.

Salesperson

- The salesperson's license was revoked and an administrative penalty in the amount of $13,000 was assessed.

Failure to Disclose a Defect and Signing Without Authorization

Facts:

In April 2008, a broker entered into a verbal agreement to represent a client in the negotiation and purchase of residential real property. The broker was successful in locating an ideal property for the client, and a sales contract was executed for the property's purchase. Closing was scheduled in April 2008.

A home inspection for the property was ordered by the client. A pest inspection was included with the home inspection. The pest inspection company conducted an inspection of the property. At the time of the pest inspection, the broker, in the absence of the client, visited the property and delivered payment for the pest inspection service to the pest inspection company. The pest inspection company submitted the pest inspection report for the property to the broker. The pest inspection report was not provided to the client.

The pest inspection report noted active and previous infestation of the property by subterranean termites. The pest inspection report also noted swarming termites, termite mud, and termite damage in the front bedroom area of the property. The broker did not provide the pest inspection report to the client nor did he inform the client of the results.

Prior to closing, the broker signed, without proper written authorization from the client, the client's name to an amendment of the sales contract. The amendment provided a reduction in the purchase price of the property, which was negotiated based on several items, including the cost of treatment for termites. The seller signed the amendment, and the sale for the property closed with the client taking ownership of the property. After closing, the client discovered the existence of termites on the property. The client submitted a complaint to TREC.

Conclusions:

- The broker failed to disclose to the client a defect (termite damage) known to the broker that would be a significant factor to a reasonable and prudent buyer in making a decision to purchase real property, in violation of Texas Occupations Code §1101.652(b)(4).
- The broker engaged in conduct that is dishonest or in bad faith or that demonstrates untrustworthiness by signing the client's name to a contract amendment without the knowledge of or authorization from the client, in violation of Texas Occupations Code §1101.652(b)(2).

Orders:

The broker's license was suspended for a period of 3 years. The 3-year suspension was probated under the following terms and conditions:

- The broker must comply with Chapter 1101 of the Texas Occupations Code and with the Rules of the Commission.
- The broker must fully cooperate with the Commission's Standards & Enforcement Services in completing its investigation of any complaints which may be filed against the broker.
- The broker must complete 30 hours in agency law, as defined by Texas Occupations Code §1101.003(a)(1), from a school or provider approved by or acceptable to TREC and that these hours are in addition to the Mandatory Continuing Education (MCE) hours required for the next renewal of the broker's Texas real estate license.
- The broker must pay an administrative penalty of $3,500 to TREC.

Broker Supervision of Sponsored Salesperson

Facts:

Two separate complaints were filed against a broker who was accused of not properly supervising sponsored salespersons.

Salesperson One: The broker, through his salesperson, executed a property management contract. On behalf of the owner, the salesperson executed a lease for a term of a year with a monthly rental payment of $1,400 and collected a $1,400 security deposit. The money was never deposited into a trust account. The salesperson suddenly informed the property owner she was unable to fulfill her management of the property. The owner requested return of the final month's rental payment and security deposit. The owner received $1,000 of the final month's rental only. The salesperson acknowledged her failure to return the $400 balance for rent and $1,400 for the security deposit. The salesperson surrendered her license.

Salesperson Two: The broker, through his salesperson, negotiated a listing agreement. Under the listing agreement, the seller agreed to pay the salesperson 5 percent of the sales price or 4 percent if the salesperson was the sole salesperson in the transaction. Shortly thereafter, the salesperson began representing a buyer. The salesperson had the buyer sign and initial a blank Residential Buyer/Tenant Representation Agreement. The salesperson proceeded although the agreement was not completely filled out. Further, the salesperson prepared a Nonrefundable Buyer Agency Retainer document and required the buyer to sign it. The salesperson told the buyer that such a retainer is typical business practice. The document provided for a nonrefundable $4,000 retainer from the buyer. The buyer paid the retainer directly to the salesperson.

The salesperson negotiated a contract between the buyer and seller without properly forming the intermediary relationship. The salesperson amended the Buyer Representation Agreement by altering the terms to include that the broker would receive 5 percent of the gross sales price and the buyer would receive credit for $6,500 paid to the broker. Additionally, the amended terms stated that if the buyer failed to close, the $6,500 would not be refunded and would be considered commission paid.

The salesperson amended the Buyer Representation agreement for a third time by changing the terms. The new terms required the buyer to pay the broker's fees of the greater of 6 percent of the sales price or $6,500 plus a $275 transaction fee. The salesperson was to receive compensation from both parties to the transaction per the listing agreement and the amended buyer representation agreement. The salesperson amended agreements and attempted to unilaterally amend those agreements when previous terms were no longer to his benefit. The buyer and seller refused to agree to any additional changes to their respective representation agreements. When the transaction under the terms of the representation agreement were no long in the benefit of the salesperson, he intentionally obstructed the closing of the transaction, and the transaction failed to close.

Conclusions:

- The broker acted negligently or incompetently in the supervision of salesperson 1 in violation of Texas Occupations Code §1101.652(b)(1) and is cause for the suspension or revocation of the broker's real estate license and is further cause for the assessment of an administrative penalty against the broker pursuant to Texas Occupations Code §1101.701.
- The Broker acted negligently or incompetently in the supervision of salesperson 2 in violation of Texas Occupations Code §1101.652(b)(1) and is cause for the suspension or revocation of the broker's real estate license and is further cause for the assessment of an administrative penalty against the broker pursuant to Texas Occupations Code §1101.701.

Orders:

The broker's license was reprimanded and was subject to the following terms and conditions:

- The broker must comply with Chapter 1101 of the Texas Occupations Code and with the Rules of the Commission.
- The broker fully cooperates with the Commission's Standards & Enforcement Services in completing its investigation of any complaints which may be filed against broker.
- The broker agrees to testify at any SOAH hearing upon timely request from TREC on any complaints currently opened against him.
- The broker shall pay the sum of $1,800 to satisfy salesperson's failure to remit rental payment and security deposit.
- The broker shall pay an administrative penalty of $7,000 to the Texas Real Estate Commission.

Failing to Forward Funds and Commingling Funds in Property Management

Facts:

A broker began collecting monthly rents and security deposits and managed properties for several years until October of 2009 when several owners' checks were returned for insufficient funds. The broker blamed this on errors caused by the brokerage's computer being stolen, bad bookkeepers who paid several vendors twice, and a big property owner client terminating its management agreement with the LLC, which caused a shortage of trust funds. When his promises to make the checks good did not materialize and additional money became due, the owners began canceling their management agreements. The owners were unable to obtain rents due nor the security deposits being held by the broker. Several property owners filed complaints with TREC. Some of the owners obtained judgments against the broker and LLC brokerage and were later reimbursed through the Real Estate Recovery Fund. The LLC was later forfeited by the Secretary of State for failure to pay franchise taxes.

The broker initially failed to respond to TREC but later admitted utilizing the property owners' money for unauthorized purposes and not reimbursing them.

Conclusions:

- Both the broker and LLC brokerage failed to properly account for or remit funds remitted to a license holder that belonged to another being held in trust in violation of Texas Occupations Code §1101.652(b)(9).
- Both the broker and LLC brokerage commingled money belonging to others with the license holder's own money, which must be maintained in a trust account, and which may not be used to pay operating expenses or withdrawn for any purpose other than proper disbursement of the money held in trust in violation of Texas Occupations Code §1101.652(b)(10).
- Both the broker and LLC brokerage engaged in conduct which was dishonest or done in bad faith by failing to keep clients informed of financial difficulties or the inability to pay money due under the property management agreements in violation of Texas Occupations Code §1101.652(b)(2)
- Both the broker and LLC brokerage, by failing to provide information sought by TREC within a reasonable time, were in violation of Texas Occupations Code §1101.652(a)(6).

Orders:

- The broker's license was revoked and the broker assessed a $60,000 administrative penalty.
- The LLC brokerage's license was revoked and assessed a $60,000 administrative penalty.

Appendix

Chapter 1 – The Canons of Professional Ethics

The duties of fidelity, integrity, and competency are aspirational goals expressed in the preamble to the Code of Ethics of the National Association of REALTORS® and the Code of Ethics of the CCIM Institute (Certified Commercial Investment Member).

The Code of Ethics of the National Association of Real Estate Brokers (Realtists) imposes a duty on Realtists to protect the public against misrepresentation, unethical practices or Fraud in their Practices (Part I, §3).

- NAR's Code of Ethics and the CCIM Code of Ethics prohibit their members from the following:
- Denying equal professional services to any person on the basis of protected class,
- Being a party to any agreement or plan to discriminate on the basis of protected classes,
- Discriminating in their employment practices on the basis of protected classes,
- Volunteering information regarding racial, religious, or ethnic composition of any neighborhood,
- Engaging in any activity that may result in panic selling, and
- Printing or distributing material that indicates any preference or limitation or discrimination based on a protect class (Art. 10).
- CCIM members may provide demographic information when involved in the sale or lease in commercial property if the information is needed to complete the transaction and is obtained from a recognized, reliable, independent, and impartial source (SP10-3).
- Part I, §2 of the Realtist Code of Ethics provides that a Realtist should never be instrumental in establishing, reinforcing or extending restrictions that limit the use or occupancy of property to any racial, religious or national origin groups.

The duty to treat other parties to a transaction honestly is also found in Article 1 of the NAR Code of Ethics and the CCIM Code of Ethics, and is expressed as a theme in the Realtist Code of Ethics.

Chapter 2 – Agency Relationships

- The duty to disclose who the agent represents at the first contact with the other party in the transaction or the other party's agent is also expressed in NAR's and CCIM's Codes of Ethics (SP 16-10, 11 & 12).

- The NAR and CCIM Codes of Ethics require the members to advise their clients of any potential for the member to represent more than one party in the transaction. This communication is required at the time a listing or buyer representation agreement is signed (SP 1-12 & 13).
- NAR's and CCIM's Codes of Ethics prohibit members from selling or acquiring an interest in real estate for themselves, their immediate families, members of their firms, or entities in which they have an ownership interest without making their true position known (Art 4.). Such disclosures must be in writing before signing a contract (SP 4-1). Part I §9 of the Realtist Code of Ethics requires the Realtist to disclose if he or she has a personal interest in the property being purchased.
- NAR's and CCIM's Codes of Ethics prohibit the member from receiving any commission, rebate or profit on expenditures without the client's knowledge and consent (Art 6). Any referral fees received for referring a person to a service provider must be disclosed to the client or customer to whom the recommendation is made.

- The prohibition against receiving compensation from more than one party without the knowledge and consent of all parties is also found in Article 7 of NAR's and CCIM's Codes of Ethics and in Part I, §6 of the Realtist Code of Ethics.
- The prohibition against interfering with the agency relationship of another broker is also found in Article 16 of NAR's and CCIM's Code of Ethics and Part II, §7 of the Realtist Code of Ethics.
-

Chapter 5 – Advertising

- Article 12 of NAR's and CCIM's Codes of Ethics require members to: (1) present a true picture in their advertisements; and (2) disclose their professional status (broker, REALTOR®, etc.). The advertising of inducements is permitted if the advertisements clearly state any conditions required to obtain the inducement (SP 12-3). Advertisements of listed property must disclose the firm's name (SP 12-5).

Additional Legal Update and Hot Topics

Sponsoring Broker's Executive Summary of the New Trec Regulations

"To Do" List

1. Advise sales people of their scope of authorized activities in writing. YOU'RE STILL RESPONSIBLE FOR PERMITTED ACTIVITIES BEYOND THAT SCOPE.
2. Review <u>all</u> advertising for all sponsored licensees [See §535.2 (g)].
3. Establish in writing who in your office can be a team leader or supervisor [See §535.2 (e)]. YOU'RE STILL RESPONSIBLE FOR ALL ACTIVITIES.
4. Keep the following records for <u>four years</u> [See §535.2 (h)]:

   - All Disclosures (IABS, Seller's, Disclosure of Agency Relationships).
   - All compensation agreements of any kind.
   - All work files.
   - All contracts, exhibits, and addenda.
   - All receipts and disbursements involving compensation.
   - All property management contracts.
   - All appraisal information.
   - All agreements which must be in writing and signed by both between sponsoring broker and sponsored salespeople.

5. Prepare a written policy and procedure manual [See §535.2 (i)]:
   - Confirms the four-year record-keeping policy set out in Paragraph 4 above.
   - Has a procedure that maintains all licenses as current. CALENDAR THEM.
   - Confirms that all compensation must be paid through the sponsoring broker; no "secret commissions" (paid to party not represented by the licensee) will be tolerated.
   - Confirms that fees cannot be shared with an unlicensed corporation or LLC created by a licensee for the purpose of collecting fees on behalf of a licensee [See §535.4 (f)].
   - Establishes a trust account that cannot be coming led with the operating account and has appropriate controls [See §535.2 (i) (7)].
   - Prohibits the use of a service provider who utilizes a contract that prohibits the licensee from offering similar services from another similar provider. THIS REQUIRES THE USE OF TREC Form RSC-1, DISCLOSURE OF RELATIONSHIP WITH RESIDENTIAL SERVICE COMPANY (SEE §535.148).

6. Make sure all licensees disclose in <u>all</u> transactions, IN WRITING, when applicable, that the licensee is engaging in a real estate transaction:
   - On his or her own behalf
   - On behalf of a business entity in which the licensee owns more than 10 percent of that entity
   - On behalf of the licensee's spouse, parent, or child (See§535.144).

7. Set up a procedure for immediately delivering all mail to sponsored salespersons [See §535(k)].

Texas Contracts

The following Real Estate Commission forms are currently promulgated for use by all real estate licensees, and their use is required in all transactions to which the form is applicable.

1. TREC 9-9 Unimproved Property Contract
2. TREC 20-10 One-to-Four Family Residential Contract (Resale)
3. TREC 23-11 New Home Contract (Incomplete Construction)
4. TREC 24-11 New Home Contract (Completed Construction)
5. TREC 25-8 Farm and Ranch Contract
6. TREC 30-9 Residential Condominium Contract (Resale)

Addendums for the above-referenced forms are also promulgated and required for use by licensees in all transactions in which the form is applicable:

1. TREC 10-5 Addendum for Sale of Other Property by Buyer
2. TREC 11-6 Addendum for "Back-Up" Contract
3. TREC 12-2 Seller's Release of Liability and VA Restoration of Entitlement
4. TREC 15-4 Seller's Temporary Residential Lease
5. TREC 16-4 Buyer's Temporary Residential Lease
6. TREC 26-5 Seller Financing Addendum
7. TREC 28-1 Environmental Assessment, Threatened or Endangered Species, and Wetlands Addendum
8. TREC 32-2 Condominium Resale Certificate
9. TREC 33-1 Notice for Coastal Area Property
10. TREC 34-3 Addendum for Property Located Seaward of the Gulf Intercoastal Waterway
11. TREC 36-6 Addendum for Property Subject to Mandatory Membership in an Owners' Association
12. TREC 37-3 Resale Certificate for Property Subject to Mandatory Membership in an Owners' Association
13. TREC 38-3 Notice of Termination of Contract
14. TREC 39-6 Amendment to Contract
15. TREC Consumer Information Form
16. TREC 40-4 Third-Party Financing Condition Addendum for Credit Approval
17. TREC 41-1 Loan Assumption Addendum
18. TREC 44-0 Addendum for Reservation of Oil, Gas, and Other Minerals
19. TREC 45-0 Short Sale Addendum

Other forms are also currently promulgated by the Texas Real Estate Commission:

1. TREC OP-C Notice to Prospective Buyer
2. TREC OP-H Seller's Disclosure of Property Condition
3. TREC OP-I Texas Real Estate Consumer Notice Concerning Recognized Hazards
4. TREC OP-K Information About Brokerage Services
5. TREC OP-L Lead-Based Paint Addendum
6. TREC OP-M Non-Realty Items Addendum
7. RSC 1 Disclosure of Relationship with Residential Service Company

A few of the most commonly used forms are printed at the back of this text. All of the current forms are available at the Texas Real Estate Commission's Web site and can be downloaded at no cost. Its Web site is http://www.trec.state.tx.us. A licensee should visit this Web site frequently, as TREC uses it to update all of their rules and regulations, forms, and other pertinent consumer information. Put it on your "favorite places" list on your computer, and visit it often.

Computerized Forms

The Texas Real Estate Commission regulations provide that computer-driven printers can print forms, provided these guidelines are followed:

- The computer file or program containing the form text must not allow the end user direct access to the text of the form and may only permit the user to insert language in blanks in these forms.

- Typefaces or fonts must appear to be identical to those used by the Commission in printed forms of the particular form.

- The text and number of pages must be identical to that used by the Commission in printed proofs of the particular form.

- The spacing, length of blanks, borders, and placement of text on the page must appear to be identical to that used by the Commission in printed proofs of the form.

- The name and address of the person or firm responsible for developing the software program must be legibly printed below the border at the bottom of each page in no less than six-point type and no larger than ten-point type.

- The text of the form must be obtained from a proof of the form bearing a control number assigned by the Commission.

The control number of each proof must appear on all forms reproduced from the proof and may be reproduced with only the following changes or additions:

- The business name or logo of a broker, organization, or printer may appear at the top of the form outside the border.
- The broker's name may be inserted in any blank provided for that purpose.

Practicing Law

The Texas Real Estate Commission requires all licensees to use promulgated forms, when appropriate, in all real estate transactions. There are common questions and concerns that merit emphasis. Although this provision may seem too basic to review, please understand that the Texas Real Estate Commission takes a very strong position against the concept of brokers practicing law.

Please note the existing provision of the Texas Real Estate License Act regarding the practice of law:

Sec. 1101.654.(a) A license granted under the provisions of this Act shall be suspended or revoked by the commission on proof that the licensee, not being licensed and authorized to practice law in this state for a consideration, reward, pecuniary benefit, present or anticipated, direct or indirect, or in connection with or as a part of his employment, agency, fiduciary relationship as a licensee, *drew* a deed, note, deed of trust, will, or *other written instrument that may* transfer or *anywise affect the title to or an interest in land*, except as provided in the subsections below, or *advised or counseled* a person as to the validity or *legal sufficiency of an instrument* or as to the validity of title to real estate.

(b) Notwithstanding the provisions of this Act or any other law, the completion of contract forms which bind the sale, exchange, option, lease, or rental of any interest in real property by a real estate broker or salesperson incident to the performance of the acts of a broker as defined by this article does not constitute the unauthorized or illegal practice of law in this state, provided the *forms have been promulgated for use by the Texas Real Estate Commission* for the particular kind of transaction involved, or the forms have been prepared by an attorney-at-law licensed by this state and approved by said attorney for the particular kind of transaction involved, or the *forms have been prepared by the property by an attorney-at-law licensed by this state and approved by said attorney for the particular kind of transaction involved*, or the forms have been *prepared by the property owner* or prepared by an attorney and *required by the property owner*.

Note that the provisions only allow a broker to use:

- the promulgated forms

- forms prepared by an attorney for the particular kind of transaction involved

- forms prepared by the property owner or prepared by an attorney and required by the property owner

Use of any other form will be practicing law without a license. If you are in doubt, call the Texas Real Estate Commission. Adaptation of a form to "make it fit" to a transaction is also a violation.

Another word of caution: When filling in the blanks or the special provisions of the promulgated form, if any information is inserted that could be construed to be legal advice or affecting the legal rights of the party, it will probably be construed as practicing law. The insertions in these areas of the contract are for business provisions only. If there is a concern as to filling in the blanks or the legality of certain special provisions, it is probably more prudent for the licensee to have the owner fill in the blank or special provision in the owner's own handwriting so it cannot be construed as the broker practicing law without a license.

Pertinent Provisions

There are general rules that apply to the interpretation of the promulgated contract forms that are commonly asked. It should be noted here that there are brokers who may not use TREC-promulgated contracts often, such as commercial real estate brokers who feel the discussion of TREC contracts may be inapplicable to them. It should be pointed out that the provisions of the TREC earnest money contracts are encountered in many commercial contracts, so discussion of each of these issues is pertinent to all real estate brokers, commercial as well as residential. In addition, TAR has introduced a number of forms that are drafted for the use of REALTOR® members that, in many cases, are very practical documents to use in a broker's practice in conjunction with the contracts. A copy of the new TREC Form 20-8 is shown on page 332 for reference.

Contingencies

It should be noted that all of the Texas Real Estate Commission-promulgated forms provide for two basic contingencies:

- Buyer's approval of title and survey.

- Buyer's ability to obtain financing.

It should be noted that the contracts, even though they contain specific performance provisions, are not binding earnest money contracts until these two contingencies have been satisfied. Therefore, the buyer is not bound to performance until the two contingencies can be removed from the contract. Technically, these contingencies are called "conditions precedent to buyer's performance."

Specific Paragraphs

Paragraph 1. Parties. This provision was revised in 2008 to make it very clear that the only parties to the contract are the buyer and the seller. The broker is not a party to the contract; the title company is not a party to the contract; only the buyer and seller are.

Paragraph 2. Property. In the most recent revision, Paragraph 2 was changed to make the definition of "property" clearer. Paragraph 2.B. identifies those items that are permanently installed and built in are labeled "improvements." What about plasma TV's and surround sound systems in your media room? The latest revisions mention that the brackets and mounts for the TV's and speakers stay with the house. Those items that are less likely to be attached to the real estate but are peculiarly adapted to the real estate in most circumstances are set out in Paragraph 2.C. and labeled "accessories." Paragraph 2.D., labeled "exclusions," provides a specific space to exclude those things that will not transfer with title to the real estate *and must be removed prior to delivery of possession*. If additional items are to be included, they must be set out in Paragraph 11. This paragraph of the contract will always change as lifestyles change.

Paragraph 4. Financing. This paragraph was significantly changed in the latest revision. Note that it provides three choices:

1. Third-Party Financing
2. Assumption
3. Seller Financing

Rather than including all of the financing provisions in the body of the contract, it now refers to the applicable addenda, which can be attached to the contract. This paragraph was recently reformatted to clarify that the contract is made subject to the lender's approval (which includes, but is not limited to, appraisal, insurability and lender required repairs) of the property (which is a contingency that continues until closing). Section 4(A)(2) is the contingency that applies only to the buyer's creditworthiness and financing approval. This contingency does have a time limit as set out in the third-party financing addendum, discussed later. If Box 4(A)(2)(b) is checked, there is no need to attach any financing condition addendum.

Paragraph 5. Earnest Money. In Paragraph 5, there is a specific provision for the buyers providing earnest money upon execution of the contract by all parties. Note, however, that the new contract states that if the earnest money is not deposited (e.g., a bad check), the buyer shall be in default, triggering the provisions of Paragraph 15. A prudent practice, however, is to request that the buyer provide a cashier's or certified check to prevent the "bouncing check" issue.

Paragraph 6. Title. The new contract provides boxes to determine who should pay for the owner's policy of title insurance. Traditionally, the seller has paid in most counties, and most listing agreements provide that the seller will pay for the title insurance. So, as a practical matter, the seller agrees to pay pursuant to the listing agreement. The contracts give us a choice! This may help if the buyer's employer pays for all closing costs, as the buyer might be able to bargain for a better sales price. Paragraph 6 also contains a significant change in the most recent revision. Note that Paragraph 6.A.(8) allows the buyer at buyer's expense to have the exception as to "discrepancies, conflicts, shortages in area for boundary lines, encroachments or protrusions, or overlapping of improvements" amended to read only "shortages in area." This provision has been commonly used in commercial contract forms, although this is the first time it has been utilized in the residential forms. The issue presented is a rather complex one, and now real estate licensees will have to become very familiar with this issue because many buyers, particularly those from out of state, might ask about this provision.

The initial issue involves title insurance coverage. The standard owner's policy of title insurance has an exception for "discrepancies, conflicts, shortages in area for boundary lines, encroachments or protrusions, or overlapping of improvements," which means that the buyer does not have title insurance coverage for most minor encroachment issues (e.g., fences, garage eaves, deck encroachments onto power line easements, roof encroachments over building lines, and misaligned driveways). Many buyers are surprised when they acquire their properties that this coverage is not provided, but the coverage traditionally has not been available under title insurance policies in Texas unless the buyer pays an additional premium (currently 5 percent of the existing title premiums on residential policies, and 15 percent on commercial policies) and provides the title insurer with a staked, on-the-ground survey. In most cases, this could mean a considerable additional expense. The old contract form did not deal with who would pay this expense or whether or not this insurance coverage was available. This new revision to the contract form clearly makes it available at the buyer's expense. As a practical matter, the title insurance company will then review the survey to determine whether there are any conflicts or encroachments. If these conflicts exist, the title insurance company may except to a specific encroachment or choose to insure against enforcement of any third party's rights regarding that encroachment by express insurance coverage. That is, the title insurance company can agree to insure against the enforcement of an easement right removal of an encroachment or protrusion so that the buyer can rest assured that he has "clear" title. If there is a complaint about any of the conflicts or encroachments, the title insurance company will defend them against that enforcement by another party.

If a licensee represents a buyer, they may want to pay particular attention to this new provision. Many buyers tend to be extremely picky, and they are firmly convinced that they do not have good title if there is a three-inch encroachment of a pool deck into a power line right-of-way. The fact is that they don't have good title if this exists, but, as we just previously discussed, the title insurance company can insure against any damages as a result of the encroachment. Some buyers, however, will worry about their ability to sell the property in the future with this encumbrance and will choose not to purchase. For the first time, this new revision in the contract helps an agent and his buyer focus on alternatives available if this condition exists.

The contract also provides that the title company does not have to deliver the commitment until 20 days after the title company receives a copy of the contract and specifies the seller's authorization for the title company to deliver the commitments and all related documents, and that they are to be delivered at the buyer's address shown on the contract. If the commitment is not delivered in a timely manner, the delivery is automatically extended for up to 15 days. In smaller counties where title companies have a more difficult time getting the commitments out, this is a tremendous relief and eliminates the problem of where to send the documents to the buyer. It puts an additional duty on the broker, however, to be sure to fill in the buyer's address at the end of the contract.

Title commitment not delivered in a timely manner? That may be a real problem! In *Humphrey v. Camelot Retirement Community*, 893 S.W.2d 55 (Tex. App.-Corpus Christi, 1994), the plaintiff sued the defendant to recover earnest money that was paid to the defendant for the purchase of a new home. The contract required that within 30 days of the date the contract was executed, the defendant "shall cause to be furnished to purchaser a standard Commitment for Owner Policy of Title Insurance." The defendant did not cause the title commitment to be furnished within 30 days required by the contract. In its failure to comply with this provision, the seller breached the contract, and the court considered that a breach that "would go to the essence of the contract" allowing for a rescission of the contract, return of the earnest money, and damages in the amount of $13,750. This court felt that delivery of the title commitment was critical!

Paragraph 6.C. has been changed significantly. Either party may provide the survey, or an old survey may be used if it is acceptable to the title company or buyer's lender. Buyer and seller must agree, however, how many days they can produce the survey, which is out of the control of both parties. A good suggestion may be to utilize the maximum number of days (the day prior to closing?) so that the buyer and seller aren't in default because of a slow surveyor. **Note another problem: If the seller checks box (1) and can't find the survey, it may constitute a misrepresentation. Be sure the survey is available before making this choice.** This paragraph has also been recently revised to require the seller to provide the Residential Real Property Affidavit promulgated by the Texas Department of Insurance. If the seller does not provide the survey in a timely manner, the buyer may obtain one at the seller's expense no later than 3 days prior to the closing date.

Paragraph 6.D. has now been amended to provide that the buyer have a fixed time to object to the commitment, exception documents, and survey. Therefore, the buyer's objection period does not begin until he has received all three documents. Buyer's failure to object within the time allowed constitutes a waiver of buyer's right to object. Nevertheless, that outside date is now the same for all three contingencies (commitment, exception documents, and survey).

Note that the contracts now have seven "Title Notices" in Paragraph 6E. The first notice advises the buyer to have an abstract of title covering the property examined by an attorney of buyer's selection or should be furnished with or obtain a title policy. This automatically provides for a licensee's compliance with Section 1101.555 of the Texas Real Estate License Act. The second disclosure concerns mandatory owners' association membership and whether or not the buyer is required to be a member of a property owners' association in his subdivision. The third notice provides for a required notice if the property is located in a municipal utility district. This is a specific notice required by the Texas Water Code regarding the additional ad valorem taxation, which is imposed on the property as a result of being located in a municipal utility district. The fourth notice gives the buyer a specific notice as required by the Texas Natural Resources Code if the property abuts highly influenced waters of this state. The fifth notice is a notification that the property may be subject to annexation as provided under the Texas Property Code. The sixth notice is a required notice that the seller of property located in a certificated service area of the utility service provider must give to a buyer. The seventh notice is a statutory required notice that a seller of a property in a public improvement district (often referred to as a PID), which cautions the buyer that a PID may make special assessments against the property located in the PID.

Paragraph 7. Property Condition. Paragraph 7.A. provides an absolute right for the buyer to have inspections and access to utility by an inspector "licensed by TREC or otherwise permitted by law to make such inspections." This may prevent the "setup" of an uncle or cousin doing a bad inspection to create a better negotiating position for the buyer. However, it does allow for a qualified engineer who is permitted by law to make such inspections, but not licensed as an inspector, to perform these inspections. Please note that this new paragraph also provides for reinspection after the repairs have been made. *Paragraph 7.A. does not make inspections or reinspections a contingency.* However, if the property does have significant defects, the buyer may have a cause of action against the seller for misrepresentation or failure to disclose those defects. You may notice also that the seller is required to permit the buyer and buyer's agents access to the property at reasonable times. **The buyer has the right to a walk-through any time prior to closing, so long as it is at a reasonable time**.

Paragraph 7.C. confirms the seller's obligation to comply with the Lead-Based Paint Disclosure. There is a box to check as to whether or not the disclosure is attached.

Federal law does not require the addendum for property constructed after January 1, 1978, property sold at foreclosure, the sale of a zero bedroom dwelling with a sleeping unit that is not separated from the living area, and housing for the elderly or disabled where children under age 6 are not expected to reside.

A clarification has been provided in Paragraph 7.D. In the old Paragraph 7.D, licensees, buyers, and sellers were often inserting into the blank spaces things that were not anticipated, such as "subject to inspection" and other vague comments that could render the contract unenforceable. Paragraph 7.D was revised to require that one of two boxes be checked. The first box deals with the property "in its present condition." We have had several appellate cases that indicate Paragraph 7.D.(1) will be construed as an "as is" provision. See *Larsen v. Langford*, 41 S.W.3d 245 (Tex. App.-Waco, 2001).

If box 7.D.(2) is checked, it means the buyer has noticed a specific item on the property (broken trapeze in the master bedroom) that needs to be repaired and specifies the repair and/or treatment that must be completed prior to closing. In theory, this creates a shift of the burden, where the buyer is agreeing to take the property either "as is" or only after the seller has made the specific repairs. So it is up to the buyer to carry out inspections during the option period.

What if a defect is discovered during the option period? At this point, the buyer has to make a choice: (1) exercise his right to terminate as set out in Paragraph 23, using TREC Form No. 38-2, or (2) propose an amendment to the contract, using TREC Form 39-6. Now the seller has the choice of either agreeing to the repairs or running the risk that the buyer will terminate the contract if the seller does not agree to the amendment. This was recently clarified by adding a "Notice to Buyer and Seller" to explain this issue to the parties.

Paragraph 7.E. provides for lender-required repairs and provides that the buyer can terminate the contract if the lender-required repairs exceed 5 percent of the sales price. If lender-required repairs are not made, the loan won't be approved, and the buyer may avoid performance by exercising the financing contingency set out in Paragraph 4, provided the buyer terminates in a timely manner. If the repair does not exceed 5 percent, what happens? As a practical matter, the buyer can't get the loan, so the deal is over, i.e., you probably can't successfully sue the buyer who can't get financing because of the condition of the house, and the seller may have liability for failure to disclose the defect.

Paragraph 7.F. provides for completion of repairs and treatments, and additionally provides that the repairs and treatments must be performed by persons who regularly provide such services, hopefully eliminating "Uncle Elmo the Handyman" from making these repairs. There is also a provision for all transferable warranties to be transferred to the buyer, at the buyer's expense.

There is an important change in this provision in the most recent revision to the contract form. Note that if the seller fails to complete any agreed-upon repairs prior to the closing date, the buyer has the right to do so and receive reimbursement from the seller at closing. This apparently is without regard to the expense, and it seems to give the buyer the unilateral right to do any repairs that are "agreed to." It also allows the closing date to be extended up to 15 days to complete those repairs and treatments. There is a practical problem to this. What if the seller won't let the buyer in to make the repairs? This may have created another area for conflict in the contract rather than resolving disputes.

Paragraph 8. Broker's Fees. Note that broker's fees under Paragraph 8 in the promulgated contract forms are nothing more than a ratification of the existence of an agreement. This refers the buyer, seller, or broker back to the original agreement to pay the commission and/or to pursue any legal remedies.

Paragraph 9. Closing. This paragraph was significantly changed, and the most recent revisions note that they still contain a 7-day extension or an automatic 7-day extension after the objection to title and survey have been assured. *There is no automatic extension to complete lender's closing requirements.* The paragraph is also more specific about items to be provided at the closing. Paragraph 9.B.(2) now provides an agreement by the buyer to provide good funds acceptable to the escrow agent at closing (not contained in the previous contract form). Note that this paragraph now contains the notice to the buyer that the seller may continue to show the property, and receive and negotiate back-up offers. This was previously in Paragraph 6 of the old form.

Paragraph 10. Possession. There is a revision in the new form that allows buyer possession of the property either (i) upon closing and funding or (ii) according to the temporary residential lease (this provision is clearer than it was in the old form). There is still no definition for what "funding" means, whether the buyer funds, or the lender funds, or if both elements of funding will be required. Often a buyer will fund his proceeds at closing, but the lender's funding may be delayed. Does the buyer still get possession in this circumstance? The contract simply does not address it.

Note that this paragraph requires the use of a TREC Temporary Lease form or an "at sufferance relationship" is created between the parties. The paragraph does not distinguish one day's occupancy versus one year's occupancy, so long as it is "temporary." Remember that this is a TREC-required form and must be utilized if it applies to your situation.

Paragraph 11. Special Provisions. Note that under Special Provisions (the infamous Paragraph 11) agents need to be very, very careful not to insert any items that may constitute the practice of law or refer to nonpromulgated forms not specifically required by the principal or his attorney.

Real estate brokers are not allowed to alter the terms of the contract, only to "fill in the blanks" of the TREC-promulgated forms. Contingencies for performance inserted into Paragraph 11 of the TREC contracts are for the insertion of business details, nothing more. Any changes to the form have to be at the direction of the principal and not at the instigation or direction of the broker; otherwise, it constitutes the practice of law. No contingency should be inserted in Paragraph 11 unless specifically directed by the principal. Even then, it is smart to have the principal write it in.

Another concern should be noted. If a contingency is truly superfluous, such as "this contract is contingent upon the approval of buyer's attorney" without further specification, it probably makes the contract a mere option (the seller can't sue for specific performance because the buyer always has an "out"). If the earnest money is also refundable, there may be no contract at all, as there is no consideration for the option. See *Culbertson v. Brodsky*, 788 S.W.2d 156 (Tex. App.-Ft. Worth, 1990).

Paragraph 12. Sales Expenses. There were some important changes to this paragraph in the most recent (2003) revisions. The most significant change, however, involved Paragraph 12.A.(1)(b), which provides for the seller to pay any additional expenses that the buyer is prohibited by FHA or VA from paying. Because there is only one contract form, this paragraph provides for certain notice items for FHA and VA that are included and do not require the use of separate contract forms. What if the amount exceeds the seller's limit? The seller has a contingency, too. Paragraph 12.B. requires the buyer to pay PMI, FHA, and VA fees.

Paragraph 14. Casualty Loss. This provision has come under additional scrutiny in recent years because of flooding damage in Houston and tornado damage in northern parts of the state. If the property is damaged or destroyed by fire or other casualty after the contract date, the seller is required to restore the property to its previous condition as soon as reasonably possible. If the seller fails to do so (due to factors beyond seller's control), the buyer has three options: (1) he can terminate the contract and receive a refund of his earnest money, (2) he can extend the time for performance up to 15 days, or (3) he can accept the property in its damaged condition with an assignment of the insurance proceeds. There is now a new provision for the seller to pay the deductible on the insurance policy.

Paragraph 15. Default. Note that in Paragraph 6.B. the *seller* (not the real estate agent or the title company) is required to deliver to the buyer within 20 days after the effective date of the contract, a commitment for title insurance and at buyer's expense, legible copies of restrictive covenants and documents evidencing exceptions in the Commitment, other than the standard printed exceptions. If the Commitment is not delivered in a timely manner, this Default paragraph gives the buyer the option to terminate the contract.

These two paragraphs have given title companies great concern over their ability to: (1) produce the Commitment in a timely manner, and (2) pay for the cost of all copies, with no explanation as to how the buyer is supposed to pay the title company (e.g., upon receipt, at closing, or C.O.D.). In some cases, the title company may not be able to deliver copies of title exceptions within 20 days (probates, out-of-state bankruptcies, heirship proceedings in a foreign country, etc.). In that event, Paragraph 6.B. allows for an automatic extension. If the Commitment is still not delivered within the 35 days, this paragraph gives the buyer the right to terminate the contract if the failure to deliver the Commitment in a timely manner is through no fault of the seller.

It should also be specifically noted that when a broker attempts to alter the Default paragraph (Paragraph 15), the seller can lose the ability to sue the buyer for specific performances by striking out the "specific performance" provisions. The contract may then become an option contract, which is performable purely at the option of the buyer. This not only materially alters the performance obligations under the contract, but also eliminates the broker's ability to sue for a commission unless the transaction closed. It may be no contract at all. See *Culbertson v. Brodsky supra.*

Paragraph 16. Mediation. Paragraph 16 provides that it is the policy of the state of Texas to encourage resolution of disputes under the contract through mediation and provides a choice for agreed mediation, eliminating the need for the Mediation Addendum with this form. Many licensees have been concerned that the buyer and seller are forced to discuss disputes even before the contract is signed. The fact is, however, that mediation resolves many disputes without having to resort to litigation, hiring lawyers, and expensive court proceedings. As most earnest money disputes involve minor differences, mediation forces the parties into a discussion of the dispute. This is less time consuming, less costly, and an easier way to resolve disputes in most circumstances. As a practical matter, most earnest money contract disputes do not involve large amounts of money, and a court will order mediation anyway.

Paragraph 17 was revised in response to a lawsuit that denied a broker's right to get attorney's fees. See *Williamson v. Guynes*, 2005 WL 675512 (Tex. App. Waco, 2005). Frequently, a broker may be a defendant in a lawsuit, win the lawsuit, and still have to bear the cost of defense, which can be substantial. This paragraph was revised to provide that, in addition to the buyer or seller, the listing broker, other broker, or escrow agent who prevails in any legal proceedings is entitled to recover reasonable attorney fees and all costs incurred. This provision now poses a risk to the plaintiff in some lawsuits. If the plaintiff fails to prove his or her case, and the broker or the title company prevails, the defendant may be awarded attorney fees and costs, to be paid by the plaintiff. Newer cases have been leaning more towards awarding attorney's fees as an agreed-to part of the contract.

Paragraph 18. Escrow. This paragraph was changed significantly in the new form. It no longer requires the signature of the broker to disburse the earnest money. In addition, if one party makes a demand for the earnest money, the escrow agent is required to give notice of that demand to the other party. If the other party doesn't respond within 15 days, the escrow agent can go ahead and disburse the earnest money to the party demanding it. This should help "clear out" a lot of escrow accounts when parties cannot be reached for response. Note that a new paragraph, 18.D., was added to provide that if a party wrongfully refuses or wrongfully fails to sign a release, the party entitled to the earnest money is also entitled to liquidated damages of three times the amount of the earnest money, plus attorneys' fees and court costs. If a party receiving the earnest money owes any creditors in the file (appraisers, surveyors, etc.) the title company is authorized to pay those bills out of the recipient's share of the earnest money.

Paragraph 20. Federal Tax Requirement. There is specific reference to foreign parties as sellers of the property and amounts of currency in connection with the real estate closing. It should be pointed out that a foreign party has specific tax requirements that put the burden on the buyer to withhold taxes for the Internal Revenue Service. Although this is not a common problem in residential transactions, foreign sellers in commercial transactions can create unique problems. These sorts of issues should be resolved early in the transaction rather than at the closing table. The same is true of cash. Federal law prohibits the deposit of large amounts of cash in the bank without justifiable reason. Title companies are therefore very reluctant to close transactions where cash or other forms of consideration (e.g., jewels) may be involved. A wise broker may want to caution parties to a real estate transaction not to engage in cash transactions, which are outside of the normal business practice. Use wired funds, cashier's checks, or certified checks, and closings will go much more smoothly.

Paragraph 21. Notices. This is a new provision put in the body of the contract to provide notices to the seller and the buyer. This is more effective than putting it at the end of the contract (past the signatures). It now makes it part of the body of the contract, and it must be filled in. This was a detail often overlooked by licensees. Putting it in the body of the contract will make that omission much less likely.

Paragraph 22. Addenda. Paragraph 22 now lists all promulgated addenda. It should be reemphasized that a nonpromulgated addendum must be prepared by an attorney or the principal because it is not an official TREC-promulgated form.

Paragraph 23. Option to Terminate. This paragraph provides an option to terminate the contract for any reason whatsoever during the option period. Note that this paragraph was recently revised to provide that the option fee can be paid within two days after the effective date of the contact, although the consideration can be "nominal." If no dollar amount is stated as the option fee or if the buyer fails to pay the option fee within the time prescribed, the buyer loses his right to terminate. Note that in this paragraph, time is of the essence, but this provision is applicable to this paragraph only.

This new paragraph is somewhat unique. It gives the buyer (in consideration for the payment of the option fee) the right to terminate the contract within the specified number of days. Note that if the blanks of this contract are not filled in, the buyer does not have the termination option; or if, for whatever reason, the buyer has not paid the option fee, there is no right to terminate and the buyer and seller have a binding contract for the sale of their real estate. Therefore, if the seller does not receive the option fee (or the check bounces) or the contract blanks are not filled in, *this is a binding earnest money contract on both parties, subject to the conditions of the agreement.* Note that the right of termination is within the stated number of days after the effective date of the contract.

The burden is on the buyer to give notice of the termination within the time specified, and there is a choice as to whether or not the option fee will be credited to the sales price at closing. The appropriate form has been promulgated by TREC as Form No. 38-1. If the buyer fails to give the notice, the right to terminate is waived. Buyer's agents, mark your calendars!

The size of the option fee is always negotiable, and it is always prudent to negotiate an option period long enough to allow for inspections and to obtain costs for repairs.

BUT. . .if the buyer finds that the need for extensive repairs exists, the buyer should give notice of termination in a timely manner, or amend the Earnest Money Contract, utilizing the TREC Amendment Form (No. 39-6). This new amendment form is discussed later in this chapter.

Paragraph 24. Consult an attorney. This is a new addition to the contract forms providing for the address, telephone, and facsimile numbers for the respective parties' attorneys. As you may recall, the old form required you to "squeeze" everything into one line.

Note also that there is a new provision at the end of the contract for the seller's receipt of the option money (if Paragraph 23 is utilized).

Third-Party Financing Addendum For Credit Approval. This recently revised addendum makes the financing contingency much clearer. Note that Paragraph 4 of the contract provides for two different contingencies; one is whether or not the property (the condition of the house, or appraised value) satisfies the lender's underwriting requirements, notwithstanding the buyer's ability to qualify for the loan. There is no time limit on this contingency; so if a lender determines on the day of closing that the property doesn't satisfy the lender's underwriting requirements, this contingency has not been satisfied. The buyer has an "out" until the day of closing, depending on the lender's underwriting requirements. There is also a provision (Paragraph 4.A.[2]) that eliminates the buyer's contingency for financing. Presumably, if Box 4.A.(2) is checked, the buyer either has the cash to close or has guaranteed financing already in place. It might be construed as a representation to the seller of the buyer's financial ability to close. If you cannot qualify for a loan after making this representation, does it become a deceptive trade practice? This may create an unexpected liability for a buyer. If there is a financing contingency, the contract requires the use of the new Third-Party Financing Addendum For Credit Approval. Note that this Addendum creates contingencies for conventional financing, Texas Veterans Housing Assistance Program Loans, FHA financing, and VA guaranteed financing. The form provides that the borrower must *make every reasonable* effort to obtain financing approval, including but not limited to, furnishing all information and documents required by the lender. Financing approval is obtained when the terms of the described loan are available and the lender determines that the buyer has satisfied all of the lender's financial requirements. Note also that if the buyer doesn't give written notice to the seller to exercise his financing contingency, the contingency is automatically removed!

The most recent amendment to this form also clarifies that financing approval of the buyer does not include the approval of lender's underwriting requirements for the property, as specified in Paragraph 4.A.1.

A recent Texas case focused on the automatic termination provision in this addendum. The seller informed the buyer that he couldn't get his loan approved and asked for an extension. The Appeals Court, citing this form, held that if the buyer could not obtain financing approval within the time specified, the contract will terminate and the earnest money returned to the buyer. *Nguyen vs. Woodley*, 273 S.W.3rd 891 (Tex. App.-Houston [14th Dist.], 2008).

Assumption. If the buyer is going to assume the loan, the contract now requires the utilization of the Loan Assumption Addendum, which, again, is similar to what is contained in the existing contract form. Note that it gives the seller the right to approve buyer's credit (rather than the lender). As in prior contract forms, if the assumed loan varies in an amount greater than $350 at closing, either party may terminate the contract, and the earnest money will be refunded to the buyer unless the other party elects to eliminate the excess by an appropriate adjustment at the closing. There are also contingencies involved in any assumption fee that may be required by the lender. If there is an existing escrow account, the escrow account is required to be transferred to the buyer without any deficiency and the buyer is to reimburse the seller for the amount of the transferred account at closing.

Seller Financing Addendum. This form was revised in 2006 to include common provisions for note payments and an interest rate. New provisions for seller's consent to a subsequent conveyance by the buyer and continued liability for the buyer if the buyer is not specifically released from liability in the subsequent conveyance were also added. There are requirements for credit documentation and credit approval, and it gives the buyer the right to prepay the promissory note holder in part at any time without penalty. It also has automatic provisions for late payment fees along with the payment provisions that are required in the promissory note. The addendum also has specific choices for the terms of the Deed of Trust regarding property transfers (due-on-transfer clauses) and tax and insurance escrows, so that the seller can be assured that the taxes and insurance are current and paid on time each year.

Addendum for "Back-Up" Contract. This was revised in 2007, and is for use in the fairly common situation where a buyer (Buyer 2) will choose to execute a contract with the seller to buy the property in the event an existing contract (with Buyer 1) should terminate. Note that Paragraph B puts the burden on the seller to notify the buyer on a specific date that the previous contract has terminated. If the seller does not notify the buyer, the contract (back-up contract with Buyer 2) automatically terminates. This addendum gives the buyer no rights other than to create a contract in the event of termination of the prior contract. A real estate licensee should be seriously cautioned not to attempt to encourage the termination of contract number 1. This may be construed as tortious interference of a contract, and the licensee may be subject to license revocation or suspension for this kind of conduct as a direct violation of Section 1101.652(6)(21) of the Texas Real Estate License Act (even if the second offer is higher than the first). It should be understood that the first contract is a binding and enforceable contract and any attempt to interfere with the (parties) performance may result in severe legal consequences.

This form provides for the parties' obligations under the "back-up" contract. The buyer is required to deposit any earnest money and option fee as provided in the "back-up" contract, but is not otherwise obligated to perform during the contingency period. The addendum now also addresses the time for the buyer to give notice of termination if the buyer exercises the option to terminate under Paragraph 23 of the contract (Buyer 1).

This creates complicating situations. Two things can happen: (1) the seller can notify the buyer that the previous contract is terminated; or (2) the buyer would need to notify the seller that the buyer terminates the back-up contract. TAR has prepared two forms to address this situation. TAR-1912 Paragraph B provides a form for the seller's notice to buyer that the previous contract is terminated. This satisfies Paragraph B of the Back-up Addendum and confirms the Seller Notification. Note that Paragraph C of the Back-up Addendum automatically terminates the contract if the seller does not notify the buyer. Notwithstanding the language, TAR has another form (TAR-1913) where the buyer acknowledges that the notification has not taken place and confirms the termination of the back-up contract. Although this may seem unnecessary, it is always good business practice to have the buyer acknowledge the termination to the seller to avoid the risk that the seller may attempt to "activate" the contract a few days later. A well-documented file of confirming documentation is always an asset should problems arise.

Addendum for Sale of Other Property by Buyer. This form was revised in 2007, and is another fairly common situation where a buyer needs to sell his house before he can commit to the actual purchase of the house that is the subject of this contract. *If your buyer has not closed on the sale of a prior home, you must use this addendum unless your buyer can confirm the ability to purchase without the sale of the prior home.* Please note that the seller may continue to show the property and consider other offers from buyers. There is in many realtor systems a special provision in MLS for this situation where the property is "under contract," but is still "on the market." Note Paragraph C. If a seller "accepts" a written offer to purchase the property (presumably this second contract will have a "back-up" addendum), the seller notifies the buyer and the buyer must remove the contingency specified in this addendum. If the buyer fails to do so, the back-up contract is terminated. Note that the buyer may only waive the contingency by notifying the seller of the waiver and depositing $_____ with the escrow agent. There is no requirement that dollars be inserted in this blank, but it is presumed that some additional funds would be deposited to show the increased commitment of the buyer. Note that if the buyer removes the contingency, there can be no financial contingency as set out in Paragraph E.

Not unexpectedly, complications arise here. To simplify these issues, TAR has also addressed the addendum under TAR Forms TAR-1912 and TAR-1913. Under Paragraph A, it acknowledges that the seller has accepted another written offer to purchase the property (again, presuming it would have a "back-up" provision). TAR Form 1912 acknowledges that the buyer must notify the seller no later than the time required under the addendum to waive the contingency and deposit the required additional earnest money. In TAR Form 1913, Paragraph A, the buyer acknowledges waiving the contingency and deposits the additional earnest money or executes his alternative of terminating the contract and refunding the earnest money. Please remember that in order to use these forms, you must be a member of the Texas Association of REALTORS®.

Addendum for Property Subject to Mandatory Membership in an Owners' Association. Logically, it's fair to provide the buyer this notice so he is not surprised with additional expenses after he moves into the property.

Subdivision Information, Including Resale Certificate for Property Subject to Mandatory Membership in an Owners' Association. This form was revised in 1999 to comply with new state legislation that requires homeowners' associations to provide certain information to purchasers. This "Subdivision Information," if not received by the buyer, gives the buyer the right to terminate the contract at any time prior to closing. After the seller delivers the Subdivision Information, the buyer has the right to terminate the contract for any reason within 7 days after the buyer receives the Subdivision Information, or prior to closing, whichever occurs first.

Addendum for Seller's Disclosure of Information on Lead-Based Paint and Lead-Based Paint Hazards. This new addendum is to comply with the federal lead-based paint disclosure statute discussed in Chapter 2. Note that there are convenient boxes for both buyer and seller to check, and this addendum presumably keeps all parties (including brokers) in compliance with the new federal law.

Buyer's and Seller's Temporary Residential Lease. These forms are new for 2006 and required for use. Note that Paragraph 4 specifies that rentals shall be paid per day. There is no longer a provision for monthly rental payment. This presumes the "temporary" nature of the residential lease. Please note also that this is required in the event it applies to your transaction. A licensee should not presume that another form would be acceptable, because these forms were specified for those particular transactions. Occupancy by the buyer (prior to closing) or seller (after the closing) without these temporary leases presumes a tenancy at sufferance, which means neither party has rights, other than to dispossess the tenant or terminate the relationship. The new revisions emphasize "residential" rather than "single family" to clarify that duplexes and quadruplexes were also included. There is also a new emphasis on property insurance (note Paragraph 16).

Amendment. This new, revised Amendment form (TREC 39-6) is for an accommodation to the parties to change the terms of their contract after it has been signed and the conditions have changed. Please note that there are now nine (a) boxes to check concerning the amendments. There is also a required additional option fee, and the buyer waives his rights to terminate under Paragraph 23 of the TREC form. If the parties choose to amend the contract for any other reason, there is no provision for that (e.g., change possession dates or other special provisions). In those situations, an attorney or the principals themselves should draft the amendment. Otherwise, a licensee may run the risk of practicing law without a license.

Notice of Termination of Contract. (TREC 38-2-see page 330). In accordance with Paragraph 23 of the contract, this is the official notice that the buyer must give in order to terminate his rights under the option provisions. There is a common problem in utilizing this notice of termination. If the seller is currently considering whether or not to amend the contract (using the new Amendment form), but does not respond in a timely manner, the buyer may be bound by the terms of the contract if he hasn't exercised his Notice of Termination in a timely manner. Particularly buyer's brokers, mark your calendar carefully to make sure that the buyer's obligation to send this Notice of Termination is done.

Effective Date

Note that the "broker" is required to fill in the date of final acceptance and the parties' addresses to the contract. This is extremely important! The Effective Date keys all the time requirements in the contract. The "broker" should note that if the contract is tendered to the title company 5 or more days after the Effective Date stated in the contract, it substantially alters the title company's ability to issue the title commitment, as well as all the other contingencies under the contract. This may create a significant liability for brokers who fail to fill in these items properly as required by the contract.

Two new addenda have been approved by the Real Estate Commission, due to current changes in the marketplace.

The first is a Short Sale Addendum, which provides for the contingency of a sale of the property at a price below the current mortgage balance. It provides that the seller should obtain the lien holder's consent, or refund the earnest money in the event the lien holder's consent is not obtained.

The second is the Addendum for Reservation of Oil, Gas, and Other Minerals. The price of oil and new technology has made oil, gas, and other minerals available in paying quantities in new areas of the state. Many of these areas are under existing subdivisions. This makes mineral rights a new bargaining chip for sellers and buyers. The problem is that this is a complicated legal issue. Most residential real estate agents are not prepared to deal with these issues. This addendum only deals with very fundamental issues of ownership and waiver of surface rights, and warns all parties to seek legal counsel before signing the contract. Note the new addenda in the appendix.

Additional New Statutes!!

Correction Instruments

There has been a lot of litigation in recent years over the use of correction deeds. These have always been an easy way of correcting defects, clerical errors, and typographical errors in documents without going through the formality of having them re-executed at another closing.

The Property Code was amended by adding Section 5.027 through 5.031 that specifically allows a correction of an ambiguity or error in an original of conveyance to transfer real property or an interest in real property.

Correction documents are put into two categories: nonmaterial and material. For nonmaterial corrections, any person who has actual knowledge of facts relevant to the correction of a recordable instrument can make nonmaterial changes that result from clerical error including:

1. A correction of an accurate or incorrect element in a legal description (distance, angle, direction, bearing, or chord, etc.); or
2. An addition, correction, or clarification of a party's name, marital status, date the conveyance was executed, recording data, or any fact relating to the acknowledgement or authentication.

The document must disclose the basis for the person's personal knowledge of the facts relevant to the correction, and then must record the document in each county where the original instrument of conveyance being corrected is recorded. If the correction instrument is not signed by each party to the original recorded instrument, a copy of the correction instrument must be sent by first class mail, email, or other reasonable means to each party to the original instrument of conveyance.

If the correction is a material one, such as:

1. A buyer's disclaimer of an interest in real property, mortgagee's consent or subordination to a recorded document, or to add land to a conveyance that correctly conveys other land; or
2. Removing land from a conveyance that correctly conveys other land; or

3. Accurately identifying a lot that was inaccurately identified as another lot; the correction instrument must be executed by each party to the recorded original instrument, and then recorded in each county where the original instrument of conveyance is recorded.

The instrument becomes effective as of the effective date of the original instrument of conveyance.

Assignment of Rentals

Texas is a lien theory state. The owner of the property has right to possession and dominion and control over the property. The lender's rights are only those of a lienholder. In the event the borrower is in default, he can collect the rents and keep them, even though he's not making any payments to the lender. This leads a very profitable result for a defaulting borrower. While this matter has been litigated in the past, there has been nothing conclusive and the question lingered on.

The 2011 legislature addressed this issue by adding a new section to the Business and Commerce Code that supports the lender's right to collect the rents in the event of a default. The statute basically says that any security instrument (deed of trust) that has an assignment of rents does create a security interest in all accrued and unaccrued rents arising from the owner's use of the property. The document must be recorded in the real property records of the county where the land is located.

To enforce the assignment, the lender could give notice to the owner of the property, notice to the tenant, or another method sufficient to enforce the assignment under other Texas law. To enforce the notice to the owner, the lender only has to provide a notice demanding that the owner pay the proceeds of any rents. The notice could be made after default or as otherwise agreed between the parties. It does not apply to homestead property.

To enforce an assignment by notice to the tenant, the lender simply provides the tenant a notice demanding that the tenant pay to the lender all unpaid accrued rents and accrued rents as they accrue. After the tenant receives the notice, the tenant is obligated to pay to the lender all unpaid accrued rents and unaccrued rents as they accrue. The tenant's payment to the lender of rents would satisfy the tenant's obligation to the owner to the extent of the payment made.

The notices must be sent by certified mail by depositing them with the U.S. Postal Service. In that situation if they are presumed to have gotten the notice on the fifth day after the notice was deposited in the U.S. Postal Service.

What does the lender do with the proceeds? They would have to apply the proceeds in the following order:

(1) to reimburse the lender's expenses of enforcement including reasonably attorneys' fees;

(2) reimbursement of any expenses incurred by the lender to protect and maintain the real property;

(3) payment of the secured obligation;

(4) payment of any obligation secured by a subordinate security interest (if they received a notice from the subordinate lienholder demanding payment of the proceeds); and then

(5) the payment of any excess goes to the owner of the property.

The new statute became effective from/on June 30, 2011.

This gives lenders significant new rights and allows them to put a lot of pressure on borrowers to strictly comply with their mortgage or they will lose their cash flow.

Disaster Remediation Contracts

Have you had trouble with hurricanes, wildfires, crazy relatives? There is a new statute for disaster remediation contractors which are persons who engage in disaster remediation for compensation after the occurrence of wide spread or severe damage related to any natural cause, including fire, flood, earthquake, wind storm, or wave action that results in a disaster declaration by the governor.

A disaster remediation contractor may not require a person to make a full or partial payment under a contract before the contractor begins the work. Nor may he require that the amount of any partial payment under the contract exceed an amount reasonably proportionate to the work performed. Any contract for a disaster remediation services must contain the following statement in conspicuous bold-face type of at least 10 pts in size:

This contract is subject to Chapter 57, Business& Commerce Code. A contractor may not require a full or partial payment before the contractor begins work, and may not require partial payments in an amount that exceeds an amount reasonably proportionate to the work performed, including any materials delivered.

Violation of the statute constitutes a Deceptive Trade Practice. See Texas Business & Commerce Code §57.001.

Deeds as Mortgages

This new statute prohibits execution of a deed to somebody that extends credit to the owner of residential real estate. it provides that a seller of residential real estate or a person who makes an extension of credit and takes a security interest or a mortgage against residential real estate may not request or require the purchaseror borrower to execute and deliver to the seller or a person making the extension of credit, a deed conveying the residential real estate to the seller or person making the extension of credit. Any deed executed in violation of that statute is voidable and if any litigation is involved, the prevailing party is entitled to recover reasonable and necessary attorney's fees.

This statute was passed to prevent lenders from having a deed-in-lieu of foreclosure executed at closings. In the event of default, the lendermerely records the executed deed. The borrower, then, has signed away his foreclosure rights under traditional mortgages.

This also appears to prohibit the mortgage technique that's been long recognized in Texas called a deed absolute as a mortgage. See §21.001, Texas Business & Commerce Code.

Homestead Issues

Almost all Texans are familiar with the traditional homestead exemptions and the protection from forced sale of a homestead by the owner's creditors. Likewise, there has always been an absolute prohibition against mortgaging the equity in one's homestead. The basic rule is that the homestead cannot be encumbered by any increase of debt over those traditionally allowed lien rights. Texas has recognized two types of homesteads, either urban or rural. The urban homestead can consist of two homesteads, a business and residential, which are construed together as one homestead under Texas law.

The lien rights that have been determined to be foreclosable against homesteads in Texas are:

- purchase money mortgage.

- home improvements, when those improvements have been properly contracted for in writing by husband and wife (or single homestead claimant, if there is no marriage) *prior* to *any* work being done.

- taxes.

- homeowners' association maintenance fund liens, if they have been reserved in the deed restrictions.

In 1995, we expanded the list of liens that are foreclosable against homesteads to include Internal Revenue Service liens, which are the debt of both spouses, general federal tax liens, and owelty liens.

Then in 1997, we were blessed with home equity liens and reverse mortgages. It is still changing!

Home Equity Liens

The new constitutional amendment has consumer-friendly protections that are mandatory and still make Texas homestead protection unique. The requirements are as follows:

Voluntary Lien. The lien can only be created under a written agreement under the consent of each owner and each owner's spouse. Section 50(a)(6)(A).

Loan to Value Cap. The amount of the equity loan plus the total of all other debt against the homestead property cannot exceed 80 percent of the market value of the property on the date the loan is closed. Section 50(a)(6)(B). *It doesn't look like a 125 percent loan is valid!*

Nonrecourse Loans. All loans will be nonrecourse (i.e., no personal liability for the homeowner beyond the homestead property) unless the homeowner obtained the loan through actual fraud. Section 50(a)(6)(C).

You can't get sued for a deficiency!

Judicial Foreclosure. A lender must file suit and obtain a judgment ordering foreclosure of the lien securing the equity loan. Section 50(a)(6)(D). The Texas Supreme Court has promulgated rules of civil procedure for expedited foreclosure proceedings for equity loans.

Fees. Loan fees (not including interest) are capped at 3 percent of the loan amount. This prohibits the owner or the owner's spouse from paying fees to any person necessary to originate, evaluate, maintain, record, insure, or service the extension of credit that exceeds, in the aggregate, 3 percent of the original principal amount of the extension of credit. Section 50(a)(6)(E).

Can lenders pay these expenses, and then add them to the loan amount? Hmm.

Lines of Credit. An equity loan may be in the form of an open-end account (i.e., line of credit).

Prepayment Penalty. Prepayment penalties are prohibited. Section 50(a)(6)(G).

Additional Collateral. A lender may not require any property other than the homestead property as collateral for an equity loan. Section 50(a)(6)(H). With the new 10-acre urban exemption, this problem has little effect on most home sites.

Agricultural Property Exemption. Property with an "agricultural use" exemption cannot be used as collateral for an equity loan unless the property is primarily used for the production of milk. Section 50(a)(6)(I).

Decrease in Market Value. Lender may not demand payment on an equity loan if there is a decrease in the market value of the homestead property. Section 50(a)(6)(J).

One Debt. The debt secured by the homestead at the time the extension of credit is made must be the only debt, except for other permitted encumbrances. Enumerated under subsections (a)(1)-(a)(5). Section 50(a)(6)(K).

Substantially Equal Payments/Full Interest Amortization. An equity loan must be repaid in substantially equal monthly payments that fully amortize the interest owed. Section 50(a)(6)(L).

Cooling Off Period. An equity loan cannot be closed until at least 12 days after the later: (1) of the date that the borrower applies for the loan; (2) or the date the lender provides the borrower a copy of the notice prescribed in the Constitution. Presumably, the most efficient procedure would be to have the loan application coupled with the notice (shown on Exhibit B). Section 50(a)(6)(M).

Location of Closing. An equity loan cannot be closed in a borrower's home; closing must occur in the office of a lender, a title company, or an attorney. Section 50(a)(6)(N).

Cross Default. A lender may not demand payment on an equity loan because of a default on another debt. Section 50(a)(6)(Q)(i).

Authorized Lenders. Equity loans can be made only by certain authorized lenders:

- A bank, savings and loan association, savings bank, or credit union doing business under the laws of this state or the United States.

- A federally chartered instrumentality or a person approved as a mortgagee by the United States government to make federally insured loans.

- A person licensed to make regulated loans as provided by statute of this state (presumably any lender that is a regulated lender licensed by the Consumer Credit Commissioner under the Texas Credit Code). See Chapter 3(a) of the Texas Credit Code.

- A person who sold the homestead to a current owner and provided all or part of the financing for the purchase.

- A person who is related to the homestead property owner within the second degree of affinity or consanguinity.

See Section 50(a)(6)(P). Note the following conditions:

- The proceeds can't be used to repay another debt except a debt secured by the homestead.

- There can be no assignment of wages as security.

- The owner may not sign the instrument if substantive terms of agreement are left to be filled in.

- The owner may not sign a confession of judgment or power of attorney to the lender or to a third person to confess judgment or to appear for the owner in any judicial proceeding.

- The lender must provide the owner of the homestead a copy of all documents signed by the owner related to the extension of credit.

- The instruments must contain a disclosure that the extension of credit is the type of credit defined by Article XVI, Section 50(a)(6), Texas Constitution.

- Upon final payment the lender is required to cancel and return the promissory note to the owner of the homestead, then give the owner, in recordable form, a release of the lien securing the extension of credit or a copy of an endorsement and assignment of the lien to a lender that is refinancing the extension of credit.

- There must be a provision that any owner or spouse may, within 3 days after the extension of credit is made, rescind the extension of credit without penalty or charge.

- The owner of the homestead and the lender must sign a written acknowledgment as to the fair market value of the homestead on the date the extension of credit is made.

- The lender or any holder of the note for the extension of credit shall forfeit all principal and interest to the extension of credit if the lender or holder fails to comply with lender's or holder's obligations under the extensions of credit within 60 days after the lender or holder is notified by the borrower of the lender's failure to comply.

This last provision may have diluted homestead protections significantly. Texas has a long history of strict enforcement of homestead protection. However, in interpreting the above provision (allowing the lender a reasonable time for failure to correct the defect) the Texas Supreme Court was very liberal in allowing lenders to correct defects. *Doody v. Ameriquest Mortgage Company* 49 S.W.3d 342 (Tex. 2001). See also *Doody v. Ameriquest Mortgage Corp.*, 242 F 3rd 286, at 289.

See Section 50(a)(6)(Q).

Anti-Flipping Provision. An equity loan cannot be refinanced more frequently than once a year. Section 50(a)(6)(M)(ii).

Anti-Redlining Provision. Any lender found by a federal regulatory agency to have engaged in "redlining" is prohibited from making equity loans. Section 50(a)(6)(P).

The 2003 Legislature passed a new joint resolution recommending an amendment to the Texas Constitution to allow refinancing of a debt secured by a homestead for extensions of home equity loans or reverse mortgages. This permits refinancing of a home equity loan with a reverse mortgage.

Home Improvement Loans

Another constitutional amendment modifies Section 50(a)(5) to provide a valid lien for work and material used in constructing new improvements thereon, if contracted for in writing, or work and material used to repair or renovate existing improvements thereon, if:

- The work and materials are contracted for in writing with the consent of both spouses.

- The contract for work and materials is not executed by the owner or the owner's spouse before the fifth day after the owner makes written application for any extension of credit for the work and materials, unless due to an emergency affecting health and safety.

- The contract for work and materials provides that the owner may rescind the contract without penalty or charge within 3 days after the execution of the contract with all the parties.

- The contract for the work and materials is executed by the owner and the owner's spouse:
    o   at the office of the third-party lender making an extension of credit for the work and materials;
    o   is an attorney at law; or
    o   a title company.

Reverse Mortgage Loans

A third constitutional amendment provides for reverse mortgages. Reverse mortgages have been available in a number of states since the mid-1970s. They work like conventional mortgages except in reverse; they pay the homeowner in regular installments (or as a line of credit one can draw down as needed) over a number of years. The loan balance of a reverse mortgage grows larger over time because the loan principal increases (as interest and other charges also accrue) each month on the total funds advanced from the mortgage company. When the homeowner leaves the home, the balance becomes due and payable, but the obligation to repay the loan is limited to the market value of the home. Effectively without recourse, the lender cannot require repayment from assets other than the home. In general, the reverse mortgage permits the borrower to retain homeownership and doesn't require repayment as long as the borrower remains in the home.

Texas law defines "reverse mortgage" as an extension of credit:

- that is secured by a voluntary lien on homestead property created by a written agreement with the consent of each owner and each owner's spouse.

- that is made to a person who is or whose spouse is 62 years or older.

- that is made without recourse for personal liability against each owner and the spouse of each owner.

- under which advances are provided to a borrower based on the equity in a borrower's homestead.

- that does not permit the lender to reduce the amount or number of advances because of an adjustment in the interest rate if periodic advances are to be made.

- that requires no payment of principal or interest until:
  - all borrowers have died.
  - the homestead property securing the loan is sold or otherwise transferred.
  - all borrowers cease occupying the homestead property for a period of longer than 12 consecutive months without prior written approval from the lender.
  - the borrower:
    - defaults on an obligation specified in the loan documents to repair and maintain, pay taxes and assessments on, or insure the homestead property.
    - commits actual fraud in connection with the loan.
    - fails to maintain the priority of the lender's lien on the homestead property, after the lender gives notice to the borrower, by promptly discharging any lien that has priority or may obtain priority over the lender's lien within 10 days after the date the borrower receives the notice, unless the borrower takes one of the following three actions: (1) He or she agrees in writing to the payment of the obligation secured by the lien in a manner acceptable to the lender; (2) He or she contests in good faith the lien by, or defends against enforcement of the lien in, legal proceedings so as to prevent the enforcement of the lien or forfeiture of any part of the homestead property; or (3) He or she secures from the holder of the lien an agreement satisfactory to the lender subordinating the lien to all amounts secured by the lender's lien on the homestead property.

- that provides that if the lender fails to make loan advances as required in the loan documents and if the lender fails to cure the default as required in the loan documents after notice from the borrower, the lender forfeits all principal and interest of the reverse mortgage, provided, however, that this subdivision does not apply when a governmental agency or instrumentality takes an assignment of the loan in order to cure the default.

- that is not made unless the owner of the homestead attests in writing that the owner received counseling regarding the advisability and availability of reverse mortgages and other financial alternatives.

- that requires the lender, at the time the loan is made, to disclose to the borrower by written notice the specific provisions contained in Subdivision (6) of this subsection under which the borrower is required to repay the loan.

- that does not permit the lender to commence foreclosure until the lender gives notice to the borrower, in the manner provided for a notice by mail related to the foreclosure of liens under Subsection (a) (6) of this section, that a ground for foreclosure exists and gives the borrower at least 30 days, or at (6) (D) (iii) of this subsection, to:
  - remedy the condition creating the ground for foreclosure.
  - pay the debt secured by the homestead property from proceeds of the sale of the homestead property by the borrower or from any other sources.
  - convey the homestead property to the lender by a deed in lieu of foreclosure.

- o that is secured by a lien that may be foreclosed upon only by a court order, if the foreclosure is for a ground other than a ground stated by Subdivision (6) (A) or (B) of this subsection.

The advances made on a reverse mortgage loan under which more than one advance is made must be made according to the terms established by the loan documents by one or more of the following methods:

- at regular intervals.

- at regular intervals in which the amounts advanced may be reduced, for one or more advances, at the request of the borrower.

- or at any time by the lender, on behalf of the borrower, if the borrower fails to pay on time any of the following that the borrower is obligated to pay under the loan documents to the extent necessary to protect the lender's interest in or the value of the homestead property:
  - o taxes.
  - o insurance.
  - o costs of repairs and maintenance performed by a person or company that is not an employee of the lender or a person or company that directly or indirectly controls, is controlled by, or is under common control with the lender.
  - o assessments levied against the homestead property.
  - o any lien that has, or may obtain, priority over the lender's lien as it is established in the loan documents.

A reverse mortgage may provide for an interest rate that is fixed or adjustable and may also provide for interest that is contingent on appreciation in the fair market value of the homestead property. Although payment of principal or interest shall not be required under a reverse mortgage until the entire loan becomes due and payable, interest may accrue and be compounded during the term of the loan as provided by the reverse mortgage loan agreement.

The borrower either can receive the proceeds as a lump sum payment at closing or can arrange equal monthly payments over the loan term. It can also be a line of credit loan, discussed in Chapter 4 of the Law Update section of the book. The loan balance increases rather than decreases over the term of the loan. The term of the reverse mortgage most likely will be indefinite. The loan comes due when the borrower no longer needs that home as a residence. This generally occurs when the borrower dies, permanently moves to a health-care facility, or moves in with their children!

A reverse mortgage can also be used to buy a home. Fannie Mae's HomeKeeper for Purchase Program allows a person over the age of 62 to purchase a home financed with a reverse mortgage. The purchase requires a substantial down payment, but there are no monthly mortgage payments as long as the homeowner remains in the house. The payments are considered loan proceeds, not income, and therefore, are not taxable.

Borrowers must receive counseling on the conditions and appropriateness of the loan to their needs and situations. Whereas Texas law now allows a home equity lien to be refinanced by a reverse mortgage, the reverse mortgage cannot take the form of a line of credit.

Who Needs a Reverse Mortgage?

Most who plan on living in their present home for as long as they are able can reap significant benefits from these types of loans, which could mean the difference between a comfortable existence or living on a very tight budget. When the borrower dies, the heirs can always pay off the loan but it may result in a much smaller amount of equity being passed to one's heirs.

Although this may be an excellent estate-planning vehicle, one should always consult experts in estate planning and retirement for making this kind of a loan.

Urban Homestead

The 1999 Legislature, subject to approval by the voters, increased the homestead exemption in the urban environment to "not more than 10 acres." (It used to be 1 acre.) The statute now also requires that the lot(s) be contiguous (not a previous requirement).

The Legislature also defined urban homestead, as property:

- located within the limits of a municipality or extraterritorial jurisdiction, or a plat in subdivision; and

- served by police protection, paid or volunteer fire protection, and at least three of the following services provided by a municipality or under contract to a municipality: electric; natural gas; sewer; storm sewer; and water.

The Fifth Circuit Court of Appeals in Rush Truck Centers v. Bouchie 324 F.3rd 780 (5th Cir. 2003), held that under the well-known canon of "inclusio unius est exclusio alterius," the legislature intentionally excluded all other factors from the rural/urban determination and, therefore, this new statute is the exclusive vehicle for distinguishing between rural and urban homesteads.

Another recent case has held that the property will be classified as urban, even if the city services were available to the property but not utilized by the homestead claimant. Smith v. Hennington, 249 S.W.3d 600, 604 (Tex. App.-Eastland 2008).

Judgment Liens

This remains a hot topic! Recall that we passed a new statute to address this issue (see Chapter 1). A good Texas case has given us some comfort in the fact that judgment liens do not attach to homesteads. In *Tarrant Bank v. Miller*, 833 S.W.2d 666 (Tex. App.-Eastland,

1992, writ denied), the homeowner sued for slander of title when the bank refused to honor the homeowner's request for a partial release of its lien. The bank had obtained a judgment against the homeowner that stopped the sale of the homeowner's homestead. The bank acknowledged the lien was unenforceable, but would not sign a release. The homeowner sued and recovered substantial damages for slander of title. This provides an excellent incentive for lien holders to release their judgment liens or be subject to a substantial damage claim in the event the sale of property is lost because of title problems.

A similar result was reached in the federal courts in In *re Henderson*, 18 F.3d 1305 (5th Cir., 1994), wherein the creditor argued that because the judgment lien did not attach, it could not create a cloud on title, and therefore, no liability should arise for the creditor who refuses to release the judgment against the homestead. The court held that because the defendant refused to release the lien on the plaintiffs' homestead, the title company refused to issue an owner's title policy, and the plaintiffs were unable to complete the sale of their home. The court noted that the decision in *Tarrant Bank* demonstrated that the judicial lien does impair the homestead exemption in a very real and practical sense. The court held that as a matter of federal law, the judgment lien creates a cloud on the title to the homestead, making it difficult, if not impossible, to obtain title insurance. It therefore "impairs" title to the property.

In a partial response to the *Tarrant Bank* case, the 1993 legislature provided another method of releasing judgment liens. The problem existed because if a person declared bankruptcy, his debts might be discharged, but the liens of record in the county in which the property was located would not be released except under specific circumstances defined under the Bankruptcy Code. Unfortunately, an awful lot of people who went through bankruptcy didn't realize the clouds on title weren't released and subsequently were stopped at the closing table because of these liens. We amended the Property Code in 1993, however, to provide that if an abstract of judgment or judgment lien is recorded before September 1, 1993, a judgment or judgment lien may be discharged from his debts under the Federal Bankruptcy Law. If the judgment or judgment lien is recorded on or after September 1, 1993, a judgment is discharged and the abstract of judgment or judgment lien is cancelled and released without further action in any court, and may not be enforced if the lien is against real property owned by the debtor before a petition for debtor relief was filed under Federal Bankruptcy Law and the debt or obligation evidenced by the judgment is discharged in the bankruptcy.

Does this mean automatic damages? *Citing Tarrant Bank*, the Texas Attorney General determined that a cloud on title results from two factors:

1. the recording and indexing of the abstract.
2. the lack of conclusive determination that the debtor's property is homestead.

The Attorney General opined that any judgment creditor's knowledge of the judgment debtor's homestead right does not constitute knowledge that the judgment lien is forever inapplicable to the homestead, nor does the creditor's refusal to release the potential lien created by the abstract of judgment constitute a claim that the creditor has a present lien on the homestead property. The Attorney General further suggested that a release of a judgment lien against the homestead should be expressly conditioned upon the closing of the specific contemplated sale of the property, and stating that the release shall be void in the event the judgment debtor ever again acquires an interest in the property, and that provisions on the face of the release of lien should include: (1) expressly conditioning the release; and (2) stating that the release shall be void in the event the debtor ever reacquires an interest in the property. See *Opinion No. DM-366 (1995)*. See also *Cadle Company v. Harvey*, 46 S.W.3d 282 (Tex. App.-Ft. Worth, 2001). The Fifth Circuit recently addressed the lien priority issue again in *United States v. Johnson*, 160 F.3d 1061 (5th Cir.-1998). Johnson continuously claimed his property was homestead and resided in it except during a period of incarceration for a 1989 criminal conviction. A judgment was obtained against him on December 24, 1986, and the abstract of judgment was recorded in Travis County. Johnson subsequently conveyed a one-half interest in the property (under an option to purchase) to Property Trading, Inc., on August 3, 1989. Property Trading, Inc., did not record the deed until October 28, 1992. The question in the case was whether or not that one-half interest conveyed was free and clear of the judgment lien. The judgment creditor alleged that the judgment lien attached to the undivided one-half interest conveyed to Property Trading, Inc., during the period between the conveyance and the recordation. The Fifth Circuit recited long-standing Texas homestead law, overruling one prior inconsistent Texas Court of Appeals case. Judgment liens do not normally attach to homestead property in Texas. Because the property was uncontestedly Johnson's homestead at the time he conveyed the one-half interest, Property Trading, Inc., took title free and clear of the judgment lien.

In another recent homestead case, a seller got a judgment lien against him, and his property was in excess of the homestead limit (one and one-half acres when, in 1999, the homestead limit was one acre). The court noted that the constitutional amendment expanding the homestead from one acre to ten acres in an urban environment was effective on January 1, 2000. The court noted that the lien was valid because it was filed before January 1, 2000, but that the creditor could not execute on it because the writ of execution was issued after January 1, 2000. *Wilcox v. Marriott*, 230 S.W.3d 266 (Tex. App.-Beaumont, 2007).

New Statute

When a person cannot pay a judgment, an abstract of judgment constitutes a lien on and attaches to all real property owned by the defendant in the county the abstract is filed. An exception is for real property exempt under Texas Homestead laws. This new law provides that a judgment debtor may, at any time, file an affidavit in the Real Property Records in the county in which the judgment debtor's homestead is located, and it serves as its release of record of a judgment then. A bona fide purchaser or mortgagee, or successor or assigns may rely conclusively on this affidavit if it includes evidence that:

the judgment debtor is sent a letter and a copy of the affidavit notifying the judgment creditor of the affidavit and judgment debtor's intent to file the affidavit; and

the letter and the affidavit were sent by registered or certified mail, return receipt requested, 30 or more days before the affidavit was filed to

(i)   the judgment creditor's last known address,

(ii)   the address appearing on the judgment creditor's pleadings,

(iii)   the judgment creditor's last known attorney, and

(iv)   the address of the judgment creditor's last known attorney as shown in the records of the State Bar of Texas, if that address is different from those pleadings.

The affidavit does not serve as a release of record if the judgment creditor files a contradicting affidavit in the real property records of the county asserting that:

- the debtor's affidavit is untrue; or

- states another reason exists as to why the judgment then attaches to the judgment debtor's property (Section 52.0012, Texas Property Code).

New Bankruptcy Rules

The federal government recently passed new bankruptcy rules involving homestead exemptions that have a significant effect on bankruptcy protection under Texas law. When one declares bankruptcy, there is a choice of going under the federal laws or state laws. Texas laws have always been so protective that all claimants have opted for the Texas homestead protection. Some (particularly Congress) have seen this Texas Homestead Protection as unfair and overly protective, when compared to other states.

The new rules apply a federal homestead cap to a debtor claiming a homestead exemption under state laws. Under these new rules, a debtor may not exempt any interest that was acquired by the debtor during the 1,215 days preceding the date of the filing of the bankruptcy petition that exceeds the aggregate of $125,000 in value of real property that the debtor (or dependent of the debtor) claims as a homestead. 11 USC §522(p)(1). In effect, if one declares bankruptcy and has acquired a homestead within the last 1,215 days (roughly 3.3 years) the homestead claimant is limited to an exemption of only $125,000 in the homestead. It only applies to homesteads acquired, not an increase in equity in the home. In re Blair 334 B.R. 374 (Bankr. N.D. Tex. 2005).

The $125,000 homestead cap also applies if the court finds the debtor-committed crimes involving a violation of the Federal Securities laws or any criminal act, intentional tort, or willful or reckless misconduct that causes serious physical injury or death to another individual in the preceding 5 years. 11 USC §522(q)(1)(B). This new penalty, however, does not apply if the debtor's homestead exemption is reasonably necessary for the support of the debtor or a dependent of the debtor. This seems to a spouse and children the right to full homestead protection, but there is no case law yet on how this provision will be interpreted.

Recent Homestead Cases

In *re Preston*, 233 B.R. 375 (Bkrtcy. E.D. Tex., 1999), TPC 41.001(a) states, "A homestead and one or more lots used for a place of burial of the dead are exempt from seizure...." Here, Preston, a single woman, claimed exemption in four burial plots valued at $2,000 each. The bankruptcy trustee objected to the exemptions.

The debtor claimed that the plain meaning of the statute was that "one or more" burial plots could be exempted. There is nothing in the statute limiting the number, although the statute before revision in 1985 limited the exemption to lots used for a single adult or family members. The court looked at the legislative intent in making the revision. Here, the legislature removed the "family" limitation from the statute because the definition of family was too restrictive and the legislature intended that an exemption be available for lots for people related to the claimant but not within the "dependency" and "support" ranges required by the court-created definition of family. Allowing exemptions for lots to benefit brothers and sisters seemed reasonable enough to the court, but expanding the statute to allow an unlimited number of exempt burial plots would be clearly contrary to the legislative intent: "The legislature had to have meant that one could claim as exempt the number of burial plots that are reasonable based on the facts and circumstances." 233 B.R. at 377.

In *re Box*, 340 B.R. 782 (S.D. Tex. 2005), the bankruptcy court considered a purported home equity loan that did not comply with the Texas Constitutional requirements for making such loans. Mr. Box had been a First State Bank (FSB) customer for over 15 years. The bank made several loans to Mr. Box's business and in August of 2003, Mr. Box liquidated his business to pay off his creditors. After the liquidation was complete, Mr. Box still owed FSB an unsecured debt of approximately $107,000.

FSB then approached Mr. Box about obtaining a home equity loan to secure the debt. Mr. Box reluctantly agreed. After executing a series of documents for the home equity loan containing recitals and affirmations that they "were not required to use the proceeds of the loan to repay another debt to the same lender," Mr. Box claimed he had never read the documents. The court found otherwise, and said that the intent of the parties was unambiguous and the intent of the parties was to make a home equity loan to collaterize the prior debt to FSB.

The court noted, however, that Mr. Box did not receive the funds. Instead, the proceeds of the home equity loan were applied to Box's preexisting debt to FSB. The court noted that the effect of the transaction was to collaterize the previously unsecured debt. Section §50(a)(6)(Q)(i) of the Texas Constitution states that "the owner of a homestead is not required to apply the proceeds of the extension of credit to repay another debt, except debt secured by the homestead or debt to another lender." The court held that the lender violated this constitutional requirement, notwithstanding the fact that the debtor signed various documents to the contrary. The court noted, "It is fundamental to Texas Homestead Law that an owner may not change the status of a homestead through false recitals or declarations." The court then concluded that because the lien did not meet the requirements set out in the Texas Constitution, the debt was only an unsecured extension of a credit.

In *Norris v. Thomas*, 215 S.W.3d 851 (Tex. 2007), the Texas Supreme Court responded to an inquiry from the 5th Circuit Court of Appeals to determine whether or not a boat qualifies as a homestead under the Texas Constitution. After reviewing a long history of Texas homestead protection, the Texas Supreme Court held that the Constitution has long since been interpreted to mean that improvements to real property must include improvements to real property as contemplated by Article 16, Section 51 of the Constitution, and that there can be no homestead rights in personalty until it is annexed to the real estate, and even at that, it must be a permanent improvement.

The court analogized the situation to a house trailer, mounted on wheels and moved into the backyard of a residence. The Court noted that the house trailer was only a homestead because it was permanently attached to the real estate and set alongside the house, essentially becoming an extra room, and that house trailers without the characteristics of permanent fixture are not protected homesteads.

In this case, dock-based connections to utilities and plumbing are sufficient for a mobile home or house trailer, but the boat retains its independent, mobile character even when attached to the dock-based amenities, because of (1) its self-contained utility and plumbing systems and (2) its own propulsion. The Court further noted that the legislature is certainly free to put a proposed amendment before the Texas voters to include boats, since amending the Texas Constitution is no Sisyphean task. (Go look up Sisyphean and surprise your friends.)

Landlord and Tenant

Waiver of Implied Warranty of Fitness

Texas is the only state where the Supreme Court has provided for an implied warranty of suitability for commercial premises. The Texas Supreme Court has also held that "as Is" provisions are also enforceable. Which controls?

In *Gym-N-I Playgrounds, Inc. v. Snider*, 220 S.W.2d 905 (Tex. 2007), the case resolves a split in the lower appeals courts as to the meaning of Davidow and as to the application of the prudential doctrine on "as Is" clauses. In *Prudential Ins. Co. of Am. v. Jefferson Assocs. Ltd.*, 896 S.W.2d 156 (Tex. 1995), the Texas Supreme Court upheld the application of an "as Is" clause in a sale agreement of commercial property, holding that it demonstrated that the cause of any injury to the buyer as a consequence of defects in the premises arose due to the buyer's failure to identify the problems, rather than the seller's failure to disclose or remedy them.

The case construes the well-known holding in *Davidow v. Inwood North Professional Group-Phase I*, 747 S.W.2d 373 (Tex. 1988). This case, based on some particularly good plaintiff's facts, concluded that commercial landlords in Texas implicitly warrant the suitability of their premises for a tenant's commercial purposes. The case involved a multi-tenant office building and a claim by a doctor occupying a relatively small portion of the building who suffered from significant structural and systems problems originating inside and outside of his leased area. The case mentioned the superior ability of a landlord to identify and remedy building problems. No court has followed Davidow, and, as the court notes here, at least four jurisdictions have rejected it expressly (Kansas, Nebraska, New Hampshire, and North Dakota).

The Davidow warranty was never as broad as the implied warranties of habitability recognized almost universally in residential leases. The court indicated that in determining whether there was a breach of the warranty, a court needed to consider: "the nature of the defect; its effect on tenant's use of the premises; the length of time the defect persisted; the age of the structure; the amount of the rent; the area in which the premises are located; whether the tenant waived the defects; and whether the defect resulted from any unusual or abnormal use by the tenant."

When the Texas Supreme Court, however, decided in Prudential that broad "as is" clauses would be recognized on freedom of contract grounds in commercial real estate sales, the stage was set for a broad reading of the lease waiver language.

The tenants in this case were long-time employees of the buildings and, in the words of the landlord, themselves "knew more about the building than anyone else." The City Code required that buildings containing combustible materials of certain kinds contain sprinkler systems, but the city inspector had not required sprinklers here, though he recommended them. Tenants were fully aware of this.

The tenants, leasing under a "hold over" clause following the end of an initial five-year term, suffered a fire that destroyed the premises. The insurer paid them for their business losses and then brought a claim against the landlord based upon various grounds, including implied warranty, and all predicated on the absence of a sprinkler system and claimed defective wiring.

But the insurers ran head on into the language of the lease dealing with waivers of warranties:

> "Tenant accepts the Premises 'as is.' Landlord has not made and does not make any representations as to the commercial suitability, physical condition, layout, footage, expenses, operation or any other matter affecting or relating to the premises and this agreement, except as herein specifically set forth or referred to and tenant hereby expressly acknowledges that no such representations have been made. Landlord makes no other warranties, express of implied, of merchantability, marketability, fitness or suitability for a particular purpose or otherwise, except as set forth herein, and implied warranties are expressly disclaimed and excluded."

The clause undoubtedly expresses the meaning that there is no implied warranty given under the lease, and does not do so in the context of transferring any repair responsibilities to the tenant. The court found the waiver enforceable, and found no implied warranty in the lease, thus resolving once and for all the enforceability of such waivers in Texas.

In *Prudential Ins. Co. of America v. Italian Cowboy Partners, Ltd.*, discussed in the MCE legal Update section, the Texas Supreme Court reversed a lower court holding, holding that the disclaimer-of-representations language written on the lease was not a disclaimer of the tenant's reliance on the property manager's oral assurance during the negotiations of the lease. The manager of the center made very specific representations that "the building was practically new and had no problems" and "the building was in perfect condition, never a problem whatsoever" and "this is my baby and I was here from the first day when they put the first brick until the last one… it's in perfect condition."

At trial, prior tenants who had occupied the same premises (and who also had vacated the premises because of the foul odors) testified that the manager "knew of the smell" and she herself had acknowledged to other people that is was "almost unbearable" and "ungodly."

Acknowledging the disclaimer of reliance on the merger clauses in the lease, the court held that these provisions do not control if there is a fraudulent inducement. The landlord also attempted to defend by saying expressions by the manager were mere expressions of opinion. The court specifically rejected this issue noting that whether a statement is an actionable statement as a "fact" or merely one of "opinion" often depends on the circumstances in which the statement is made. When a speaker purports to have special knowledge of the facts, or does have superior knowledge of the facts, a party may maintain a fraud action. Testimony indicated that the manager herself personally experienced the odor.

In a probably more surprising holding, the court upheld Texas' Implied Warranty of Suitability established in Davidow unless the Implied Warranty of Suitability is expressly waived. The Court upheld an award for special damages for lost investment, accounts payable, interest carried, in addition to rescission of the lease.

New Federal Landlord and Tenant Law!

Congress passed a new Landlord and Tenant Law that became effective May 20, 2009, which affects all foreclosures from that date through December of 2012. The new law enables a bona fide tenant who is leasing premises that are foreclosed upon, to continue occupancy during the full term of the lease unless the new owner (who purchased the property at the foreclosure sale) intends to use the property as his or her primary residence. In this case, the new owner must still give the tenant 90 days notice to vacate.

In virtually every other circumstance, the tenant is entitled to a 90-day notice to vacate. It applies not only to a federally regulated mortgage loan, but also to any dwelling or residential real property.

What is a bona fide tenant? It can't be the mortgagor, or the mortgagor's child, spouse, or parent, it must have been an arm's length transaction and for a substantially fair market value.

This creates problems for foreclosing creditors. What if it is a long-term lease? What if it has rights to sublease? Thiscould force lenders into being owners and unable to liquidate properties for an extended lease period.

Fair Housing

This is becoming a more difficult concept to discuss. The original Fair Housing statutes were passed to provide access to housing for all Americans. Their enforcement is now taking on a different focus to some federal agencies. They are using the Fair Housing Statutes as a sword rather than a shield, to punish rather than to protect. In addition, society has changed since the laws were initially passed in 1968. There is some indication that the pendulum may be swinging somewhat, as many appeals courts are beginning to encounter lawsuits that are somewhat abusive in an attempt to enforce Fair Housing laws.

The Fair Housing legislation is still the same, and is still very important. One cannot discriminate on the basis of race, color, creed, national origin, sex, familial status, and handicap status. Remember, the objective is to see that all Americans have the same right to housing. A real estate licensee is enabling that access and is critically important.

Adults Only, Familial Status

In *U.S. v. Fountainbleau*, 566 F. Supp. 2d. 726 (E.D. Tenn., 2008), an apartment complex openly admitted that it engaged in an "adults only" rental policy and actively engaged in a pattern of discriminatory conduct. The management refused to provide rental applications to families with children, refused to show available units to them, and suggested that they find another apartment complex that would accept children. Fountainbleau claimed that it qualified for an exception for discrimination on the basis of family status under the "for older persons" part of the Fair Housing Act. However, the court found that the complex "utterly failed to demonstrate any level of compliance" with the requirement that the policies and procedures of the complex demonstrated the intent to only provide housing for older people. The complex only excluded people under the age of 21, rather than excluding all under age 55. Thus, Fountainbleau did not qualify for the "older person" exemption of the FHA, and were found by the trial court to have illegally discriminated against prospective renters on the basis of family status.

The defendants claimed that they did not realize they were violating the law; however, not knowing the law is not a defense to violating it. They made the conscious decision to exclude (and, thus, discriminate against) families with children from the complex, without looking into whether or not this was legal.

Both managers and owners of Fountainbleau were found to be individually liable for violating the FHA. Although not directly involved in the discriminatory acts, the owners were "held liable for the discrimination of their agents under the theory of respondeat superior." The court cited other cases to show that "a property owner is liable for the conduct of his employees despite instructions to them not to discriminate" under the direction of his or her employer.

In *Housing Opportunities Project for Excellence, Inc. v. Key Colony No. 4 Condominium Assoc., Inc.,* 510 F. Supp. 2d 1003 (S.D. Fla., 2007), a condominium association and its manager enforced a very restrictive policy limiting the number of residents in a condo unit to four people. Plaintiffs purchased a unit while there were four people in their household, yet they were expecting the birth of another child. The property manager said this would not restrict their moving in. However, the condominium association sent the family a letter, denying that they had a right to move in based upon the occupancy restriction. The plaintiffs claimed that these actions violated the FHA protection barring discrimination based upon familial status. In response, the defendants requested the case be dismissed on the basis that they could not be held liable under the FHA.

The court held that where "the board of directors each personally and intentionally discriminated against families," state laws generally protecting nonprofit board members did not apply. Additionally, the property manager was not released from liability, since "it is clear that an employee acting in the course and scope of her employer is still liable for her own unlawful conduct." The court states it is clear from many past cases that an agent has no excuse for acting illegally whether or not the illegal acts are done under the direction of his or her employer.

In *U.S. v. Matusoff Rental Co.,* 494 F. Supp. 2d 740 (S.D. Ohio, 2007), the government sued the owner of three apartment complexes for discriminating on the basis of race and family status, thereby violating the Fair Housing Act. Mr. Matusoff instructed his employees not to rent to African-Americans and not to repair the apartments of African-Americans who already lived in the complexes. Race discrimination was standard operating procedure in the management of the apartments (between 1989 and 1997), and the court found Matusoff "engaged in a pattern and practice of discriminating against African-American tenants and applicants for apartments on the basis of their race." Thus, Matusoff was found liable to be individually liable for engaging in a pattern of race discrimination, as his actions were not sporadic, occasional, or isolated events.

The court identified 26 victims of Matusoff's violations of the FHA. Each victim was awarded either $7,500, $15,000, or $20,000 in compensatory damages (depending on the amount of harm experienced), and each was also awarded $5,000 in punitive damages. In total, Matusoff was fined $535,000. Compensatory damages of $405,000 were awarded for the emotional distress, humiliation, embarrassment, mental anguish, and out-of-pocket losses resulting from his discrimination. The additional $130,000 was awarded for punitive damages as a punishment for the court's finding that Matusoff "acted with reckless indifference to the requirements of the FHA" for a period of at least eight years.

Lender Liability—"Reverse red-lining"

In *M & T Mortgage Corp. v. Foy*, 20 Misc. 3d 274, 858 N.Y.S. 2d 567 (Supp. 2008), Foy obtained a mortgage loan on a house she owned in a predominantly Black and Hispanic area of Brooklyn. The loan was for a 30-year term with an interest rate of 9.5 percent. Foy was a military reserve officer and had served several recent active duty tours overseas. The property was evidently used for rental, at least when she was out of the country, but she alleged that it was difficult to manage the property and keep viable tenants.

Foy moved for reformation of the mortgage pursuant to New York Military Law, and apparently also alleged that the loan was racially discriminatory. The form of discrimination alleged was "reverse red-lining," under which a lender makes loans on more burdensome terms in minority areas. Apparently the court viewed this allegation as a potential violation of the Fair Housing Act. Initially the court placed the burden of proving discrimination on Foy, but in the present opinion it reverses that decision.

Thus, the court holds that a "higher priced loan" (one exceeding nine percent interest), if made to a minority borrower in a predominantly minority area, is presumed to have been discriminatory, placing the burden on the lender to show that it is not. If the lender is unable to rebut the presumption, the court says that it will impose equitable remedies, without saying exactly what they might be. It implies that it might deny the lender's right to pursue the foreclosure, or might refuse to grant a deficiency judgment.

Child Predators

In *Doe v. Miller*, 405 F. 3d 700 (8th Cir. 2005), the court represents that this is a case of first impression in U.S. courts.

In 2002, in an effort to protect children in Iowa from the risk that convicted sex offenders may reoffend in locations close to their residences, the Iowa General Assembly passed, and the Governor of Iowa signed, a bill that prohibits a person convicted of certain sex offenses involving minors from residing within 2,000 feet of a school or a registered child care facility. The district court declared the statute unconstitutional on several grounds and enjoined the Attorney General of Iowa and the county attorneys in Iowa from enforcing the prohibition.

On appeal, the Eighth Circuit Court of Appeals panel reversed. The court ruled unanimously that the residency restriction is not unconstitutional on its face.

The statute defines "sex offender" to include only persons found guilty of sexual crimes involving minors. The statute was promptly challenged in a class action brought by persons affected by the statute for themselves, other similarly situated, and other convicted sex offenders who might plan to move to Iowa. In reaching its decision that the statute was unconstitutional, the trial court reviewed maps and heard testimony from a county attorney, and found that the restricted areas in many cities encompass the majority of the available housing in the city, thus leaving only limited areas within city limits available for sex offenders to establish a residence. In smaller towns, a single school or child care facility can cause all of the incorporated areas of the town to be off limits to sex offenders. The court found that unincorporated areas, small towns with no school or child care facility, and rural areas remained unrestricted, but that available housing in these areas is "not necessarily readily available."

The appellate court, reversing the district court, stated, more or less, that the fact that a person could find few places to reside in Iowa didn't mean that a person could not travel there:

> The Iowa statute imposes no obstacle to a sex offender's entry into Iowa, and it does not erect an "actual barrier to interstate movement."... There is "free ingress and regress to and from" Iowa for sex offenders, and the statute thus does not "directly impair the exercise of the right to free interstate movement." Nor does the Iowa statute violate principles of equality by treating nonresidents who visit Iowa any differently than current residents, or by discriminating against citizens of other States who wish to establish residence in Iowa. We think that to recognize a fundamental right to interstate travel in a situation that does not involve any of these circumstances would extend the doctrine beyond the Supreme Court's pronouncements in this area. That the statute may deter some out-of-state residents from traveling to Iowa because the prospects for a convenient and affordable residence are less promising than elsewhere does not implicate a fundamental right recognized by the Court's right to travel jurisprudence."

> The Iowa residency restriction does not prevent a sex offender from entering or leaving any part of the State, including areas within 2,000 feet of a school or child care facility, and it does not erect any actual barrier to intrastate movement.... The John Does also urge that we recognize a fundamental right 'to live where you want.' This ambitious articulation of a proposed unenumerated right calls to mind the Supreme Court's caution that we should proceed with restraint in the area of substantive due process, because '[b]y extending constitutional protection to an asserted right or liberty interest, we, to a great extent, place the matter outside the arena of public debate and legislative action.'

Although the court acknowledged that there was some evidence that the statute would present a severe restriction on living accommodations for some individuals, the court concluded that the state's only burden was to show that this restriction was rationally consistent with the civil purpose of the enactment. The court cited evidence in the record that convicted sex offenders generally are not fully deterred by punishment and cannot be cured. Consequently, it was rationale for the state to protect its children by separating them as a class from places where children congregated.

Two dissenting judges concluded that the statute swept too broadly, and imposed a "banishment" result on persons who did not present the high level of threat to children that the statute was designed to address:

> There is no doubt a class of offenders that is at risk to reoffend and for whom such a restriction is reasonable. However, the restriction also applies to John Doe II, who pleaded guilty to third-degree sexual abuse for having consensual sex with a 15-year-old girl when he was 20 years old. The restriction applies to John Doe VII, who was convicted of statutory rape under Kansas law. His actions that gave rise to this conviction would not have been criminal in Iowa. The restriction applies also to John Doe XIV, who pleaded guilty to a serious misdemeanor charge in 1995 after he exposed himself at a party at which a 13- year-old girl was present. John Doe XIV was 19 at the time of his offense. The actions of these and other plaintiffs are serious, and, at least in most cases, illegal in this state. However, the severity of residency restriction, the fact that it is applied to all offenders identically, and the fact that it will be enforced for the rest of the offenders' lives, makes the residency restriction excessive.

Title Insurance

Closing Attorney's - Referral Fees

An exception has always existed in the Insurance Code for attorneys (usually in small counties) who examine titles or close transactions on behalf of a title company. They are commonly referred to as "approved attorneys" or "fee attorneys", and they would receive a portion of the premium for performing this function for the title companies, usually around forty percent of the premium. Today, some attorneys in larger metropolitan areas want to be a fee attorney so that they, too, can get a portion of the premium. The Texas Department of Insurance has recently published a commissioner's bulletin discussing these issues and classified these attorneys into two different categories. The first, described as "fee attorneys," includes attorneys who are licensed to act as escrow officers and close in the name of a title insurance company, or title agent pursuant to the Texas Insurance Code. The second, known variously by title practitioners as "outside closing attorneys," "approved attorneys" and "P-22 attorneys," includes attorneys who do not have a license to act as an escrow officer, and who close the transaction in the name of the law firm.

The first category of attorneys clearly comes under the Texas Department of Insurance rules and must comply with all the provisions of the Texas Insurance Code and related regulations promulgated by the Texas Department of Insurance; the second category, however, does not, as they are handling on behalf of the law firm rather than an insurance company. Not only do they not have to follow all the regulations, but they also can't perform a number of services which title insurance companies are allowed to perform because these attorneys are not regulated by the Department of Insurance. See commissioners Bulletin II B-0017-07.

Many consumers and real estate professionals do not understand the difference between these two categories. What is more discomforting is that these attorneys may be representing a party to the transaction as well as being the escrow officer, which creates a high potential for conflicts of interest.

This brings up another referral fee question, however. If a title company has escrow officers, why would they employ a closing attorney to close a transaction for them? Is it merely a referral fee to get the business? Referral fees are prohibited under the Insurance Code. The Texas Department of Insurance is currently looking into these issues with much greater scrutiny, as this practice has continued to expand into metropolitan areas of Texas.

In *Newington Limited v. Forrester,* 2008 WL 4908200 (N.D. Tex.), the plaintiff appointed an agent to negotiate and purchase restricted shares in a corporation, and made a $1,000,000 "good-faith" deposit in a trust account for the purchase. The trust account was controlled by defendant, an attorney who had provided legal services for the corporation for nearly ten years.

Plaintiff claims that its agent sent explicit written instructions for the defendant to hold the deposit until the negotiations were finalized, and that he only transferred the money based on the express understanding with defendant that the deposit would be held until a deal was reached. However, defendant transferred $200,000 of the deposit to a third-party creditor of the corporation's CEO.

The negotiations for purchase of the shares were ultimately unsuccessful, and defendant was only able to refund $800,000 of the deposit. Plaintiff made three further demands for payment of the balance owed, and ultimately sought recovery through various liability theories: conversion, unjust enrichment, breach of fiduciary duties, breach of trust, and money had and received.

Defendant moved to dismiss based on the premise that: (1) that the tort claims fail because plaintiff is limited to a breach of contract claim, (2) defendant and plaintiff do not have a fiduciary relationship, (3) breach of trust claim fails as a matter of law, (4) unjust enrichment is not a cause of action recognized by Texas law, and (5) money had and received claim fails because defendant didn't benefit from the $200,000.

The court found that there are circumstances where a plaintiff can sue in tort despite the existence of a contract. Defendant owed plaintiff the duties of an escrow agent under Texas law, where such duties are imposed on a holder of funds acting in an escrow type arrangement, despite the lack of a formal escrow agreement. An escrow agent owes fiduciary duties to the parties in a transaction, consisting of the duties of loyalty, full disclosure, and to exercise a high degree of care in conserving and distributing the funds only to those entitled to receive it. Acting outside of the instructions of the depositor is a breach of the escrow duties, regardless of whether a contract existed or not.

Do you see the conflict here?

Water Rights

The concept of water rights has undergone dramatic changes over the past few years. The Texas Commission on Environmental Quality (TCEQ), in one way or another, regulates every drop of water in the State. Ground water has become a third estate in land, being defined as "real property" by the 2011 legislature, V.T.C.A., Water Code, §36.002(a). Similar to oil and gas rights, water rights are now transferred from one landowner to another and may be a significant part of the negotiation of the purchase price of real property. The legislature even enacted laws to provide for value to be attributed to water rights in condemnation proceedings. Particularly in large acreage transactions, the water rights are negotiated as aggressively as oil and gas rights. There is a long involved history of Texas water rights. A few of these historical factors deserve to be discussed to put these rights in perspective. Recent legislation has made current applications of water rights so important that we will expand on those that are currently in effect. In general terms, water rights fall into two categories: ground water and surface water.

Surface Water Rights

There have been common-law theories of water rights, basically classified in three categories: **riparian rights** of land bordering a stream, **littoral rights** of land adjoining a large body of water, and a governmental-controlled use of water through **prior appropriation**. Texas falls basically into this third category, since Texas has specific statutory guidelines for the use, enjoyment, and appropriation of its water resources. The Texas Water Rights Adjudication Act provides the exclusive means by which water rights may be recognized. In re Adjudication of Water Rights of the Brazos III Segment of the Brazos River Basin, 746 S.W.2d 207 (Tex. 1988). These laws with respect to water rights are contained in the state Water Code, which basically gives all water rights to the state. It does not recognize any riparian rights in the owner of any land the title to which passed out of the State of Texas after July 1, 1895, V.T.C.A., Water Code, §11.001(b), although current owners who can trace their riparian rights to a date prior to that date may still claim them.

The Texas Supreme Court has held, however, that the vested right to that water is only a **usufructuary** use of what the state owns. A usufruct has been defined as the right to use, enjoy, and receive the profits of property that belongs to another. In re The Adjudication of the Water Rights of the Upper Guadalupe Segment of the Guadalupe River Basin, 642 S.W.2d 438 (Tex. 1983).

Ownership of Waterways. In establishing the ownership of waterways, the Texas Water Code specifies that the water of the ordinary flow, underflow, and tides of every flowing river, natural stream, and lake, and of every bay or arm of the Gulf of Mexico; and the storm water, flood water, and rainwater of every river, natural stream, canyon, ravine, depression, and watershed in the state are the property of the state. In addition, all water imported from any source outside the boundaries of the state for use in the state, and which is transported through the beds and banks of any applicable stream within the state or by utilizing any facilities owned or operated by the state, is also the property of the state, V.T.C.A., Water Code, §11.021. Texas holds the title to the waters in a navigable stream in trust for the public. In re Upper Guadalupe, supra.

The state may authorize the use of state water, which may be acquired by the process of appropriation from the Department of Water Resources in the manner and in the preference provided for by statute. Once the permit has been obtained from the Department of Water Resources, the right to use the state water under that permit is limited not only to the amount specifically appropriated, but also to the priority of purposes specified in the appropriation. One should always try to use this appropriation, since all water not used within the specified limits is not considered as having been appropriated and the owner may lose his right to that appropriation. Therefore, if one doesn't use his appropriation in the current year, it may be limited or prohibited in future years. This theory encourages the beneficial use of water as a conservation measure. The nonuse of appropriated water is equivalent to waste, since the water would then run unused into the sea.

Conflicting Claims. All persons having an appropriation by the state must file by March 1 of each and every year a written report to the Department of Water Resources on forms prescribed by the department or be subject to a statutory penalty. If the appropriation has been given to two conflicting claimants, the first in time is first in right, V.T.C.A., Water Code, §11.027. The only exception to the doctrine of appropriation is that any city or town can make further appropriations of the water for domestic or municipal use without paying for the water.

One can acquire an appropriation through a process similar to adverse possession, however. When a person uses water under the terms of a certified filing or permit for a period of three years, he acquires title to his appropriation against any other claimant of the water. Conversely, if any lawful appropriation or use of state water is willfully abandoned during a three-year period, the right to use the water is forfeited and the water is again subject to appropriation, V.T.C.A., Water Code, §11.029.

Ground Water

The majority of water in Texas is ground water, and is a real property interest. It includes percolating water, underground flow, artesian water and well water. Ground water is owned by the owner of the property with two exceptions: (1) the landowner only has the right to pump the water and (2) regulatory programs of underground water conservation districts that have the legislative right to regulate the use of ground water. The historical right to use the ground water by the landowner is designated as the **Rule of Capture**, which means that the owner of the land can pump unlimited quantities of water from under the land. It is also severable and can be reserved by the owner in a subsequent sale of the property, City of Del Rio v. Clayton Sam Colt Hamilton Trust,269 S.W.3d 613 (Tex. App.—San Antonio 2008, writ. den.). The ground water, however, is subject to state regulations. Cipriano v. Great Spring Waters of America, Inc., 1 S.W.3d 75 (Tex. 1999). The TCEQ has established a number of local water conservation districts to regulate the use of ground water. To date, they have mostly regulated the use of ground water pumping where it has caused land subsidence. However, the legislature has given the local conservation districts expanded powers to regulate any number of different ways. This area of water law will be constantly expanding because of our legislative power to regulate in the public interest. Barshop v. Medina County Underground Water Conservation District, 925 S.W.2d 618 (Tex. 1996).

Wind Farms

Texas has become the nation's leading source of wind power. Wind energy leases usually pay a royalty fee which is based on the percentage of the gross revenue generated from the sale of the electricity. Wind alone, however, does not seem to be susceptible to ownership, so its value must be based on the value after the investment has been made by harnessing that power.

Texas has always subscribed to the ownership theory which says that we own the fee simply interest up through the earth and the sky. Can these be separated similar to mineral rights and water rights? At least so far Texas has not had a case that has resolved the issue of severability of wind rights. One issue which has been litigated is the unsightliness of the turbines. Do they constitute a nuisance under Texas law because they diminish the scenic beauty of the surrounding land? At least one case has held that it is not a cause of action under Texas law, *Rankin vs. FPL Energy*, LLC, 266 S.W.3rd 506 (Tex. App.-Eastland 2008).

This is a brand new area of the law, and it is evolving very quickly. Can one own the wind? There are areas of Texas that are very conducive to sustained high wind. Most of these areas are remote, sparsely populated areas. The mechanics of getting the wind-generated power to populated areas is a challenging concept. Notwithstanding this difficulty, the question still remains: if a party purchases 3,000 acres to create a wind farm, can another person purchase the adjacent 3,000 acres and set up windmills in front of the existing wind farm? Could an adjacent owner build anything that would hinder the free flow of wind through that wind farm? These and many other questions are on the horizon for this new source of energy. There will be a lot of new law in this area over the next few years.

As the inquiry relates to federal, state, tribal, and local government records, the review includes searching for records in databases pertaining to nearby and adjoining properties as well as records concerning the subject property. There is no distance from the boundary that is specified by the rules, and may be modified and the judgment of the environmental professional to accounts for such factors as development and geological conditions. For commercial real estate brokers, this is a significant change. In many cases, there were pending sales that had to have second environmental inquiries because the contract wasn't closed by November 1, 2006, therefore a new inquiry had to be maintained after November 1, 2006, to comply with the new rules.

There's an interesting question: What if the adjoining land owners won't allow inquiries? In these situations, the environmental professional may inspect the property by other means, including aerial imagery.

It reminds me of the environmental professional who was pulled from the tree. He suffered severe damage because wood particles were wedged into his body as a result of the extrication. He went to the hospital for treatment, and the surgeon responded that he couldn't remove natural forestry products from sensitive locations without EPA approval, and therefore couldn't help.

Mortgage Fraud

There is hardly a more pervasive problem in lending today than of mortgage fraud. It almost always involves a conspiracy between a loan originator and an appraiser. Additional conspirators can include a buyer's broker (it can also be the mortgage broker), a title company, and the seller's real estate agent. An additional conspirator could be the purchaser of the loan in the secondary market who is encouraging loan originators to make loans as fast as possible so they can be sold to investors in the secondary market. Many of these loans are sold with very little due diligence as to the quality of the borrower or credit scores. Let's talk about the potential fact situations.

The Fact Situations

While not illegal on their face, "flip" closings have been blamed for a number of mortgage fraud transactions in which the title company was allegedly complicit, resulting in fines in the millions of dollars against various underwriters throughout the United States levied both by the Department of Housing and Urban Development and by the States' Department of Insurance. One cannot be too careful to note the "red flags," which can turn a seemingly simple transaction into active mortgage fraud against a lender:

The "Flip"

In a "flip" transaction, it is usually the use of a straw man established in the middle of the transaction. For instance, in an A to B to C transaction, B would be a mere nominee (phony company) who is buying at a low price from a legitimate seller, but selling it at a much higher price to a buyer, either legitimate or another straw man. The fraud involved is a phony appraisal that reflects property value much higher than its real sales price, and a loan application to a lender loaning far more than what the property is worth. The problem is that the sale from B to C has to close before the sale from A to B so that funds are available to pay A. For instance, if it is a $400,000 initial sales price, and a $600,000 conveyance from B to C, the lender has to fund on the $600,000 in order to get to $400,000 to pay A. The straw man (B) nets the $200,000. Under most computer programs the transaction is caught because you can't close the second transaction until the first transaction is closed (B is not in title yet). In an effort to appease the greed, however, the escrow officer may override the program or use no program at all (filling out the closing documents by hand). In this case, it's difficult to defend if a lender discovers the fraud. The escrow officer has to step out of standard office procedure in order to complete the transactions. If the A to B transaction closes at one title company, and the B to C transaction closes at another, it may be easier to juggle the timing, but the "conspiracy" net grows!

The Old Switch

In this mortgage fraud, the buyer and seller agree to change the sales price in the contract and the seller kicks money back to the buyer at the closing. In this scenario, the house is sold for $400,000 and appraised for $600,000; the buyer then returns to the seller and asks that they increase the sales price to $600,000 so he can get the higher loan and pocket the difference. The seller then has to agree to kick back the excess proceeds to the buyer either in cash or through a "soft second lien," which will never be repaid. Once again, we have a lender making a loan for more than the property is worth, putting money in the buyer's pocket and destroying the loan-to-value ratio that the lender had anticipated. The problem with this scenario is that the seller is happy to do it and the real estate broker too is happy to do it, because the seller ultimately gets his agreed sales price and doesn't care that the buyer profits in the transaction. In addition to this, the seller and the broker make their sale! The buyer never makes one mortgage payment and moves on to his next transaction.

The Contractor's Scheme

In this scenario, the buyer is supposedly going to do a substantial amount of improvements to the property; he gets a bid from a contractor (a straw company) and then pays that contractor at closing… who turns out to be the buyer. Using the same example, it's a $400,000 purchase, a $200,000 home improvement and the loan is based on the inflated $600,000. There is no construction loan! The deal is closed and funded, the contractor turns out to be a front for the buyer, and no improvements are ever made. Again, the buyer never makes one mortgage payment, puts the money in his pocket, and moves on to the next transaction.

The Ultimate Lie

In this scenario, there is a borrower who simply lies to the lender. At the closing, the lender provides his loan application that may include income tax returns, W-2s, paycheck stubs, and a number of other back-up documents for the borrower's application. The problem is when the loan application information (submitted by the borrower earlier in the loan application process) turns out to be completely false, and if the title company doesn't properly check picture identifications, or confirm signatures of the applicant and their spouse. It could be aiding and abetting the fraudulent loan application process.

The Innocent "Investor"

A smart mortgage broker encourages uninformed, first-time investors to invest in a home. He will set up the mortgage plan; he will get them a good price (often buying homes in bulk from a builder with a low sales volume) and help the new investor "get rich quick" by investing in real estate. Many of these investors are foreign and easily duped by a glib-tongued mortgage broker who is licensed by the state and can apparently be trusted. The broker even pays buyer $1,000.00, then sets up a "flip" transaction where the broker takes the money out of the middle, and sets up a loan for the new investor who can't really afford to make the monthly payments. He often promises to lease the property and manage it for the investor in order to make it an easy closing. After closing, when no tenants are obtained, the buyer determines that the loan broker made a significant amount of money on the transaction, and the investor can't afford to make the monthly payments when no tenant can be found. The investor has been duped, but is personally liable for a significant mortgage loan.

"Trust Me"

In this scam, elderly or uninformed homeowners may be facing a foreclosure and, once again, are desperate for relief. In this fraud, the investor requests that the homeowner place the land in a trust with the investor (or investor's lackey) as a trustee, which gives them complete control over the ownership of the property. The owner may maintain a "beneficial" interest, or they may assign their beneficial interest to another investor in the trust. In almost every case, an investor third then takes complete control of the property, and the homeowner is not really aware of the impact of signing these odd-looking documents. In the homeowner's mind, it has not triggered the "due on transfer" clause of their mortgage, and they trust the smooth-talking investor. After the homeowner can no longer pay the investor, keep up their lease payments, or whatever their relationship happens to be, the investor simply informs the homeowner that they no longer own the property and he is free to resell it at a profit, although he is happy to inform them that he has "saved their credit."

Believe it or not, there are seminars that teach people how to do this scam. Similar to the "Flip" scam, the entire transaction may be technically legal, with paperwork in apple pie order, but the homeowner is duped with a wink and a nod.

Identity Theft

Another scheme has recently surfaced wherein the fraud perpetrator will search the real property records and find the name of somebody who is deceased, the name of a corporation or LLC, and they will assume the identity of the individual, the manager in charge of the LLC, or an officer of the corporation. During most closings, a simple check of identify is all that is required. It's amazing how far a fake driver's license can get you, particularly when closings are handled by mail or the perpetrator (always in a hurry) signs documents and leaves in a very short period of time. In one recent case, the perpetrator listed property, had their Realtor put a sign on it, sold it at a bargain sale price, and had a very quick closing. As it turned out, the real owner had no idea that the property was on the market, and certainly did not know that it was sold. When construction began, the real owner got upset and discovered that the perpetrator had assumed their identity, sold the property, took all of the money and was now nowhere to be found. Title companies and escrow agents can be duped, just like anybody else.

Fake Check/Fast Closing

Another new fraud issue which is becoming more common is the buyer who is usually out of state and often out of the country. They have immediate cash and want to close as fast as possible. He will frequently call an attorney or real estate broker indicating that because of his absence and frequent business travels, must close quickly. He forwards a cashier's check from an out-of-state bank to aid in the quick closing process. The buyer's representative (attorney or broker) proudly tenders the check to the title company as "certified funds" or a "cashier's check" to prove availability of funds to confirm the closing. The title company deposits the funds, closes the next day and funds the sales price to the seller who promptly disappears with his cash.

The next day or so, the title company is informed that the cashier's check, in fact, was a fake. There are no funds available and the title company has to cover the losses. This is a new "red flag." All cashier's checks, certified checks, and teller's checks, should be tendered to the drawee bank and the funds in the title company's account confirmed before completing the closing.

Who's Liable?

The fraud is typically uncovered when the buyer refuses to make any payments (or doesn't make one payment!) and the lender pursues foreclosure. If the lender is an investor, he may look to the loan originator as the fraudulent party for selling him a loan that the loan originator knew was a bad (or maybe non-existent) applicant. There is usually a pattern to these fraudulent transactions, and they can almost always be tied to a loan originator working in concert with an appraiser. The appraiser, however, only gives an opinion of value and therefore it is hard to find liability with the appraiser, provided his opinion can be justified.

The real estate brokers may have some potential liability, particularly if the buyer's representative is also the loan broker. This tends to lead to conflicts of interest wherein a real estate broker loses as a sale (and his share of the commission) if the buyer does not qualify for the loan. In situations where there is excess money being funded back to the buyer at the closing, there is a concern that both buyer's broker and the seller's broker may have some liability if they "turn a blind eye" to an obvious fraud being committed on the lender because of over-inflated appraisals, suggested contract prices, or false debtor information. By the way, these issues are being criminally prosecuted as well as civilly prosecuted in the courts today.

The title company seems to be in the middle of everything! While the title company tends to be a disinterested third party, they are present when the closing takes place, and when the instructions from the lender are tendered and the parties sign the documents. Remember though that as a disinterested third party they cannot take sides in representing one party against another and courts have held that the traditionally fiduciary escrow duties are somewhat limited to the instructions of the parties because the title company necessarily serves two conflicting parties. One bad case has arisen, however, *Home Loan Corporation v. Texas American Title Company*, 191 S.W.3d 728 (Tex. App. -Houston [14th Dist.], writ applied for) wherein the Court held that the title company was a fiduciary to all parties of the transaction and had a 100 percent duty of disclosure to all parties of the transaction. While this case seems to be very troublesome, and is currently on appeal to the Supreme Court, it may have a significant on how title companies handle escrows in the future.

Note the following list of "Red Flags":

- Investors making offers of significantly above asking price, particularly on property that has been on the market for a long time.

- Investor/buyer/mortgage officers telling buyers that they can acquire appraisals in excess of the sales price.

- Investors claiming property as their primary principal residence, which is to be owner occupied.

- Investors and/or sellers receiving excess sales proceeds after acquiring the property.

- Use of for-sale-by-owner transactions to circumvent the use of real estate professionals.

- Use of inexperienced or unsupervised licensees.

- Undisclosed concessions at the closing table.

- Not knowing the source or actual amount of the buyer's down payment, inflated appraisals, false information about the borrower's credit, and undisclosed rebates to an unknown third party.

- Secret second mortgages, earnest money deposits paid outside of closing.

- Double contracting, closing the sale on one tract while closing the loan on the second, higher priced contract.

When any of the foregoing become apparent, the advice is easy: get out of the transaction. If you are an escrow officer, don't close the transaction. While one may forego a commission or a title insurance premium, it is a lot cheaper than what may be a cost of defense at a later date.

Closings can be complicated. Buyers, sellers, and even real estate agents often misunderstand how many issues are handled at closing. Good escrow officers require a lot of communication skills, accounting skills, and ability to stay cool in a frequently difficult environment where buyers and sellers don't know each other. The lender or agent may be forcing some issues. Then there are the title problems! It is not a business for sissies.

RESPA

New RESPA rules were adopted on November 17, 2008, by the Department of Housing and Urban Development. Effective January 16, 2009, all third parties' charges paid by title agents must be separately itemized and cannot exceed the amount actually paid to the service provider. The new rule does permit any provider to use an average charge calculation to collect the amount due for a service billed by a third-party provider that is paid for by the borrower or the seller provided this "average charge calculation" meets the criteria of the new rule (it's easier just to pass their actual cost if you know them). Another amendment to the rules affects affiliated businesses. The rule still prohibits participants in affiliated business to require the use of an affiliated business. However, under the new rule, a settlement service provider may offer combined services at a price lower than the sum of individuals' service without triggering "required use" concerns if: (1) the use is optional to the consumer; and (2) the lower price is not made up of higher costs elsewhere in the transaction. This allows a settlement service provider to provide economic incentives. The rule does not apply to homebuilders, as they are not settlement service providers.

Another amendment provides for a new good faith estimate of closing costs and provides for "tolerances" for variations of those costs. Origination fees, lender costs, and transfer of taxes are subject to zero tolerance and may not increase. Settlement services recommended by the lender are subject to a 10-percent tolerance between the Good Faith Estimate (GFE) and the closing. Individual services that are provided as a part of the settlement may exceed the tolerance as long as the total of the tolerances does not exceed 10 percent. If the loan originator violates the GFE requirements the new rules provide an opportunity to cure any violation of the tolerance if the lender reimburses the borrower of the amount by which the tolerance is exceeded.

Effective January 1, 2010, lenders and mortgage brokers are required to use a new GFE to a potential borrower within three days after loan application. The new GFE must state dates and terms of the loan and charges for the loan. The quoted terms and prices in the GFE must be available for at least ten business days after the GFE is issued. The cost quoted in the GFE is subject to "tolerances" lender charges for taking, underwriting, and processing the application. The points for origination fees and the real property transfer tax must be exact and fall under the category of "zero tolerance." When the lender requires the settlement service provider or provides settlement services from a list of providers for title services and title insurance the tolerances are allowed to increase as much as 10 percent over the original GFE. If the borrower chooses providers (including title insurance) the escrow amounts, per diem interest and homeowner's insurance, there is unlimited tolerance, as the provider has no control over the costs.

The new rule also publishes two new HUD-1 and HUD-1A forms. The first page is unchanged but the second page added information to make the forms more closely follow the information set out in the GFE.

For the first time, the HUD-1A discloses the agent's portion of the title premium along with the underwriter's portion of the title premium. This is not disclosed in the GFE, but HUD felt that it was important to disclose it on the final settlement statement so that the consumer could better understand their title charges.

Right to Cure

The rules give the loan originator the opportunity to cure any violation by reimbursing the borrower in any amount in which the tolerance has over exceeded. This reimbursement may be made at settlement or within 30 calendar days after settlement.

Texas Deceptive Trade Practices Act: One New Change!

At one time, virtually every lawsuit brought against a real estate broker in Texas included some cause of action under the Texas Deceptive Trade Practices Act. Tort reform has helped to change this a little.

Any consumer can maintain a deceptive trade practices action for one of the following violations designated in Section 17.50 if it is a **producing cause** of damages:

- the use or employment by any person of a false, misleading, or deceptive act or practice that is specifically enumerated in the subdivision of Subsection (b) of Section 17.46 of this subchapter (certain of these specific provisions will be discussed later).

- breach of an express or implied warranty.

- any unconscionable action or course of action by any person.

- the use or employment by any person of an act or practice in violation of Article 21.21, Texas Insurance Code, as amended.

A producing cause requires proof of: (1) actual causation and fact, (2) the fact that but for the defendant's conduct the plaintiff's injury would not have occurred, and (3) the act or omission being a substantial factor in bringing about injury, and thus, liability should be imposed. The plaintiff only has to show producing cause and does not have to show that the harm was foreseeable. Section 17.50 was amended in 1995 to provide for "**economic**" damages rather than "actual" damages, or damages for mental anguish. The amount of economic damages is found by the trier of fact (jury, or judge, if there is no jury). If the trier of fact finds that the conduct of the defendant was committed "**knowingly**," the consumer may also recover damages for mental anguish, as found by the trier of fact, and the trier of fact may award not more than three times the amount of economic damages; or if the trier of fact finds the conduct was committed **"intentionally,"** the consumer may recover damages for mental anguish, as found by the trier of fact, and the trier of fact may award not more than three times the amount of damages for mental anguish and economic damages.

"Intentionally" is actual awareness, or flagrant disregard of prudent and fair business practices.

"Economic damages" means compensatory damages for pecuniary loss, including costs of repair and replacement. The term does not include exemplary damages or damages for physical pain and mental anguish, loss of consortium, disfigurement, physical impairment, or loss of companionship and society.

"Knowingly" means actual awareness of a falsity, deception, or unfairness of an act or practice giving rise to the consumer's claim or, in an action brought under a breach of an express or implied warranty as provided in Section 17.50, actual awareness of the act or practice constituting the breach of warranty, but actual awareness may be inferred where objective manifestations indicate the person acted with actual awareness.

These new amendments are part of our new tort reform, limiting the overwhelming damages that were in the old statute.

Definitions

As you may recall, there are certain key definitions that apply to real estate brokers under the Texas Deceptive Trade Practices Act:

- "Goods" are defined as tangible chattels or **real property** purchased for lease or use Section 17.45[1]).

- "Services" means work, labor, or services purchased or leased for purchase, including services furnished in connection with the sale or repair of goods (Section 17.45[2]).

- "Consumer" means an individual, partnership, corporation, or governmental entity that seeks or acquires by purchase or lease any goods or services (Section 17.45[4]).

- "Unconscionable action or course of action" means an act or practice that, to a consumer's detriment, takes advantage of the lack of knowledge, ability, experience, or capacity of a person to a grossly unfair degree.

Other Important Provisions

Section 17.42 Waivers

The 1995 Legislature made major changes in the DTPA as it pertained to waivers. A waiver is now valid and enforceable if: (1) the waiver is in writing and is signed by the consumer; (2) the consumer is not in a significantly disparate bargaining position; and (3) the consumer is represented by legal counsel in seeking or requiring the goods and services. Section 17.42(a)(1).

The waiver is not effective if the consumer's legal counsel is directly or indirectly identified, suggested, or selected by a defendant or an agent of the defendant.

To be effective, the waiver must be: (1) conspicuous and in boldface of at least ten points in size; and (2) identified by the heading "Waiver of Consumer Rights," or words of similar meaning and in substantially the following form:

> Waiver of Consumer Rights
>
> "I waive my rights under the Deceptive Trade Practices-Consumer Protection Act, Section 17.41 et seq., Business & Commerce Code, a law that gives consumers special rights and protections. After consultation with an attorney of my selection, I voluntarily consent to this waiver."

Unlike the old statute, it does not require the signature of the consumer's attorney. Section 17.44

This subchapter states that the DTPA shall be liberally construed and applied to promote its underlying purposes, which are to protect consumers against false, misleading, and deceptive business practices, unconscionable action, and breaches of warranty and to provide effective and economical procedures to secure such protection.

Section 17.49 Prohibited Claims (This is new!)

Section 17.49 prohibits a claim for damages based on the rendering of a professional service, the essence of which is the providing of advice, judgment, opinion, or similar professional skill. **This exemption now specifically applies to real estate brokers.** The exemption does not apply, however, to: (1) an express misrepresentation of the material fact; (2) an unconscionable action or course of action, the failure to disclose information and violation of §17.46(b)(24); or (3) a breach of an express warranty that cannot be characterized as advice, judgment, or opinion. See §17.49(c).

The statute prohibits a claim for damages, under Section 17.49(f) of the DTPA, for a claim arising out of a written contract, if the contract relates to a transaction involving total consideration by the consumer of more than $100,000 if the consumer is represented by legal counsel and the contract does not involve the consumer's residence. Similarly, the act also exempts claims arising from a transaction, a project, or a set of transactions relating to the same project, involving total consideration by the consumer of more than $500,000, other than a cause of action involving a consumer's residence, even if the consumer is not represented by a legal counsel.

"The Laundry List"

We previously discussed the application of Section 17.46(b) as a violation of the DTPA. There are twenty-six specific violations enumerated in 17.46. Many of these are specifically applicable to the real estate brokerage business and will be emphasized here.

- Representing that goods are original or new if they are deteriorated, reconditioned, reclaimed, used, or secondhand. Sec. 17.46(b)(5).

- Representing that goods or services are of a particular standard, quality, or grade, or that goods are of a particular style or model, if they are of another. Sec. 17.46(b)(7).

- Disparaging the goods, services, or business of another by false or misleading representations of facts. Sec. 17.46(b)(8).

- Making false or misleading statements of fact concerning the reason for, existence of, or amount of price reductions. Sec. 17.46(b)(11).

- Representing that an agreement confers or involves rights, remedies, or obligations that it does not have or involve or that are prohibited by law. Sec. 17.46(b)(12).

- Knowingly making false or misleading statements of fact concerning the need for parts, replacement, or repair service. Sec. 17.46(b)(13).

- Misrepresenting the authority of the salesperson, representative, or agent to negotiate the final term of a consumer transaction. Sec. 17.46(b)(14).

- Representing that work or services have been performed on or parts replaced in goods when the work or services were not performed or the parts not replaced. Sec. 17.46(b)(21).

- The failure to disclose information concerning goods or services that was known at the time of the transaction, if such failure to disclose such information was intended to induce the consumer into a transaction into which the consumer would not have entered had the information been disclosed. Sec. 17.46(b)(24).

This last "laundry list" item is tough. Unlike affirmative misrepresentations, where the law imposes a duty on the seller to know whether an affirmative statement is true, this duty does not arise when the seller fails to reveal information about which he does not know. To prove a DTPA action for failure to disclose information concerning goods or services, plaintiffs must show that the information: (1) was known at the time of the transaction, (2) was intended to induce the plaintiffs into a transaction, and (3) had it been disclosed, would have caused the plaintiffs not to enter into the transaction. There is no duty of disclosure under the DTPA if a defendant fails to disclose material facts and merely should have known. *Kessler v. Fanning* (953 S.W.2d 515, 521, Tex. App.-Fort Worth, 1997).

Although the court cannot suspend a broker's license under the DTPA, there are a number of pertinent corresponding provisions of the Real Estate License Act that provide that a licensee can have his or her license revoked or suspended for:

■ making a material misrepresentation, or failing to disclose to a potential purchaser any latent structural defect or any other defect known to the broker or salesperson. A latent structural defect and other defects do not refer to trivial or insignificant defects but refer to those defects that would be a significant factor to a reasonable and prudent purchaser in making a decision to purchase, Section 15(a)(6)(A).

■ soliciting, selling, or offering for sale real property under a scheme or program that constitutes a lottery or deceptive practice, Section 15(a)(6)(I).

■ pursuing a continued and flagrant course of misrepresentation or making a false promise through agents, salesperson, advertising, or otherwise, Section 15(a)(6)(C).

■ failing to make clear, to all parties to a transaction, which party he is acting for, or receiving compensation from more than one party except with full knowledge and consent of all parties, Section 15(a)(6)(D).

■ inducing or attempting to induce a party to a contract of sale or lease to break the contract for the purpose of substituting in lieu thereof a new contract, Section 15(a)(6)(M).

■ guaranteeing, authorizing, or permitting a person to guarantee that future profits will result from a resale of real property, Section 15(a)(6)(K).

■ acting in the dual capacity of broker and undisclosed principal in a transaction, Section 15(a)(6)(J).

■ accepting, receiving, or charging an undisclosed commission, rebate, or direct profit on expenditures made for a principal, Section 15(a)(6)(H).

Unconscionable Action or Course of Action

This portion of the statute has been interpreted as meaning "taking advantage of the consumer's lack of knowledge to a grossly unfair degree," which seems to be tailor-made for suing brokers because of their superior knowledge of the marketplace, and would be particularly applicable to brokers when they are acting in their capacities as principal when dealing with a consumer who is held to a much lower duty of care. Note *Chastain v. Koonce* and *Wyatt v. Petrila*, discussed later in this chapter.

Brokerage Cases Interpreting the DTPA

Under the Deceptive Trade Practices Act, the consumer has been held to have a duty of care of being ignorant, unthinking, and credulous, *Spradling v. Williams*, 566 S.W. 561 (Tex., 1978). Brokers have been held to provide services of an expert who has been tested and found to be such, *Holloman v. Denson*, 640 S.W.2d 417 (Tex. Civ. App.-Waco, 1982). The result is sometimes referred to as "disparity in bargaining position," and a real estate licensee should not take advantage of those who are less qualified. This poses an interesting question: Can a real estate licensee be held liable for selling a house for too high a price? What if it is his or her own house? (Particularly if there is a failure to disclose information.) Some discussion was given to this in the case of *Wyatt v. Petrila*, 752 S.W.2d 683 (Tex. App. -Corpus Christi, 1988), wherein there is a lengthy discussion involving gross disparity between value received and consideration paid as an unconscionable action under the DTPA. In that case, a disparity of $50,000 in a house costing $625,000 was not considered to be "gross," as a matter of law.

There has never been much concern over whether or not the seller could sue the broker for misrepresentation of services either for sale or management of the property, Lerma v. Brecheisen, 602 S.W.2d 318 (Tex. Civ. App.-Waco, 1980). *Henry S. Miller Management Corp. v. Houston State Associates*, 792 S.W.2d 128 (Tex. App.-Houston [1st Dist.], 1990).

In *Cameron v. Terrell & Garrett, Inc.*, 618 S.W.2d 535 (Tex., 1981), the Texas Supreme Court held that the purchaser could sue the broker for misrepresentation in calculating the square footage of a house.

New case concerning square footage!

Although not a deceptive trade practices case, *Trenholm v. Ratcliff*, 646 S.W.2d 927 (Tex., 1983) wiped out any defense of a broker maintaining "mere opinion" as a defense. This may be particularly true when one of the parties has superior knowledge to the other or superior access to information. Representations as to matters not equally open to parties are legally statements of fact and not opinions. *Robertson v. United New Mexico Bank at Roswell*, 14 F.3d 1076 (5th Cir., 1994).

In *Pleasant v. Bradford*, 2008 Westlaw 2544814 (Tex. App. 6/26/08), a listing broker listed a house for sale and prepared an MLS sheet that disclosed the square footage of the house as approximately 1850 sq. ft. She obtained this information from the local county assessor. It was the custom to put square footage information in MLS listings, although not required. It was also the custom to reveal in the listing the source of the information, e.g., "per Bell County Assessor's Office." But in this case, allegedly because of a scrivener's error by an employee of the broker's office, this qualification did not appear next to the square footage information on this particular MLS sheet. The computerized MLS listing automatically computed a "per square footage" price that was part of the information on the sheet.

The buyers looked at the house with a selling broker, and in one way or another got the selling broker's MLS listing sheet, which was also not an unusual event. The buyers maintained at trial that they were attracted to the house because, although it needed repair, its price was substantially lower per square foot than that of other houses in the neighborhood.

Because the sellers were anxious to close the deal and because buyers could not get a loan until they received confirmation of the husband's residency contract at a local hospital, the parties executed a contract that permitted the buyers to occupy the home on a rental basis before closing, during which time they did substantial repairs and renovation. When they did get the confirmation and applied for a loan, however, the bank appraisal indicated (accurately, unfortunately) that the house was in fact 1571 square feet. Buyers closed on the house and sued broker for the difference between the value of the house at its true size and the value of the house at the size represented. A jury found for the buyers and awarded them the difference of about $2,500. Plus, the buyers got attorney's fees. The broker appealed.

The court of appeals affirmed. The broker first argued on appeal that buyers had not relied on the broker's representation because there was evidence that buyers had indeed checked the assessment department's Web site on their own and saw the (erroneous) square footage report. The court conceded that indeed there was Texas authority that said that there must be evidence of reliance and that if a party, after receiving a misrepresentation, independently checks out the facts, there may be no factual link between the representation and the actual reliance. In this case, however, there was evidence that the buyers, encouraged by their broker, had gone to the Web site not to check the square footage but to look for any evidence of defects in the property so that they could understand why the per square foot price was so much less than other houses. They incidentally saw the square footage information, but the purpose of their checking the Web site was not to verify that information. Consequently, the jury could have found that they were still relying, at least in part, on the selling broker's representation.

The broker next pointed out that the buyers had signed a document provided by the selling broker, which contained the following statement:

> "The Buyer is advised to verify all information important to him/her and to ask the appropriate questions of the appropriate authorities himself/herself or through an attorney with respect to important issues such as … size of structure … Any statements with respect to problems or with respect to the availability or existence of any of these items which were made by the REALTOR® and his/her associates were made based on information given to the REALTOR® by the Seller/Owner and/or government agencies, and/or others, and there is no intention that the Buyer rely on the statements of the REALTOR® and his/her associates, and the Buyer is urged to confirm any such statements on his/her own.
>
> Having read the foregoing disclaimer, I/we, the prospective Buyer(s), by my/our signature(s) below, state that I/we have not relied upon any statement given to me/us by the REALTOR® and/or his/her associates with regard to the property, and my/our decision to make an offer on the property and to subsequently purchase the property is based on my/our independent decision with or without legal counsel."

The court ruled that it was a jury issue whether this constituted a statement that the buyers were not relying upon the "listing broker's" representations, as opposed to only the representations made by their selling broker. The court noted that the statement quoted above did not constitute a waiver of a right to make a claim or bring a lawsuit and at best could only be construed as an assertion of nonreliance. To this extent, the question was properly presented before the jury. The jury, of course, had found for the buyers on the point.

Ridco v. Sexton, 623 S.W.2d 792 (Tex. Civ. App.-Ft. Worth, 1981) wipes out any defense of mere puffing as a defense or cause of action under the act. There was a recent Texas case, however, that indicated that "mere puffing" was not a representation and therefore not actionable, *Autohaus, Inc., v. Aguilar*, 794 S.W.2d 459 (Tex. App.-Dallas, 1990). In that case, it was determined that "good" was only a general term of approval and the term "probably" is "relatively likely but not certain" and statements that are too general cannot be actionable. It should be noted that the Texas Supreme Court refused to hear the case but specifically did not approve or disapprove of the lower court's opinion. *Aguilar v. Autohaus, Inc.*, 800 S.W.2d 853 (Tex., 1991). Puffing is still a dangerous practice.

Kelley v. Texas Real Estate Commission, 671 S.W.2d 936 (Tex. Civ. App.-Houston, 1984) held a broker liable even though the misrepresentations were innocent and unknowing; a plaintiff is not required to prove a licensee's knowledge of the falsity of the misrepresentation. *Henry S. Miller v. Bynum*, 797 S.W.2d 51 (Tex. App.-Houston [1st Dist.], 1990). The new DTPA amendments may have made a big difference in these cases.

Ramsey v. Gordon, 567 S.W.2d 868 (Tex. Civ. App.-Waco, 1978) wipes out any defense of an agent claiming he is a principal in a transaction. *Weitzel v. Barnes*, 691 S.W.2d 598 (Tex., 1985) wipes out the defense of using "as is" in an earnest money contract, but the holding has been somewhat limited after the *Prudential case*, discussed later. See also *Wyatt v. Petrila*, discussed earlier.

Canada v. Kearns, 624 S.W.2d 755 (Tex. Civ. App.-Beaumont, 1981) held the broker liable for the misconduct of his or her agent even though the broker received no fee. If the sponsoring broker is not sued, though, there's a different result. In *Miller v. Keyser*, 90 S.W.3d 712 (Tex., 2002), the court was determining whether an agent or a disclosed principal could be held liable for passing along false representation. The court held that, because the DTPA allows a consumer to bring suit against "any person," the agent can be held personally liable for the misrepresentation he or she makes when acting within the scope of employment.

The case revolves around the sale of lots in Pearland, Texas, which backed up to Brazoria County's Drainage District, located on the back 20 feet of each lot. Each buyer knew that the drainage easement was on the lot, but the agent (salesperson) represented to the homeowners that the lots were oversized and that they were, in fact, larger than the lots of a competing builder in the subdivision. The homeowners paid a premium for these "oversized" lots. After their homes were built, the buyers received a letter from the Brazoria County Drainage District, telling them that all fences in the easement must be removed at the owner's expense. As a result, the homeowners sued. Through a series of procedural maneuvers, the only defendant left was the salesperson, Barry Keyser, who argued that a corporate agent couldn't be held personally liable for company misrepresentations (apparently assuming under Texas law that everything he did was on behalf of the corporation that held his license).

The court disagreed, noting that Keyser personally made the representations about the size of the lot and the location of the fence. He was the only person with whom the homeowners had any contact. Based on the plain language of the statute, Keyser was liable for his own DTPA violations.

Keyser then claimed that his misrepresentations were innocent (apparently relying on information given to him by the sponsoring broker). The court noted, however, that the DTPA does not require the consumer to prove that the employee acted knowingly or intentionally in order to create liability. Keyser was liable even if he did not know his representations were false or even if he did not intend to deceive anyone. The court held that the homeowners did have a right to seek indemnification from the employer and, therefore, could have sued the employer, brought into the case as part of their defense.

ECC Parkway Joint Venture v. Baldwin, 765 S.W.2d 504 (Tex. App.-Dallas, 1989) held that a broker's failure to disclose a height restriction on property supported a purchaser's cause of action against the broker for fraud, negligent misrepresentation, and breach of fiduciary duty as well as a violation of the Texas Deceptive Trade Practices Act. The course of action was upheld notwithstanding the deed restrictions being of record in the county courthouse and the purchaser accepting the deed subject to all restrictions of record in the county. The **failure to disclose** is a very difficult defense for brokers, as it often involves what the broker "should have known" but didn't disclose, as well as the actual failure to disclose. To prevail at trial, the plaintiffs must prove: (i) a failure to disclose information concerning goods or services; (ii) which was known at the time of the transaction; (iii) which was intended to induce them into the transaction; and (iv) that they would not have entered into the transaction if the information had been disclosed. *O'Hern v. Hogard*, 841 S.W.2d 135 (Tex. App.-Houston [14th Dist.], 1992). The 1995 amendments to the Texas Real Estate License Act may give more relief in this area, however. Haney v. Purcell Company, Inc., 770 S.W.2d 566 (Tex., 1989), although not a brokerage case, held a seller of real estate liable for failing to disclose that there was an unrecorded cemetery in the purchaser's backyard.

The criteria for a violation of the act appears to be found in circumstances where the knowledge of the agent, in conjunction with the consumer's relative ignorance, operates to make the slightest divergence from mere praise (by the agent) into representations of fact (as understood by the consumer). *Chrysler Plymouth City, Inc., v. Guerrero*, 620 S.W.2d 700 (Tex. App.-San Antonio, 1981).

In Century 21 Page One Realty v. Naghad, 760 S.W.2d 305 (Tex. App.-Texarkana, 1988) a broker listed "no known defects" in the listing agreement, and there was no other communication with the purchaser prior to the sale. The court held that both parties (the seller and broker) benefitted and both were jointly and severally liable because both parties benefitted from the misrepresentation.

Nix v. Born, 870 S.W.2d 635 (Tex. App.-El Paso, 1994) held that where the broker did not tell the seller that he had an interest in the partnership/buyer, the broker's fiduciary duty had been breached and upheld a jury award for lost profits and exemplary damages.

In *Chastain v. Koonce*, 700 S.W.2d 579 (Tex., 1985) the Texas Supreme Courtalso addressed criteria for "unconscionable action" or course of action under 17.45(5). It requires "taking advantage of a consumer's lack of knowledge to a grossly unfair degree, thus, requires a showing of intent, knowledge, or a conscious indifference" at the time the misrepresentation was made.

Sanchez v. Guerrero, 885 S.W.2d 487 (Tex. App.-El Paso, 1994) is a frightening case! The Guerreros saw a vacant house in El Paso, which was listed by Century 21 Casablanca Realty. The Guerreros executed an earnest money contract with $500 for earnest money. The deal was ultimately closed, making the Guerreros the owners of their "dream house." The same evening, the Guerreros saw a television news program about a woman who had been tried and acquitted of child molestation charges, which allegedly occurred in the Guerreros' new home. The Guerreros sued the real estate brokers, alleging that they knew that the woman had lived there and withheld the information from the appellees in an attempt to induce appellees to complete the transaction, and that this is a violation of the Texas Deceptive Trade Practices Act. The jury found that Sanchez (the broker) knowingly engaged in false, misleading, or deceptive acts or practices and that they knowingly engaged in the unconscionable action or course of action and that such action is a producing cause of damages to the Guerreros. The court discussed an excellent explanation of failure to disclose information under the DTPA and the unconscionability provisions of the DTPA. It ultimately held that the real estate broker took advantage of the Guerreros' lack of knowledge of real estate to a grossly unfair degree and supported mental anguish damages as being recoverable because the conduct was committed knowingly.

The jury awarded the Guerreros the sum of $120,000, which consisted of $20,000 for the closing costs and $100,000 for their mental anguish.

There were two distinctly different facts presented to the court. The purchaser alleged that he requested information about the prior ownership of the home (the title was currently held by the Veterans Administration). The real estate broker denied that particular conversation ever took place. However, the appeals courts have a very difficult time reversing a finding of the jury because they are the final arbiter of the facts.

In *Lefmark Management Company v. Old*, 946 S.W.2d 52 (Tex., 1997), a widow of a customer killed during an armed robbery of a shopping center store sued the store, the shopping center owners and managers, and the former property manager of the shopping center. The Texas Supreme Court reiterated the general rule that a landowner must use reasonable care to make the premises safe for the use of business and invitees. However, on the date of the indicated, Lefmark, as a previous manager, did not own, occupy, manage, possess, or otherwise have any control of the shopping center. The court held that a management company does not have a duty to disclose a dangerous condition to a subsequent management company.

Okay. This is a California case, but it gives "stigma" a whole new meaning. In *Shapiro v. Sutherland* (1998 WL 333914 [Cal. App. 2 Dist.]), a purchaser of residential property from a relocation management service sued the relocation service and the former owners who had sold the property, alleging fraudulent misrepresentation and material nondisclosure.

The prior owner had occupied the property for 15 years and was transferred to the new location. The company's relocation policy allowed the relocation company to purchase the property for a preestablished price. The homeowners entered into the home purchase agreement with the relocation company, which had purchased the property for $349,000. The owners executed the deed, which was signed and notarized, but left a blank as to the name of the grantee. The documents were then transferred to the relocation company. The owners executed the state-mandated disclosure form that included the following question: "Are you aware of any... (11) neighbor noise problems or other nuisances?" The homeowners responded "no."

The record reflected that the owners' next-door neighbors were, over a period of years, a source of disturbing noises and commotion. The owners had called the police on a number of occasions. The relocation company did not know of these matters.

The court here held that there was a common law duty of disclosure "where a seller knows the facts materially affecting the value or desirability of the property...and also knows such facts are not known to or within the reach of the diligent attention and observation of the buyer, the seller is under a duty to disclose them to the buyer," citing the earlier California case of *Alexander v. McKnight*, 7 Cal. App. 4th 973, 977 (1992). The court held that California law provides specific seller disclosure requirements. It contains questions concerning neighborhood noise problems, and should have been disclosed truthfully. In essence, the owner was held liable for failing to disclose a noisy neighbor. Does this mean that a noisy neighbor can stigmatize the neighborhood? Hopefully, the precedent in this case will be limited to California!

NUISANCE; Diminished Property Value?

In *Smith v. Kansas Guest Service Co.*, et al, 169 P. 3d 1052, real property owners brought a class action against the operator of a gas storage facility, asserting claims of negligence and nuisance and seeking injunctive relief and damages for diminished property values that resulted from an escape of natural gas from the facility. There was an explosion in downtown Hutchinson, Kansas, in January of 2001, and it was determined that escaped gas migrated underground through a porous geological formation and rose to the surface in Hutchinson through abandoned brine wells that were not properly plugged. After the source of the problem was identified, the leak was remedied.

The issue presented to the Kansas Supreme Court was whether or not a property owner can collect damages under either a negligence or a nuisance theory for a diminution in the property's market value caused by the stigma or market fear resulting from an accidental contamination, where the property owner has not proved either a physical injury to the property or an interference with the owner's use and enjoyment of the property. In holding that the owner could not, the court acknowledged that even though stigma damages may be recoverable, remote, speculative and conjectural damages are not to be considered. Having determined that there was no physical injury to the properties in question, the court's second focus was whether or not the landowners showed interference in the use and enjoyment of the property, and held that they did not. The court noted other jurisdictions holding the same way: Virginia, Arkansas, California, Kentucky, Mississippi, North Carolina, Pennsylvania, Utah, and Wyoming.

This case apparently follows the more traditional logic of legal history. What damage have you suffered because you are "afraid" of something that has happened or might happen, without showing a physical injury or an interference with the use or enjoyment of the property? These damages are very difficult to prove.

In *Smith v. Herco, Inc.*, 900 S.W.2d 852 (Tex. App.-Corpus Christi, 1995, writ denied), Smith purchased a townhouse for $64,000. Herco told Smith he would be deeded the unit "wall to wall" and gave Smith a warranty deed. When he attempted to resell the townhouse, he learned that one corner of the townhouse, indicating a portion of the interior, extended into the common area of the development. Smith could not obtain a deed from all the other townhouse owners. Therefore, he stopped making mortgage payments, and the townhouse eventually foreclosed.

Smith sued the seller and surveyor under DTPA and for breach of contract and warranties. The trial court found that both defendants had affirmatively misrepresented that the plaintiff would receive title to the entire unit. Specifically, the court held that the deed and statements that Smith would own all of the unit were false. Regardless of the reason, when a good real estate does not have the characteristics it is represented to have, or does not perform as represented, the injury to the consumer is the same.

The Court of Appeals affirmed the trial court judgment for $87,600 in damages, $30,016 in attorney's fees, and $87,890 in prejudgment interest. The damages represented $32,000 for loss in value of the unit and $57,600 for damage to the plaintiff's credit rating.

In *McFarland v. Associated Brokers*, 977 S.W.2d 427 (Tex. App.-Corpus Christi, 1998), the purchaser brought suit against the defendant (listing broker) for violations of the DTPA, negligence, and fraud. The purchaser had requested the inspection of the home prior to closing, which was performed by a real estate inspection company. The inspector neither discovered nor reported any major roof damage. On the same date as the inspection, however, the purchaser discovered water in the light fixture in the closet in the master bedroom, indicating there was a roof leak. The purchaser requested that the roof be repaired at the seller's expense with the assurance that the repair work would be guaranteed for at least 1-year.

Repairs were made by a contractor who assured the purchaser that the roof was in good shape and extended a 1-year warranty on the repairs. The purchaser closed the sale, moved into the house, and discovered that the roof was still leaking. The purchaser then brought suit against the listing broker for damages, alleging the broker's knowing concealment, nondisclosure of known defects, and the nondisclosure of false representations made by the sellers.

The broker defended by saying that the broker was not the cause of the damage, alleging that:

■ a contract addendum eliminated their liability (it stated that the buyer had not relied upon any representations or statements made by the real estate agent).

■ the inspection was performed by the buyer.

■ the buyer discovered the leakage.

■ the buyer had an agreement and warranty with the roof; therefore, the broker could not have been the cause of the damage. The trial court entered judgment in favor of the broker and awarded the broker $19,200 for legal services, plus additional amounts for appeal.

The Court of Appeals reversed the trial court, holding that an independent inspection was not, in and of itself, enough to constitute a new and independent basis for the purchase of the dwelling. The court seemed to infer that if the buyer had subsequently agreed to take the property "as is," then the case may have gone the other way. The case was then remanded to the trial court for a full trial on the merits.

Rosas v. Hatz, 147 S.W.3d 560 (Tex. App.-Waco, 2004, no pet.). While a broker has no duty to inspect the property and disclose all facts that might affect its value or desirability, one who knows all the facts and provides false information, or one who makes a partial disclosure and conveys a false impression, may be liable for negligent misrepresentation. Fraud and DTPA claims also require a false representation.

The Rosas' claim that the broker, Hatz, told Mrs. Rosas that the house had been "partially rewired" and the plumbing "replaced or redone" and that this constitutes an affirmative mis-representation due to the wiring and plumbing problems discovered afterwards. Hatz's representation to Mrs. Rosas that the house had been rewired and the plumbing "redone" gives rise to a reasonable inference that any problems with the house had been fixed. This statement, in combination with the evidence that the seller's tenant told Hatz of a leak in the home, creates a fact issue as to whether Hatz's statements were affirmative representations of false information. Thus, there is more than a scintilla of evidence that Hatz made affirmative misrepresentations.

Brokers; Can You Represent Two Buyers?

In *Zuazua v. Tibbles*, 150 P.2d 361 (Mont. 2006), Stone, an agent of the Coldwell Banker agency, had on July 8 executed a form with Zuazua that identified Stone as a buyer's agent for Zuazua. Two days later, Zuazua authorized Stone to submit an offer on a property. Two days after that, Stone signed another buyer's agency agreement with Moritzky and submitted an offer on the same property on that same day. Even though two days had passed since the supposed presentation of the first offer, the seller testified that he evaluated both offers and accepted Moritzky's.

Zuazua sued in federal court, and the court referred to the Montana court the question of whether the Montana statute prohibits a buyer's agent from submitting two offers from two different clients on the same property.

The Montana Supreme Court, in a split decision, found that the requirement in the statute that the buyer's broker work "solely in the best interests of the buyer" was dispositive of the question, and it ignored other language, emphasized heavily by the three dissenters, that implicitly authorized buyer's brokers to submit offers from different brokers, subject to the injunction that the broker could not disclose to either client the terms of the other bid. The Montana Real Estate Commission had already issued rules permitting the submission of competing offers by the same agent. Both sides agreed that the statute did not expressly address the practice.

The Supreme Court limited its decision to the behavior of the individual agent and would have permitted the agent in question to designate (with client's consent) another agent in the same office to move forward on an offer. Indeed, one commentator on the case suggested that, if the result stands, agents might be well advised to designate different "submitters" for each of the buyers, so that the designated buyer's agent can maintain comfortable relations with both buyer clients after the issue is resolved. (Remember that the seller might reject both offers, leaving both clients still looking.)

In *Rivkin v Century 21 Teran Realty LLC*, 858 N.Y.S. 2d 55 (N.Y. 2008), a buyer was looking for a lakefront property in a certain area that had special meaning to him. He contacted Luborsky, an agent for Teran, a real estate broker, and got Internet information about a certain property listed for $100,000. He realized that this might be his dream property, and told Luborsky as much, authorizing Luborsky to make a verbal offer of $75,000 before he had even visited the property, but indicating that he would not be in a position to sign a contract until he had made such a visit. Luborsky contacted the listing broker and made the offer.

Three days later, the buyer visited the property and, although the improvements were, in his view, "tear down," the site was perfect, and he authorized Luborsky, on the agent's advice, to make a written offer of $75,000, expecting a counter offer or an invitation for final highest bids. He told Luborsky that he was willing to go to the asking price to get the property. He also signed an agency disclosure that stated, as required by New York law, that the "buyer's agent acts solely on behalf of the buyer" and has "without limitation, the following fiduciary duties to the buyer: reasonable care, undivided loyalty, confidentiality, full disclosure, obedience and a duty to account."

Over the weekend following, Luborsky told the buyer that other offers had been received, and the buyer indicated that he would go higher. So Luborsky agreed that he would contact the selling broker and ask whether a counteroffer or a "highest and best" solicitation would be forthcoming.

Unbeknownst to either buyer or Luborsky, another buyer, the Martins, were also interested in the property. The Martins had been working with another agent from Teran, Luborsky's office, and had submitted a full price unconditional offer on the property, which the sellers ultimately accepted, despite the buyer's and Lubrosky's attempts to communicate an unconditional overbid. The buyer made several direct contacts with one of the sellers, who consistently referred him to the selling broker, who ultimately informed the buyer that the property had in fact been sold through an offer from Teran, the buyer's own brokerage firm.

The buyer brought this lawsuit claiming that Teran and Luborsky and the other agent had all violated the exclusive fiduciary duty set forth in the disclosure and required by New York law.

This was apparently an issue of first impression since the law had been amended and the buyer brokers began to appear on the scene. The court concluded that the statute sometimes used the term "broker" and sometimes used the term "agent," and that the term "agent" referred only to an individual. It concluded that Luborsky owed an exclusive duty of loyalty to the buyer, and could not have acted on behalf of another client, but another agent in the office could represent a competing buyer:

> "An individual buyer's agent acting on behalf of multiple clients bidding on the same property cannot negotiate an optimal purchase price for all of them. The buyers' interest conflict; the agent's representation is inevitably compromised. But two buyer's agents simply affiliated with the same real estate brokerage firm and acting on behalf of different buyers bidding on the same property generally do not present comparable risks…they only earn commissions for sale to their own clients. As a result, in this situation the agents have every reason to negotiate in their clients' best interest."

The court also noted that a brokerage with an agency relationship with a seller would have the right to show other competing properties to potential buyers, even if those properties are listed for sale with the same brokerage firm, but suggested that a seller's agent would have a duty to disclose that it intended to do so.

Defenses Under the DTPA

Statutory Defenses

Section 17.506. There are several defenses to damages under the Deceptive Trade Practices Act. If the defendant can prove that before consummation of the transaction, he gave reasonable and timely notice to the plaintiff of the defendant's reliance on:

- written information relating to the particular goods and service in question obtained from official governmental records, if the written information was false or inadequate and the defendant did not know and could not reasonably have known of the falsity or inaccuracy of the information.

■ written information relating to the particular goods or service in question obtained from another source if the information was false or inaccurate and the defendant did not know of the falsity or inaccuracy of the information.

■ written information concerning a test required or prescribed by a government agency, if the information from the test was false or inaccurate and the defendant did not know and could not reasonably have known of the falsity or inaccuracy of the information.

Apparently the term "and could not reasonably have known of the falsity or inaccuracy" imposes upon the real estate broker this duty of care to at least investigate the information to determine whether or not it was true.

Section 17.505

Under the DTPA, a consumer must give the defendant a specific complaint and amount of actual damages at least 60 days prior to filing of the lawsuit. If the lawsuit is filed without the 60-day notice, the effect of filing the petition is the same as providing the written notice, as it gives the defendant 60 days from filing of the lawsuit to serve his defense.

It also provides that during that 60-day period the consumer has to give the defendant permission to inspect the product that is the source of the complaint. If the consumer fails to produce the product for inspection, his damages are limited.

■ The notice required apparently does not have to meet any formal requirements as it is to purely "inform the seller of the consumer's complaint and thus therefore provide an opportunity for the parties to settle the matter without litigation." *North American Van Lines v. Bauerele*, 678 S.W.2d 229 (Tex. Civ. App.-Ft. Worth, 1984). The "specific complaint" can be relatively general in description. *Jim Walters Home, Inc., v. Valencia*, 690 S.W.2d 239 (Tex., 1985).

■ The notice, however, must state a specific monetary amount of damages. *Sunshine Datsun v. Ramsey*, 687 S.W.2d 652 (Tex. Civ. App.-Amarillo, 1984).

■ If the defendant gives a tender offer to settle the conflict within the time allowed, it is a defense to the potential treble damage exposure. DTPA Sec. 17.50(d). It should also be noted that any tendered offer made by the defendant during the 60 days must also include the attorney's fees in addition to the actual damages claimed by the plaintiff. *Cail v. Service Motors, Inc.*, 660 S.W.2d 814 (Tex., 1983). The 1989 amendment to the Deceptive Trade Practices Act also specifically prohibits any attempts to offer the settlement offer as evidence before a jury.

Section 17.5051 Compulsory Mediation

This section provides for compulsory mediation and offers of settlement through mediation. Under this new procedure, a party may, no later than the 90th day after the date of service of the pleading, file a motion to compel mediation in a dispute. After the motion is filed, the court must, no later than 30 days after the motion is filed, sign an order setting the time and place of the mediation. The mediation must be held within 30 days after the date the order is signed, unless the parties agree otherwise. A party, however, may not compel mediation if the amount of economic damages claimed is less than $15,000, unless the party seeking to compel the mediation agrees to pay the cost of the mediation. Offers made during the mediation are treated very similarly to those under §17.505.

Section 17.555

This provision extends indemnity and contributions under the act to encompass all possible damages under the act and can be considered a very effective defense under the rights to the fact situation. The statute provides that the defendant may seek contribution or indemnity from one whom, under statute law or at common law, may have liability for the damaging event of the consumer complaint. This would allow the defendant to implead the seller, property inspector, or other person who may be determined to have the ultimate liability. The statute also provides for the defendant to get reimbursement for reasonable attorney's fees and costs.

The legislature also made an attempt to limit some of the licensee's liability through an amendment to the Texas Real Estate License Act. The act now provides the licensee is not liable for misrepresentation or concealment of material fact made by a party in a real estate transaction, or made by his subagent in a real estate transaction unless the licensee knew of the falsity of the misrepresentation or concealment and failed to disclose the licensee's knowledge of the falsity of the misrepresentation or concealment. *V.T.C.A. Occupations Code* §1101.805. This seems to impose an "actual knowledge" requirement on the broker and eliminates the ability to impute liability for what the broker "should have known." Note, however, that the new provisions do not diminish the real estate broker's liability for the broker's acts, nor the acts or admissions of the broker's salespersons.

Section 17.49 – Mere opinion of a professional (now specifically including real estate licenses) is not actionable unless one of the exemptions applies (note page 193).

Case Law Defenses

1. *Didn't say it.* One effective defense has been when the agent never made the representation, *Newsome v. Starkey*, 541 S.W.2d 468 (Tex. Civ. App.-Dallas, 1976); *Ozuna v. Delaney Realty*, 593 S.W.2d 797 (Tex. Civ. App.-El Paso, 1980, writ ref'd n.r.e.); *Stagner v. Friendswood Dev. Co., Inc.*, 620 S.W.2d 103 (Tex., 1981); *Micrea v. Cubilla Condominium Corp.*, 685 S.W.2d 755 (Tex. Civ. App.-Houston, 1985).

2. *Didn't know.* The courts will not hold an agent to the duty of care of failing to reveal information that he does not know, *Robinson v. Preston Chrysler Plymouth, Inc.*, 633

S.W.2d 500 (Tex., 1982). *Steptoe v. True, ante.* The real estate agent has also been held not liable when the plaintiff was not relying on the real estate agent's representations because of the plaintiff's own inspections of the property prior to acquisition, *Lone Star Machinery Corp. v. Frankel*, 564 S.W.2d 135 (Tex. Civ. App.-Beaumont, 1978). This defense may also apply to any consumer who hires his or her own inspector. *Pfeiffer v. Ebby Halliday*, 747 S.W.2d 887 (Tex. App.-Dallas, 1988).

3. *Not me.* If the broker is not a party to the earnest money contract, he will not be held responsible for his principal's default or misconduct. *Baxter & Swinford, Inc., v. Mercier*, 671 S.W.2d 139 (Tex. Civ. App.-Houston, 1984). As a general rule, the broker has no right, duty, or power to affect a principal's decision, and he has no duty except to forward information to the principal. *James Shore v. Thomas A. Sweeney & Associates*, 864 S.W.2d 182 (Tex. App.-Tyler, 1993).

4. *I told him.* If the seller discloses a defect and the buyer buys anyway, there may also be a defense. *Zak v. Parks*, 729 S.W.2d 875 (Tex. App.-Houston, 1987).

In *Cendant Mobility Services Corporation v. Falconer*, 135 S.W.3d 349 (Tex.App.-Texarkana 2004, no pet.). The Gregg County house purchased by Kenneth S. Falconer turned out to be a nightmare. Falconer purchased the house in 1999 through Cendant Mobility Services Corporation, a relocation firm selling the property for the prior owners, the Gunnelses. After the purchase, and a severe drought, Falconer began to see damage to interior and exterior walls and floors revealing serious and widespread structural flaws. Falconer sued Cendant, asserting causes of action for fraud and violation of the DTPA, claiming that Cendant failed to disclose that the house's foundation had shown evidence of substantial movement in the past and that Cendant provided only a portion of the relevant engineer's report for his review. The evidence reveals, however, that Falconer's initials appear on each page of the previous homeowner's real estate disclosure and an engineer's structural inspection report.

Despite Falconer's admission that he received and initialed at least those portions of the documents describing the foundation's condition, he nevertheless maintains that he was misled by Cendant's agent. He testified he would not necessarily characterize what she affirmatively told him about the house as a misrepresentation of the information available to her, but believed she misled him by selectively informing him of certain portions of the disclosures and reports, omitting the fact that substantial movement had taken place in the past. Instead, she reportedly pointed out from the seller's disclosure statement only that minor settlement had occurred in the past and then jumped forward to the last two sentences of the engineers' report, indicating that the foundation was stable, that the house was structurally sound, and that no additional repairs were warranted. In answer to the question: "Do you expect Cendant to sit down and read each—the contract through line by line with you?", he said: "If that's what it takes."

Despite Falconer's belief that Cendant's agent should have explained every detail of the contract, including any disclosures or attached reports, this is simply not the law. Even where there exists a fiduciary relationship—which did not exist here—there is no duty under the DTPA requiring sellers to orally disclose the contents of a written contract. The information provided in the seller's disclosure and the engineers' report was clear and unambiguous and subject to Falconer's review before signing. It is well settled that the parties to a contract have an obligation to protect themselves by reading what they sign. Unless there is some basis for finding fraud, the parties may not excuse themselves from the consequences of failing to meet that obligation. In this case, there was no evidence of fraud. The evidence was that he had everything in front of him and didn't read it. The failure of one party to read a contract, or any of the materials appertaining to it, however, does not equate with a failure of the other party to disclose the information contained within the four corners of that contract. Absent showing Cendant misrepresented the information disclosed in written form, Falconer was obligated to protect himself by reading the contract. He cannot now be excused from the consequences of failing to meet that obligation.

5. *Too vague. Autohaus v. Aguilar, supra*, held that a description of "good" was too general to be actionable, as was the statement that the consumers would "probably" have no problems with the item they were purchasing. Another recent case has also held that a "good house" that "had been repainted," a "roof put on," "new carpet," "a good buy," "a good value," "built on a good foundation," "a sound foundation," "in a good neighborhood," "house had been inspected," did not hold an agent liable for failing to disclose that there was a geological fault in the neighborhood when the broker had no knowledge of the fault. *Hagans v. Woodruff*, 830 S.W.2d 732 (Tex. App.-Houston [14th Dist.], 1992).

6. *Not my job*. In a very good case, the Court of Appeals held that §15(a)(6)(A) does not impose a duty on agents to inspect listed properties or to make an affirmative investigation for visible defects, *Kubinsky v. Van Zandt Realtors, et al.*, 811 S.W.2d 711 (Tex. App.-Ft. Worth, 1991, writ den.), particularly when the buyers retained their own agent *and* inspector in purchasing the home. Note a similar holding following the Kubinsky case in the Hagans' case, referenced earlier.

Another exception may be available when the circumstances and information from another source are correct, although the agent's information was incorrect, *Mikkelson v. Quail Valley Realty*, 641 P.2d 124 (Utah, 1982); or, that the principal still has the duty to read and understand his own contract, *Jones v. Maestas, supra, but see Phillips v. JCM, supra*; and *Wilkenson v. Smith, supra.*

In *Bartlett v. Schmidt*, 33 S.W.3d 35 (Tex. App.-Corpus Christi 2000, writ denied), Schmidt bought some land from sellers, who were represented by their broker, Bartlett. Schmidt wanted the property for use as a shipbuilding facility, where he intended to build ocean-going vessels. Pursuant to the contract, Schmidt was given a title commitment. The commitment showed some restrictive covenants that affected adjacent property, but that did not restrict commercial development on his property. The title company failed to show various amendments to the restrictions that, in fact, did prohibit commercial use of the property. Schmidt consulted with his lawyer and then bought the property. When he began laying the foundation for a shipbuilding enterprise, he was advised that the property had been annexed by the adjacent subdivision and was now limited to residential use only. Schmidt sued the seller, the broker, and the title company. The title company settled.

The trial court held that Bartlett was liable for fraud, negligent misrepresentation, and DTPA violations.

Both fraud and negligent misrepresentation require a showing of *reliance*. Here Bartlett argued that because Schmidt had consulted with his lawyer before buying the property, that consultation was an independent investigation that negates his claims. The decisions that support this notion are based on the notion that the buyer's decision to undertake a separate investigation indicates that he is not relying on representations about the property. Here, before he bought the property, Schmidt asked third parties to review conveyancing documents to be sure there were no restrictions on his intended use. He did this after he heard Bartlett's representations about the property. So the court held, relying on the third parties' representations, not on Bartlett's representations. Reliance on the title company's two external assessments of the feasibility of purchasing property was held to introduce a "new and independent" cause of the buyer's damages, thus negating the producing cause element of a DTPA claim. See also *Steptoe v. True*, 38 S.W.3d 213 (Tex. App.-Houston [14th Dist.], 2001).

7. *"As Is." The Prudential Insurance Company of America v. Jefferson Associates, Ltd.*, 896 S.W.2d 156 (Tex., 1995). In 1984, the Prudential Insurance Company of America sold a four-story office building in Austin, Texas, to F.B. Goldman, who later conveyed to Jefferson Associates, Ltd., a limited partnership of which Goldman was a partner. Goldman was an experienced investor and had bought and sold several large investment properties on an "as is" basis. Before bidding on the building, Goldman had it inspected by his maintenance supervisor, his property manager, and an independent professional engineering firm. Prudential's representative told Goldman that the building was "superb," "superfine," and "one of the finest little properties in the city of Austin." Goldman's original architects reviewed the specifications in 1987, some 3 years after the sale, and found nothing to indicate that the building contained asbestos. The building, however, had a fireproofing material called MonoKote® that contained asbestos. There was no evidence that Prudential actually knew that the Jefferson building contained asbestos before Goldman filed the lawsuit.

The contract to purchase the building contained the following provisions:

> As a material part of the consideration for this Agreement, seller and purchaser agree that purchaser is taking the Property "AS IS with any and all latent and patent defects and that there is no warranty by seller that the property is fit for a particular purpose. Purchaser acknowledges that it is not relying upon any representation, statement, or other assertion with respect to the property condition, but is relying upon its examination of the property. Purchaser takes the property under the express understanding that there are no express or implied warranties (except for limited warranties of title set forth in the closing documents). Provisions of this Section 15 shall survive the Closing;" and

- Purchaser hereby waives an action under the Texas Deceptive Trade Practices Act.

The Texas Supreme Court held that by agreeing to purchase something "as is," a buyer agrees to make his own appraisal of the property and to accept the risk that he may be wrong. The court noted that the sole cause of buyer's injury in said circumstances, by his own admission, is the buyer himself, as he has agreed to take the full risk of determining the value of the purchase. Rather than pay more, a buyer may choose to rely entirely upon his own determination of the condition and value of the purchase. In making this choice, he removes the possibility that the seller's conduct will cause this damage. The court qualified its holding, though, that the "as is" language is not determinative in every circumstance and would not apply if: (1) the buyer is induced to make a purchase because of fraudulent representation or concealment of information by the seller; (2) the buyer is impaired by the seller's conduct, such as obstructing an inspection; or (3) the "as is" clause is merely an incidental or "boilerplate" provision. In order for the "as is" clause to be enforceable, it must be an important basis of the bargain and apparently set out in some distinctive type style, such as ten-point type.

The court also noted that there was no evidence that Prudential actually knew of the asbestos and restated Texas law as it relates to Deceptive Trade Practices Act:

- a seller has no duty to disclose facts he does not know.

- a seller is not liable for failing to disclose what he only should have known.

- a seller is not liable for failing to disclose information he did not actually know.

Concerning the statements made by the Prudential representative, the court held that they were merely puffing and could not constitute fraud, unless the maker knew it was false when he made it or made it recklessly without knowledge of the truth. The court also noted that the problems of asbestos had been well known and publicly discussed for years when Goldman bought the building, and, therefore, Goldman's agreement to buy the building "as is" precluded him from recovering damages against Prudential.

As to the Deceptive Trade Practices Act, the court noted that the "as is" provision does not violate the prohibition against consumer's waiver under the DTPA, noting that "Goldman's agreement does not say he cannot sue Prudential for violating the DTPA; it says he cannot win the suit. He cannot win because he has asserted facts which negate proof of causation required for recovery."

Justice Gonzales noted that the court "returns to reason by reinstating reliance as an essential part of producing cause in a DTPA claim premised on a representation."

Does this theory apply to home sellers and buyers? Probably so.

In *Smith v. Levine*, 911 S.W.2d 427 (Tex. App.-San Antonio, 1995), the Smiths leased a house to Mr. Grissom, who was interested in buying the house. Grissom hired an inspection company to do a foundation analysis. It reflected that the foundation was defective. Grissom discussed the report with Mr. Smith and offered to give him a copy in exchange for paying part of the fee. The seller refused, indicating that the report "would have no value to us." The Smiths later listed the house with a real estate agent and did not mention the defective foundation on the agent's questionnaire. After the listing agreement expired, the Smiths put the house on the market themselves, describing the house as being in "excellent" condition. When showing the house, the Smiths also assured the purchasers that visible cracks were superficial. The purchasers (Mitchells) hired an engineer to do a "walk through" inspection, which also indicated that the cracks were minor and superficial.

The Mitchells later listed the house with a REALTOR® who secured a contract with a new purchaser. This second purchaser hired the same inspector who did the original inspection showing the foundation as being defective. What a coincidence!

The jury found that the Smiths knowingly engaged in a "false, misleading, or deceptive act or practice," as well as "unconscionable acts or course of action," both of which were the producing cause of damages to the Mitchells. The court affirmed that the jury was entitled to find that the Smiths knew the foundation was defective because of the original inspection.

The earnest money contract also contained an "as is" provision. The court held, however, citing the Prudential case, that "as is" is not a defense to a cause of action where a party is induced to enter into the contract because of fraudulent misrepresentation or concealment of information by the seller.

The Prudential case seems to be an open door to provide "as is" as a defense under the Deceptive Trade Practices Act, shifting the burden to the buyer. Later cases have indicated that the "as is" language in the earnest money contract must be clear, not "boilerplate," and should be in bold, ten-point type to be sure the buyer or reader of the contract would not have overlooked the provision. For instance, one case has indicated that the "as is" provision should emphasize the buyer's sole reliance on his own inspection to preclude causation under the Deceptive Trade Practices Act. It is also helpful if the buyer has an attorney, which seems to reinforce the ability to use "as is" as a defense. See *Erwin v. Smiley*, 975 S.W.2d 335 (Tex. App.-Eastland, 1998).

In *Fletcher v. Edwards*, 26 S.W.3d 66 (Tex. App.-Waco, 2000), the Fletchers filed suit against Edwards alleging that Edwards (a real estate agent) represented to them that they could get a water connection to the lot that they ultimately purchased, when they could not obtain the necessary connection because of a lack of easements across an adjoining lot. The trial court prevented a summary judgment in favor of the broker, and the Fletchers appealed. The court noted the parties' dispute—whether Edwards affirmatively represented to them that the water was available to the lot or Edwards maintained that he never told the Fletchers the water service was available to the lot, but told the Fletchers that they needed to check with a water company. The Fletchers signed an "Acceptance of Title" agreement at closing that contained an "as is" clause. The Fletchers asserted that the "as is" clause was not applicable in DTPA cases. The court noted that in the earnest money contract the Fletchers contractually bound themselves to accept the property "in its present condition." The court held that this is an agreement to purchase the property "as is" (this is the standard language in the TREC Form, paragraph 7.D.2). The court noted that the "as is" negates the causation essential to recovery for DTPA. However, it does not bind a buyer who is induced to enter in the agreement because of fraudulent misrepresentation. The court went on to hold that the Fletchers could prevail under a common law fraud claim if they could show that Edwards recklessly made the alleged representations as positive assertions without knowledge of the truth.

The court affirmed the fact that the defendant was entitled to judgments as a matter of law on the claim for exemplary damages under the DTPA and common law because of the "as is" defense, but they reversed the trial court's holding as to fraudulent inducement.

In *Larsen v. Langford & Associates, Inc.*, 41 S.W.3rd 245 (Tex. App.-Waco, 2001), involves the second "as is" case out of the Waco Court of Appeals. A real estate broker (Larsen) and his wife, who had access to the Multiple Listing Service, were looking for a house in Corsicana, Texas. The house was described as historic, built in 1913, and needing work. The property was listed with Carlene Langford & Associates, Inc. The broker, representing himself, requested to see the home. No one from the Langford office accompanied the Larsens to the home. They ultimately entered into a residential Earnest Money Contract to purchase the home for $65,000 through an assumption of the seller's loan. Langford was the seller's broker. The buyer's broker represented himself. The buyers admitted learning of problems with the home before closing and also agreed to receiving a Seller's Disclosure Form before the closing and before signing the final inspection. The sellers did not fill out some parts of the Seller's Disclosure Form. The buyer, however, never requested that they complete the form.

After closing, the broker/buyer alleged common law fraud, negligent misrepresentation, and violations of the DTPA. The court noted that all four cases of action were predicated on the reliance of the buyer on a representation made by the seller or the seller's agent. The court further noted that the box 7.D.2 was checked, which indicated that the home was purchased "as is." The listing broker also prepared another document that was signed by the buyers at closing that included the following clauses:

> I/We have been advised by the named REALTOR®/Real Estate Company to make any and all inspections of the subject property either by myself or anyone that I wish to employ, such as a licensed real estate inspector.

> I have made all inspections or have had an employee of my choice to make them for me. I accept the property in its present condition and am satisfied with the inspections and any repairs that were required.

> Brokers and sales associates shall not be liable or responsible for any inspections or repairs pursuant to this Contract and Addendum even in an event of a problem that has been overlooked by any or all parties involved in this transaction.

The court noted that enforceability of the "as is" agreement is determined: (1) in light of the sophistication of the parties, (2) by the terms of the "as is" agreement, (3) by whether the "as is" clause is freely negotiated, (4) by whether it was an arm's length transaction, and (5) by whether there was a knowing misrepresentation or concealment of a known fact. The court noted that the transaction was conducted at arm's length and that both parties were similarly knowledgeable and sophisticated parties in the real estate business, *particularly in light of the fact that the buyer acted on his own behalf as a broker*. The court also noted that the "as is" language was found in two separate documents, the preprinted Earnest Money Contract and the Final Inspection and Disclosure Form. The court held that by signing both agreements, the Larsens (buyers) explicitly agreed that they would accept the property in its present condition without requiring any repairs by the seller, that they had made their own inspection, and that they would relinquish Langford of any liability for the repairs known or unknown by the seller. The relevant contract provisions were clearly unambiguously demonstrated. Because the Larsens agreed to rely solely upon themselves, their own inspections, or the inspectors they chose and because the agreement affirmatively negated the element of each claim that the Langfords' conduct caused them any harm, the court further found that there was no inducement for the buyer to buy the house based on representations made by the broker and that the "as is" language effectively waived their rights to prevail under an allegation under the Deceptive Trade Practices Act.

In *Cole v. Johnson*, 157 S.W.3d 856 (Tex. App.-Ft. Worth, 2005), purchasers sued a seller for nondisclosure of certain information regarding the foundation of their home. At closing, the purchaser signed a document indicating that the sales price was being lowered $2,000 in lieu of foundation repairs, agreed that the sellers would be held harmless for any present or future repairs, and further agreed that the property was being purchased in an "as-is" condition. Other documents were provided to buyers at or prior to closing, totaling fifty-five pages of documentation relating to the foundation repairs. In the seller disclosure form, the seller represented that they were not aware of any undisclosed defective conditions, and that they were unaware of any current defective conditions to the drainage on the property. After the closing, there was a telephone conversation between the buyers and the sellers in which the seller indicated that the foundation work had failed. The buyers sued the seller based solely on this verbal allegation of nondisclosure.

The trial court awarded a summary judgment to the sellers, including attorney's fees. The court found that the purchasers were aware that there was no foundation warranty on the premises, they were aware that the property had an extensive history of foundation problems and foundation work. The court further found that they were aware that the foundation work had not cured the foundation problems because the foundation had continued to move and that there were numerous references in the reports given to the buyer that indicated there were continuing slab problems. The court noted the seller of a house is charged only with disclosing such material facts as to put a buyer exercising reasonable diligence on notice of a condition of the house, and that it was obvious, even to a layman, that the foundation had not corrected all of the problems and that they were ongoing at the time of the inspection reports that had been given to the buyer.

The court further noted that the use of the "as-is" provision is enforceable depending on the "totality of the circumstances" surrounding the agreement and that absent fraud, the "as-is" agreement is enforceable. The court found no fraud in this transaction at all.

Cherry v. McCall, 138 S.W.3d 35 (Tex.App.-San Antonio 2004, pet. pending). The Cherrys bought a home from the McCalls. After the Cherrys bought the home, they discovered a walled-in room in the basement. The room was filled with trash, including rusty plumbing fixtures, bathtubs, sinks, commodes, boards, pipes, rocks, and used building materials. The trash was damp and contaminated with mold.

The Cherrys brought a declaratory judgment action, seeking declaration that (1) the McCalls breached the contract, and (2) the walled-in room constitutes a mutual mistake justifying rescission. The McCalls answered by general denial. The McCalls also asserted the "as is" provision of the contract as an affirmative defense.

The Cherrys argued that the "as is" clause is unenforceable under the "totality of the circumstances" test set out by *Prudential*. The Cherrys do not allege that the McCalls fraudulently induced them to buy the house or concealed knowledge about the hidden room, nor do they allege that they were prevented from making their own inspection. Rather, they argue that their lack of sophistication, the fact that the "as is" provision was not negotiated but a standard boilerplate provision, the high price the Cherrys paid for the property, and the fact that the defect was hidden are all factors indicating that the "as is" clause is unenforceable under the "totality of the circumstances."

The court disagreed. While there is some evidence indicating that Mrs. Cherry, who had never handled the details of purchasing a home on her own before, was less sophisticated than the McCalls, who owned rental properties, there is no evidence that the Cherrys and the McCalls entered into the contract from unequal bargaining positions or that the transaction was not made at arm's length. Additionally, there is no evidence to support the Cherrys' argument that the "as is" provision was not freely negotiated. In fact, Mrs. Cherry confirmed in her deposition testimony that she "agreed to purchase the property in its current condition" and that she "accepted the risk" that the property might be deficient. Because the Cherrys contracted to accept the property "as is," they cannot, as a matter of law, prevail on their breach of contract claim.

In order to be entitled to a declaratory judgment that the contract was made under a mutual mistake, the Cherrys had to prove: (1) a mistake of fact, (2) held mutually by the parties, (3) which materially affects the agreed-upon exchange. Under section 154 of the Restatement (Second) of Contracts, however, a party bears the risk of mistake when the risk is allocated to him by agreement or when he knowingly treats his limited knowledge of the facts surrounding the mistake as sufficient. Here, the risk of mistake was allocated to the Cherrys by agreement when they contracted to accept property "in its current condition." Accordingly, their claim of mutual mistake fails as a matter of law.

The Cherrys argue, however, that the contract itself is invalid because a mutual mistake prevented the "meeting of the minds" necessary to the formation of a valid contract. Again, the court disagreed. Mrs. Cherry confirmed in her deposition testimony that she "agreed to purchase the property in its current condition" and that she "accepted the risk" that the property might be deficient. Thus, the evidence confirms that a meeting of the minds did take place, i.e., though neither party knew of the hidden room when it entered into the agreement, both parties agreed to place the risk of any unknown defects on the Cherrys.

There are exceptions to the "as is" rule. In *Kupchynsky v. Nardiello*, 230 S.W.3d 685 (Tex. App.-Dallas, 2007), Nardiello sued Kupchynsky and FGH Homebuilders, Inc., in connection with construction defects on a house. FGH was the builder of the home, and George Kupchynsky was the vice president of the company, but lived in the house as his residence. He contracted to sell the house to Nardiello, who obtained home, foundation, and termite inspections while the contract was pending. The residence featured two tiled balconies, one in the front and the other in the back of the house. Nardiello closed the transaction, and approximately five months later, the back balcony began to leak in several places. Nardiello sued after discovering that the balconies had been leaking "for quite some time" and the galvanized metal pans in the balcony were rusted and had holes. Construction experts concluded during the trial that the home was not built in a good, workmanlike manner.

At trial, the jury found that the defendants engaged in false, misleading, or deceptive acts and further made a negligent misrepresentation on which the purchasers relied. Kupchynsky's defense was that the plaintiffs had gotten independent inspections, and therefore they could not have relied on his representation as a matter of law. The trial court found otherwise, however, noting that the buyer may have relied on an expert's opinion, but (1) they did not renegotiate the price based on that opinion, and (2) the plaintiffs followed the inspector's recommendation and questioned Kupchynsky about the moisture that had accumulated in the balcony. Therefore, they could not have relied on the inspector alone.

A more confusing part of the case is that there was an "as is" provision (Paragraph 7.D. of the standard TREC form), which the court held did not negate the cause of action as a matter of law and that it was not an "as is" provision, "given the totality of the circumstances and the nature of the transaction." This contradicts two other courts of appeals cases. There is a vigorous dissent that 7.D. was an "as is" provision, and was not an exception to the "as is" rule, if there was no fraud in the inducement on behalf of the seller of the property. In another similar case a seller misrepresented the cash flow of an apartment project and the court considered it a fraudulent inducement and not subject to the "as is" defense. San Antonio Properties, L.P. v. PSRA Investments, Inc. (Tex. App.-San Antonio, 2008).

Licensed Real Estate Property Inspectors

The Real Estate License Act provides for a program of inspectors to inspect and report on the condition of real property. In the event an inspector engages in conduct that constitutes fraud, misrepresentation, deceit, or false pretenses, there are statutory procedures for recovering money from the Real Estate Inspection Recovery Fund. This also provides a "safe harbor" for real estate agents to refer the purchaser to a real property inspector, particularly as to the technical, mechanical defects in the property. It also gives the purchaser another party to rely on, rather than the representations of the real estate agent, particularly in light of the holding in Ozuna, Kubinsky, and Stagner cases.

There is some authority, however, that such recommendations may result in liability; see *Diversified Human Resources Group, Inc., v. PB-KBB, Inc.,* 671 S.W.2d 634 (Tex. Civ. App. Houston, 1984).

Ooh. Interesting Issue!

In *Head v. U.S. Inspect DFW, Inc.,* 159 S.W.3d 731 (Tex. App.-Ft. Worth 2005, no pet.), a home purchaser brought action against a home inspector for breach of contract, reach of implied warranty, negligence, and breach of DTPA for failure to discover and disclose roof problems. Inspector defended DTPA claims by raising as affirmative defense the professional services exemption of Tex. Bus. Com. Code Ann. §17.49(c) precluding claims arising out of advice, judgment, opinion, or similar professional skill. The inspector stated in the report that the roof was "performing its intended function," but it was not a misrepresentation of fact, but an expression of professional opinion.

The court noted that the inspector's contract provided that inspection would be conducted by "licensed real estate inspector." The inspector was assisted in inspection of roof by an apprentice inspector. This was some evidence that the services provided were nonconforming with the express warranty given on who would conduct the inspection.

But wait! The inspection contract limited the liability of inspector for breach of contract or negligence to the contract price of inspection ($348.27). The court held that the homeowner and inspector were free to contractually limit liability in absence of controlling public policy precluding enforcement of the agreement. With many providers of inspection services available, there was no disparity of bargaining power between the parties that made the limitation unconscionable. In view of the small fee paid to the inspector for a visual inspection of house, there were legitimate commercial reasons for limiting liability.

Could brokers do the same thing??? Hmm.

Seller Disclosure Forms

Similar to the real estate inspectors, a defense can be created for the licensee if the seller disclosed the defects. The theory behind this is that if the purchaser knows of the defect but buys anyway, he may have lost his right to sue for damages. See *Zak v. Parks,* 729 S.W.2d 875 (Tex. App.-Houston, 1987); *Dubow v. Dragon,* 746 S.W.2d 857 (Tex. App.-Dallas, 1988); *Pfeiffer v. Ebby Halliday,* 747 S.W.2d 887 (Tex. App.-Dallas, 1988). This may be particularly true in light of the new statutory Seller's Disclosure Statement.

In 1993, the Texas Legislature added a new section to the Property Code that now requires the seller of residential real property, comprising not more than one dwelling unit, to give the purchaser of the property a written notice in a form.

The notice is to be completed with the best of the seller's knowledge and belief as of the date the notice is completed and signed. If the information required is unknown to the seller, the seller should indicate that fact on the notice and stay in compliance with the section. This probably does not mean, however, that the seller can be blind to an obvious defect and say he doesn't know. Disclosure of a defect is required for a broker under §1101.652(b)(3) & (4) of the License Act! **The statute does not apply** to any transfers:

- pursuant to a court order.

- by a trustee in bankruptcy.

- to a mortgagee by a mortgagor or successor in interest.

- by a mortgagee or a beneficiary under a deed of trust who has acquired the real property by sale conducted pursuant to a power of sale under a deed of trust or a sale pursuant to a court-ordered foreclosure or has acquired the real property by deed in lieu of foreclosure.

- by a fiduciary in the course of the administration of a decedent's estate, guardianship, conservatorship, or trust.

- from one co-owner to one or more other co-owners.

- made to a spouse or to a person or persons in the initial line of consanguinity of one or more of the transferors.

- between the spouses resulting from a decree of dissolution of marriage or a decree of legal separation or from a property settlement agreement incident to such a decree.

- to or from any governmental entity.

- of new residences of not more than one dwelling unit that have not previously been occupied for essential purposes.

- of real property where the value of any dwelling does not exceed 5 percent of the value of the property.

The notice must be delivered by the seller to the purchaser on or before the Effective Date of an executory contract (signing the Earnest Money Contract) binding the purchaser to purchase the property. Note that the broker is required to fill in the Effective Date on the TREC forms. If the contract is entered into without the seller providing this required notice, the purchaser may terminate the contract for any reason within 7 days (by the 6th day!) after receiving the notice. A new issue exists, however. What if the seller never delivers the notice? What if the disclosure form is given on the Effective Date but before buyers had a chance to review it—can the buyer then not revoke?

A provision of the new statute parallels a similar change in the Texas Real Estate License Act, that a seller or seller's agent (does it apply to a buyer's broker?) has no duty to make a disclosure or release information related to whether a death by natural causes, suicide, or accident unrelated to the condition of the property occurred on the property. Note that the Texas Real Estate License Act says that a licensee has no duty even to *inquire about* whether death occurred on the property under these circumstances. Presumably, a seller would not need to inquire! How would a licensee know that the death was exempt from disclosure, however, if the licensee didn't inquire? One may want to put the "death disclosure" on the seller's disclosure form so that the broker has no need to inquire.

Seller's Disclosures in the Courts

Drainage Problems

In *Kessler v. Fanning*, 953 S.W.2d 515 (Tex. App.-Ft. Worth, 1997, no writ history to date) in connection with buying a house, the buyers received the required Property Condition Disclosure Statement. With respect to the questions on the statement about improper drainage or previous structure repairs, the sellers had answered "no." There appears to have been no other statements about drainage or structure made by the sellers. The buyers had the house inspected and detected no drainage problems during the inspection, even though it was raining at the time.

After moving into the house, the buyers noticed some real drainage problems. They sued the sellers, alleging DTPA violations.

The first question on appeal was whether any statement by the sellers was the producing cause of the Fannings' injury. In order to recover under the DTPA, the consumer must prove that the deceptive act was the producing cause of damages. The Fannings testified that, if they had known of the drainage problem, they would not have bought the house. The sellers claimed that the inspection of the property by the buyers was an intervening factor that broke the causal connection. The court held in favor of the buyers as to the issue of producing cause. The possibility of an independent investigation that might have uncovered fraud does not preclude recovery damages for fraudulent misrepresentations.

The second question was whether the statutorily required disclosure statement continued misrepresentations of fact or was merely a statement of opinion. The form stated that it was "not a substitute for inspections or warranties" and that it contained "representations made by the owner(s) based on owner's knowledge." The sellers claimed that these statements showed that the disclosures were merely statements of opinion or mere puffing, and not actionable misrepresentations. Whether a statement is opinion or not depends on (i) the specificity versus vagueness of the statement, (ii) the comparative knowledge of the parties, and (iii) whether the representation pertains to a past versus a future condition. The court held that the disclosure statement was not vague, was not based on equivalent knowledge by the parties, and pertained to past as opposed to future conditions. Thus, it did amount to a misrepresentation rather than merely a statement of opinion. Similarly, in *Blackstock v. Dudley*, 12 S.W.3d 131 (Tex. App.-Amarillo, 1999), a seller was sued for allegedly failing to disclose plumbing problems prior to the purchase. The home was inspected, but the court held that the plumbing defects were not, and because of their nature could not, have been discovered. The court noted that there is conflicting testimony as to what was actually said about the condition of the house. The jury resolved those conflicts in favor of the plaintiffs, and when the jury makes a decision, the court is highly unlikely to reverse that decision if there is even a scintilla of evidence that exists in support of the jury findings. That is the risk of the courthouse! In *Fernandez v. Schultz*, 15 S.W.3d 658 (Tex. App.-Dallas, 2000), Mr. Fernandez, a real estate agent, bought a house from HUD. He personally examined the property and purchased it on September 1, 1995. The real estate agent testified that he was familiar with the signs of termite infestation and denied seeing any evidence of termites in the house before he bought it. Fernandez remodeled the house, utilizing Mr. Nova, who testified that he noticed evidence of active termites and informed Fernandez about the termites, but Fernandez told him to continue his work making cosmetic repairs.

Fernandez offered the house for sale, gave the buyer (Schultz) a Seller's Disclosure of Property Condition dated October 29, 1995, which indicated that Fernandez had no knowledge of any active termites, termite damage, or previous termite treatment. Upon the Schultzes' inspection, they discovered evidence of previous termite treatment along the front porch. Fernandez agreed to have "spot" termite treatment done for the exterior of the house.

Following the purchase, the Schultzes discovered several swarms of termites inside their home and, ultimately, paid for full treatment by a different pest control company. Schultz sued under the Texas Deceptive Trade Practices Act alleging that Fernandez "knowingly" violated the DTPA. Fernandez defended by saying that there was a professional inspection, which relieves him from liability as a seller upon sale of the house, relying on *Dubow v. Dragon*. The court distinguished the holding in *Dubow*, however, noting that in Dubow the independent inspection resulted in a re-negotiation of the sales contract, relying on the professional opinions and quotes of their inspector. This was not the case here. The contract was never re-negotiated based in reliance on the inspection. Therefore, the seller still had liability for failing to disclose the termite problem.

Seller didn't know

There may be some relief in sight. In *Bynum v. Prudential Residential Services, et al.*, 129 S.W.3rd 781 (Tex. App.-Houston [1st Dist.] 2003), parents sued on behalf of their children to hold various Prudential entities (relocation company), inspectors and sellers, alleging violations of the Deceptive Trade Practices Act. They alleged that the home was remodeled without getting building permits. The contract for sale to the Bynums included an "as is" clause. The court held that there was no evidence that Prudential had actual knowledge that the sellers had remodeled their home without the necessary permits and, therefore, the buyers were not entitled to have the "as is" clause set aside on grounds of fraudulent misrepresentation or concealment.

As it related to the Seller's Disclosure Form, the court held that the Homeowner's Disclosure Form, standing alone, is not evidence that the McNamaras knew that their Disclosure Statement to the Bynums was false. The McNamaras apparently did not know much about construction, did not inquire as to the necessity of building permits, so it did not follow that they had actual knowledge that permits were required to remodel their bathrooms. In upholding the "actual knowledge" standard, the court said that there was no evidence that the McNamaras actually knew that they had remodeled without the necessary permits. The court further noted long-standing Texas law that when a buyer purchases "as is," he is agreeing that there is no express or implied warranties and that the buyer is relying only on his own examination of the property.

An important issue was raised concerning the Homeowner's Disclosure Form. The court held that the law (Section 5.008 of the Property Code) requires only that the form be completed to the best of seller's belief at the time the Notice is completed and signed, and there was no duty to provide continuing updates as to matters within the form.

Problems Duty to disclose

In *Sherman v. Elkowitz*, 130 S.W.3d 316 (Tex. App.-Houston [14th Dist.] 2004), the question posed for the court was whether the listing agent for the seller of the home could be liable for alleged misrepresentations and nondisclosures in a disclosure notice required by the legislature. In May of 1998, the Shermans purchased a home; Elkowitz acted as listing agent for the Shields and assisted them with the sale of the property to the Shermans. The Shields completed and provided to the Shermans a Seller's Disclosure Notice as required by Texas law, in which they just identified cracks in the driveway as a known defect needing repair and also disclosed a treatment for termites in 1990. The Shermans had the property inspected before agreeing to the purchase.

After purchasing the property, the Shermans discovered various defects in the property and eventually learned that the Shields (the sellers) had sued the previous owner for failing to disclose the same defects the Shermans had discovered. They then brought suit against the Shields claiming that the Shields and Elkowitz were required to disclose the alleged defects and the earlier lawsuit. In the trial court, the Shermans obtained a favorable judgment against the Shields, but the trial court handed a directed verdict for Elkowitz.

The disclosure notice was the same form provided by the Texas Association of REALTORS® that noted that the notice was not a substitute for inspections and was not a warranty. There is an additional notice in the disclosure that states that the broker has relied on the notice as true and correct and has no reason to believe that it is false. The Shermans placed emphasis on the statement that "there was no reason to believe it was false."

The court noted that the broker would have a duty to come forward only if he had any reason to believe that the seller's disclosures were false or inaccurate, and the notice makes it clear the disclosure is by the seller, not by the seller and the broker, and is merely statement of the broker's knowledge concerning the seller's disclosures. The court noted that the only way the broker could be held liable for the statement in the notice is if it were shown to be untrue.

There were two other issues: (1) that there was a defect that was corrected and not disclosed; and (2) the broker's duty to disclose the prior lawsuit. The court noted that repairing corrected defects does not prove their continued existence, therefore, one could logically conclude that there was no duty to disclose defects that had been repaired.

The court went on to hold that as a matter of law, brokers are not required to disclose prior lawsuits and that the disclosure only requires to a current lawsuit. That statutory form did not require disclosure of a lawsuit that was not pending.

Structural Repairs

In *Robertson vs. Odom*, 296 S.W.3d 151 (2009), Robertson purchased a townhouse in which the replacement stucco exterior had been improperly installed. Robertson sued the seller of the house, and the seller's Realtor (Barnes). Robertson's townhouse was a part of a complex in which they were removing synthetic stucco and installing a "hard-coat" stucco exterior. Unbeknownst to Odom (the Seller) the new hard-coat stucco contained several latent installation defects. Odom prepared a Seller's Disclosure Notice in which he represented that he was unaware of other structural repairs to the property.

The REALTOR® informed the buyer that the original synthetic stucco had been replaced and was "better than new." Robertson was skeptical and instructed his property inspector to carefully examine the stucco. The inspector reported no problems with the stucco and Robertson purchased the townhouse. The trial court awarded a take nothing judgment and Robertson appealed because of the seller's failure to disclose structural repairs and alleging that the broker's representation of "better than new" created liability for the seller. The court noted that the Property Code does not define structural repair as it relates to seller's disclosures, but relied on several other references under the Property Code to determine that a structural repair refers to a repair to a low-bearing portion of the residence. This defect was not a structural repair and did not need to be disclosed in that portion of the Seller's Disclosure Notice.

Damages Under the DTPA

As previously discussed, the statutory damages recoverable under the Deceptive Trade Practices Act were changed in 1995 and now include:

■ the amount of economic damages found by the trier of fact. In addition, the court may award two times that portion of the actual damages if it does not exceed $1,000. If the trier of fact finds that the conduct of the defendant was committed knowingly, the trier of fact may award no more than three times the amount of actual damages in excess of $1,000.

■ an order adjoining such acts or failure of act.

■ orders necessary to restore to any part of the suit any money or property, real or personal, which may have been acquired in violation of this subchapter.

■ any other relief that the court deems proper, including the appointment of a receiver or the revocation of a license or certificate authorizing the person who engages in business in this state if the judgment has not been satisfied within 3 months of the date of final judgment. The court may not revoke or suspend a license to do business in the state or appoint a receiver to take over the affairs of the person who has failed to satisfy judgment if the person is a licensee of or regulated by a state agency that has the statutory authority to revoke or suspend a license or to appoint a receiver or trustee. [Emphasis added.] It has further been held that the treble damages must be found by the trier of the fact and is not an automatic award. *Martin v. McKee Realtors, Inc.,* 663 S.W.2d 446 (Tex., 1984).

A recent 1999 Amendment to the Texas Deceptive Trade Practices Act eliminates the requirement that attorney's fees be reasonable in relation to the amount of work expended.

Apparently, this opens the door now for the court to award contingency fees to plaintiffs rather than requiring fees to be "reasonable."

This case may greatly limit plaintiff's suits if the plaintiff's attorney is unwilling to settle for an hourly rate paid at the successful conclusion of the case. Contingency fees are still legal, but the ability to recover them from the defendant is now greatly limited.

Negligent Misrepresentation

Another cause of action beginning to permeate cases involving real estate brokers is negligent misrepresentation. When alleging negligent misrepresentation, the parties seeking the remedy must prove that: (i) a representation is made by the defendant in the course of his business for a transaction in which he has a pecuniary interest; (ii) the defendant provides "false information" for the guidance of others in their business; (iii) the defendant did not exercise reasonable care or competence in obtaining or communicating the information; and (iv) the plaintiff suffers pecuniary loss by justifiable reliance on the representation. *O'Hearn v. Hogard,* 1992 W.L. 324462 (Tex. App.-Houston [14th Dist.], 1992).

In the case of *Hagans v. Woodruff,* 830 S.W.2d 732 (Tex. App.-Houston [14th Dist.], 1992), the court, in reasoning similar to *Aguilar, supra,* held that the false information must be provided by the broker to the plaintiff but that general comments, such as the house was in a "good neighborhood," are not an all-encompassing negligent representation that no faults exist in the neighborhood.

Following the reasoning of the *Kubinsky, supra,* the court held that a broker has no legal duty to inspect listed property and disclose all facts that might affect its value or desirability. In this case, there was a fault line running through the neighborhood. Licensees should continue to be very cautious, however. The court in *Hagans* also followed the *Bynum* court's theory that any false representation tied to the broker creates a cause of action under the

DTPA as well as for negligent misrepresentation. The key defense seems to be that the agent, after reasonable investigation, did not know that the information was "false."

Real Estate Recovery Fund

The plaintiff is also guaranteed solvency of any real estate licensee defendant under the Real Estate Recovery Fund. Any party that has been held to be an aggrieved party can recover for the wrongful act of real estate agents, Texas *Real Estate Commission v. Century 21 Security Realty, Inc.*, 598 S.W.2d 920 (Tex. Civ. App.-El Paso, 1980). The recovery fund is also liable for attorney's fees, *Texas Real Estate Commission v. Hood*, 617 S.W.2d 838 (Tex. Civ. App.-Eastland, 1981). Any valid claim for a recovery out of the fund may result in a suspension of the broker's or salesperson's license, and the license cannot be reinstated until he or she has repaid the recovery fund in full plus interest at the current legal rate. The recovery fund is limited to the aggregate of $50,000, including attorney's fees, in the same transaction or $100,000 against any one licensed real estate broker or salesperson. Only actual damages (not treble damages) may be recovered out of the fund. *State v. Pace*, 640 S.W.2d 432 (Tex. Civ. App.-Beaumont, 1982).

Regarding liability insurance, the Texas standard policy form for omissions and errors for real estate might not cover violations of the DTPA!! *St. Paul Ins. Co. v. Bonded Realty, Inc.*, 583 S.W.2d 619 (Tex., 1979). Another word of caution: Many insurance policies do not provide coverage for damages in excess of actual damages. This may mean that a real estate broker does not have insurance coverage for punitive damages, exemplary damages, or multiple damages under the Deceptive Trade Practices Act. Be sure to check your policy for this coverage.

Economic and Finance Update Federal and State

Economic Update—Introduction

The field of real estate finance includes many related subjects. Similarly, there are many economic factors that affect real estate. However, this chapter is limited to key changes that have occurred over the past two to three years that have had an effect on Texas real estate licensees and the real estate market.

The Federal Reserve Bank provides financial and economic data in a publication commonly known as the Beige Book. This report is published eight times per year. Each Federal Reserve Bank gathers anecdotal information on current economic conditions in its District through reports from Bank and Branch directors and interviews with key business contacts, economists, market experts, and other sources. The Beige Book summarizes this information by District and sector. An overall summary of the twelve district reports is prepared by a designated Federal Reserve Bank on a rotating basis. The information given here is condensed from the report based on information collected before October 19, 2011.

To keep current with the information provided in this publication, access either of these Web sites:

http://www.federalreserve.gov/FOMC/BeigeBook/2011/
http://www.federalreserve.gov/FOMC/BeigeBook/2012/

Beige Book Summary Of All Districts

Reports from the twelve Federal Reserve Districts indicate that overall economic activity continued to expand in September 2011, although many Districts described the pace of growth as "modest," "slight" and contacts generally noted weaker or less certain outlooks for business conditions. The reports suggest that consumer spending was up slightly in most Districts, with auto sales and tourism leading the way in several of them. Business spending increased somewhat, particularly for construction and mining equipment and auto dealer inventories, but many Districts noted restraint in hiring and capital spending plans. By sector, manufacturing and transportation activity was reported to have increased on balance. A few Districts also reported slight improvements in construction and real estate activity; nonetheless, overall conditions for both residential and commercial real estate remained weak. Districts reporting on nonfinancial services cited mixed results with activity varying widely by industry.

Loan demand by and large moved lower, with the exception of an increase in mortgage refinancing in many Districts. Crop conditions at harvest were generally less favorable than a year ago. In contrast, energy and mining activity continued to strengthen in several Districts, with the exception of some storm-related slowdowns in the Gulf of Mexico. Cost pressures eased in the majority of Districts, though there was some further pass-through of earlier increases to downstream prices. Wage pressures remained subdued outside of a few exceptions in which firms noted having difficulty finding appropriately skilled workers.

Consumer Spending and Tourism. Consumer spending was up slightly in September. The majority of Districts reported increases in auto sales, with the largest improvements in San Francisco and New York. Several Districts noted a greater availability of new vehicles as the supply disruptions that had plagued auto dealerships in the aftermath of the Japanese disaster subsided. Contacts in the Cleveland, New York, Philadelphia, and Dallas Districts indicated that demand for used cars remained high and that some models were still scarce. A large number of Districts reported that nonauto retail sales were flat to down in September 2011 but a few, such as Philadelphia, Richmond, and Dallas noted an increase in customer traffic late in the month and into early October.

Business Spending. Business spending increased somewhat from the previous report. However, contacts in a number of Districts reported that a weaker and more uncertain economic outlook had increased caution and was weighing on future spending plans. Philadelphia, Richmond, and Chicago indicated that many retailers were reluctant to build inventories ahead of the holiday season, pointing to recent declines in consumer confidence. Auto dealers were an exception, as they continued to replenish inventories that ran low in the aftermath of the production disruptions caused by the Japanese disaster.

Nonfinancial Services. Reports regarding nonfinancial services were mixed in September. Richmond noted slower overall activity, and St. Louis cited reduced demand for telecommunications, media, and education services. Demand for accounting and legal services was reported to have been unchanged in both Dallas and San Francisco. On the positive side, contacts in St. Louis reported that demand for business support services increased, and Boston reported strong business conditions for economic consulting firms involved with litigation work and advertising firms helping to market financial services.

Manufacturing and Transportation. Contacts indicated that manufacturing and transportation activity increased since the last report in most Districts. A large number of Districts reported higher production of autos and other transportation-related equipment. Cleveland, Atlanta, and Chicago noted increases in auto production, and Boston, Richmond, Chicago, and St. Louis all cited robust activity for auto suppliers. Dallas reported healthy demand for nondefense transportation goods. Boston, Richmond, Kansas City, and San Francisco indicated continued growth in commercial aviation and aerospace manufacturing. Steel production rose in Cleveland and Chicago, and in a number of Districts metal manufacturers' new orders also rose.

Real Estate and Construction. All twelve Districts reported that real estate and construction activity was little changed on balance from the prior report. Residential construction remained at low levels, particularly for single-family homes. That said, Philadelphia, Cleveland, and Minneapolis noted small increases in single-family construction, and construction of multifamily dwellings continued to increase at a moderate pace in Boston, Philadelphia, Cleveland, Kansas City, Dallas, and San Francisco. Home sales remained weak overall, and home prices were reported to be either flat or declining across all of the Districts. In contrast, rental demand continued to rise in a number of Districts. Commercial real estate conditions remained weak overall, although commercial construction increased at a slow pace in most Districts.

Banking and Finance. Financial activity was reported to have weakened some since the last report. Dallas noted that the improvement in financial conditions had stalled, and Chicago indicated a further tightening of credit conditions, particularly for financial firms. In addition, New York reported noticeably weaker activity in the securities industry. Loan volumes were either flat or down slightly in most Districts. Consumer loan demand moved lower according to respondents in Cleveland, Chicago, and Kansas City, and it held steady in New York and San Francisco. However, New York, Philadelphia, Cleveland, Richmond, Chicago, and Kansas City all noted an increase in mortgage refinancing activity given lower mortgage rates, and Cleveland also noted continued strength in auto lending and increased demand for business loans.

Agriculture and Natural Resources. Contacts generally reported that crop conditions at harvest were less favorable than a year ago, although results varied by and within Districts. Lower yields than a year ago were reported for major crops in the Chicago, Minneapolis, and Dallas Districts and in most of the Kansas City District. Even so, yields were large enough to alleviate worries about shortages. Corn, soybean, and wheat prices moved down, while some contacts noted higher prices for cotton. Drought conditions persisted in the Atlanta, Kansas City, and Dallas Districts, and pastures were in worse shape than a year ago in many areas.

Employment, Wages, and Prices. Respondents indicated that labor market conditions were little changed, on balance, in September 2011. Several Districts cited only limited and selective demand for new hires. Cleveland, Richmond, Atlanta, Chicago, and Kansas City all noted that firms in some sectors that were hiring more broadly (such as manufacturing, transportation, and energy) were also experiencing difficulties in finding appropriately skilled or qualified labor.

Respondents in the Boston, Richmond, Atlanta, and Chicago Districts indicated that hiring was being restrained by elevated uncertainty or lower expectations for their future growth. New York reported that deteriorating business conditions in the finance industry had led to a pull back in hiring with some layoffs anticipated in the months ahead.

Eleventh District—Dallas

The Eleventh District economy continued to expand at a modest pace since the last report. Manufacturing activity was mixed. Service sector activity held mostly steady, although retailers noted a recent pick-up in sales. There were some signs of improvement in the housing sector, and apartment demand remained brisk. Office and industrial leasing activity continued to increase, but commercial real estate investment activity fell. Loan demand was mostly unchanged, according to financial contacts. The energy sector continued to expand at a strong pace, while agricultural conditions deteriorated further. Many responding firms across industries noted their outlooks were less optimistic, reflecting uncertainty about the U.S. and global economies.

Prices. Price pressures eased slightly since the last report. Most firms said input prices were unchanged or down, although retailers noted some increases in apparel and jewelry prices. Raw materials prices were flat or down. The exception was food producers who noted increased prices for some inputs. Contacts in the agricultural sector said commodity prices moved down since the last report. The price of West Texas Intermediate (WTI) held between $80 and $90 per barrel for most of the survey period, but slipped under $80 by early October. As the driving season ended, the price of on-highway diesel and gasoline fell by 11 and 16 cents per gallon, respectively.

Labor Market. Employment levels held steady at most responding firms, although there were several reports of slight hiring activity. Staffing firms continued to note steady demand at high levels. Most primary metals manufacturers reported increases in payrolls and some continue to look for additional workers. Scattered reports of hiring came from contacts in the legal, auto sales, airline, and transportation manufacturing industries. Contacts in food manufacturing and financial services said hiring activity had abated. Wage pressures remained minimal, although upward pressure was noted by select retail, lumber and transportation manufacturing firms.

Manufacturing. Reports were mixed among construction-related firms, but most contacts described demand as steady during the reporting period. Several responding firms said ongoing public projects were buoying activity. Fabricated metals firms noted a slight pickup in demand and two lumber producers noted a pickup believed to be due to home improvement projects and demand from homebuilders. Construction related outlooks were mostly unchanged, with a slow recovery expected.

Respondents in high-tech manufacturing said that sales growth remained positive but continued to slow and new orders declined. Demand weakened across consumer and business markets and throughout most regions of the world. Producers of consumer electronics are reportedly very cautious about demand over the holidays and into the first half of next year, and have reduced their orders for semiconductors. Because of the decline in new orders, respondents in the high-tech sector expect sales to weaken over the next six months. Reports from paper manufacturers were mixed. Box producers noted orders from the food and beverage industry had fallen, but demand from retailers had picked up. One paper firm said strong demand was leading to lower inventories. Outlooks were mostly downbeat, due to fluctuations in the stock market and speculation about another recession. Nondefense transportation manufacturers said demand held steady at pretty good levels and is up significantly from a year ago. Responding firms were cautiously optimistic in their outlooks, noting troubles at the national level had not impacted them yet. Food producers said sales were flat since the last report and outlooks were positive, although firms were not hiring because of concerns about current U.S. economic conditions. Petrochemical demand weakened in September. Ethylene spot prices fell despite two large plants shutting down. Domestic demand for polyethylene is weak, and the strong dollar has cut off exports to Asia and Europe. Exports to Latin America also weakened as Asian producers offered prices low enough to displace U.S. exports. Refiners said demand for refined products fell slightly as summer ended. Margins remain strong but have narrowed.

Retail Sales. Retail sales growth slowed over most of the reporting period but picked up in the final weeks of September. A long hot summer led to delayed fall clothing purchases, however, contacts said cooler weather recently spurred seasonal sales. The higher end of the market continues to fare better than lower price point offerings. Eleventh District growth trended roughly in line with the nation, according to one large retailer. Expectations are for modest growth this holiday season. Automobile sales were steady with some slowdown in traffic attributed to economic concerns caused by pessimistic headlines. Despite concerns, customers continue to buy vehicles. Inventories are somewhat light but at appropriate levels for the most part. Used car supply remains constrained resulting in high prices. Expectations are for a continued moderate pace of sales growth.

Services. Overall demand for staffing services continued to hold steady at high levels. One contact noted a slight pull back that was characterized as "fear driven." Direct hires continue to outpace temporary placements. Outlooks were mixed, with half of the respondents more cautious and half more positive. Even contacts with positive outlooks expressed concern about the upcoming election cycle and regulatory uncertainty. Accounting firms said demand for accounting services remained steady. Outlooks were unchanged, but one contact noted the next few months will be telling, as customers appear to be waiting for greater clarity about the economy and possible regulations. Demand for legal services remained unchanged. Most transportation services firms said demand held steady or rose, but many firms' outlooks weakened further since the last report. Intermodal cargo volumes were flat, and contacts say outlooks are negative for 2012. Railroad firms said volumes increased during the reporting period, but that the numbers were somewhat artificially inflated due to capacity coming back online after the flooding in the northern U.S.

Container volumes declined modestly over the past three months, but picked up in August. Small parcel shipments held steady in August, but shipping firms have lowered expectations of growth this year. Airline traffic was reportedly holding up well and has been flat to slightly improved over the last six weeks in terms of passenger volume. Demand for travel to Latin America remains strong and travel to Japan is weak. Airline industry outlooks are positive, but more uncertain.

Construction and Real Estate. Contacts in the housing sector noted some improvement, although most characterize conditions as choppy. Inventories of existing homes declined since the last report, and new home inventories remain lean. Most contacts say sales are better, although many note the strict lending environment, along with nervousness about the path of the U.S. economy, is keeping many would-be buyers on the sidelines. Apartment demand continued to rise since the last report, and contacts are positive in their outlooks. While construction has increased, demand has kept up, and respondents believe it will be a year or two before much of the new product is available. Apartment rents continued to increase.

Commercial real estate contacts said demand for office space remained strong overall during the reporting period, but that in recent weeks clients have deferred decisions to expand.

Demand for industrial space was being spurred by lease renewals rather than the expansion by existing tenants. Real estate investment activity declined in August amid uncertainty.

Financial Services. Financial firms reported relatively flat loan demand overall. National banks noted modest increases in loan demand, although contacts were uncertain the gains would continue. Regional banks said loan demand was flat, and loan pricing remained competitive. Still, outstanding loan quality continued to hold up, according to contacts. The improvement in lending conditions noted in the last report has stalled due to both the modest level of demand and more caution in supplying loans to anyone but the most creditworthy of borrowers.

Energy. Drilling activity remains strong. Contacts in the energy sector said oil field activity is at high levels and expanding. The Texas rig count rose by 11 during the reporting period. Despite the strength, many noted concern about the recent dip in the price of oil and U.S. and global economic weakness.

Agriculture. Drought in the Eleventh District remained severe during the reporting period, particularly in Texas where more than 85 percent of the state is in exceptional drought. Already poor grazing and stock water conditions deteriorated further, forcing many ranchers to sell off part or all of their herds. The drought caused low yields and record-high abandonment rates for some crops, including cotton. Export demand for beef continued to grow while the volume of exports for most crops was lower than six weeks ago. There was growing concern about continued drought conditions and the negative impact of low soil moisture on 2012 crop production.

The Federal Reserve Bulletin

The *Federal Reserve Bulletin* was introduced in 1914 as a vehicle to present policy issues developed by the Federal Reserve Board. Throughout the years, the *Bulletin* has been viewed as a journal of record serving to provide data generated by the Board back to the public. Authors from the Federal Reserve Boards' Research and Statistics, Monetary Affairs, International Finance, Banking Supervision and Regulation, Consumer and Community Affairs, Reserve Bank Operations, and Legal divisions contribute to the contents published in each issue. The *Bulletin* includes topical research articles, legal developments, Report on the Condition of the U.S. Banking Industry, and other general information.

The tables that appeared in the Financial and Business Statistics section of the *Bulletin* (1914-2003) are now published monthly as a separate print publication titled *Statistical Supplement to the Federal Reserve Bulletin*.

Since 2006, the *Bulletin* is published on the Board's public Web site on a continuing basis, as it becomes available. The quarterly paper version of the *Bulletin* is no longer published. However, the Board will print an annual compendium. To access the *Bulletin*, utilize the following link:

http://www.federalreserve.gov/pubs/bulletin/default.htm

Interested parties may subscribe to "The Federal Reserve Board E-mail Notification Service." The e-mail notification service alerts subscribers to newly available testimonies, speeches, articles, and reports in the *Federal Reserve Bulletin*, the *Statistical Supplement to the Federal Reserve Bulletin*, and press releases and other items (Consumer Credit, Flow of Funds, Industrial Production and Capacity Utilization, and Senior Loan Officer Survey statistical releases). The message provides a brief description and a link to the recent posting.

The Texas Job Market

On Tuesday, July 26, 2011, the headlines on the front page of USA Today carried these words: "Need a Job? Move to Texas." The subtitle stated that "Finding work may not be all that simple, but it sure seems that way. While the nation's job growth has limped along since the economic recovery began two years ago, the Lone Star State is enlarging payrolls in Texas-size fashion."

The background picture behind the headlines showed Occidental Petroleum's Goldsmith field near Midland, Texas. The company led a rush to find oil on land after the BP oil spill in the Gulf of Mexico in 2010.

The article went on to say that from June 2009 to June 2011 the state added 262,000 jobs, or half the country's 524,000 payroll gains, according to the Federal Reserve Bank of Dallas and the Bureau of Labor Statistics. Even by a more conservative estimate that omits states with net job losses, Texas advances make up 30 percent of the one million additions in the 34 states with net growth. The article goes on to state that Texas' big gains are partly a reflection of its population growth. But the recent job gains are outpacing the rate of population growth in Texas, the nation's second largest state, with 25 million residents which is about 8 percent of the U.S. population.

The state's payrolls have risen 2.9 percent since the end of the recession, third behind North Dakota and Alaska and far outpacing the USA's 0.4 percent growth, according to the Bureau of Labor Statistics. Also, Texas' unemployment rate of 8.2 percent is well below the nation's 9.2 percent. Moody's economist Ed Friedman says that "For one large state to grow (jobs) so much faster than the rest of the nation is very unusual."

What is Driving Texas' Job Growth?

Economists point to an array of factors, including high energy prices that set off an oil drilling frenzy, rising exports, and a conservative banking industry that helped the state sidestep the housing crash. Yet while energy has been a spark—employment in natural gas, oil, and other mining sectors rose by 45,000, or 23 percent since the recession ended—growth has been broad-based. During the past two years, professional and business services added 74,000 jobs; education and health care gained 91,000; and leisure and hospitality grew by 29,000 according to the Bureau of Labor Statistics.

State officials cite a pro-business climate that is drawing scores of businesses from high-cost states a trend that took on urgency for firms that got lean in the economic downturn. Texas has no state or corporate income tax and keeps regulations at a minimum to allow businesses to grow quickly. Tort reform has helped reduce or limit frivolous law suits. The state has doled out more than $600 million in grants and investments since 2003 to recruit out-of-state companies and help Texas firms expand.

Are There Negatives?

Texas ranks 44th in the United States in per-student expenditures and 43rd in high school graduation rates. Seventeen percent of Texans lived below the poverty level in 2009, compared to 14 percent for the nation. The state leads the nation with the highest percentage of the population with no health insurance, and was ninth in income inequality in the mid 2000s, according to the latest data available from the Economic Policy Institute. The state's relatively low wages, particularly for low-skilled jobs, stems in part from its status as a right-to-work state with little unionization. That seems to dampen consumer spending and limits economic growth. In June 2011, average hourly earnings for private-sector employees in Texas were about 5 percent lower than the U.S. average.

Mark Doutzer, chief economist at Texas A&M's Real Estate Center, says the state's lower pay helps compete in a global economy. "Either you choose to have low-wage jobs or you choose to have no jobs at all. The state's reasonable cost of living makes it possible for many residents to live comfortably on lower salaries. For example, the Dallas area ranks 10th in housing affordability among 82 metro areas with more than one million residents, and Houston ranks 15th according to the Demographia International Housing Affordability Survey. This is partly because of Texas' abundance of cheap land, which is also another draw for firms looking to relocate.

Other Reasons For Texas' Robust Job Growth

The Energy Boom: Oil prices have nearly tripled since early 2009. High prices spark more exploration and production. Technological breakthroughs have let companies extract natural gas embedded in shale deposits. Barnett Shale in Fort Worth is one of the United States' largest gas fields, and drilling began at the Eagle Ford Shale in South Texas in 2008. Each rig employs a few dozen workers and leads to hiring by engineering firms, pipeline builders, and other services.

Exports: Overseas shipments by Texas' strong computer, electronics, petrochemical, and other industries rose 21 percent in 2010 compared with 15 percent for the nation, according to the Dallas Federal Reserve Bank. Texas also benefits from its proximity to Latin America countries that are big importers of U.S. goods. The surge creates jobs for Texas manufactures and ports.

No Housing Crash: Texas never had a housing boom but also avoided the bust that decimated consumer credit and home construction in much of the nation. While prices of single-family homes more than doubled from January 2000 to their mid-2000s peak in cities, such as Los Angeles and Las Vegas, they rose less that 27 percent in the Dallas/Ft. Worth market, according to S&P/Case-Shiller Home Price Index. Meanwhile, Texas banks burned by the savings and loan crisis in the 1980s were less eager than those in other states to approve risky mortgages. Texas law limits mortgage debt, including home equity loans, to 80 percent of the home's value.

Texas still was hit by the recession. Annual permits for single family homes declined by 59 percent from their 2005 peak but that's less than the nation's 73 percent plunge, according to the Real Estate Center. Similarly, employment fell 4 percent in the downturn. The USA's overall drop was 6.3 percent. Texas has recovered 380,000 jobs since its December 2009 low and is now just 54,000 shy of its 10.6 million peak.

Population Growth: Texas' population grew by 4.3 million, or 21 percent, during the past decade, more than twice the national pace. About half the total was because of births, but Texas also gained 849,000 residents via state-to-state migration, second only to Florida. Texas benefits from a virtuous cycle: More people are moving to Texas for work, generating consumer demand that creates still more jobs. That has expanded the workforce keeping the unemployment rate at 8.2 percent, ranked just 26th in the nation, despite the strong payroll advances.

One recent arrival moved from Philadelphia to Austin in July of 2011. He was a high school counselor in Philadelphia but moved to Austin to be nearer to his family. Within two weeks he had a job as a rehabilitation specialist for a growing outpatient facility for the mentally ill. When he arrived in Austin he expected to be looking for a job for four or five months.

Companies Searching for Possible Relocation: Corporate giants including Fluor, Toyota, and Medtronic recently moved headquarters or operations to Texas. Also, eBay, AT&T, Samsung, and Cirrus Logic have expanded to Texas. Samsung added about 700 jobs in Austin since 2010, enlarging a plant that makes chips for smartphones. Area business leaders, meanwhile, have aggressively courted out-of-state companies.

In July 2011 the Dallas Regional Chamber sent a letter to 50 Illinois businesses urging them to consider a move to Texas. The letter included a side-by-side comparison of the two states that notes Illinois recently raised corporate and personal income taxes and highlighted Texas' lower housing, labor, and other expenses. The Dallas Chamber typically targets states with heavy duty business taxes, personal taxes, and regulatory mindsets.

Texas has particularly tried to lure high-tech California companies to lower-cost technology corridors in Austin, Dallas, and San Antonio. Medtronic, the Minneapolis-based medical device giant, has moved customer support from the Los Angeles area to San Antonio over a 22-month period creating over 750 jobs in Texas. Medtronic was drawn by labor costs that are "significantly lower" than those in Los Angeles and a large, high-quality workforce. Another attraction was the more affordable real estate and the lack of state corporate tax, though the latter was a minor factor. The company, which also received $14 million in incentives from the state, chose San Antonio from among more than 900 U.S. cities evaluated. The $14 million incentive was comparable with other offers.

Other Effects: The corporate relocations and expansions are having a ripple effect on restaurants, hospitals, and other service businesses. Winstead, a Dallas law firm with about 270 lawyers statewide, has added 50 since 2010 to handle the extra workload from firms, such as Comerica Bank that have moved to Texas the last few years. After cutting staff in 2009 and 2010, DeMontrand Automotive in Houston has hired about 20 employees in mid 2011 in response to a 20 percent jump in revenue. DeMontrand has gained about 50,000 jobs through July 2011.

Texas Economic Condition By Industry and Metropolitan Area

The Real Estate Center at Texas A&M publishes a "Monthly Review of the Texas Economy" by Ali Anari and Mark G Dotzour. The following information was derived from the September 2011 edition. This information is available to the public as well as all Texas Real Estate Licensees.

Texas continues to outperform the United States in job creation. Texas gained 271,400 nonfarm jobs from August 2010 to August 2011, an annual growth rate of 2.6 percent compared with 1 percent for the United States. The state's private sector added 284,200 jobs, an annual growth rate of 3.3 percent compared with 1.6 percent for the nation's private sector (Table 4-1). Texas jobs created from August 2010 to August 2011 accounted for 21.1 percent of total nonfarm jobs created in the United States.

Texas' seasonally adjusted unemployment rate increased to 8.5 percent in August 2011 from 8.2 in August 2010. The nation's rate decreased from 9.6 to 9.1 percent (Table 4-1). Table 4-2 shows Texas industries ranked by employment growth rate from August 2010 to August 2011. Table 4-3 shows the relative importance of the state's industries based on number of employees.

All Texas industries except the information industry and the state's government sector had more jobs in August 2011 than in August 2010 (Table 4-2). Higher oil prices continue to help the state's mining and logging industry, ranking first in job creation among the state's industries. This industry posted an annual employment growth rate of 17.4 percent from August 2010 to August 2011 (Table 4-2). The average number of active rotary rigs increased from 708.4 in August 2010 to 875.8 in August 2011 according to Hughes Tool Co.

The state's construction industry ranked second in job creation, adding 31,500 jobs from August 2010 to August 2011, a 5.5 percent rate increase (Table 4-2). Job gains consisted of 7,100 in construction of buildings, 10,600 in heavy and civil engineering construction, and 13,800 in specialty trade contractors.

The state's professional and business services industry gained 54,800 jobs from August 2010 to August 2011, an annual growth rate of 4.3 percent (Table 4-2). Job gains consisted of 45,400 jobs in the state's administrative and support services industry, 9,200 jobs in the professional, scientific, and technical services industry, and 200 in the state's management of companies and enterprises industry.

169

The state's leisure and hospitality industry (arts, entertainment, recreation, accommodations, and food services) gained 36,100 jobs from August 2010 to August 2011, an annual growth rate of 3.5 percent (Table 4-2).

The other services industry (repair and maintenance, personal and laundry services, religious, civic, and professional organizations) gained 11,600 jobs over the year, a 3.2 percent increase (Table 4-2). The state's education and health services industry added 39,500 jobs from August 2010 to August 2011, an annual growth rate of 2.8 percent (Table 4-2). The state's health services industry gained 44,300 jobs while the state's education industry lost 4,800 jobs.

The state's manufacturing industry gained 22,000 jobs from August 2010 to August 2011, an annual growth rate of 2.7 percent (Table 4-2). Job gains comprised 19,400 jobs in the state's durable manufacturing and 2,600 jobs in the state's nondurable manufacturing. Major job gains in the state's durable goods manufacturing industry were in fabricated metal product manufacturing (9,600 jobs), machinery manufacturing (9,800), computer and electronic product manufacturing (1,800), transportation equipment manufacturing (2,100), and primary metal manufacturing (1,000). Major job losses in the state's durable goods manufacturing industry were in nonmetallic mineral product manufacturing (1,600), furniture and related product manufacturing (200), electric equipment, appliance, and component manufacturing (800), and wood product manufacturing (1,000). Major job losses in the state's nondurable manufacturing industry were in printing and related support manufacturing (1,300), petroleum and coal products manufacturing (400), plastic and rubber manufacturing (200), paper manufacturing (500), and chemical manufacturing industry (1,300).

The state's trade industry gained 38,700 jobs from August 2010 to August 2011, a 2.4 percent increase (Table 4-2). Job gains consisted of 13,700 in the wholesale trade and 25,000 jobs in the retail trade industry. Trade is the state's largest industry after government, accounting for 15.9 percent of nonfarm employment (Table 4-3).

The state's transportation, warehousing, and utilities industry gained 9,300 jobs over the year, a 2.2 percent growth rate (Table 4-2).

The state's financial activities (finance, insurance, real estate, rental and leasing services) added 11,400 jobs from August 2010 to August 2011, an annual growth rate of 1.8 percent (Table 4-2). Job gains consisted of 7,700 jobs in the state's real estate, rental and leasing industry and 3,700 in the state's finance and insurance industry.

The state's government sector lost 12,800 jobs from August 2010 to August 2011, an annual decline rate of 0.7 percent (Table 4-2). Government job losses consisted of 800 in state government, 8,700 in the state's federal government, and 3,300 in the state's local government.

The state's information industry (Internet service providers, web search portals, publishing industries and broadcasting and telecommunications) lost 7,300 jobs from August 2010 to August 2011, a 3.8 percent rate decrease (Table 4-2).

Texas Metropolitan Statistical Areas

All Texas metro areas except Abilene and Texarkana had more jobs in August 2011 than in August 2010. Victoria ranked first in job creation, followed by Odessa, Lubbock, McAllen-Edinburg-Mission, and Midland.

The Austin-Round Rock-San Marcos metro area's annual employment growth rate from August 2010 to August 2011 was 2 percent, ranking it 11th (Table 4-4).

The Dallas-Plano-Irving metro area posted an annual employment growth rate of 1.7 percent in August 2011 (Table 4). The metro area ranked 14th in employment growth rate (Table 4-4).

The Fort Worth-Arlington metro area's annual employment growth rate from August 2010 to August 2011 was 1.8 percent, ranking it 12th (Table 4-4).

The Houston-Sugar Land-Baytown metro area posted an annual employment growth rate of 2.6 percent for the period and ranked 9th among Texas metro areas in employment growth rate (Table 4-4).

The San Antonio-New Braunfels metro area had a 1.8 percent annual employment growth rate, ranking it 12th (Table 4-4).

The state's actual unemployment rate in August 2011 was 8.5 percent. Midland had the lowest unemployment rate followed by Amarillo, Odessa, Lubbock, San Angelo, and College Station-Bryan (Table 4-5).

Table 4-1 Texas and U.S. Labor Markets

Nonfarm Employment	August 2011	August 2010	Change Absolute	Percent
Texas	10,593,200	10,321,800	271,400	2.6
United States	130,906,000	129,624,000	1,282,000	1.0
Private Employment	August 2011	August 2010	Absolute	Percent
Texas	8,831,000	8,546,800	284,200	3.3
United States	110,140,000	108,396,000	1,744,000	1.6
	Actual		Seasonally Adjusted	
Unemployment Rate	August 2011	August 2010	August 2011	August 2010
Texas	8.5	8.3	8.5	8.2
United States	9.1	9.5	9.1	9.6

Sources: Texas Workforce Commission and Bureau of Labor Statistics

Table 4-2 Texas Industries Ranked by Employment Growth Rate from August 2010 to August 2011

Rank	Industry	August 2011	August 2010	Change Absolute	Percent
1	Mining and Logging	247,300	210,700	36,600	17.4
2	Construction	605,700	574,200	31,500	5.5
3	Professional & Business Services	1,341,800	1,287,000	54,800	4.3
4	Leisure & Hospitality	1,063,000	1,026,900	36,100	3.5
5	Other Services	374,300	362,700	11,600	3.2
6	Education & Health Services	1,429,100	1,389,600	39,500	2.8
7	Manufacturing	837,400	815,400	22,000	2.7
8	Trade	1,679,500	1,640,800	38,700	2.4
9	Transportation, Warehousing, Utilities	429,900	420,600	9,300	2.2
10	Financial Activities	635,500	624,100	11,400	1.8
11	Government	1,762,200	1,775,000	−12,800	−0.7
12	Information	187,500	194,800	−7,300	−3.8

Sources: Texas Workforce Commission and Real Estate Center at Texas A&M University

Table 4-3 Texas Industries' and Government Shares of Employment

Industry	August 2011	August 1990
Mining and Logging	2.3	2.3
Construction	5.7	5.0
Manufacturing	7.9	13.4
Trade	15.9	17.9
Transportation, Warehousing, Utilities	4.1	4.3
Information	1.8	2.5
Financial Activities	6.0	6.5
Professional and Business Services	12.7	9.2
Education and Health Services	13.5	9.6
Leisure and Hospitality	10.1	8.7
Other Services	3.5	3.8
Government Sector	16.6	16.7

Sources: Texas Workforce Commission and Real Estate Center at Texas A&M University

Table 4-4 Texas Metropolitan Areas Ranked by Employment Growth Rate August 2010 to August 2011

Rank	Metro Area	Percent Growth Rate
1	Victoria	5.9
2	Odessa	3.8
3	Lubbock	3.5
4	McAllen-Edinburg-Mission	3.2
4	Midland	3.2
6	Longview	3.0
6	Corpus Christi	3.0
8	College Station-Bryan Texas	2.7
9	Houston-Sugar Land-Baytown	2.6
10	Tyler	2.3
11	Austin-Round Rock-San Marcos	2.0
12	San Antonio-New Braunfels	1.8
12	Fort Worth-Arlington	1.8
14	Dallas-Plano-Irving	1.7
14	El Paso	1.7
14	Amarillo	1.7
17	Waco	1.5
18	Beaumont-Port Arthur	1.3
19	Sherman-Denison	0.9
20	San Angelo	0.7
21	Killeen-Temple-Fort Hood	0.6
21	Laredo	0.6
23	Wichita Falls	0.3
24	Brownsville-Harlingen	0.2
25	Texarkana	0.0
26	Abilene	–4.7

Source: Texas Workforce Commission

Finance Update

As reported in the Beige Book quoted earlier, financial activity was reported to have weakened some in the middle of 2011. Dallas noted that the improvement in financial conditions had stalled, and Chicago indicated a further tightening of credit conditions, particularly for financial firms. In addition, New York reported noticeably weaker activity in the securities industry. Loan volumes were either flat or down slightly in most Districts. Consumer loan demand moved lower in numerous areas of the country while holding steady in other areas. Many areas noted an increase in mortgage refinancing activity given lower mortgage rates.

Table 4-5 Texas Metropolitan Areas Ranked by Unemployment Rate, August 2011

Rank	Metro Area	Unemployment Rate, Percent
1	Midland	4.8
2	Amarillo	5.9
3	Odessa	6.5
4	Lubbock	6.6
5	San Angelo	6.8
6	College Station-Bryan	6.9
7	Victoria	7.1
8	Abilene	7.2
8	Longview	7.2
10	Austin-Round Rock-San Marcos	7.3
11	Wichita Falls	7.6
12	San Antonio-New Braunfels	7.8
13	Texarkana	8.0
14	Waco	8.1
15	Corpus Christi	8.2
16	Fort Worth-Arlington	8.3
16	Tyler	8.3
18	Dallas-Plano-Irving Texas	8.4
19	Killeen-Temple-Fort Hood	8.5
19	Laredo	8.5
21	Houston-Sugar Land-Baytown	8.6
22	Sherman-Denison	8.8
23	El Paso	10.6
24	Beaumont-Port Arthur	11.5
25	Brownsville-Harlingen	12.5
26	McAllen-Edinburg-Mission	12.6

Source: Texas Workforce Commission

The following discussions focus on major factors that affect real estate financing. Fannie Mae, Freddie Mac, Ginnie Mae, FHA/HUD, and VA have profound influences on mortgage lending, so it is important to examine what each of these entities is doing to enhance the mortgage lending industry.

Fannie Mae—Federal National Mortgage Association

Fannie Mae is working to help the U.S. housing market get back on stable ground. They plan to accomplish this by replenishing the funds that lenders need to make new loans, refinance existing loans, and finance multifamily housing at affordable rates. During the housing crisis, many mortgage investors left the market or scaled back their activity. Fannie Mae remains committed to providing liquidity and stability to the housing market in all economic conditions.

Supporting Homeownership

The following is a quote from the Fannie Mae Web site: "For Americans who are ready to buy a home, we believe they should have access to affordable, sustainable options. We have provided nearly $1.7 trillion in single-family funding since 2009, while establishing stronger and more sustainable lending standards. This has helped more than seven million families buy homes or refinance their loans since the beginning of 2009."

Single-Family

Fannie Mae's single-family acquisitions include several products that address specific housing needs. For instance, during 2010, Fannie Mae purchased:

$831 million in mortgages targeted specifically to lower- income and/or first-time home buyers through banks and state housing finance agencies
$944 million in mortgages secured by manufactured homes
$138 million in single-family mortgages in rural areas

Multifamily Rental Housing

In the wake of the housing crisis, many Americans today have grown more cautious about homeownership. As a leading provider of debt financing to the multifamily mortgage market, Fannie Mae works to ensure that quality affordable housing is available to those who prefer to rent versus buy. Their multifamily activities reach far beyond conventional rental properties. They also focus on cooperative housing, rent-restricted housing targeted to lower-income populations, seniors housing, and more. In conjunction with their multifamily lender and housing partners, they have provided $49 billion in debt financing for the rental housing market since 2009.

Multifamily

In 2010, Fannie Mae's multifamily mortgage business provided more than $1.4 billion in affordable lending, including:

$643 million in mortgages that preserved over 14,000 rent-restricted affordable units
$804 million in financing that supported over 11,000 units of rental housing to targeted populations, including nearly 1,300 units for the homeless and more than 6,700 units for elderly who rely on Medicaid.

Supporting Affordable Housing

Fannie Mae helps provide financing to enable Americans to buy or rent quality affordable housing. From 2010 through June 2011 they supported single-family and multifamily lending that served more than 1,126,000 low-income families, including more than 134,000 very low-income households. Fannie Mae also offers specialized mortgage financing solutions that help increase the supply of affordable owned and rental housing as well as preserve the existing inventory of homes

Economy at a Crossroads—According to Fannie Mae's Economics & Mortgage Market Analysis Group.

Despite recent marginally positive economic trends, the economy is stuck in a slow growth scenario that is expected to continue for a relatively extended period. According to Fannie Mae's (FNMA/OTC) Economics & Mortgage Market Analysis Group, economic growth is expected to be no greater than 2 percent through the end of 2012—a growth rate that makes the economy very vulnerable to any external shock that could trigger a downturn, the most likely of which remains contagion of the Greek sovereign debt crisis to other economies in Europe. External factors coupled with uncertainty surrounding the degree of domestic fiscal austerity, including the scheduled expiration of various tax cuts and unemployment benefits, and the impact of forthcoming regulations remains a factor in determining how fast the economy will grow. In turn, the Group continues to gauge expectations of a recession by the end of next year at close to fifty-fifty.

"In this type of environment, the housing market remains very sluggish and consumers' willingness to dig into their savings to purchase big ticket items is very low," said Fannie Mae Chief Economist Doug Duncan. "There's been a little seasonal cyclical pickup in housing activity recently as spring and summer sales are generally stronger than fall and winter, but leading indicators point to housing sales bouncing near the bottom at least through the end of 2012."

"Home prices are a key factor for any positive movement in the housing market, and the large inventory of distressed homes working their way through the market is putting downward pressure on prices. Now that we are entering a traditionally weak seasonal sales period, we expect home prices to show renewed declines after firming for several months," Duncan stated.

For an audio synopsis of the October 2011 Economic Outlook, listen to the podcast on the Economics & Mortgage Market Analysis site at www.fanniemae.com. Visit the site to read the full October 2011 Economic Outlook, including the Economic Developments Commentary, Economic Forecast, and Housing Forecast. Follow FNMA on Twitter: http://twitter.com/FannieMae

Freddie Mac—Federal Home Loan Mortgage Corporation

Freddie Mac was chartered by Congress in 1970 with a public mission to stabilize the nation's residential mortgage markets and expand opportunities for homeownership and affordable rental housing. Their statutory mission is to provide liquidity, stability, and affordability to the U.S. housing market. They participate in the secondary mortgage market by purchasing mortgage loans and mortgage-related securities for investment and by issuing guaranteed mortgage-related securities, principally those called PCs. The secondary mortgage market consists of institutions engaged in buying and selling mortgages in the form of whole loans (i.e., mortgages that have not been securitized) and mortgage-related securities.

The Current Landscape

Freddie Mac is operating under a conservatorship that began on September 6, 2008, conducting its business under the direction of the Federal Housing Finance Agency (FHFA). They are focused on meeting the urgent liquidity needs of the U.S. residential mortgage market, lowering costs for borrowers, and supporting the recovery of the housing market and U.S. economy. By continuing to provide access to funding for mortgage originators and, indirectly, for mortgage borrowers and through their role in the federal Making Home Affordable program, they are working to meet the needs of the mortgage market by making homeownership and rental housing more affordable.

Helping Families Keep Their Homes

Freddie Mac is both mindful and appreciative of the federal financial support received, and as an institution in conservatorship, they are highly focused on being good stewards of this support. In their efforts to accomplish these objectives they currently offer the following programs:

Fixed Rate Mortgage Plans
15-, 20-, and 30-year Fixed-rate Mortgages
Affordable Merit Rate® Mortgages
Alt 97
A-minus Mortgages
Cash-out Refinance Mortgages
Condominium Unit Mortgages/Streamlined Condo Review
Construction Conversion Mortgages
Financed Permanent Buy-down Mortgages
Investment Property Mortgages
Loans with Secondary Financing
Manufactured Homes
Mortgages for 2- to 4-unit Properties
Mortgages for Newly Constructed Homes
Mortgages with Temporary Subsidy Buy-down Plans
Newly Built Home Mortgages
No Cash-out Refinance Mortgages
Relief Refinance Mortgages SM – Same Servicer
Relief Refinance Mortgages – Open Access
Renovation Mortgages
Rural Housing Service Section 502 Leveraged Seconds
Seller-owned Modified Mortgages
Super Conforming Mortgages
Adjustable-Rate Mortgages
A-minus Mortgages
Cash-out Refinance Mortgage
CMT-indexed ARMs
Cost-of-Funds Indexed (COFI) Rate-Capped ARMs

Financed Permanent Buy-down Mortgages
Home Possible® Mortgages
Investment Property Mortgages
LIBOR-indexed ARMs
Loans with Secondary Financing
Manufactured Homes
Mortgages for 2- to 4-unit Properties
Mortgages with Temporary Subsidy Buy-down Plans
No Cash-out Refinance Mortgages
Relief Refinance Mortgages – Same Servicer
Relief Refinance Mortgages – Open Access
Seller-owned Converted Mortgages
Seller-owned Modified Mortgages
Super Conforming Mortgages
Balloon/Reset Mortgages
Balloon/Reset Mortgages (5- and 7-year)
A-minus Mortgages
Cash-out Refinance Mortgages
Investment Property Mortgages
Loans with Secondary Financing
Mortgages for 2- to 4-unit Properties
Mortgages with Temporary Subsidy Buy-down Plans
No Cash-out Refinance Mortgages
Seller-owned Modified Mortgages
Government-sponsored Offerings
Guaranteed Rural Housing Mortgages
HUD-Guaranteed Section 184 Native American Mortgages
RHS Leveraged Seconds
Veterans Affairs (VA) Mortgages

One of the most important roles that Freddie Mac plays today is to provide continuous liquidity and to keep mortgage funds flowing. With the housing markets and broader economy still recovering, keeping the mortgage markets liquid and stable is critical. Together, Freddie Mac and Fannie Mae provide most of the liquidity to the housing market —purchasing or guaranteeing roughly two-thirds of home loans originated in the first nine months of 2011.

Freddie Mac purchased or guaranteed $259 billion in mortgage loans and mortgage-related securities in the first nine months of 2011. Through this funding, Freddie Mac helped:

1 million families buy a home during one of the most challenging credit markets in years.

Other Benefits

Freddie Mac's role in the housing finance system has additional benefits for homeowners, lenders, and the housing market as a whole:

Lower mortgage rates: Freddie's liquidity contributes to lower mortgage rates for 30-year fixed-rate conforming mortgages relative to the "jumbo" mortgage loans we aren't allowed to buy. Over the last year, millions of borrowers have taken advantage of the lowest mortgage rates in five decades to buy and refinance homes.

The 30-year fixed-rate mortgage: Freddie helps make possible the freely pre-payable 30-year fixed-rate mortgage on a scale that's unique to this country. The pre-payable fixed-rate mortgage is the first choice for many consumers because it protects them from upward swings in interest rates and allows them to refinance whenever they want without penalty. By providing stability, certainty, and flexibility in this way, the pre-payable fixed-rate mortgage is a real economic asset for the nation.

A "backstop bid" for mortgage lenders: Freddie's lender customers know there will always be a buyer for their loans—which gives them the confidence to keep lending in any environment and in turn helps to stabilize the market.

Freddie serves the market in good times and bad: They are an important counter-cyclical influence that stays in the market even when purely private capital has pulled out. This has been proven time and again—particularly during the events of recent years.

Other Resources

http://www.freddiemac.com/pmms/

Ginnie Mae—Government National Mortgage Association

For more than 40 years Ginnie Mae has provided liquidity and stability to the nation's housing system. Through its mortgage-backed securities (MBS) program, the only one of its kind to carry the full faith and credit of the U.S. government, Ginnie Mae serves as the principal financing arm for government loans and ensures that funds can flow into the mortgage market. The strength and dependability of the Ginnie Mae MBS attracts investors from around the globe and allows lenders access to capital, so they can make new mortgage loans that allow for safe and affordable housing for Americans.

Ginnie Mae's simple model and conservative approach enables it to accomplish its mission of supporting the federal government's role in promoting and expanding housing in America. During the past two years alone, the corporation's issuance activity during the housing crisis has circulated nearly $800 billion in liquidity into the U.S. housing mortgage finance market, while generating a profit of more than $1 billion for taxpayers. In July 2010,

Ginnie Mae surpassed $1 trillion in remaining principal balance outstanding for the first time in its history.

The following is a message from President Theodore W. Tozer to The Honorable Shaun Donovan, Secretary, U.S. Department of Housing and Urban Development at the end of 2010:

"In yet another challenging year for the housing finance system, Ginnie Mae continued to provide stability to the capital markets as well as a solid foundation for mortgage finance participants. Ginnie Mae is well positioned to sustain this support based on a number of important program, operational, and risk management enhancements. In meeting the current countercyclical demand for liquidity, Ginnie Mae has served its mission through a disciplined conservative approach that enables it to remain a self-sustaining entity that protects U.S. taxpayer dollars.

The foundation of the Ginnie Mae business model is the simple pass-through security. Ginnie Mae does not actively invest in mortgage-backed securities (MBS) or whole loan portfolios for investment purposes. Therefore, it is not subject to the mark-to-market losses often associated with these assets, nor does it need sophisticated derivatives to hedge interest rate risk. Ginnie Mae MBS offer the full faith and credit guaranty of the U.S. government. This is the means by which it attracts capital from global sources and channels it to finance housing nationwide.

In July 2010, Ginnie Mae reached a new milestone by surpassing $1 trillion in outstanding principal balance for the first time in its history. In Fiscal Year 2010, Ginnie Mae guaranteed $413 billion in securities, which represents the corporation's efforts to finance nearly 1.9 million homes for families across the country. Included in this year's volume are significant multifamily projects, primarily apartment buildings that provide affordable rental homes.

Since the onset of the credit crisis, Ginnie Mae has taken an active role in working with other government agencies involved in stabilizing the credit and housing markets. In particular, Ginnie Mae worked closely with the Federal Deposit Insurance Corporation (FDIC) to manage the orderly transition of Ginnie Mae portfolios of depositories placed in FDIC receivership. Additionally, Ginnie Mae published an All Participants Memorandum clarifying its role with regard to loan modifications and the process by which loans may be repurchased from a Ginnie Mae security. For issuers in good standing or nondefaulted issuers, Ginnie Mae is not involved in either the loss mitigation or loan modification process. Ginnie Mae has accumulated substantial reserves over the years and throughout the housing crisis has remained profitable. That is no small accomplishment given the difficulty of the recovery from the prolonged economic turmoil and the instability of the housing market. There is no government or industry MBS market player that is safer and more secure than Ginnie Mae. The nation's reliance on Ginnie Mae during the current financial crisis highlights our vital role, mission, and continued support of housing in America."

HUD/FHA

Potential Changes to FHA Single-Family Loan Limits beginning October 1, 2011, from Implementation of the Housing and Economic Recovery Act of 2008:

I. Introduction

Barring Congressional action, Federal Housing Administration (FHA) loan limits will revert back to loan limits determined under the Housing and Economic Recovery Act (HERA) for loans insured by FHA on or after October 1, 2011. As a result, FHA loan limits would likely decline in 669 of the 3,334 counties or county equivalents that are eligible for FHA insurance. A complete list of FHA loan limits for the 669 potentially affected counties and county equivalents can be accessed by visiting the FHA website. The remaining 2,665 counties are unlikely to experience a change in loan limits. This Market Analysis Brief discusses the location and impact of the potential loan limit declines as initial guidance to the industry and consumers. Additional information and analysis may be shared in the coming months.

FHA loan limits restrict the size of mortgages that can be insured by the FHA. Prior to 2008, the National Housing Act, as amended in 1998 Mortgagee Letter 1998-28, required that FHA mortgage limits be set at 95 percent of the median house price in that area. However, FHA loan limits could not exceed 87 percent or go lower than 48 percent of the conforming mortgage limit established by the Government Sponsored Enterprises (GSE) in any given area. For the high-cost states and territories (Alaska, Guam, Hawaii, and the Virgin Islands), the National Housing Act allowed mortgage limits to be 150 percent of the national ceiling.

To mitigate the effects from the economic downturn and the sharp reduction of mortgage credit availability from private sources, Congress temporarily increased FHA loan limits in 2008. The Economic Stimulus Act (ESA) enacted in February 2008 stipulated that FHA loan limits be set temporarily at 125 percent of the median house price in each area.

The FHA loan limits could not exceed 175 percent of the 2008 GSE conforming mortgage limit of $417,000; nor be lower than 65 percent of the same 2008 GSE conforming loan limit for a residence of applicable size for any given area. Also, ESA stipulated that mortgage limits for Alaska, Guam, Hawaii, and the Virgin Islands be adjusted up to 150 percent of the national ceiling.

ESA loan limits apply to all FHA mortgages endorsed beginning March 1, 2008 under the following sections of the National Housing Act: Section 203(b) FHA's basic 1-4 family mortgage insurance program, Section 203(h) Mortgages for disaster victims, Section 203(k) Rehabilitation mortgage insurance, Section 203(c) Condominium units, and Section 203(e) Property in declining areas. ESA does not affect mortgage limits on Home Equity Conversion Mortgages (HECM) Section 255. Five months after passing ESA, Congress enacted the HERA in July 2008, which established the Federal Housing

Finance Administration (FHFA) and assigned FHFA the responsibility to establish conforming mortgage limits for the nation and for high-cost areas.

Since 2009, the national conforming mortgage limit has been set at $417,000. Mortgage limits under HERA are set at 115 percent of the county with the highest median house price within that MSA but cannot exceed 150 percent nor be lower than 65 percent of the GSE conforming mortgage limit. Similar to previous regimes, Section 214 of the National Housing Act applies in HERA. This section allows mortgage limits for Alaska, Guam, Hawaii and the Virgin Islands to be 150 percent higher than the ceiling.

Seven months after passing HERA, Congress enacted the American Recovery and Reinvestment Act (ARRA) in February 2009. ARRA stipulated that FHA loan limits for 2009 be set in each area at the higher dollar amount when comparing loan limits established under 2008 ESA requirements and limits calculated for 2009 under HERA. These loan limits have since been extended by Congress each year, most recently through the Continuing Appropriations Act of 2011, and are the limits that are currently in effect for FHA loans. Barring Congressional action FHA loan limits will revert back to loan limits determined under HERA for loans insured by FHA on or after October 1, 2011.

HERA loan limits apply to all FHA mortgages endorsed after January 1, 2009 under the following sections of the National Housing Act: Section 203(b) FHA's basic 1-4 family mortgage insurance program, Section 203(h) Mortgages for disaster victims, Section 203(k) Rehabilitation mortgage insurance, and Section 203(c) Condominium units. HERA also stipulates that Home Equity Conversion Mortgages (HECM) insured on or after November 6, 2008 will face a national mortgage dollar amount limit equal to the national conforming limit. In 2008, the national conforming mortgage limit was $417,000. For high-cost areas the mortgage limits for HECMs were allowed to increase up to 115 percent or $625,500 whichever is less.

ARRA loan limits apply to all FHA mortgages endorsed after January 1, 2010, under the following sections of the National Housing Act: Section 203(b) FHA's basic 1-4 family mortgage insurance program, Section 203(h) Mortgages for disaster victims, Section 203(k) Rehabilitation mortgage insurance, and Section 203(c) Condominium Units.

II. Market Impact of Potential Loan Limit Declines

To determine the number of borrowers and loans that may be affected by the implementation of HERA loan limits, FHA evaluated the number of loans in calendar year 2010 and calendar year 2011 to date that had a principal balance at time of endorsement that is greater than the corresponding HERA limit for that jurisdiction.

For the United States as a whole, approximately 3 percent of loans by count (33,301) and 6 percent by dollar volume ($14.2 billion) endorsed in calendar year 2010 would not have been endorsed had HERA limits been in effect. In calendar year 2011 to date

(January through April), approximately 2 percent of endorsed loans by count (6,673) and 7 percent by dollar volume ($2.8 billion) would have been affected.

It is important to note that streamline refinance loans would not be affected by any reduction in area loan limits. Loans insured prior to October 1, under higher loan limits, would still be eligible for streamline refinancing in the future, even if their outstanding balances remain above the loan limits in effect at that time.

Additionally, loan limits for the FHA reverse mortgage program, HECM, are established under separate legal authority from loan limits for the forward loan program. Loan limits beginning on October 1, 2011, for HECM loans are currently under review and additional guidance will be provided in a subsequent communication to borrowers and the industry.

III. Geographic Location and Impact of Potential Loan Limit Declines

The magnitude of the decline in an area's loan limits does not directly correlate to the number of borrowers who might be affected. For example, 44 municipios in Puerto Rico may experience a $221,000 decline in loan limits, the largest decrease of any county or county equivalent. This corresponds to a potential impact of 4 percent by loan count and 10 percent by dollar volume of FHA loans endorsed in calendar year 2010 in Puerto Rico. Loans originated in Puerto Rico represented less than 1 percent of all FHA loans endorsed in calendar year 2010 by both loan count and dollar volume.

Separate loan limits are set for 2-, 3-, and 4-unit properties. Those limits would also decline in the identified areas. Through ESA, FHA loan limits for multiple unit properties are set at a multiple of the 1-unit limit: 128 percent for 2-unit properties, 155 percent for 3-unit properties, and 192 percent for 4-unit properties. In comparison, Connecticut may experience the greatest percentage impact, 8 percent by loan count and 15 percent by dollar volume of FHA loans endorsed in calendar year 2010, but would experience loan limit declines ranging from as low as $1,100 in Windham County to as high as $133,750 in Fairfield County. Loans originated in Connecticut represented just over 1 percent of all FHA loans endorsed in calendar year 2010 by both loan count and dollar volume.

When analyzed by potential impact on loan counts, nine states may experience declines that are greater than 5 percent: Arizona, California, Colorado, Connecticut, District of Columbia, Massachusetts, Maine, New Hampshire, and Oregon. When evaluated by potential impact on dollar volume, eight states may experience declines that are greater than 10 percent: Arizona, California, Connecticut, District of Columbia, Massachusetts, New Hampshire, Nevada, and Puerto Rico.

The Dodd-Frank Wall Street Reform and Consumer Protection Act

Years without accountability for Wall Street and big banks have produced the worst financial crisis in the United States since the Great Depression. The loss of millions of jobs, failed businesses, a drop in housing prices, and wiped out personal savings have created an environment for financial reform. The Dodd-Frank Wall Street Reform and Consumer Protection Act is one of the most complex pieces of legislation ever written. It represents perhaps the greatest legislative change to financial supervision since the 1930s. President Obama's signature on July 21, 2010, made the Dodd-Frank Wall Street Reform and Consumer Protection Act the law of the land.

The Act now enters the regulatory implementation period of its development. Only a small number of the requirements of the Act are effective right away, and Congress projected the Act to become operational over a period of time. Regulators, over the next 6 to 18 months, will enter into an intense period of rulemaking. Many of the Act's new reforms and implementation issues are currently unclear and are subject to rule-making processes and various statutorily directed studies. The Act, according to the law firm of Davis Polk & Wardwell LLP, requires 243 rulemakings and 67 studies.[1] Mortgage loan originators consequently must keep current with the many rulemaking activities that evolve during the implementation of Dodd-Frank. The Act is a work in progress. Mortgage loan originators must stay informed of the regulations as they are adopted.

Financial institutions are already beginning to address the historic reform that will grow out of the general framework established by the Act. In particular, mortgage loan originators are also beginning to change their behavior in response to these new regulations and to the rules issued by other regulators. Following is a brief summary of Titles IX, X and XIV of the Dodd-Frank Act, which are of particular interest and relevance to the mortgage industry. Residential mortgage loan originators are just beginning to understand the Act's many facets and its full impact.

Title IX Investor Protections and Improvements to the Regulation Of Securities

Subtitle C—Improvements to the Regulation of Credit Rating Agencies

Findings

Congress believes that credit rating agencies, including Nationally Recognized Statistical Rating Organizations ("NRSROs"), are matters of national public interest because of the reliance placed on credit ratings by investors and regulators. Credit rating agencies play a

---

[1] Davis Polk & Wardwell, Summary of the Dodd-Frank Wall Street Reform and Consumer Protection Act, Enacted into www.davispolk.com/.../070910_Financial_**Reform_Summary**.pdf · Retrieved January 19, 2011.

"gatekeeper" role in the debt market similar to that of auditors and securities analysts in the equity market, justifying a similar level of public oversight and accountability. (§ 931)

New Requirements and Oversight of Credit Rating Agencies (§ 931-939H).

New Office (§ 932(p)). Creates an Office of Credit Ratings at the SEC with expertise and its own compliance staff and the authority to fine agencies. The SEC is required to examine Nationally Recognized Statistical Ratings Organizations at least once a year and make key findings public.

Disclosure (§ 931(a)(3)). Requires Nationally Recognized Statistical Ratings Organizations (NRSRO)to disclose their methodologies, their use of third parties for due diligence efforts, and their ratings track record.

Conflicts of Interest (§ 931(5)). Prohibits compliance officers from working on ratings, methodologies, or sales; installs a new requirement for NRSROs to conduct a one-year look-back review when an NRSRO employee goes to work for an obligor or underwriter of a security or money market instrument subject to a rating by that NRSRO; and mandates that a report to the SEC when certain employees of the NRSRO go to work for an entity that the NRSRO has rated in the previous twelve months.

Compliance Officer (§ 932(a)(5)(A)). An NRSRO's designated compliance officer may not perform credit ratings or marketing or sales functions, participate in developing ratings methodologies or models, or participate in establishing compensation levels (except for compliance personnel).

Compliance Report (§ 932(a)(5)(B)(5)). The Act requires an annual report to be submitted to the NRSRO and SEC by the designated compliance officer addressing compliance with securities laws and the NRSRO's policies and procedures. This report must describe material changes to the NRSRO's code of ethics and conflict of interest policies and must include a certification of accuracy and completeness.

Qualifications for Ratings Analysts (§ 936). The SEC must issue rules to ensure persons employed to perform ratings are tested for knowledge of the rating process and meet standards of training, experience and competence necessary to produce accurate ratings.

Subtitle D—Improvements to the Asset-Backed Securitization Process (§ 941)

Credit Risk Retention (§ 941). Requires federal banking agencies and SEC to jointly prescribe rules requiring securitizers to retain economic interest of at least five percent of credit risk of assets they securitize. Regulations must include separate requirements for different asset classes, and may allocate retention amount between originator and securitizer. HUD and Federal Housing Finance Agency must participate in joint rulemaking process for residential mortgage backed securities (MBS) risk retention requirements.

The statute (§ 941(e)) requires an exemption for "qualified residential mortgages," which shall be defined by regulators based on statutory criteria to ensure sound underwriting and lower risk of default such as:

- o Documentation of borrower's financial resources;
- o Debt-to-income standards;

- Mitigating potential for payment shock on adjustable rate mortgages through product features and underwriting standards;

- o Mortgage insurance or other credit enhancements to reduce risk of default; and

- Prohibiting use of loan features that have been demonstrated to exhibit a higher risk of borrower default.

Title X—Bureau Of Consumer Financial Protection

Subtitle A—Structure, Funding, Formation, and Relationship with Other Agencies

Title X establishes the Bureau of Consumer Financial Protection (§ 1001(a)) as an independent entity housed within the Federal Reserve. The new Bureau regulates consumer financial products and services in compliance with the Act (§ 1002(5)).

The Bureau is headed by a director who is appointed by the President, with the advice and consent of the Senate, for a term of five years (§ 1001(c)). The Bureau is subject to financial audit by the Government Accountability Office (GAO) (§ 1017(a)(5)(A)) and must report to Senate Banking Committee and the House Financial Services Committee bi-annually (§ 1016(b)).

The Fed is prohibited from interfering with matters before the Director, directing any employee of the Bureau, modifying the functions and responsibilities of the Bureau or impeding an order of the Bureau (§ 1012(c)(2)). The Bureau is separated into five units (§ 1013(b)):

Research (§ 1013(b)(1))

Community Affairs (§ 1013(b)(2))

Complaint Tracking and Collection (§ 1031(b)(3))

Office of Fair Lending and Equal Opportunity - ensuring equitable access to credit (§ 1013(b)(4))

Office of Financial Literacy - promoting financial literacy among consumers (§ 1013(b)(5))

Within the Bureau, a new Consumer Advisory Board (§ 1014(a)) assists the Bureau and informs it of emerging market trends. This Board is appointed by the Director of the Bureau, with at least six members recommended by regional Fed Presidents (§ 1014(b)). Elizabeth Warren was the first appointee of the President as an adviser to get the Bureau running.

Subtitle B—Jurisdiction

The Bureau has authority to examine and enforce consumer protection regulations for:

"Very Large" Banks, Thrifts, and Credit Unions - The Bureau shall have certain supervisory and enforcement authority regarding insured depository institutions and insured credit unions with more than $10 billion in assets. These financial institutions will be subject to the Bureau's rulemaking, supervisory, and enforcement authority regarding the consumer financial protection laws the Bureau enforces. The Bureau is also charged with reporting to the IRS any tax noncompliance it uncovers (§1025).

"Other" Banks, Thrifts, and Credit Unions - Smaller insured depository institutions and insured credit unions, with $10 billion or less in assets, will be subject to the Bureau's rulemaking authority, but existing banking agencies continue to have supervisory and enforcement authority, except that the Bureau will have the authority to:

- require reports from such entities;
- refer suspected violations law to other agencies;
- report tax noncompliance; and include its examiners in the reviews conducted by other agencies (§1026).

Covered Persons and Nondepository Covered Persons - A "covered person" is any person that engages in offering or providing a consumer financial product or service, and any affiliate of such person that acts as a service provider to that person. (§§ 1002(6), 1024) (see "Definition of Financial Product or Service" and "Definition of Consumer Financial Product or Service" below).

The Bureau shall generally have supervisory and enforcement authority over a nondepository covered person that (§ 1024(a)(1)):

- offers or provides origination, brokerage, or servicing of loans secured by real estate for use by consumers primarily for personal, family, or household purposes, or loan modification or foreclosure relief services in connection with such loans (§1024(a)(1)(A)),
- is a larger participant [in the] market for other consumer financial products or services, as defined by the rule (§ 1024(a)(1)(B)),
- that the Bureau reasonably determines, by order after notice and an opportunity to respond, is engaged in conduct that poses risks to consumers regarding the offering or provision of consumer financial products or services (§ 1024(a)(1)(C)),

- offers or provides a consumer private education loans under Truth in Lending Act §140, 15 U.S.C. § 1650 (§ 1024(a)(1)(D)), or
- offers or provides a consumer a payday loan. (§1024(a)) (§ 1024(a)(1)(E))

The Act provides the Bureau with significant authorities and responsibilities including:

- Providing timely/understandable information, protecting against unfair, deceptive, and abusive practices and enforcement (§ 1021(b)(1));
- Collecting, investigating, and responding to consumer complaints (§ 1021(c)(2));
- Conducting financial education programs out of special office of financial literacy (Office of Financial Education) (§ 1013(d));
- Researching, monitoring, and publishing information relevant to functioning of consumer financial products and services markets to identify risks to consumers (§ 1021(c)(3));
- Operating two special offices, one for military personnel (Office of Service Member Affairs) (§ 1013(e) and one for older Americans (Office of Financial Protection for Older Americans) (§ 1013(g));

Exercising authorities including Issuing rules, orders, and guidance implementing Federal consumer financial protection laws (§ 1021(c)(5)).

Subtitle C—Areas of Substantive Authority

Enumerated Consumer Protection Laws (§1002(12))

The Bureau will become responsible for writing rules, implementing, and enforcing the following federal laws:

- Alternative Mortgage Transaction Parity Act of 1982 (12 U.S.C. §3801 et seq.);
- Consumer Leasing Act of 1976 (15 U.S.C. §1667 et seq.);
- Electronic Fund Transfer Act, except for §920 (15 U.S.C. §1693 et seq.), except with respect to §920 of that Act;
- Equal Credit Opportunity Act (15 U.S.C. §1691 et seq.);
- Fair Credit Billing Act (15U.S.C. §1666 et seq.);
- Fair Credit Reporting Act (15 U.S.C. §1681 et seq.), except with respect to §§615(e) and 628 of that Act (15 U.S.C. §§1681m(e), 1681(w);
- Home Owners Protection Act of 1998 (12 U.S.C. §4901 et seq.);
- Fair Debt Collection Practices Act (15 U.S.C. §1692 et seq.);
- FDIA §43(b)-(f) (12 U.S.C. §1831t(c)–(f));
- Gramm-Leach-Bliley Act (§§502 through 509) (15 U.S.C. §§6802– 6809) except for §505 as it applies to §501(b);
- Home Mortgage Disclosure Act of 1975 (12 U.S.C. §2801 et seq.);
- Home Ownership and Equity Protection Act of 1994 (15 U.S.C. §1601 note);
- Real Estate Settlement Procedures Act of 1974 (12 U.S.C. §2601 et seq.);
- S.A.F.E. Mortgage Licensing Act of 2008 (12 U.S.C. §5101 et seq.);
- Truth in Lending Act (15 U.S.C. §1601 et seq.);

- Truth in Savings Act (12 U.S.C. §4301 et seq.);
- Omnibus Appropriations Act §626, 2009 (Public Law 111–8), §1002 (12, 14); and
- Interstate Land Sales Full Disclosure Act (15 U.S.C. §1701).

Combined Mortgage Loan Disclosure

The Bureau of Consumer Financial Protection ("Bureau") must propose a single integrated model disclosure that combines the disclosures required by the federal Truth-in-Lending Act ("TILA") with the good faith estimate, the Department of Housing and Urban Development ("HUD") special information booklet, and the HUD-1 or HUD-1A settlement statement required by the federal Real Estate Settlement Procedures Act of 1974 ("RESPA"). The Bureau must propose the model disclosure within one year after the designated transfer date unless the Bureau determines that any proposal issued by the Board of Governors of the Federal Reserve System ("Board") and HUD carries out the same purpose (§ 1032(f)).

Subtitle H—New Government Studies and Reports

Amendments to the Home Mortgage Disclosure Act

Title X significantly amends requirements for data to be submitted under HMDA to include:

- Age of applicants (§ 1094(3)(A)(i));
- Total points and fees (§ 1094(5)(A));
- Difference between the APR and a benchmark rate determined by the Bureau (§ 1094(5)(B));
- The actual or proposed term in months of the mortgage loan (§ 1094(6)(D),
- Value of the real property securing the loan (§ 1094(6)(A));
- Length of any introductory rate period (§ 1094(6)(B));
- The presence of contractual terms or proposed contractual terms that would allow payments other than fully amortizing payments during any portion of the loan term (§ 1094(6)(C));
- The channel through which the application was received, such as retail, broker or other (§ 1094(6)(E));
- The Secure and Fair Enforcement for Mortgage Licensing Act of 2008 ("SAFE Act") unique identifier for the loan originator (§ 1094(6)(F));
- A universal loan identifier (§ 1094(6)(G));
- The parcel number of the property to be pledged (§ 1094(6)(H));
- The credit score of the applicants (§ 1094(6)(I));
- Such other information as the Bureau may require (§ 1094(6)(J)).

Study and Report on Credit Scores

The Bureau shall conduct a study on the nature, range, and size of variations between the credit scores sold to creditors and those sold to consumers by consumer reporting agencies that compile and maintain files on consumers on a nationwide basis (as defined in section 603(p) of the Fair Credit Reporting Act 15 U.S.C.1681a(p)) and whether such variations disadvantage consumers (§ 1078(a)).

The Bureau shall submit a report to Congress on the results of the study conducted under subsection (a) not later than 1 year after the date of enactment of this Act (§ 1078(b)).

Title XIV—Mortgage Reform and Anti-Predatory Lending Act

Subtitle A—Residential Mortgage Loan Origination Standards

Prohibition on Steering Incentives

Prohibits mortgage originator from receiving from any person, or any person from paying mortgage originator, directly or indirectly, compensation that varies based on terms of loan (other than amount of principal) (§ 1403(c)(1)).

A mortgage loan originator may not receive from any person other than the consumer (and no person other than the consumer, who knows or has reason to know that a consumer has directly compensated or will directly compensate a mortgage originator may pay a mortgage originator) any origination fee or charge except bona fide third party charges not retained by the creditor, mortgage originator, or an affiliate of the creditor or mortgage originator (§ 1403(c)(2)(A)).

This prohibition is intended to make illegal yield spread premiums or other similar compensation based on terms including rate that would cause originator to "steer" borrower to particular mortgage products.

Exception

A mortgage originator may receive from a person other than the consumer an origination fee or charge, and a person other than the consumer may pay a mortgage originator an origination fee or charge (§ 1403(c)(2)(B)), if:

- The mortgage originator does not receive any compensation directly from the consumer (§ 1403(c)(2)(B)(i)) and
- The consumer does not make an upfront payment of discount points, origination points, or fees, however denominated (other than bona fide third party charges not retained by the mortgage originator, creditor, or an affiliate of the creditor or originator), except that the Board may, by rule, waive or provide exemptions to this clause if the Board determines that such waiver or exemption is in the interest of consumers and in the public interest (§ 1403(c)(2)(B)(ii)).

Regulations

The Federal Reserve Board shall prescribe regulations prohibiting mortgage originators from:

- Steering any consumer to loan that (§ 1403(c)(3)(A)):
- consumer lacks reasonable ability to repay (§ 1403(c)(3)(A)(i)) or
- has predatory characteristics or effects such as equity stripping, excessive fees, or abusive terms (§ 1403(c)(3)(A)(ii));
- Steering any consumer from a "qualified mortgage to not qualified mortgage when consumer qualifies for qualified mortgage (§ 1403 (c)(3)(B);
- Abusive or unfair lending practices that promote disparities among consumers of equal creditworthiness but of different race, ethnicity, gender, or age (§ 1403(c)(3)(C));
- Mischaracterizing credit history of consumer or residential loans available to consumer (§ 1403(c)(3)(D)(i));
- Mischaracterizing or inducing mischaracterization of appraised value of property securing extension of credit (§ 1403(c)(3)(D)(ii)).

If unable to suggest, offer, or recommend to consumer a loan that is not more expensive than the loan for which consumer qualifies, discouraging consumer from seeking mortgage from another originator (§ 1403(c)(3)(D)(iii)).

Rules of Construction

No provision of this subsection shall be construed as:

- Permitting any yield spread premium or other similar compensation that would, for any residential mortgage loan, permit the total amount of direct and indirect compensation from all sources permitted to a mortgage originator to vary based on the terms of the loan (other than the amount of the principal) (§ 1403(c)(4)(A));
- Limiting or affecting the amount of compensation received by a creditor upon the sale of a consummated loan to a subsequent purchaser (§ 1403(c)(4)(B));
- Restricting a consumer's ability to finance, at the option of the consumer, including through principal or rate, any origination fees or costs permitted, under this subsection, or the mortgage originator's right to receive such fees or costs (including compensation) from any person, so long as such fees or cost do not vary based on the terms of the loan (other than the amount of the principal) or the consumer's decision about whether to finance such fees or costs (§ 1403(c)(4)(C)); or
- Prohibiting incentive payments to a mortgage originator based on the number of residential mortgage loans originated within a specified period of time (§ 1403(c)(4)(D)).

Maximum Liability

Establishes mortgage originators are liable for violations of new Section 129B of Truth in Lending Act including duty of care and prohibition against steering incentives. The maximum liability for violation of the steering prohibitions shall not exceed the greater of actual damages or three times the total direct and indirect compensation or gain accruing to the mortgage originator in connection with the subject mortgage loan, plus costs (§ 1404).

Subtitle B – Minimum Standards for Mortgages

Ability to Repay

Lenders are prohibited from making residential mortgages without having made a reasonable, good faith determination based on verified and documented information that, at the time of consummation, the consumer has a reasonable ability to repay the loan according to its terms, along with all applicable taxes, insurance, and assessments (§ 1411(a)(1)).

Safe Harbor and Rebuttable Presumption of Ability to Repay for Qualified Mortgage

Any creditor with respect to a residential mortgage, and any assignee of such loan, may presume that a loan has met the "ability to repay" requirements if it is a "qualified mortgage."

Qualified Mortgage Definition

The term "qualified mortgage" means any residential mortgage loan:

- There is no negative amortization (§ 1412(b)(2)(A)(i)(I)).
- Repayment of principal cannot be deferred by the consumer (note an exception with respect to certain balloon loans) (§ 1412(b)(2)(A)(i)(II)).
- There is no balloon payment (note an exception with respect to certain balloon loans). For this purpose, a "balloon payment" is one where a scheduled payment is more than twice as large as the average of earlier scheduled payments (§1412(b)(2)(A)(ii)).
- The income and financial resources relied upon to qualify the consumer are verified and documented (§ 1412(b)(2)(A)(iii)).
- If the loan has a fixed rate, the loan must be underwritten on the basis of a fully amortizing loan that takes all applicable taxes, insurance, and assessments into consideration (§ 1412(b)(2)(A)(iv)).
- If the loan has an adjustable rate, the loan must be underwritten on the basis of the maximum rate that is permitted under the loan during the first five years and a payment schedule that fully amortizes the loan over the scheduled term, taking into consideration all applicable taxes, insurance, and assessments (§ 1412(b)(2)(A)(v)).

- The loan must comply with any Board regulations or guidelines relating to debt-to-income ratios or residual income (§ 1412(b)(2)(A)(vi)).

The total points and fees for the loan may not exceed 3 percent of the total loan amount. With regard to the application of the points and fees test, note the following (§ 1412(b)(2)(A)(vii)):

For which loan term does not exceed 30 years, except as such term may be extended by the Board such as in high-cost areas (§ 1412(b)(2)(A)(viii)) and

In case of a reverse mortgage (except for purposes of subsection 9 (a) of section 129C, to extent that such mortgages are exempt altogether from those requirements), a reverse mortgage which meets standards for a qualified mortgage, as set by the Board (§ 1412(b)(2)(A)(ix)).

3 Percent Limit – Calculation of Points and Fees – Qualified Mortgages

Certain bona fide discount points paid by the consumer may be excluded in computing the points and fees, as follows:

- up to and including 2 bona fide discount points may be excluded if the interest rate to be discounted does not exceed by more than 1 percent the Average Prime Offer Rate (§ 1412(b)(2)(C)(i)(I));
- up to and including 1 bona fide discount point may be excluded if the interest rate to be discounted does not exceed by more than 2 percent the Average Prime Offer Rate (§ 1412(b)(2)(C)(i)(II));
- the bona fide discount points must be "knowingly" paid by the consumer for the purpose of obtaining the interest rate reduction, and must actually result in a bona fide reduction of the interest rate (§ 1412(b)(2)(C)(iii)); and
- the interest rate reduction must be "reasonably consistent with established industry norms and practices for secondary market transactions (§ 1412(b)(2)(C)(iv)).

The "Average Prime Offer Rate" is defined to mean the average prime offer rate for a comparable transaction as of the date on which the interest rate is set, as published by the Board (§ 1412(b)(2)(B)).

Defense to Foreclosure

A creditor may assert a defense to a judicial or nonjudicial foreclosure initiated by a creditor, assignee, or holder of a mortgage based on:

- a violation of the prohibition on steering incentives (§ 1413(k)(1)) or
- the ability to repay standards, without regard to the time limit on a private action for damages under the Truth in Lending Act. (§ 1413(k)(1))

Claim can lead to actual damages, statutory damages, and enhanced damages including return of finance charges (§ 1413(k)(2)(A)).

Prohibition on Certain Prepayment Penalties

A residential mortgage loan that is not a qualified mortgage may not require a prepayment penalty for paying all or part of the principal after the loan is consummated (§ 1414(c)(A)), nor may an adjustable rate mortgage or certain other mortgages based on the degree to which the APR for the mortgage exceeds the average prime offer rate for a comparable transaction (§ 1414(c)(B)).

A qualified mortgage may not impose prepayment penalties in excess of:

- During the first year, 3 percent of the outstanding balance (§ 1414(c)(3)(A));
- During the second year, 2 percent of the outstanding balance (§ 1414(c)(3)(B)),
- During the third year; 1 percent of the outstanding balance (§ 1414(c)(3)(C)).
- After the end of the 3-year period beginning on the date the loan is consummated, no prepayment penalty may be imposed on a qualified mortgage (§ 1414(c)(3)(D)).

A creditor may not offer a consumer a residential mortgage allowing for prepayment penalties without also offering a mortgage with no prepayment penalty term. (§1414(c)(3)(D)).

Subtitle D—Office of Housing Counseling

"Expand and Preserve Homeownership Through Counseling Act."

Office of Housing Counseling Office

The Office of Housing Counseling (the "Office") is established as part of HUD (§ 1442(g)).

The Director is appointed by the Secretary of HUD, and heads the Office. The Director shall perform wide range of activities including research, public outreach, and policy development related to counseling as well as establishment, coordination and administration of HUD counseling related programs and other activities authorized under Act (§ 1442(g)(3)(A)(i)(ii)).

Advisory Committee

The Secretary of HUD shall appoint a nonpaid advisory committee to assist the Director, of not more than 12 members, each to serve a term of 3 years (§1442(g)(4)).

Study of Defaults and Foreclosures

The Secretary of HUD shall conduct an extensive study of the root causes of default and foreclosure of home loans, and examine the role of escrow accounts in helping prime and nonprime borrowers to avoid defaults and foreclosures, and the role of computer registries of mortgages, including those used to trade mortgage loans. The Secretary shall submit a preliminary report to Congress within 12 months of the Date of Enactment, and a final report within 24 months (§ 1446).

Mortgage Information Booklet

The Director of the Bureau of Consumer Financial Protection ('Director') shall prepare, at least once every 5 years, a booklet to help consumers applying for federally related mortgage loans to understand the nature and costs of real estate settlement services. The Director shall prepare the booklet in various languages and cultural styles, as the Director determines to be appropriate, so that the booklet is understandable and accessible to homebuyers of different ethnic and cultural backgrounds. The Director shall distribute such booklets to all lenders that make federally related mortgage loans (§ 1450(a)).

Each booklet shall detail in plain and understandable language the following information (§ 1450(b)):

A description and explanation of the nature and purpose of the costs incident to a real estate settlement or a federally related mortgage loan. The description and explanation shall provide general information about the mortgage process as well as specific information concerning, at a minimum (§ 1450(b)(1)):

- balloon payments (§ 1450(b)(1)(A));
- prepayment penalties (§ 1450(b)(1)(B));
- the advantages of prepayment (§ 1450(b)(1)(C)); and
- the trade-off between closing costs and the interest rate over the life of the loan (§ 1450(b)(1)(D)).

An explanation and sample of the uniform settlement statement (§ 1450(b)(2)).

A list and explanation of lending practices, including those prohibited by the Truth in Lending Act or other applicable Federal law, and of other unfair practices and unreasonable or unnecessary charges to be avoided by the prospective buyer with respect to a real estate settlement (§ 1450(b)(3)).

A list and explanation of questions a consumer obtaining a federally related mortgage loan should ask regarding the loan, including whether the consumer will have the ability to repay the loan, whether the consumer sufficiently shopped for the loan, whether the loan terms include prepayment penalties or balloon payments, and whether the loan will benefit the borrower (§ 1450(b)(4)).

An explanation of the right of rescission as to certain transactions provided by sections 125 and 129 of the Truth in Lending Act (§ 1540(b)(5)).

A brief explanation of the nature of a variable rate mortgage and a reference to the booklet entitled 'Consumer Handbook on Adjustable Rate Mortgages', published by the Director, or to any suitable substitute of such booklet that the Director may subsequently adopt pursuant to such section (§ 1450(b)(6)).

A brief explanation of the nature of a home equity line of credit and a reference to the pamphlet required to be provided under section 127A of the Truth in Lending Act (§ 1450(b)(7)).

Information about homeownership counseling services made available pursuant to section 106(a)(4) of the Housing and Urban Development Act of 1968 (12 U.S.C. 1701x(a)(4)), a recommendation that the consumer use such services, and notification that a list of certified providers of homeownership counseling in the area, and their contact information, is available (§ 1450(b)(8)).

An explanation of the nature and purpose of escrow accounts when used in connection with loans secured by residential real estate and the requirements under section 10 of his Act regarding such accounts (§ 1450(b)(9)).

An explanation of the choices available to buyers of residential real estate in selecting persons to provide necessary services incidental to a real estate settlement (§ 1450(b)(10)).

An explanation of a consumer's responsibilities, liabilities, and obligations in a mortgage transaction (§ 1450(b)(11)).

An explanation of the nature and purpose of real estate appraisals, including the difference between an appraisal and a home inspection (§ 1450(b)912)).

Notice that the Office of Housing of the Department of Housing and Urban Development has made publicly available a brochure regarding loan fraud and a World Wide Web address and toll-free telephone number for obtaining the brochure (§ 1450(b)(13)).

Home Inspection Counseling

Subtitle D requires HUD to take necessary actions to inform potential homebuyers of the availability and importance of obtaining an independent home inspection (§ 1451(a)(1)). Such actions shall include:

- Publication of the HUD/FHA form HUD 92564–CN entitled "For Your Protection: Get a Home Inspection", in both English and Spanish languages (§ 1451(a)(1)(A));
- Publication of the HUD/FHA booklet entitled "For Your Protection: Get a Home Inspection", in both English and Spanish languages (§ 1451(a)(1)(B));
- Development and publication of a HUD booklet entitled "For Your Protection—Get a Home Inspection" that does not reference FHA-insured homes, in both English and Spanish languages (1451(a)(1)(C)); and

- Publication of the HUD document entitled "Ten Important Questions To Ask Your Home Inspector", in both English and Spanish languages (§ 1451(a)(1)(D)).

Warnings to Homeowners of Foreclosure Rescue Scams

Subtitle D provides funds to the Neighborhood Reinvestment Corporation to provide notice, to delinquent borrowers, of the dangers of fraudulent activities associated with foreclosure.

Subtitle F—Appraisal Activities

Property Appraisal Requirements

Subtitle F requires physical appraisal for higher-risk mortgage by certified appraiser that performs work in accordance with Uniform Standards of Professional Appraisal Practice (USPAP) (§ 1471(a)(1)). Also, requires second appraisal if property was previously purchased within 180 days of subject purchase (§ 1471(a)(2)(A)). The cost of any second appraisal required may not be charged to the applicant (§ 1471(a)(2)(B)). Subtitle F also requires creditors to provide to consumer one copy of each appraisal conducted for higher-risk mortgage, at least three days prior to closing, without charge (§ 1471(c)).

Higher-risk mortgage means any first lien residential mortgage loan with an APR that exceeds average prime offered rate (APOR) for a comparable transaction by 1.5 percentage points or more for mortgage loan having original principal obligation that does not exceed conforming loan limit (§ 1471(f)(2)(A)), 2.5 percentage points or more for jumbo loan having a principal obligation that is greater than conforming loan limit (§ 1471(f)(2)(B)), and 3.5 percentage points or more for subordinate lien residential mortgage loan (§ 1471(f)(2)(C)).

Appraisal Independence Requirements

It shall be unlawful

- To compensate, coerce, bribe, or otherwise attempt to influence an appraiser for the purpose of causing the results to be based on any factor other than the appraiser's independent judgment (§ 1472(b)(1));
- To mischaracterize the results of an appraisal (§ 1472(b)(2));
- To encourage a targeted value in order to facilitate a mortgage (§ 1472(b)(3)) and
- To withhold or threaten to withhold payment for properly provided appraisal services (§ 1472(b)(4)).

Exceptions

The independence requirements shall not be construed as prohibiting a mortgage lender, mortgage broker, mortgage banker, real estate broker, appraisal management company, employee of an appraisal management company, consumer, or any other person with an interest in a real estate transaction from asking an appraiser to undertake 1 or more of the following (§ 1472(c)):

- Consider additional, appropriate property information, including the consideration of additional comparable properties to make or support an appraisal (§ 1472(c)(1)).
- Provide further detail, substantiation, or explanation for the appraiser's value conclusion (§ 1472(c)(2)).
- Correct errors in the appraisal report (§ 1472(c)(3)).

Penalties

Subtitle E establishes civil penalties of up to $10,000 per day for first violations (§ 1472(k)(1)) and $20,000 for subsequent violations (§ 1472(k)(2)).

Mortgage Disclosure Improvement Act

The Federal Reserve Board revised Regulation Z (Truth in Lending) to incorporate amendments found in the Mortgage Disclosure Improvement Act ("MDIA"). Compliance with the following MDIA amendments was mandatory on July 30, 2009:

Early disclosure requirements apply to all loans that are subject to RESPA and are secured by a consumer's dwelling. Therefore, early disclosure requirements now also cover refinances and home equity loans. Early disclosures are required to be delivered or placed in the mail not later than three business days after the lender receives the loan application, and at least seven days before consummation of the transaction.

If the annual percentage rate provided in the early disclosures is no longer accurate (based on the applicable tolerances), corrected disclosures of all changed terms must be provided no later than three business days before the date of consummation. Final disclosures must be provided at the time of consummation of the transaction.

The TIL must be re-issued continually until within tolerance (125 percent). The three-day waiting period is based on the date the TIL is received. The three-day waiting begins each time a TIL is issued until within tolerance. Early TILA disclosures and corrected TILA disclosures must contain the following notice:

"You are not required to complete this agreement merely because you have received these disclosures or signed a loan application."

A consumer may waive the provision for the seven business day and three business day waiting periods if the consumer has a bona fide personal financial emergency that must be addressed before the end of the waiting period.

Lenders are prohibited from imposing a fee on the consumer in connection with a loan before the consumer receives the required early disclosures, except for a credit report.

A business day is defined two ways:

1. General Business Days – days in which a mortgage loan originator's office is open to the public for carrying out their normal business functions.
   a. Mailing of Disclosures
2. Rescission Business Days – All calendar day except Sunday and legal holidays.
   a. Seven-Day waiting period prior to consummating the mortgage loan
   b. Three-Day waiting period prior to consummating the mortgage loan

Truth In Lending Act—TILA

Changes to TILA Advertising Requirements

The Federal Reserve Board, in 2008, approved a final rule, which amends Regulation Z (Truth in Lending), for home mortgage loans to better protect consumers and facilitate responsible lending. The new rules went into effect on October 1, 2009, and are intended to protect consumers from unfair or deceptive acts. The rule establishes additional advertising standards. The advertising rules now require additional information about rates, monthly payments, and other loan features. The final rule bans seven deceptive or misleading advertising practices.

The Board implemented rules to prohibit the following seven deceptive or misleading practices in advertisements for closed-end mortgage loans:

1. Advertisements that state "fixed" rates or payments for loans whose rates or payments can vary without adequately disclosing that the interest rate or payment amounts are "fixed" only for a limited period of time, rather than for the full term of the loan;
2. Advertisements that compare an actual or hypothetical rate or payment obligation to the rates or payments that would apply if the consumer obtains the advertised product unless the advertisement states the rates or payments that will apply over the full term of the loan;
3. Advertisements that characterize the products offered as "government loan programs," "government-supported loans," or otherwise endorsed or sponsored by a federal or state government entity even though the advertised products are not government-supported or -sponsored loans;
4. Advertisements, such as solicitation letters, that display the name of the consumer's current mortgage lender, unless the advertisement also prominently discloses that the advertisement is from a mortgage lender not affiliated with the consumer's current lender;
5. Advertisements that make claims of debt elimination if the product advertised would merely replace one debt obligation with another;
6. Advertisements that create a false impression that the mortgage broker or lender is a "counselor" for the consumer; and

7. Foreign-language advertisements in which certain information, such as a low introductory "teaser" rate, is provided in a foreign language while required disclosures are provided only in English.

Higher Priced Mortgage Loans

On July 30, 2008, the Board of Governors of the Federal Reserve Board (the "Board") published a final rule amending Regulation Z. The main purposes of the rule are to protect consumers from unfair, deceptive, abusive lending practices and to provide consumers with timely disclosures.

Definition of Higher-Priced Mortgages Loans

The category of "higher-priced mortgage loans" is defined by Regulation Z as consumer credit transactions secured by consumers' principal dwellings that for first-lien loans are 1.5 percentage points above the average prime offer rate issued by Freddie Mac, and for second-lien loans are 3.5 percentage points over the same index. The Board will obtain or, as applicable, derive average prime offer rates for a wide variety of types of transactions from the Primary Mortgage Market Survey® (PMMS) conducted by Freddie Mac, and publish these rates on at least a weekly basis.[2]

Prohibitions for Higher-Priced Mortgage Loans

Higher-priced mortgage loans are subject to the following restrictions under Regulation Z:

Prohibit a lender from making a loan without regard to borrowers' ability to repay the loan from income and assets other than the home's value. A lender complies, in part, by assessing repayment ability based on the highest scheduled payment in the first seven years of the loan.

Require lenders to verify the income and assets they rely upon to determine repayment ability. Lenders cannot rely on income or assets not verified. Lenders must verify the assets or income it relied on in approving the higher-priced mortgage loan using reasonably reliable third-party documentation.

Prepayment penalties are prohibited entirely on any higher-priced mortgage loan (and Section 32 Loans) where the payment can change during the first four years following consummation. Prepayment penalties are limited to two years on any higher-priced mortgage loan where the payment is fixed for at least the first four years following consummation.

Require creditors to establish escrow accounts for property taxes and homeowner's insurance for all first-lien mortgage loans. Creditors may offer a borrower the opportunity to cancel the escrow after the first 12 months following consummation.

---

[2] Mortgage Bankers Association, "Summary of Federal Reserve's Final Home Ownership and Equity Protection Act (HOEPA) Rule Amending Regulation Z (Truth in Lending)", July 2008.
http://www.mortgagebankers.org/files/Advocacy/2008/HOEPARuleSummaryJuly18.pdf

Corescore

Mortgage companies and other lenders soon will know a lot more about would-be borrowers than what is contained in credit reports. With the new CoreScore, lenders can look into credit behavior that potential borrowers often try to hide. This new credit report lets lenders dig deeper. For example, it will report evictions, tardy child support payments, tax liens, rent-to-own contracts, and missing homeowner association dues.

Information such as this is an important indicator of whether a borrower is likely to make the house payments, but it is often missing from the traditional credit report, which is typically just a view of a borrower's credit record over the years. Traditional credit reports can be as much as 90 days behind in logging late payments or other transgressions. However, CoreScore data are updated daily, giving lenders a practically up-to-the-minute picture, at least in credit reporting terms, of someone's credit conduct.

One example of an advantage of CoreScore's benefits would be exposing a situation where a borrower attempts to borrow money from a high cost payday lender so they have enough cash to cover the closing costs on a new home mortgage. CoreScore is going to know and so will the lender. Another example would be where a potential borrower failed to make court ordered alimony payments. The prospective borrower conveniently forgot to tell the mortgage company when they applied for a loan. However, CoreScore will know.

CoreScore became available in November 2011. It is provided by CoreLogic, a provider of consumer, financial, and property information and analyses. The Santa Ana, California based company claims the largest and most comprehensive collection of real estate, rental, and public record information in the country. Launched from The First American Corporation, CoreLogic combines the leading providers of financial, property, and consumer information, analytics and business intelligence into one dynamic new company. CoreLogic contends that their clients can gain the perspective necessary to identify, understand, and take decisive action.

It starts with their proprietary information and expertise, billions of pieces of public and private sector data, plus the sharp minds of more than 6,500 dedicated employees. Leveraging these resources, CoreLogic is able to deliver world-class products, services, and solutions to fit their client's specific business needs. CoreLogic's resources include:

Dynamic Information - They maintain the most comprehensive business database in the United States with continuously updated data from more than 3.5 billion public documents, over 500 million transactions, and 70 million mortgage applications, just to name a few.

Advanced Analytics - Their proprietary analytics algorithms and predictive modeling capabilities enable them to analyze information on multiple levels, helping clients make informed decisions that yield extraordinary competitive results.

Unique Insights - Working with over 40,000 clients in the public and private sectors has given CoreLogic a vast storehouse of real-world experience to draw upon in helping clients create effective solutions that target their unique needs.

Comprehensive Data - CoreLogic's data library combines property and mortgage information; legal, parcel, and geospatial data; motor vehicle records; criminal background records; national coverage eviction information; payday lending records; credit information; and tax records. Their platforms support a constantly changing regulatory environment.

Expert Analysis - As a leading provider of predictive decision analytics products and services, they have made significant investments in human capital, their PhD-level economists, computer scientists, geospatial scientists, technologists, behaviorists, and networking experts continually update and refine the science behind their algorithms.

Innovative Services - CoreLogic is building distinctive business services around information analysis. Their expanding portfolio gives clients new tools for approaching critical decisions with enhanced transparency on multidimensional business problems.

Collaborative Consulting - They partner closely with clients to create custom solutions, tailored to their individual needs. Their professional services and information and analytics products fit each client's unique workflow to produce the insights needed to stay ahead.

The company adds public record transactions and new trade lines in an average of 23 days. Obviously the new credit report is aimed at helping lenders make more informed credit decisions by uncovering behavior applicants would rather lenders not know about. A preliminary analysis of more than 250,000 credit reports on mortgage applicants found one in thirteen was missing such information as other properties owned and whether they were encumbered, as well as inquiries and charge-offs from online lenders.

But CoreScore works the other way too, by identifying hidden performance that could improve a consumer's credit profile. Again, that's because the report covers information that does not show up in traditional credit reports. Landlords, for example, usually do not report whether a tenant has paid their rent on time every month for the last three years. Likewise, cell phone companies typically do not report timely payments. Sometimes loans from credit unions do not show up either. Such timely payments can be just as telling as untimely ones.

Consequently, CoreScore can be a great help for lenders, especially among "thin file" borrowers who have little or no conventional credit histories. CoreScore is not intended to replace traditional credit reports but rather to complement them. The data it supplies cover property ownership, mortgage obligations, legal filings, tax payment status, rental applications, evictions, inquiries and charge-offs from nontraditional lenders, child support obligations and consumer-specific bankruptcies, liens and judgments.

Although these things generally are not available from traditional credit-reporting agencies, one or more can significantly impact your credit score, sometimes by raising that all important number, but more likely by lowering it. Testing found one in three applications in which material information was missing, nearly one in four had open but unreported mortgage obligations and one in five had open but unreported trade lines that were either derogatory or delinquent. These items could have impacted the borrower's debt-to-income ratio had their lenders known about them.

FICO, formerly Fair Issac Corp., is the company behind the credit scoring systems used by the three main repositories – TransUnion, Experian, and Equifax. It also built the industry standard FICO 8 Mortgage Score. No mention of FICO would be complete without reporting the company has inked deals with four of the country's top mortgage servicers to identify borrowers at the greatest risk of walking away from their loans, even though they can afford to continue making their payments.

FICO won't say how it does it, only that "the technology exists" to find borrowers before they walk away and reverse the trend toward what's known as "strategic defaults." Those who walk out on their loans are typically "underwater," meaning their homes are worth less than what borrowers owe on them.

Reverse Mortgages

The Department of Housing and Urban Development (HUD) through the FHA created one of the first reverse mortgage programs in America. HECM is a FHA's reverse mortgage program which enables consumers to withdraw some of the equity in their home. The HECM is a safe plan that can give older Americans greater financial security. Many seniors use it to supplement social security, meet unexpected medical expenses, and finance home improvements.

A reverse mortgage is a mortgage loan that allows older homeowners to convert a portion of their home equity into cash without selling the home. All borrowers must be at least 62 years of age or older to qualify. The borrower must live in the home at least six months of each year and must either own the home outright or have a low mortgage balance that can be paid off at the closing with the proceeds from the reverse mortgage. The loan amount depends on the borrower's age, the equity in the home, and the market value of the home.

Reverse mortgages aren't like traditional and home equity loans that require the borrower to make regular payments until the debt is settled. A reverse mortgage gives the senior borrower money from the equity in their home in the form of a loan that isn't paid back until the borrower no longer uses the home as a principal residence. For example, if the borrower sells the home, does not live in the home for an extended period of time, or dies.

Reverse mortgages have been available to homeowners for several years and are becoming a popular way for seniors to tap into their home equity. In particular, the generation known as the Baby Boomers (born between 1946–1964), have begun to retire in large numbers and have increasingly looked at a reverse mortgage as a means to provide funds necessary to maintain their standard of living. With rising costs of living and a dwindling budget to accommodate the elderly and disabled, lenders will see increased usage of the reverse mortgage in the future. As aging Baby Boomers enter retirement age and beyond, opportunities to serve this segment of the population have risen. People are living longer and as a result have needed to make adjustments to their finances as they have exceeded their savings.

Many baby boomers are considering taking out a reverse mortgage as they begin to turn 65 and consider what they want to get out of their lives as senior citizens. Boomers are known for being active and involved in the community, travel, family, and more. A reverse mortgage may be able to provide them with the funds that they need in order to continue to live life to the fullest.

FHA Home Equity Conversion Mortgage

Legislative History

The Housing and Community Development Act of 1987 established a Federal mortgage insurance program, Section 255 of the National Housing Act, to insure home equity conversion mortgages. The program is administered by the Department of Housing and Urban Development (HUD). Pursuant to the 1987 Act, the Department was authorized to insure 2,500 HECMs. These 2,500 reservations of insurance authority were allocated among the 10 HUD Regions in proportion to each Region's share of the nation's elderly homeowners. The Regional Offices of Housing then distributed the reservations among lender applicants using a random drawing method. The Omnibus Budget Reconciliation Act of 1990 (P.L. 101-508, 11/5/90) increased the Department's insurance authority to 25,000 mortgages; accordingly, the reservation system was terminated, and all FHA approved lenders are now eligible to participate in the HECM program.

Purpose of the Program

The FHA's HECM is designed to allow older homeowners convert equity into cash without selling their homes. HECM loans are made by banks, credit unions, and other typical mortgage lenders. The program insures what are commonly referred to as reverse mortgages and is intended to enable elderly homeowners to convert the equity in their homes to monthly streams of income and/or lines of credit.

Characteristics of the Mortgage

There is no income qualifying or credit scoring to get a reverse mortgage. All you need is ownership and sufficient equity.

Unlike a traditional "forward" residential mortgage, which is repaid in periodic payments, a reverse mortgage is repaid in one payment, after the death of the borrower, or when the borrower no longer occupies the property as a principal residence.

The HECM has neither a fixed maturity date nor a fixed mortgage amount.

If the lender is unable to make payments to the borrower, HUD will assume responsibility for making payments until the lender is able to resume. If the lender will not be able to make any future payments, HUD will make payments for the remainder of the mortgage.

The mortgage proceeds paid by the lender and/or HUD will be secured by first and second mortgages on the property. These liens will allow the lender and HUD to recover any losses up to the value of the property when the borrower dies, or no longer maintains the property as a principal residence

Nonrecourse

A consumer safeguard for the senior and heirs is that there is no personal liability with reverse mortgages. Plainly stated, the borrower(s) or borrower's heirs or estate will never owe more on the property than the value of the property. When the proceeds from a sale of the property are insufficient to pay off the loan balance then the lender will take the loss difference or most likely use the MIP to file a claim for the insurance to make us the difference. The object is for the heirs or estate never to have to come out of pocket for the property.

Maximum Claim Amount: The lesser of Appraised Value, Sales Price, or national Mortgage Limit

Maximum Loan Amount: The national FHA loan limit for HECM is $625,500

Mortgage Insurance Premium (MIP)

The borrower will be charged mortgage insurance premiums to reduce the risk of loss in the event that the outstanding balance, including accrued interest, MIP, and fees, exceeds the value of the property at the time that the mortgage is due and payable.

Types of mortgage insurance premiums

HECM Standard

- A one-time nonrefundable initial MIP equal to 2% of the maximum claim amount will be assessed at closing. It may be paid in cash by the borrower or may be added to the outstanding balance. It must be remitted by the lender to HUD before the loan can be endorsed.
  - o No Refunds
- A monthly MIP equal to one-twelfth (1/12) of the annual rate of 1.25% of the outstanding balance will be assessed throughout the life of the loan. The MIP will be added to the outstanding balance and remitted to HUD monthly by the lender.

HECM Saver

- A one-time nonrefundable initial MIP equal to 1% of the maximum claim amount will be assessed at closing. It may be paid in cash by the borrower or may be added to the outstanding balance. It must be remitted by the lender to HUD before the loan can be endorsed.
  - o No Refunds

- A monthly MIP equal to one-twelfth (1/12) of the annual rate of 1.25% of the outstanding balance will be assessed throughout the life of the loan. The MIP will be added to the outstanding balance and remitted to HUD monthly by the lender.

HECM Saver vs HECM Standard

FHA designed the HECM Saver as an alternative to the HECM Standard for the purpose of lowering loan closing costs to the consumer. The program is designed for those who would like to borrow a smaller amount than what is currently available with the HECM Standard. The amount of equity a borrower can access with the HECM Saver is less than with the HECM Standard. For example, if a 74 year old homeowner using the HECM Standard initially accesses 68.9% of their home equity, then the same homeowner using the HECM Saver can only draws out 52.9%.[3] Since the initial loan balance is significantly smaller, using the HECM Saver can leave the borrower with more equity in their home. Alternately, the HECM Standard can allow the borrower to access more equity.

Transaction Types

- Traditional (Equity in current property used to obtain a new HECM loan)
- Purchase (HECM loan proceeds used to purchase a principal residence)
- Refinance (Refinance of an existing HECM loan with a new HECM loan)

Borrower Eligibility

- 62 years of age or older
- Property used as collateral must be primary residence
- No delinquencies on any federal debt, CAIVRS, LDP/GSA]
- Completion of HECM Counseling

Eligible Properties

- Single Family Residences
- HUD-approved Condominiums
- Manufactured home built after June 15, 1976
- Planned Unit Developments or PUDs
- 1-4 units, borrower(s) must occupy one of the units
- existing mortgages must be paid off at closing because the HECM has to be in first position home must meet FHA minimum property standards (HECM may be used to make required repairs/updates if the cost is within program limits)

Ineligible Properties

- Cooperatives

---

[3] *Making the Pro's and Con's of Reverse Mortgages Clear,* *http://reversemortgageguides.org*, Retrieved May 31, 2011.

- 5 or more units
- Non principle residences
- Any property currently in bankruptcy

Property Requirements

- The borrower(s) are still required to pay the annual taxes and property insurance. FHA also requires the property be maintained to the minimum property standards.

Eligible Payment Plans

- Loan proceeds in a home equity conversion mortgage (HECM) or "reverse mortgage" are paid out according to a payment plan selected by the borrower. The borrower has the choice of receiving the mortgage proceeds through five basic payment plans:
- **Tenure** - Under this payment plan, the borrower will receive equal monthly payments from the lender for as long as the borrower lives and continues to occupy the property as a principal residence.
- **Term** - Under this payment plan, the borrower will receive equal monthly payments from the lender for a fixed period of months selected by the borrower.
- **Line of Credit** - Under this payment plan, the borrower will receive the mortgage proceeds in unscheduled payments or in installments, at times and in amounts of the borrower's choosing, until the line of credit is exhausted.
- **Modified Tenure** - Under this payment plan, the borrower may combine a line of credit with monthly payments for life, or for as long as the borrower continues to live in the home as a principal residence. In exchange for reduced monthly payments, the borrower will set aside a specified amount of money for a line of credit, on which he or she can draw until the line of credit is exhausted.
- **Modified Term** - Under this payment plan, the borrower may combine a line of credit with monthly payments for a fixed period of months selected by the borrower. In exchange for reduced monthly payments, the borrower will set aside a specified amount of money for a line of credit, on which he or she can draw until the line of credit is exhausted.

The borrower will be able to change the type of payment plan throughout the life of the loan.

The borrower may change the term of payments, may receive an unscheduled payment, may suspend payments, may establish or terminate a line of credit, or may receive the entire net principal limit (i.e., the difference between the current principal limit and the outstanding balance) in a lump sum payment.

With all payment plans, the lender must be able to make lump sum payments up to the net principal limit at the borrower's request.

Repayment

- Due and payable when:
  - Death of last surviving mortgagor
  - The loan is repaid when the last borrower permanently moves out of the home in excess of 12 months
  - Conveyance of title and property (property no longer serves as principal residence)
  - Failure to pay property charges (Insurance and Taxes)
  - Failure to perform mortgage obligations
- Payment of claim when outstanding balance exceeds the appraised value (subject to claim amount)

Fees (100% Financing of all Fees)

- Origination Fee: $2,500 Floor - $6,000 Ceiling
- Third Party Fees
  - Appraisal
  - Title search and Insurance
  - Surveys, Inspection
  - Recording Fees
  - Mortgage Taxes, Credit Checks, etc.
- Servicing Fees
  - Fixed - $30.00
  - Annual ARM - $30.00
  - Monthly ARM - $35.00

Independent Counseling – Mandatory

One of the most important of all the consumer safeguards set up by HUD and AARP is the mandatory counseling session with a counselor approved by the U. S. Department of Housing and Urban Development (HUD). These counselors are not employees of the lenders the government but third party agencies that schedule sessions by phone and face to face. There is normally a fee involved, but in some cases, can be deferred. No lender or originator can provide guidance on the selection or scheduling of counseling appointments. These counselors are there to make sure the senior(s) understand the entire reverse mortgage process, are aware of financial implications for them and their heirs and estate, and have all their questions and concerns answered.

Social Security, Medicare, Medicaid

- Funds received from a reverse mortgage do not generally affect Social Security, pension payments, or Medicare. Please check with your financial advisors concerning Medicad and Supplemental Security Income.

Minimum Disclosure Requirements

- Regulation Z Truth in Lending (TIL)
- Good Faith Estimate (GFE)
- Total Annual Loan Cost (TALC)
- Anti-Churning (refinance transactions only)

Additional Resources

Federal Reserve Board

20th Street & Constitution Ave., N.W.
Washington, DC 20551
Washington, DC 20410
www.federalreserve.gov

Nation Center of Home Equity Conversion

360 N. Robert Street, #403
St. Paul, MN 55101
www.reverse.org

Urban Development (HUD)

451 7th Street SW
Washington, DC 20410
202-708-1112
www.hud.gov

Federal Trade Commission

Customer Response Center
600 Pennsylvania Avenue, NW
Washington, DC 20580
877-382-4357
www.ftc.gov

Updated VA Funding Fee

Purpose

President signed H.R. 2646, Veterans Health Facilities Act Capital Improvement Act of 2011 on October 5, 2011. The bill includes a provision resulting in funding fees reverting to the same rates that existed prior to October 1, 2011, for loans closed October 6, 2011, through and including November 17, 2011. Rates for loans closed prior to enactment of H.R. 2646 and for loans closed on or after November 18, 2011, are discussed below.

1. Fee Changes

a. Loans closed October 1 through October 5, 2011: Funding fees for loans closed on these dates will be those cited in the Department of Veterans Affairs (VA) Circular 2611-12, dated September 8, 2011.

b. Loans closed October 6 through and including November 17, 2011: Funding fees for loans closed during this period, will be the same rates in effect prior to October 1, 2011. The fees can be found in the VA Lender's Handbook, Chapter 8, Topic 8.

c. Loans closed on or after November 18, 2011: Funding fees for loans closed on or after November 18, 2011, will be reduced as shown on the attached Exhibit A.

d. Funding fees for other loans: Funding fees for Interest Rate Reduction Refinancing Loans (IRRRLs) and Assumptions will not change. They will remain at .50 percent.

2. Possibility of Future Funding Fee Changes

VA believes it is likely that Congress will pass other legislation in the coming weeks that will make additional changes to the funding fee structure. Should this occur, VA will immediately publish a notice on www.benefits.va.gov/homeloans and the VA Funding Fee Payment System (FFPS), and release another Circular once any such bill becomes law. Lenders should closely monitor VA FFPS for information on funding fee changes.

3. Waiver of the Difference in Funding Fees

For cases in which lenders have closed loans based on lower funding fees cited in the Good Faith Estimate (GFE) rather than the higher fees provided in HR 2646, the Secretary, under existing authority, will waive the difference in the fees. Specifically, VA will waive the right to collect the difference in fees (between the lower October 1 rates and the higher H.R. 2646 rates) for loans for which a GFE was prepared prior to October 6 based on the lower fees and that was closed after the enactment of H.R. 2646. Instructions on how to process and obtain that waiver are forthcoming, via a Circular.

More information about HUD and its programs is available on the Internet at www.hud.gov and espanol.hud.gov.

Longer Term Loans

The 30-year fixed-rate mortgage is the most common home loan in America today. But 5 percent of all new mortgages in the United States (25 percent in California) are now being written for a term of 40 years. And the 40-year mortgage, first introduced in 2005, has since been surpassed in length by the 50-year mortgage. Known as "hybrid ARMs," the 40- and 50-year loans being offered in the mortgage market begin as fixed-rate mortgages but must be converted to an annual adjustable-rate mortgage (ARM) after a specified term. Most 50-year loans require conversion to an annual ARM either five or ten years after origination.

Lenders typically charge an increasing interest rate premium as a loan's amortization period is extended. No hard and fast rule exists to determine the amount of this premium. A reasonable premium is assumed to be 25 basis points or a quarter percent increase in the interest rate for each increment the loan's amortization period is extended. These premiums theoretically compensate for the lender's money being tied up for a longer time, assuming the borrower keeps the loan through final maturity. In reality, most mortgages are refinanced or paid off when the home is sold well before full amortization occurs.

In an article in the October 2006 edition of Tierra Grande, Harold Hunt compares numerous attributes of 15-year, 30-year, 40-year, and 50-year loans. Table 4-8a, Table 4-8b, Table 4-8c, and Table 4-8d shows some of the results of Dr. Hunt's comparisons. Using the popular 30-year loan as the benchmark, monthly payments, outstanding loan balances, and the amount of interest and principal paid on 15-year, 40-year, and 50-year loans were compared. The borrower's goal was assumed to be lower monthly payments rather than purchasing a larger home with the same payment amount. In this way, any offsetting effects from increased property taxes and insurance were eliminated. Monthly payments were calculated to include principal and interest only. Fixed-rate mortgages that fully amortize in 15, 40, and 50 years were compared with the 30-year note.

Dr. Hunt's comparisons assume a $100,000 loan at a 6.25 percent interest rate for 30 years, 6 percent for 15 years, 6.5 percent for 40 years, and 6.75 percent for 50 years. Based on the assumptions given, the 15-year mortgage is significantly less affordable than the 30-year, requiring a payment higher by $228.14 per month. The 40-year note's monthly payment is $30.26 less than the 30-year. Extending the amortization period from 40 to 50 years results in a mere $2.83 in further payment reduction. Clearly, the payment difference between a 40-year and a 50-year loan is negligible in this case.

Table 4-8a Total Interest Paid and Percent Difference from 30-Year Loan

Loan

Terms	After 3 Years	Diff.	After 5 Years	Diff.	After 7 Years	Diff.	After 10 Years	Diff.
30-year @ 6.25%	$18,419.47		$30,280.27		$41,753.84		$58,123.78	
15-year @ 6%	$16,852.86	−8.50%	$26,640.51	−12.00%	$35,097.44	−15.90%	$44,911.79	−22.70%
40-year @ 6.5%	$19,340.97	5.00%	$32,032.59	5.80%	$44,536.00	36.70%	$62,880.42	8.20%
50-year @ 6.75%	$20,173.91	9.50%	$33,525.97	10.70%	$46,787.10	12.10%	$66,479.14	14.40%

Source: Real Estate Center, Texas A&M University

Table 4-8b Total Principal Paid and Percent Difference from 30-Year Loan

Loan

Terms	After 3 Years	Diff.	After 5 Years	Diff.	After 7 Years	Diff.	After 10 Years	Diff.
30-year @ 6.25%	$3,746.35		$6,662.76		$9,966.41		$15,762.29	
15-year @ 6%	$13,525.99	261.00%	$23,990.90	260.10%	$35,786.53	259.10%	$56,351.03	257.50%
40-year @ 6.5%	$1,735.48	−53.70%	$3,094.82	−53.60%	$4,642.34	−53.40%	$7,374.40	−53.20%
50-year @ 6.75%	$800.61	−78.60%	$1,431.58	−78.50%	$2,153.47	−78.40%	$3,435.95	−78.20%

Source: Real Estate Center, Texas A&M University

Table 4-8c Outstanding Balances

Loan

Terms	After 3 Years	Diff.	After 5 Years	Diff.	After 7 Years	Diff.	After 10 Years	Diff.
30-year @ 6.25%	$96,253.65		$93,337.24		$90,033.59		$84,237.71	
15-year @ 6%	$86,474.01	10.20%	$76,009.10	18.60%	$64,213.47	28.70%	$43,648.97	48.20%
40-year @ 6.5%	$98,264.52	−2.10%	$96,905.18	−3.80%	$95,357.66	−5.90%	$92,625.60	−10.00%
50-year @ 6.75%	$99,199.39	−3.10%	$98,568.42	−5.60%	$97,846.53	−8.70%	$96,564.05	−14.60%

Source: Real Estate Center, Texas A&M University

Table 4-8d Monthly Payment and Difference from 30-Year Loan

Loan

Terms	After 3 Years	Diff.
30-year @ 6.25%	$615.72	15-year
@ 6%	$843.86	$228.14
40-year @ 6.5%	$585.46	($30.26)
50-year @ 6.75%	$582.63	($33.09)

Source: Real Estate Center, Texas A&M University

The difference in interest paid on the four loans is noteworthy but not vastly different. Borrowers choosing the 15-year loan would pay 8.5 to 22.7 percent less total interest than a 30-year borrower depending on the holding period. The 50-year borrower would pay 9.5 to 14.4 percent more. There is a considerable difference in principal reduction. A 15-year borrower pays in 257 to 261 percent more principal than a 30-year borrower, depending on the holding period. A 50-year borrower pays about 78 percent less principal than a 30-year borrower during the first ten years.

The result is a wide variation in outstanding balance. The most extreme results occur when loans are held for ten years. The 15-year loan's balance is paid down to $43,648. By contrast, the 30-year and 50-year outstanding balances decline to only $84,237 and $96,564, respectively.

Continued Payment Of Private Mortgage Insurance

A controversial subject that has caused a number of lawsuits over the years is whether a borrower is obligated to pay the premium for private mortgage insurance (PMI) after the loan amount declines to less than 80 percent of the property value. The 80 percent Loan To Value Ratio (LTVR) figure is used because lenders do not require PMI coverage if the borrower puts 20 percent or more down.

Since 1997, state law requires lenders to provide borrowers with an annual notice that they may cancel PMI whenever the loan balance is 80 percent or less of current fair market value of the home. Whether an appraisal of the property is required to determine "current fair market value" is not addressed.

A later federal law [the Homeowners Protection Act (HPA)] passed in July 1998, effective July 29, 1999, covering PMI applies only to loans originated on or after July 29, 1999. It requires lenders to notify consumers of their right to cancel private mortgage insurance when the equity in their homes reaches 20 percent. Lenders may ask for an appraisal to prove property value. The law exempts FHA and VA loans. It does not preempt any state statutes in effect before January 2, 1998.

Furthermore, the bill provides for automatic cancellation at three different levels, depending on the size and risk of the mortgage. These levels are as follows:

1. For most conventional loans, automatic cancellation is made when the loan reaches 78 percent of the original value of the property.
2. For high-risk mortgages that do not exceed conforming loan limits, automatic cancellation is triggered at the midterm of the loan.
3. For high-risk mortgages that are above the conforming loan limit, trigger for cancellation is 77 percent LTVR.

Because cancellation of PMI at 80 percent LTVR could require an appraisal, many homeowners wait until the 78 percent of original value triggers automatic cancellation.

Secure and Fair Enforcement for Mortgage Licensing Act Of 2008

This Act, also known as SAFE Mortgage Licensing Act of 2008, encourages the states to establish a Nationwide Mortgage Licensing System and Registry for the residential mortgage industry through the Conference of State Bank Supervisors (CSBS) and the American Association of Residential Mortgage Regulators (AARMR). The Act sets forth procedures, requirements (including education and testing), and standards for mandatory registration and state licensing of mortgage loan originators.

The federal banking agencies jointly, through the Federal Financial Institutions Examination Council, are required to develop and maintain a system for registering depository institution employees as registered loan originators with the Registry. In addition, the Act directs the Secretary of HUD to establish and maintain a backup licensing and registration system for loan originators operating in a state that either (1) does not, after a certain period of time, have a licensing and registering system for loan originators that meets the requirements of this Act or (2) does not participate in the Registry.

Under the Act, the HUD secretary is required to establish and maintain a backup licensing, supervisory, and tracking system for loan originators if the Registry fails to meet the requirements and purposes of this Act. It also declares that this Act does not preempt state law that provides greater protection to consumers than is provided under this Act. It directs the HUD secretary to study and report to Congress on the root causes of default and foreclosure of home loans.

Background

The CSBS and the AARMR began working in a joint effort to accomplish a system that meets *all* the needs of the states in 2003. The State Regulatory Registry (SRR) and LLC comprised of CSBS and AARMR members, was established on September 29, 2006, to develop and operate a nationwide system for state regulators in the financial services industry.

The National Mortgage Licensing System Registery (NMLSR) was launched in January 2008 with seven states initially participating. Implementation was on time and within the budget. As of August 2009, there were 31 states/territories on the National Mortgage Licensing System Registry (NMLSR) with a total of 49 expected to join by July 2010. The Texas SML signed a letter of intent to participate in the NMLSR on September 24, 2008. As of September, 2009, the Texas SML was developing a strategy for transitioning to the NMLSR.

Each licensee would be responsible for entering information into the system and for keeping his or her record updated; SML staff will not have authority to modify a licensee's record, though they can modify status changes and explanatory notes. The SML licensing specialists will work from information in the NMLSR as work-flow items to review and approve or disapprove a license. Current fees will go from a two-year base to a one-year base.

NMLSR Processing Fees

NMLSR Processing Fees (not including SML fees), initial set-up fees for new and existing licensees:

- **MU1**—Establishing a sole proprietorship, company, limited partnership, or limited liability company record: **$100**
- **MU2**—Establishing a control person or direct/indirect owner record: **No charge**
- **MU3**—Establishing a branch address: **$20**
- **MU4**—Establishing a mortgage loan originator record: **$30**

Texas Department of Savings and Mortgage Lending—Implementation of the SAFE Mortgage Licensing Act and Transition to the NMLSR

With regard to the licensing requirements of mortgage brokers and loan officers, Texas has one of the most restrictive licensing frameworks in the nation. The current Texas licensing requirements are:

- Pass a prelicensing exam (58 percent overall pass rate);
- Meet prelicensing education (0-90 hours) and ongoing continuing education (0-15 hours) requirements biennially;
- Prove net worth of $25K or $50K bond (MBs only);
- Not have been convicted of a crime determined to be of concern to THE commissioner in order to conduct lending activity;
- Satisfy the commissioner as to moral character, including integrity, honesty and trustworthiness; and
- Not be under any violation of court or state order.

If approved, a two-year license will be issued.

Approval Requirements of Financial Service Companies and Agents (MBL Act) require that the registered financial services company:

- Be a depository institution exempt from §156.202(1)(A) or (B) and chartered by the OTS or OCC, or be a subsidiary or affiliate of the institution;
- Post $1M surety bond;
- Provide an acceptable business plan; and
- Pay yearly registration fee NTE $350,000.

Registered Financial Services Agent Requirements

- Conduct loan origination exclusively for the registered FSC
- Pass criminal history and professional license investigation

Registration Requirements of Mortgage Bankers (MBR Act):

- Unconditional direct endorsement underwriting authority granted by HUD;
- Seller or servicer of Fannie Mae or Freddie Mac; or
- Issuer for Ginnie Mae;
- Yearly registration;
- Loan originator—employees are not required to have individual registration or licensing to conduct business; and
- No authority beyond consumer complaints.

Requirements for Registration:

- Undergo criminal background checks
- Furnish details regarding personal history and experience
- Complete application with NMLSR
- Renew registration annually

Additional Licensing Requirements:

- Attend prelicensing education of at least 20 hours
- Pass prelicensing examination

Time frame for states to implement Act requirements:

- Within one year (NLT July 30, 2009);
- If a state does not implement SAFE, HUD would take responsibility for the state to meet SAFE requirements;
- Project implementation time frames for Texas will be discussed later; and
- HUD may grant limited extensions if reasonable efforts are being made to meet requirements—Texas SML will not require an extension.

Background Checks—Criminal History:

- The licensee has not been convicted of, or pled guilty or nolo contendere to, a felony in a domestic, foreign, or military court:

During the seven-year period preceding the date of the application or at any time if the felony involved fraud, dishonesty, a breach of trust, or money laundering.

- Every mortgage loan originator will need to provide a new set of fingerprints for an FBI criminal history report regardless of any past fingerprinting.

Background Checks—Personal History and Experience:

- Look-back period is ten years for criminal, regulatory, civil, and financial actions or disclosures

Exceptions include certain felonies, license revocations, lifetime bans

- Credit report obtained from a consumer reporting agency

States may determine how information will be used in licensing decisions

- Administrative, civil, or criminal findings by any governmental jurisdiction

Has not had a residential loan originator license revoked by any government jurisdiction

Approval of Providers, Courses, and Instructors Transfers to NMLSR

- NMLSR has developed provider/course/instructor requirements
- NMLSR will approve or disapprove, and collect fees for processing

No exemptions for other occupational licenses

Minimum 20 hours must include:

- Three hours of federal mortgage related laws and regulations
- Three hours of ethics, including fraud, consumer protection, and fair lending issues
- Two hours related to lending standards for the nontraditional mortgage product marketplace

Current licensees must meet these requirements.

- With submitted education certificates the commissioner has discretion to certify licensee meets the requirements—NMLSR charges $15.
- Licensees not eligible for certification must complete 20 hours of NMLS-approved prelicensure education before filing for a license with NMLSR.

The SAFE prelicensing test consists of a national component and state-specific components. The tests were developed by NMLSR's education and testing provider, FINRA, and PearsonVUE with state regulators and industry subject matter experts participating in the development. The national test requires a passing score of 75 percent out of 90 questions; the cost for the test is $92 and the test is now available.

The state test requires a passing score of 75 percent out of 45-55 scored questions; the state test cost is $69. The Texas NMLS state test will be available in May 2010. The current MB/LO Examination is acceptable until the Texas SML State Component is available. The commissioner can certify that a licensee meets the state component with prior passage of the Texas test. There is a $5 fee for this certification. There are limits on how many times one can take the exam during a specific time. There is an expiration date if licensee fails to maintain valid license for five years or longer. Current licensees must meet this requirement.

Requirements for Continued Licensure:

- Must comply with financial requirement by paying into the Mortgage Industry Recovery Fund
- Each residential mortgage company shall submit to the NMLSR—reports of condition referred to as Mortgage Call Reports
- Replaces current annual report submission required of mortgage brokers
- Probably available for the collection of calendar year 2010 production information

Requirements for Renewing a License:

All licenses expire annually on December 31 of each year. To renew the license, the licensee

1. Must continue to meet minimum license standards
2. Continue education of eight hours that must include:
   - Three hours of federal mortgage related laws and regulations
   - Two hours of ethics, including fraud, consumer protection, and fair lending issues
   - Two hours on lending standards for the nontraditional mortgage product
   - Licensee may receive credit for the course only in the year in which course is taken
   - May not take the same course multiple times and receive credit in current or subsequent years
   - No exemptions for holding certain other Texas occupational licenses

Investing IRA Dollars in Real Estate

Most people are familiar with the concept of their retirement funds being invested in stocks, bonds, mutual funds, and other traditional investment vehicles. However, more people are looking to diversify their portfolio by investing their retirement funds in real estate. This can be done if the investor has a self-directed IRA.

A self-directed IRA is like other IRAs in every respect, except that it allows account holders to direct their own investments. Account holders can buy and sell investment real estate while deferring the tax consequences. Real estate practitioners can earn commissions by helping investor clients buy and sell real estate through self-directed IRAs.

The IRS allows retirement money to be used to buy real estate in any form: houses, raw land, office buildings, shopping centers, and so on. The holder can buy property and develop it or hold the property to sell at a profit at a later date. Once the property is sold, all proceeds go back into the IRA, which continues to grow tax-deferred.

Properties can be bought, sold, or used as rental property in a self-directed IRA. For rentals, all maintenance and improvement costs, taxes, insurance, and property management fees must be paid from the IRA, and all rental income must go back into the IRA. However, that rental income becomes part of the IRA balance and may be used to buy other types of investments, such as mutual funds, stocks, bonds, CDs, and T-bills.

Custodians typically require that any real estate purchased through an IRA be bought outright with no financing. In addition, the property must be used for investment purposes only and cannot be used personally while maintained in the IRA.

Public Improvement Districts (PIDs)

When a subdivision, a community, or an area with common interests has a need for capital improvements, such as street improvements, water, sewer, drainage, bulkheads, sand socks, or any other infrastructure, finding the funds may be problematic. Public Improvement Districts may be excellent vehicles for obtaining the necessary funds.

Many communities along the Gulf Coast feel that sand socks may be very beneficial in protecting their property against hurricanes and tidal surges. Sand socks are large "socks" that are filled with sand and augment the benefits of the sand dunes. In areas where the sand 294 socks have been installed, they have suffered less property damage than those areas without sand socks. For example, the GeoTubes in front of Pirates Beach in Galveston provided more protection against Hurricane Claudette (2003) and Rita (2005) than the traditional sand dunes provided other properties. That is the good news, but the bad news is that the sand socks can be very costly. The cost in some areas could be as much as $10,000 per lot. As a one-time assessment this could be prohibitive; however, if it could be paid for over 10 or 20 years, it would be far less burdensome to the property owners.

To attempt to borrow the money for the improvements would be virtually impossible because there is no entity that the lender could look to for repayment. An excellent vehicle for financing such improvements is a PID or Public Improvement District. If over 50 percent of the property owners in a discrete area petition the city for formation of a PID, the city will schedule a public hearing. Based on the results of the hearing, the city will decide whether to create the PID.

The city then issues bonds to raise money to pay for the improvements. The property owners create the management plan and establish budgets for the district but the city is in total control of the district. Once the public infrastructure is constructed, each property owner in the area will be charged or assessed its pro-rata share of the total cost. When the construction is completely finished, the city will hold a public hearing to present the cost of the project and the assessment amount for each lot. Once the public hearing is held, the city will levy the assessment. Once the assessment is levied, it does not change. The assessment lies between a tax lien and a first mortgage lien in priority.

How Can This Assessment Be Paid?

A PID assessment can be paid in one of three ways:

1. The property owner can pay it in full at closing and will not have any further annual payments; or

2. The property owner can pay the assessment in annual installments over 5, 10, or 20 years (the payout can be over any period of time established by the PID); or

3. The property owner may incorporate the PID amount into their home loan, there by including the PID amount into their monthly mortgage payment. This assumes the PID is a residential area and that the homeowner has worked this out with their mortgage company. PIDs can also be used to finance the infrastructure of a new development.

How Is This Assessment Different from a MUD (Municipal Utility District) Tax?

A MUD has the authority to construct public infrastructures, sell bonds to finance the infrastructure, and to levy a tax each year in an amount sufficient to pay the bonds and operate the MUD. Each year the tax rate can vary and as the MUD builds out, additional bonds can be sold, extending the life of the MUD. In a PID, each property that benefits from the improvements pays only for its particular pro-rata share of the cost. Once the PID assessment is paid, the property owner does not pay a portion of expansions in the subdivision. PID bonds can be sold, but only the revenue from existing PID assessments can be used to repay the bonds.

Management Districts

The property owners in a large commercial area of a major Texas city desired to make some extensive capital improvements to enhance the attractiveness of the area. The improvements consisted of massive arches across the major streets in the area, attention-getting signage, landscaping, and other items to give the area a unique character. To pay for the improvements by special assessment would have been a big burden on the property owners and collection of the assessments could not be enforced. As with PIDs, any attempt to borrow the money for the improvements was virtually impossible because there was no entity for the lender to hold responsible.

The property owners chose to form a management district as a vehicle for financing the improvements. A management district is somewhat similar to a PID with certain exceptions. The creators of the management district maintain control of the project as opposed to the PID being run by the city. Also, the formation is different in that the management district is established by the state legislature. Probably the big advantage of a management district is the flexibility of operation once the district has been formed. There are 26 such districts in the city of Houston alone.

Real Estate Center

Real estate licensees have an advantage in Texas through the benefits of a Real Estate Center that actively supports the industry with its research and education programs. It has made available to licensees a substantial library of information on the many facets of real estate. The information is in the form of numerous publications covering topics from appraisal to zoning and a reservoir of real estate price data. The Center's staff is willing to explore new fields of information that are helpful to all real estate licensees.

Under the direction of Gary Maler, the Center continues to expand its outreach throughout the state. Its professional staff is frequently called upon to meet with local organizations to explain economic, marketing, and legal questions pertinent to real estate issues. Their most current contribution to the industry is the creation of the new mandatory MCE courses, the 3-hour legal update, and the 3-hour ethics segment.

Periodically the Center holds a one-day refresher seminar to which all Texas real estate instructors are invited in cooperation with the Texas Real Estate Teachers Association (TRETA).

The Center is funded by real estate licensees. A portion of each license paid to the Texas Real Estate Commission is reserved for the operation of the Center at Texas A&M University in College Station. The 1995 legislature set the Real Estate Center's annual portion of licensee fees at $20 for brokers and $17.50 for salespersons. Although the funding varies with the number of licensees paying fees each year, the average annual budget is now about $2 million. Because of this method of financing, every licensee has a vested interest in the Center.

Real Estate Center Advisory Committee

To maintain close contact with the real estate community, the Center has an Advisory Committee consisting of nine members appointed by the governor. Six are real estate brokers licensed for at least 5 years, representing each of the following specialties: brokerage, finance, improvements, residential properties, commercial properties, and industrial properties. The other three members represent the general public. In addition, the chairperson of the Texas Real Estate Commission or a designee is an ex officio member.

Publications

Texas real estate licensees automatically receive Tierra Grande, a quarterly magazine detailing research results and trends. This publication now includes Judon Fambrough's "Law Letter."

Upon request, licensees may receive Trends, an 8-page monthly statistical report on the 27 major Texas markets.

More than 12,000 pages of free news, information, and statistical data are available on the Center's Web site at http://recenter.tamu.edu. Real Estate Center Online News (RECON) is a free weekly update of Texas-relevant real estate news; signing up can be done on their Web site.

Much of the information in this chapter has been obtained from data and publications available on the Texas Real Estate Web site. All of the recent editions of Tierra Grande are available in their entirety. There are also many other resources that are available to the real estate professional as well as the general public. The Center does an excellent job of researching current trends in real estate, particularly as they affect Texas. Real estate license fees provide funding for this valuable asset and therefore licensees should take advantage of this resource.

The Center also has several videotapes on a variety of topics. A free catalog is available for the asking. Contact:

Publications
Real Estate Center
Texas A&M University
College Station, Texas 77843-2115
Phone: 979-845-2031
Fax: 979-845-0460
E-mail: info@recenter.tamu.edu Web site: http://recenter.tamu.edu

Environmental Issues in Real Estate

Environmental Issues

Environmental concerns are a continuing issue in commercial and residential real estate transactions. Residential properties have not been subject to as much environmental concern, but this may be changing. Fairly new discoveries of brain damage to growing children caused by chemicals left in the environment by government projects and industry have caused great concern and some decline of land value in such areas.

Although real estate agents are not expected to be environmental experts, the same disclosure rules apply here as with other facts about a property. That is, *if environmental information is known to the sales agent and would affect a prudent purchaser's decision to buy, it must be disclosed.* Therefore, licensees should be familiar with the nature of these problems as well as the laws and regulations that are intended to protect the consumer and the environment.

The number of laws, how they overlap, and the many agencies involved with implementation make a clear understanding very difficult. Yet failure to comply properly with these laws and regulations can result in massive liabilities and/or the "taking" of property without compensation. In addition, many violations call for criminal penalties. Adding to the dilemma, these laws are, for the most part, broadly written with purposes ill defined, creating substantial potential for innocent and unknowing violations.

For the past three decades, most studies and research about the environment have focused on the detrimental effect that humans have had on it. Indeed, in the 1970s, federal and state laws were directed at protection of the environment from such acts as dumping waste, which inflicted long-term damage on the land, water, and air people depend on for their livelihood. Little study was given to the damaging effects that certain elements of the environment could have on people.

Recognition of the harm some chemicals can bring to humans has been somewhat overshadowed by the recent advances in medicine and diagnostic instruments. These advances have overcome many health problems and will prolong life. Publicity about new vaccines and medical techniques has dominated the news, indicating that better health will result from increased knowledge.

What has been overlooked in too many cases are the possible damaging effects that chemicals in the ground, air, and water may have on a child's physical development while growing up. Studies of children's development have produced concern, but no hard results yet. A child's growth is influenced by so many factors—poverty, parental neglect, inadequate schooling, poor diet, the wrong peers—that it is very difficult to assign actual damage to any one cause.

Even so, enough examples of chemical damage affecting a child's brain development have surfaced to warrant further study. As areas have been discovered that may be the cause of such brain damage, the economic effect on the land has been substantial.

Recently a federally funded study at the State University in New York-Oswego showed that babies who had significant amounts of Polychlorinated Biphenyls (PCBs) in their umbilical cords performed more poorly than unexposed babies in tests assessing visual recognition of faces, the ability to shut out distractions, and overall intelligence. In the 1980s, studies performed on young monkeys for Health Canada indicated that substances such as PCBs and mercury caused cancer or birth defects—the only problems for which they were tested in the United States. The studies also suggested that even at very low levels, these substances could affect the developing human brain.

EPA's Seven Priorities

A year after taking office, Lisa P. Jackson, Administrator of the EPA (http://blog.epa.gov/administrator), announced her seven priorities for 2010 and subsequent years. Listed below are the seven key themes to focus the work of the EPA:

1. **Taking Action on Climate Change**: Last year saw historic progress in the fight against climate change, with a range of greenhouse gas reduction initiatives. The EPA will continue this critical effort and ensure compliance with the law. Using the Clean Air Act, the EPA will finalize their mobile source rules and provide a framework for continued improvements. They will build on the success of ENERGY STAR to expand cost-saving energy conservation and efficiency programs.

2. **Improving Air Quality**: American communities face serious health and environmental challenges from air pollution. The EPA has already proposed stronger ambient air quality standards for ozone, which will help millions of American breathe easier and live healthier. Building on that, EPA will develop a comprehensive strategy for a cleaner and more efficient power sector, with strong but achievable emission reduction goals for SO2, NOx, mercury, and other air toxics.

3. **Assuring the Safety of Chemicals**: One of EPA's highest priorities is to make significant and long overdue progress in assuring the safety of chemicals in the nation's products, environment, and bodies. Using the EPA's streamlined Integrated Risk Information System, they will continue strong progress toward rigorous, peer-reviewed health assessments on dioxins, arsenic, formaldehyde, TCE, and other substances of concern.

4. **Cleaning Up Our Communities**: In 2009 EPA made strong cleanup progress by accelerating the Superfund program and confronting significant local environmental challenges like the asbestos Public Health Emergency in Libby, Montana and the coal ash spill in Kingston, Tennessee. They are committed to maximizing the potential of the brownfields program, particularly to spur environmental cleanup and job creation in disadvantaged communities.

5. **Protecting America's Waters**: Water quality and enforcement programs face complex challenges, from nutrient loadings and stormwater runoff, to invasive species and drinking water contaminants. The EPA will continue comprehensive watershed protection programs for the Chesapeake Bay and Great Lakes. Recovery Act funding will expand construction of water infrastructure, and the EPA will work with states to develop nutrient limits and launch an Urban Waters initiative.

6. **Expanding the Conversation on Environmentalism and Working for Environmental Justice**: The EPA is building strong working relationships with

tribes, communities of color, economically distressed cities and towns, young people and others. The EPA's revitalized Children's Health Office is bringing a new energy to safeguarding children through all of our enforcement efforts.

7. **Building Strong State and Tribal Partnerships**: States and tribal nations bear important responsibilities for the day-to-day mission of environmental protection, but declining tax revenues and fiscal challenges are pressuring state agencies and tribal governments to do more with fewer resources.

The Environment and the Economy

Much of the legislation aimed at protecting the environment is not new. Many basic laws were written in the 1970s. However, since the various laws were enacted, a stream of regulations issued by designated agencies has expanded, in many instances, the scope of legislation, making it broader and even more complex. In order to better protect landowners against unnecessary rules and legislation, the 1995 Texas Legislature passed some limitations on state laws and regulations (covered in a later section).

Because it has a direct impact on land value, environmental risk has become an added factor in all real estate transactions. One of the problems is that environmental damage is not always visible on the surface. It may be deep underground or seeping in from neighboring property. Nevertheless, under current law, an owner's ignorance of the problem does not relieve the landowner of liability. This is true regardless of whether the owner had any involvement in contaminating the property. However, the potential risk can be reduced by a professional investigation *prior* to acquiring a property (explained more fully in a later section).

Environmental Assessments for Home Loans

Home loans must be distinguished from residential loans. The term *residential* can include multi-family properties, which are treated as commercial properties with regard to environmental issues. It is owner-occupied dwellings that have been granted, by an Environmental Protection Agency rule, a broad exemption from liability for cleanup of toxic waste sites. In "Policy Toward Owners of Residential Property at Superfund Sites," issued in July 1991, the EPA stated it would not hold homeowners liable for cleanup costs unless an owner knowingly contaminated the property or failed to cooperate with the EPA in its cleanup efforts (for example, by not permitting the EPA access to the Superfund site).

The EPA's policy statement is not a statutory exemption. Rather, it is intended only as guidance for EPA enforcement employees. In other words, the EPA's policy does not amend the Superfund statute, which means homeowners can still be held liable for cleanup costs should the agency decide to rescind the policy. An appraisal for a home loan is expected to report any obvious contamination in or near the property evaluated. Furthermore, homeowners generally are prevented by their mortgage agreement from storing hazardous materials on the property and are required to report to the mortgagee any charges of environmental violations against the homeowner.

Environmental Assessments for Commercial Loans

Almost all commercial loan applications must now include an environmental site assessment. This includes multi-family dwellings. Precisely what is meant by "an environmental site assessment" is not clearly defined, and requirements vary with different lenders. However, this is changing.

The assessment outlined in the Superfund Act that is identified as a defense for an *innocent landowner* is called a *Phase I Assessment*. The scope of Phase I is limited to those hazardous materials specifically creating cleanup liability under the Superfund Act. It does not include all possible environmental problems, such as wetlands or the presence of endangered species. Thus, another term, *environmental site assessment*, has come to mean a broader approach than the more limited Phase I Assessment.

Because market terminology does not always make a distinction between a "Phase I Assessment" and an "environmental site assessment," an agent should make sure there is a mutual understanding of what is involved.

Requirements are changing. An "assessment" must be analyzed to measure future risk and in itself provides no assurance against future loss. To give better protection, lenders are now requiring environmental insurance rather than an assessment to be submitted with a commercial loan application. This insurance covers environmental liability for the collateral property if the loan defaults and contamination is found. If cleanup is required, assurance of payment by an insurance company eliminates any need for litigation. Of course, lenders like the transfer of risk and borrowers do not have to pay for the insurance if the loan is not approved.

Environmental Requirements of the Secondary Market

Whereas the secondary market is dominated by home loans, some commercial loans are moving into the hands of secondary market investors. For multi-family loans, both Fannie Mae and Freddie Mac require (in what they call a "Phase I Assessment") information on asbestos, polychlorinated biphenyls, radon, underground storage tanks, waste sites, lead-based paint, and any other hazardous contaminants. The questions, in an appendix form with the application, must be answered and filed with the loan submittal package.

For single-family loans, both agencies rely on information derived from a property appraisal. They require that an appraiser comment on any known environmental conditions that may adversely affect a property's value. This includes asbestos and urea-formaldehyde foam insulation.

In addition, the agencies also require information on the proximity of the mortgaged property to industrial sites, to waste or water treatment facilities, as well as to nearby commercial establishments using chemicals or oil products in their operations. Although appraisers are not considered to be experts on environmental hazards, they are expected to provide "early warnings" of properties harboring potential environmental problems.

Freddie Mac also requires that an appraiser consider environmental factors in reaching a conclusion as to the property's value.

It is becoming more common for lenders with residential and commercial loans to include environmental covenants in the mortgage instruments. For instance, the documents could prohibit a borrower from using hazardous substances on a pledged property. The Fannie Mae/Freddie Mac revised single-family mortgage document requires the borrower to promise to abide by state and federal environmental laws and to refrain from storing or using hazardous materials on the mortgaged property. In addition, the borrower must promise to notify the lender if an investigation or a lawsuit involving hazardous substances is filed against the property.

BOMA International Honored with Green Leadership Award

Bisnow on Business, a Washington, D.C.-based electronic news publisher, awarded the Building Owners and Managers Association (BOMA) International the 2008 Green Leadership Award in recognition of BOMA's commitment to promoting sustainability and energy efficiency among its members. The first annual award was given to 20 organizations in 5 categories, real estate, legal, tech, medical, and trade association, that have implemented impressive green initiatives and are leading the way on sustainability.

BOMA International is the leader in energy efficiency and sustainable initiatives that have helped BOMA member organizations lower energy consumption, reduce greenhouse gas emissions, and save on energy costs. The BOMA Energy Efficiency Program® (BEEP), an operational excellence program developed in partnership with the EPA's ENERGY STAR®, teaches property managers no- and low-cost strategies for reducing energy usage in commercial buildings. To date, more than 10,000 commercial real estate professionals have been trained through BEEP.

BOMA was also recognized by Bisnow for its successful Market Transformation Energy Plan and 7-Point Challenge, a challenge to the industry to reduce energy consumption in commercial buildings by 30 percent by 2012. Through the Challenge, BOMA has called upon its members to work in coordination with building management, ownership, and tenants to achieve the goals of the Challenge. The challenge includes benchmarking energy performance, providing education to property professionals to ensure equipment is properly maintained, performing energy audits, and leading community efforts to reduce commercial real estate's role in global warming. More than 100 BOMA member companies and local associations have endorsed the challenge.

Green Commercial Real Estate Lease

Other green achievements include the publication of the industry's first green lease, the premier resource on "greening" a commercial real estate lease. Also included is the launch of the Sustainable Operations Series (SOS) program, a new education program that builds on BEEP and includes additional practical ways to green building operations. An additional achievement is a collaboration with the Clinton Climate Initiative to develop a ground-breaking energy performance contract model to help building owners perform major energy retrofits to the existing building marketplace. Also considered a green achievement is the development of a partnership with the Department of Energy in the newly established Commercial Real Estate Energy Alliance (CREEA), which will pursue energy efficiency technologies that will transform energy use in the commercial building market.

BOMA International Simplifies Going Green

In October 2008, BOMA announced the launch of the next generation of green education for commercial real estate professionals, the Sustainable Operations Series (SOS). The program consists of four 90-minute Webinars that teach practical strategies and address industry best practices for implementing green commercial building operations. Created by the authors of the award-winning BOMA Energy Efficiency Program® (BEEP), BOMA's SOS program takes sustainability education to the next level by cutting through the overwhelming amount of information on sustainable practices and clearly demonstrating how green operations can effectively enhance the bottom line, improve tenant satisfaction and benefit the environment.

The four new course offerings are the following:

- **Course One: Making Sense of Sustainable Operations**—Covers the basics of greening commercial building operations, defining key terms, exploring the best approaches, and explaining green certification programs.
- **Course Two: Strategies for Reducing and Reusing Building Resources**—Highlights two key components of any good sustainable operations plan: how to reduce consumption of resources—from electricity and gas to paper and metals—and how to inventively reuse resources that have been consumed.
- **Course Three: Rethinking Recycling; Beyond Paper and Cans**—Going beyond typical paper and aluminum can recycling, learn how to identify building materials (from construction waste to light bulbs to office equipment) that can be recycled cost-effectively.
- **Course Four: How Green Is My Building? Tools for Measuring the Total ROI of Sustainability**—The final course demonstrates how to measure total ROI on sustainability (from impact on net operating income to tenant retention) and shows you how to "sustain sustainability" to continuously improve building performance.

Broker Designation—EcoBroker®

If more and more green buildings are being built, and consumers are increasingly satisfied with green buildings, the logical conclusion is that green real estate professionals should have more opportunities to help facilitate these transactions. EcoBroker® training ideally positions the broker as the most qualified real estate professional to handle these kinds of deals. Becoming an EcoBroker® can also help the broker capitalize on the continued vitality of green building.

The education requirements for becoming an EcoBroker® are extensive. EcoBroker® is a premiere green designation program for real estate professionals. EcoBroker Certified® professionals help clients market properties with green features, save money, and live comfortably through energy efficiency and environmentally sensitive choices.

Founded in 2002, EcoBroker® was the first and remains the largest green real estate training and communications program in the world. With members in all 50 United States, Canada, Mexico, the Caribbean, Central America, and New Zealand, EcoBroker® and its members serve real estate consumers, communities, and the environment with a level of care, commitment, and follow-up. With the benefit of oversight from the Association of Energy and Environmental Real Estate Professionals (AEERP), EcoBroker® training and communications provide professionals with the resources to be constructive green ambassadors in an ever-changing business and consumer world.

EcoBroker® offers education and tools to real estate professionals that in turn help consumers take advantage of energy efficiency and environmentally sensitive design in real estate properties. Through EcoBroker®'s unique energy and environmental curriculum, real estate professionals acquire the knowledge and resources to become Certified EcoBroker®s. These real estate professionals assist clients in their pursuit of properties that provide affordability, comfort and a healthier environment by, among other things, reducing carbon footprints.

In order to earn the EcoBroker® Designation, licensed real estate agents must fulfill a straight-forward set of requirements. The most important requirement of EcoBroker® Certification is the completion of the energy, environmental, and marketing training programs. For information on how to become an EcoBroker® please access the following website: http://www.ecobroker.com/eb/requirements.aspx

For more information on these and other "Green" topics, please visit the following websites:

Green Homes: A Bright Spot in the Housing Market
http://www.fypower.org/res/news/green-homes.html

VC (Venture Capital) Calls Green Building Technologies "Bright Spot" in Economy
http://energypriorities.com/entries/2008/11/ nancy_floyd_greenbuild.php

GreenSource. Green Housing Is Bright Spot on Otherwise Gloomy Market
http://greensource.construction.com/news/080725GreenHousing.asp

The Architects Newspaper. What Recession?
Green firms see bright future in dark times
http://www.archpaper.com/e-board_rev.asp?News_ID=2950

Wind Energy

In an article entitled "Against the Wind" in the October, 2008, edition of *Tierra Grande*, Judon Fambrough discusses numerous aspects of wind energy. Some of the topics that are discussed here include environmental concerns, nuisance problems, property tax abatements, construction time for wind farms and transmission lines, regulating wind development, and federal estate tax complications.

Environmental Concerns

Even though wind energy is renewable and apparently environmentally beneficial, it seems as though there are some who oppose the wholesale conversion of wind energy into electricity. Perhaps the most vocal opposition to wind energy comes from environmentalists, who object to the destruction caused when birds and bats collide with the spinning wind turbine blades.

An article with the headline "Texas Coast Wind Farms May Put Birds at Risk" appeared in the January 2, 2008, issue of *Houston Chronicle*. The article focused on two wind power projects under construction on the Kenedy Ranch in Kenedy County. The projects will generate about 388 megawatts—enough electricity to power 90,000 homes. A report issued by EDM International Inc. using methodologies developed by the U.S. Fish and Wildlife Service, concluded that the projects could result in the largest and most significant avian mortality event in the history of wind energy.

The Coastal Habitat Alliance Inc., formed in June 2007 to protect the Texas Gulf Coast, filed federal and state lawsuits in December 2007 seeking to halt construction of the two wind farms. The suit alleges that state officials and developers violated the Federal Coastal Zone Management Act by building the farms without an environmental review or permit. Loss of scenic beauty and possible harm to the bat population resulted in a moratorium on wind development in Gillespie County. Edwards County, with its significant bat population in the Devil's Cave, may follow suit.

Several lawsuits were filed against landowners and wind farms in the Sweetwater-Abilene area alleging they constituted an unreasonable interference with the use and enjoyment of nearby property. Loss of view and noise were two of the primary complaints. At the trial level, the lawsuits proved unsuccessful. Texas case law supports the free use of property in a legal, non-nuisance manner. The Real Estate Center's publication entitled *Obstruction of View, Light or Air* summarizes the pertinent case law.

The Texas courts have repeatedly ruled that the owner of real estate may, in the absence of restrictions or other regulations, erect a building, wall, fence or other structure on the premises, even if it obstructs a neighbor's vision, light, or air and even if it depreciates the value of a neighbor's land. The court dismissed the issue of the wind farm's visual degradation by granting the defendants summary judgment. This was appealed.

The trial basically ended when a landowner near the wind farm testified that noise from jet engines at Dyess Air Force Base about 20 miles away drowned out any noise from nearby wind turbines. In August 2008, the 11th Court of Civil Appeals upheld the trial court's decision to grant the defendants summary judgment regarding wind farm's visual impact. Ruling on case precedents, the court said, "Matters that annoy by being disagreeable, unsightly, and undesirable are not nuisances simply because they may to some extent affect the value of property."

Property Tax Abatements

A looming question for Texas wind-farm developers is whether property tax abatements, typically granted by the local county commissioners, will be available. Four conditions are critical to wind-farm development. First, the federal 1.9-cent income tax credit for each kilowatt hour of electricity generated must be in place. The credit is good for 10 years if one kilowatt of electricity is generated by a tower before December 31, 2008, the date the credit expires.

Second, there must be sufficient wind to generate the electricity. Texas has six classes of wind power potential. A region needs to rank class three or higher for wind development. Most of the favorable regions are located in West Texas. (See http://www.seco.cpa.state. tx.us/zzz_re/re_study1995.pdf)

Third, there must be sufficient transmission lines to move the electricity to population centers. And, finally, wind developers need to receive property tax abatements from local officials. In March 2008, the Texas Attorney General (AG) rendered an opinion calling into question wind farms' eligibility for tax abatements.

In Texas, when fixtures and improvements are not owned by the property owner, but by a lessee, for example, the wind company, they are classified as personal property, not real property. Personal property is not eligible for tax abatements under the Texas Tax Code (TC). A month after the AG rendered the opinion, two opponents of wind farms filed a lawsuit against the Taylor County Commissioners Court. The suit alleges tax abatements for the wind farms in that county are illegal because of the personal property classification.

The AG opinion and ensuing lawsuit create uncertainty with respect to past and future property tax incentives deemed vital for wind development in Texas. The Texas Legislature may address the issue in 2009. Tax abatements, if granted, are good for a maximum of 10 years.

Construction Time for Wind Farms and Transmission Lines

Construction time for wind farms is out of sync with construction time for transmission lines needed to transport the electricity. It takes about a year to build a wind farm, but about five years to construct transmission lines to send power to cities. Presently, the capacity to generate electricity in the favorable wind regions exceeds the capacity to move it, resulting in "stranded" electricity.

To alleviate the problem, the 2005 Texas Legislature implemented Section 39.904(g) of the Texas Utilities Code. It directs the Public Utility Commission (PUC), after consulting with appropriate organizations, including the Electric Reliability Council of Texas (ERCOT) to:

- designate Competitive Renewable Energy Zones (CREZs) and
- develop a plan to construct transmission capacity necessary to deliver electricity, in the most beneficial and cost effective manner, to customers from each CREZ.

The code further specifies that ERCOT, the Texas power-grid operator, study the need for increased transmission and generation capacity throughout the state and file a report with the legislature no later than December 31 of each even-numbered year. The results of the studies are intended to provide guidelines for placement of future transmission lines. The installation of the transmission lines will have a tremendous impact on wind development in the regions where the lines are located.

On July 17, 2008, the PUC announced preliminary approval for construction of a massive grid to transmit wind power from West Texas and the Panhandle. The action opens the door for a far-reaching web of transmission lines that, when completed, will create the capacity to transmit an additional 18,456 megawatts. The estimated $5 billion project will take four to five years to complete and will add five dollars monthly to Texas residential consumers' utility bills.

Regulating Wind Development

Another issue discussed in Judon Fambrough's timely and thought-provoking article is that of regulation. One of the items on the agenda for the 2009 Texas Legislature is the possible regulation of wind development. Hearings are already under way. Presently, wind development is unregulated in this state. One question the legislators must answer before imposing any regulations is whether wind is a natural resource. The Texas Constitution mandates that the Legislature pass laws for the *conservation and development* as well as the *preservation and conservation* of all natural resources in the state.

However, the constitution does not define the term *natural resources*. The Texas Natural Resources Code is of no help. It states that "the conservation and development of all the natural resources of this state are declared to be a public right and duty." And "the protection of water and land of the state against pollution or the escape of oil or gas is in the public interest." The only mention of wind in the Texas Constitution deems it more or less a nuisance. The legislature has created *wind erosion districts* which grant the power to create conservation and reclamation districts.

The constitutional language needs some legal interpretation. Do the two words in the constitutional phrase *conserve and develop* apply separately or together? The wording does not say *conserve and/or develop* but *conserve and develop*. While regulating the development of wind sounds reasonable, the conservation of it may not, especially to residents of West Texas.

Federal Estate Tax Complications

Landowners face the loss of special-use valuation when leasing their land for wind farms. The Internal Revenue Code permits farms and ranches to be valued for the purpose of federal gift and estate taxes on the basis of their present use, not their highest and best use. To qualify, several requirements must be met. For one, the deceased should have materially participated in the farm or ranch operations for the five years prior to death. In addition, the "qualified heirs" must continue to materially participate in operations for an additional 10 years after the deceased's death.

Material participation requires active involvement in management and an assumption of the associated financial risks. Cash leasing of the land is prohibited, but crop sharing is permitted. When an estate elects to use the special-use valuation, the IRS imposes a tax lien on the property for10 years. The lien secures repayment of the deferred taxes in the event the deceased's heirs fail to materially participate. If this occurs, a recapture of the tax savings is triggered with a possible foreclosure on the tax lien.

The federal tax lien makes it difficult, if not impossible, for farms and ranches to obtain third-party financing unless the IRS agrees to subordinate the lien. In a recent San Angelo case, a property was subject to the tax lien imposed by Section 6166. The heirs entered a wind lease. The lease required the landowners to get all preexisting liens released or subordinated. When the landowner asked the IRS for a subordination agreement, the IRS not only refused but viewed the wind lease as a disqualifying *cash lease* that triggered the recapture of the tax savings.

The prohibited "cash leases" are generally viewed as leases connected with farm or ranch operations, and not for wind development. If the IRS continues to take this position, it will have a chilling effect on wind energy development. When a wind lease is negotiated, consultation with knowledgeable legal and tax professionals is recommended.

Maker of Energy Production Equipment Setting up Shop in West Texas

As wind farms gain support as a viable source of renewable energy, Martifer Group has made plans to break ground on a $40 million wind tower manufacturing plant in San Angelo. The Portugal-based company expects to have its plant up and running in a year. The plant is projected to bring 225 jobs to the area in the next three years.

According to company officials, the facility will produce 400 towers a year by 2013. Each turbine will retail for about $4 million. The city offered Martifer $5.6 million in incentives and tax abatements, including money for buying the land for the 340,000-sf plant, which will be off Old Ballinger Highway on the city's northern edge. Tom Green County has offered an additional $2 million in abatements. The state, in addition to $945,000 from the Texas Enterprise Fund, is negotiating millions of dollars in rail improvements with the Texas Pacifico Railroad.

Ingleside Wind Technology School

Texas State Technical College (TSTC) has opened a new 8,633-square-foot education center that will offer the first wind technology classes in the college system. TSTC has a five-year, $87,000 lease on the building from the Port of Corpus Christi. The Renewable Energy Education Center's opening is a sign of the growing footprint of wind energy in South Texas.

The skills obtained there in hydraulics, pneumatics, electronics, and motor controls are transferable to other industries, including oil and gas. The center positions the Coastal Bend to help serve a growing demand for technical jobs in both land- and offshore-based wind power.

The center is an extension of programs offered in Harlingen and Sweetwater. Texas State Technical College claims a job placement rate of more than 90 percent for its graduates. Demand for wind technicians is so high that companies recruit students long before they finish the program, according to Regent Gene Seaman.

South Texas accounts for 13 percent, or 1,200 megawatts, of the state's 9,541 megawatts of wind capacity, according to the Electric Reliability Council of Texas.

Financing Solar Power

The sun's energy is clean, cheap, and plentiful, but the up-front costs of installing solar panels once presented a daunting barrier to entry for many companies. Fortunately, a financing tool known as **Power Purchase Agreements (PPAs)** is clearing the path. Though the details vary from state to state and from company to company, PPAs are based on the same general framework:

- A third-party solar company funds, installs, and maintains a solar energy system for the participating business.
- The solar company then sells electricity to the business, usually on a 15- to 20-year fixed-rate contract, often at prices lower than those typically offered for electricity by the local utility.

In California, Macy's used a mix of PPAs and traditional solar panel purchases to put solar arrays on the rooftops of 26 stores—while upgrading its lighting, heating and cooling, and energy-management systems to boost efficiency. The result is an estimated 40% reduction on its utility bills and an estimated 88,450 metric tons annual reduction in CO_2 emissions.

Other major companies, including Wal-Mart, Whole Foods, Kohl's, Staples, Target, Kinkos, Google, and Microsoft, have also entered into PPAs with various providers. The benefits, for both business and the environment, are multiple:

- Eliminate the financial barrier to entry normally associated with solar power.

- Reduce demand for conventional energy sources.
- Cut CO_2 emissions.
- Add renewable power to the grid.

At a time of volatile energy prices, PPAs also give companies predictable electricity bills and the opportunity to save money on operating costs. Industry analysts predict PPAs will gain 65 to 75 percent market share for commercial solar installation in 2008 alone. However, continued growth is dependent upon the expansion of state and federal solar incentives. PPAs are currently most prevalent in states with favorable government programs, like California and Hawaii.

Valley Town Earns Accolades

San Benito, a valley town tucked away in the southern tip of Texas, has garnered statewide attention for its renewable energy efforts. The Valley town has received the Texas Renewable Energy Industries Association's renewable energy project of the year award for the solar array that will help power its new water treatment plant. Funding for the $325,000 photovoltaic system came from the Environmental Protection Agency through a grant to the Texas General Land Office and its Renewable Energy Program.

Texas Environmental Quality Incentives Program (EQIP)

The Environmental Quality Incentives Program (EQIP) is a voluntary conservation program that promotes agricultural production and environmental quality as compatible national goals. Through EQIP, farmers and ranchers may receive financial and technical help to install or implement structural and management conservation practices on eligible agricultural land. EQIP was reauthorized in the Food, Energy and Conservation Act of 2008 (Farm Bill). The Natural Resources Conservation Service (NRCS) administers EQIP. Funding for EQIP comes from the Commodity Credit Corporation.

Texas 2012 Environmental Quality Incentives Program

NRCS will rank all eligible applications received for 2012 funding. Applications are being accepted at local USDA service centers across Texas. For more information about EQIP, visit the **National NRCS EQIP** web page. To locate the designated service centers visit **http://www.tx.nrcs.usda.gov/programs/eqip/12/index.html**

How EQIP Works in Texas

EQIP is a continuous sign-up program that allows landowners or operators to apply for financial and technical assistance for the application of specific conservation practices. Higher priority will be given to those applications that address national, state and local priorities and provide higher cost efficiency. The NRCS in Texas supports the locally led process through local work groups and provides EQIP funding to every county. The State Technical Committee and Local Work Groups have concurred in the practices eligible for financial assistance to treat the identified resource concerns. In Texas, financial assistance funds will be used to address both the local high priority practices identified by the Local Work Group and the statewide resource concerns identified by the State Technical Committee. Landowners and operators will choose the practices and evaluation system that best fits their needs. Payments for installed practices and management incentives will be made in accordance with the posted payment schedule for the conservation practice activity planned. The payment rate for each practice activity is on a per unit basis. The payment schedule for Limited Resource Farmers and Ranchers (LRFR), Socially Disadvantaged Farmers and Ranchers (SDAFR) and Beginning Farmers and Ranchers (BFR) are set at higher levels than the standard rates. A separate payment schedule has been developed for LRFR, SDAFR, BFR, and qualified participants with increased payment rates. A contract containing an EQIP Plan of Operations will be developed on applications that are accepted into the program. The minimum contract period will be one year following implementation of the last conservation practice but cannot exceed 10 years. Technical assistance will be provided by NRCS or, if desired, by a private Technical Service Provider (TSP) funded by NRCS.

Producer Eligibility

In order to be considered an agricultural producer eligible for EQIP, there must be an annual minimum of $1,000 of agricultural products produced and/or sold from the operation. Agricultural producers of non-industrial private forest land are exempt from the $1,000 requirement. There are, however, circumstances that may limit an individual's or entity's participation; these include:

- Federal and state governments and political subdivisions thereof, are not eligible.
- The applicant must be in compliance with highly erodible land and wetland conservation provisions.
- The individual or entity may not be eligible due to Adjusted Gross Income provisions.

Eligibility Criteria

In order to be eligible to signup for EQIP the applicant must be determined to be an eligible producer by the NRCS. The land offered for EQIP must also be determined eligible by NRCS. Eligible land is land that has a resource concern identified by a certified conservation planner that can be addressed through application of eligible conservation practices. The participant must complete and sign all necessary forms including the NRCS-CPA-1200.[1] Eligibility forms and documentation required by the FSA must be submitted to FSA prior to NRCS acceptance of the application. Payment eligibility is contingent on the producer not starting the practice prior to having an approved EQIP contract signed by the appropriate Commodity Credit Corporation (CCC) representative unless granted prior approval by the NRCS State Conservationist.

---

[1] Applications are accepted year around and funding of applicants varies throughout the year.

Ranking Pools

Eligible persons may select to apply in either the county base program, which reflects approved recommendations by the Local Work Group, or in one of the approved Statewide Resource Concerns based on recommendations by the State Technical Committee. The base program will vary from county to county depending on the priorities set at the local level. The State Resource Concerns to be addressed in 2009 are listed below. Check the link for state information to find the high priority counties and eligible practices.

- Water Quantity – Brush Management
- Water Quantity – Irrigation
- Water and Air Quality – AFO/CAFO
- Wildlife Habitat
- Invasive Species
- Water Quality – South Central Texas
- Plant Condition – Reforestation

Principal Environmental Problems

The need for adequate environmental information is becoming critical in any transaction involving commercial property. As cited earlier, there are constraints on homeowners using or storing hazardous materials on the premises. This brings up these questions: Exactly what comprises an environmental problem? What is the origin of these problems, and what is being done to mitigate the dangers?

The balance of this chapter is devoted to outlining the problems, explaining the principal federal and state laws and regulations that are being applied, and identifying the major impact these changes are having on property values affecting owners and lenders.

To examine the kinds of environmental problems created by pollution, recent developments are studied under the following nine categories. Each category is defined by law, and the principal agencies responsible for implementation of the law are identified.

1. Lead poisoning
2. Indoor air pollution
3. Toxic waste sites
4. Wetlands protection
5. Endangered species protection
6. Underground storage tanks
7. Electromagnetic forces
8. Mold
9. Carbon monoxide

Lead Poisoning

Lead is a heavy, relatively soft, malleable, bluish-gray metal. It cannot be broken down or destroyed. Because of the ease with which it can be shaped, it has been used for centuries as pipe and other building materials. More recently, it has been alloyed for use as solder to secure pipe joints and as a component of paint. Paint containing high levels of lead was found to be more durable and to look fresher longer.

Although lead was useful in buildings, its ingestion by humans can only do harm. Lead can be more damaging to children up to 7 years of age than to adults because children have higher rates of respiration and metabolism. Lead can be most damaging to the brain. Testing in the first and second grades found that children with the lowest IQs, academic achievement, language skills, and attention spans were the children with the highest levels of lead.

Lead was banned for use in paint in 1977, but lead-based paint can be found in nearly 75 percent of occupied houses built prior to 1978. About 3.8 million units are deemed to be serious hazards to their occupants. Its victims are poisoned by lead dust in the house and lead particles in the soil, not by peeling paint chips.

Nevertheless, in May 1997, the Centers for Disease Control and Prevention reported a drop in the number of children under age 6 who had high levels of lead in their blood. From 1988 to 1991, 1.7 million children were so afflicted, dropping to 1 million in the period 1991 to 1994. The reasons for this decline are attributed to federal initiatives to end the use of lead in gasoline, lead solder in the seams of food cans, and lead-based paint in homes.

1996 Lead-Based Paint Rule

On March 6, 1996, HUD and the EPA issued a joint final rule that requires sellers and renters of houses built before 1978 to disclose to potential buyers or tenants the presence of lead-based paint hazards in housing. Texas has a promulgated contract addendum covering this disclosure for use with TREC-promulgated contract forms, which is reproduced in the Appendix.

Texas Law on Lead-Based Paint

The 1997 Texas Legislature expanded lead abatement by passing its House Bill 729, which gives more authority to the Texas Department of Health to control lead paint abatement in *all pre-1978 child-occupied facilities*, not just *target housing*. This includes child care facilities, daycare centers, preschools, kindergartens, and any other facility visited at least 2 days a week for more than 3 hours, or at least 60 hours annually, by children 6 years of age or younger.

Federal Law for Building Renovators

Effective June 1, 1999, *renovators of dwellings* built before 1978 must give owners or occupants a copy of an EPA document whenever more than 2 square feet of paint will be disturbed. This disclosure is in addition to those listed above. The new law requires renovators to provide owners or occupants with the HUD pamphlet *Protect Your Family from Lead in Your Home* at least 60 days prior to any paint-disturbing activities and to obtain proof of delivery by getting signatures. Alternative means of proof may be used when signatures cannot be obtained.

EPA/Lead Web Site

An excellent resource for information on lead issues is www.epa.gov/lead/. On this website, the following links can be found:

- *Basic Information (Información Básica)*
- *Facts about lead*
- *Health effects of lead*
- *Where lead is found*
- *Where lead is likely to be a hazard*
- *How to check your family and home for lead*
- *What you can do to protect your family*
- *Are you planning to buy or rent a home built before 1978?*
- *Renovating, repairing or painting a home, child care facility or school with lead-based paint*
- *Other EPA pamphlets on lead*

Other links of importance:

- *Where You Live* - Get contacts for lead information in each EPA regional office.
- *Renovation, Repair and Painting* - Learn about EPA's lead-safety rules and lead-safe work practices.
- *Lead Professionals* - Read about EPA requirements for lead-based paint abatement for known hazards, inspection, and risk assessment.
- *Grants* - Read about EPA's grant programs to fund lead poisoning prevention activities in local communities and across the nation.
- *Lead in the News* - Read about recalls, lead in toys and children's jewelry and more.
- *Rules and Regulations* - Read about EPA regulations and policy guidance on lead abatement, cleanup, risk assessment, and remodeling and renovations.
- *Resource Center* - Access links to additional information sources on lead from other EPA offices and organizations involved in efforts to reduce lead exposure.
- *Lead Hotline*
- *Download media documents and soundbites.*

Case Study—"Lead Court"

Philadelphia, like many older US cities, has an exceptionally large amount of older housing stock. Over 90 percent of houses there were built before the 1978 ban on lead paint, according to Dr. Carla Campbell, an associate teaching professor at the Drexel University School of Public Health. Dr. Campbell was the principal investigator on a new study that explores the effectiveness of an innovative law enforcement strategy. The purpose of the strategy is to increase the compliance rate with lead remediation ordered by the Philadelphia Department of Public Health (PDPH). The study was initiated to decrease hazardous exposures to lead in the homes of children with elevated blood lead levels.

The PDPH investigates all cases that meet the definition of elevated blood lead levels in children, and mandates remediation if significant sources of lead risk are found in the child's house. Despite such efforts to address the high prevalence of elevated BLLs, a large backlog formed from Philadelphia properties that were not in compliance with the lead remediation ordered by the Philadelphia Department of Public Health.

To solve this backlog, an innovative enforcement solution was devised, namely the Philadelphia Lead Court, a special judicial court devoted exclusively to hearing cases where owners had violated local health codes regarding lead exposure. In preparation for their duties, judges and city lawyers involved with the cases received background information on lead exposure and lead poisoning by health department staff members.

Before the formation of the court, only 6.6 percent of properties were remediated within one year of the initial failed inspection, using data from all properties with one-year or more of uncensored follow-up. With the Lead Court in place that number jumped to 76.8 percent. This is a significant increase in compliance (with a p value of < 0.001).

Using a longitudinal analysis, the study also found a very slow rate of additional successful remediation over time in the pre-Court period. Even four years after the initial failed inspection, fewer than 20 percent of properties had attained compliance, compared to 81 percent eventual compliance in the Court period cases.

The take-away message is simple, said Dr. Campbell: "Lead Court is very effective. This model could be replicated in other cities with problems with high prevalence of housing with lead hazards and difficulties in enforcement, and children's lives could be made safer."

8th Circuit Declines Review of EPA's Order on Lead-Based Paint Disclosure Requirements

On January 24, 2002, the 8th Circuit dismissed an appeal filed by Billy Yee on June 28, 2001. The court never reached the merits of the appeal as the dismissal was based on EPA's jurisdictional argument. EPA contended, and the Court accepted, that Billy Yee filed his appeal with the 8th Circuit one day late, that the case should be dismissed for lack of jurisdiction. On May 29, 2001, the EPA Environmental Appeals Board handed down its final decision in the matter of Billy Yee, a case involving a St. Louis landlord's violations of the TSCA Lead-Based Paint Disclosure Rule. In the decision, the EAB upheld Chief Judge

Biro's initial decision in its entirety, including the Chief Judge's findings regarding liability and the assessment of a $29,700 penalty.

The case involved Mr. Yee's failure to provide lead-based paint disclosure information to a tenant prior to her becoming obligated under lease, in violation of the Lead-Based Paint Real Estate Notification and Disclosure Rule. After moving into the low income property the tenant discovered that five of her young children had become severely lead poisoned. As a result, the children were hospitalized on several occasions to undergo blood chelation therapy to reduce the impacts of the lead poisoning, from which the children will continue to suffer harmful effects for the remainder of their lives. The home had been inspected and was found to contain several lead-based paint hazards accessible to the children.

Indoor Air Pollution

Formaldehyde Gas

Formaldehyde is a colorless, toxic, water-soluble gas with a strong, pungent, pickle-like smell. It can be emitted by a number of building materials, such as urea-formaldehyde foam insulation (UFFI) and formaldehyde-based adhesives used in pressed wood, particleboard, plywood, shelves, cabinets, and office furniture. It can also be found in some draperies and carpeting. This gas can cause health problems ranging from minor eye, nose, and throat irritation to serious effects such as nasal cancer.

Such problems are not normally found in the average building, but pose greater problems in manufactured or mobile homes, extremely energy-efficient houses, tightly constructed newer office buildings, and even schools. Only manufactured homes are required to carry warning labels if they contain products made with formaldehyde. Buyers of manufactured homes must sign statements acknowledging the presence of formaldehyde-based materials. Other buildings have no such requirements. Thus, in other buildings, a real estate agent must disclose any known presence of UFFI or a harmful concentration of formaldehyde gas-producing materials.

Testing

Testing for formaldehyde gas is accomplished in two ways: by a professional or by a testing device. An accurate device called PF-1 is made by Air Quality Research in Research Triangle Park, North Carolina. The PF-1 is a small glass vial that is left in place for 1 week, then sent back to the company for analysis. Two sell for about $59 with analysis and for about $36 without analysis. The company's phone number is 919-918-7191.

Remedies

The best solution to the formaldehyde problem is removal of the gas-emitting material. This may, however, be an extremely complex and expensive process. Increasing ventilation or lowering the temperature and humidity inside a building can reduce the concentration of gas. Another effective procedure is to seal particleboard and other wood products with paints or veneers.

Radon Gas

In 1989, the administrator of the EPA, William Reilly, pronounced radon "the second leading cause of cancer in this country." The EPA estimates that radon causes as many as 20,000 deaths each year. The hazard was not discovered until 1984, when an engineer working on construction of the Limerick Nuclear Plant in Pennsylvania was found to be bringing radiation *into* the plant from his home!

Radon is an invisible radioactive gas. A person cannot smell it, feel it, or see it. Outside it is virtually harmless because it dissipates. It becomes a problem only inside a building, when it accumulates into dangerous concentrations. Radon comes from decaying uranium. Uranium can be found in many places—the earth's soil, black shale, phosphatic rocks, and even granite. It can be found in areas that have been contaminated with industrial wastes, such as by-products of uranium or phosphate mining.

The danger arises when such materials are located directly underneath an inhabited building and the gas seeps inside. Entry into a building can be through cracks in the slab or openings found around pipes. The gas can also enter through well water. In building areas that lack adequate ventilation (for example, a basement), the gas can become concentrated and dangerous.

Although the materials that cause radon gas are widely dispersed, they are not found everywhere. Clues about its possible presence can be obtained from local, state, and federal environmental and health officials or from information gathered about other buildings in the local neighborhood. Although any building can contain radon gas, well-insulated and energy-efficient homes experience higher levels of contamination. If the presence of radon is suspected, air tests should be made.

Testing

The simplest test involves using an activated charcoal filter canister, which can be purchased at hardware stores or home centers. The canister is placed in the basement or at ground level of the building for 4 to 7 days, then returned to a laboratory for analysis. (Radon is not normally a problem in the upper floors of a building.) If professional testing is preferred, the EPA has a list of proficient radon testing contractors. If the building tested is being offered for sale, full disclosure of the test results must be given to prospective buyers.

Remedies

Several remedies reduce the problem of radon gas pollution. Basement floor cracks and pipe openings can be sealed to prevent further seepage. Ventilation devices alone may be sufficient to reduce the radon concentration to a minimal level.

Asbestos

Asbestos is a group of naturally occurring mineral fibers found in rocks. It has been used in such products as patching compounds, wood-burning stoves, siding, roofing shingles, and vinyl floors. Asbestos has a number of advantages. It can strengthen a material, provide thermal insulation, provide acoustical insulation on exposed surfaces, and fireproof a product or material. However, it has at least one disadvantage: it can kill you. That fact has been known since 1924! In that year, the *British Medical Journal* published a report by W.E. Cooke about a young woman who had worked with asbestos and died with extensively scarred lungs.

Asbestos can cause asbestosis, a noncancerous disease that scars the lung tissues. It can also cause several different kinds of cancer in the lungs, esophagus, stomach, and intestines. Yet it is a difficult type of pollution to assess accurately. Media attention to the problems of asbestos as a health hazard in schools and office buildings has increased concern. The same problems can exist in homes, although this concern has received less attention. Nevertheless, recent studies have indicated that the real danger lies with loose asbestos rather than that occurring in hard form.

Construction materials have contained asbestos for hundreds of years. When bonded with another hard material, asbestos can be relatively harmless. This nonfriable condition, common in asbestos siding, usually poses no threat unless drilled or sanded, thus releasing fibers. It is the efforts to remove hard asbestos materials by disturbing them that can cause health hazards.

Soft or crumbling forms (i.e., friable asbestos) pose greater risks. Damaged asbestos insulation around pipes or ceiling tiles may release airborne microscopic fibers. These fibers may, even after many years, cause respiratory diseases. No conclusive studies to date have shown that a health hazard is caused from the ingestion of food or water containing asbestos or that the fibers can penetrate the skin. Asbestos becomes dangerous only when it breaks down and fibers are released into the air.

In a recent court case, it was ruled that even though the National Emission Standards for Hazardous Air Pollutants for Asbestos (Asbestos NESHAP) call for "visible emissions," it does not require the visible observation of particulate asbestos material, only the visible observation of the emissions, which contain invisible particles. The court ruled against the defendant who rehabilitated brake shoes that may have contained asbestos and fined the defendant $50,000. *United States v. Midwest Suspension & Brake*, 49 F3d 1197 (6th Cir., 1995).

Testing

As buyer/investor, seller, or agent, it is important to know whether homes or buildings in the neighborhood have been found to contain asbestos. If there is an indication of problems, an EPA-certified asbestos inspector can determine from bulk samples whether materials contain asbestos. Once a laboratory analysis determines the material's content, the buyer and seller can consider management plan options. Full disclosure to a potential buyer is mandatory.

Economic Consequences

Discovery of asbestos can be a building owner's nightmare. Aside from the problems associated with federal and state laws regarding the handling of asbestos-containing materials, a real problem lies in the economic risks associated with its presence.

Two risks are dominant: (1) the potential of health-related lawsuits and (2) the potential lack of tenants due to fear of the presence of asbestos. This translates into a lower value for the building and difficulty in obtaining adequate insurance coverage. Even so, when faced with such a dilemma, building owners may consider an asbestos management plan as suggested by the EPA.

Tort Versus Trust *Legal Newsline* reported on August 5, 2011 that tension exists between the two compensation systems for asbestos victims: the $30 billion collectively held in asbestos bankruptcy trusts, and the tort system. The issue of tort versus trust is a hot button issue.

The trusts were created to settle asbestos personal injury claims resulting from exposure to asbestos-related products mined or manufactured by the corporations. Many corporations subject to these lawsuits were forced to file bankruptcy and subsequently formed trusts. Among the more notable trusts are the Johns-Manville Corporation Trust, which was formed in 1988, and the trust formed by the U.S. Gypsum Company in 2006. The problem that has arisen is that now codefendants who are tenuously associated with asbestos are being targeted by trial lawyers.

Defendants are arguing that plaintiffs who received money from the trusts should not necessarily be getting money from both a trust and a state court case against one of these second-tier companies. This is especially true if contradictory evidence exists. However, up until now, getting claimant information from the trusts has been nearly impossible, according to sources familiar with asbestos trusts. There has been a reluctance not only to furnish information about plaintiffs, but information about the structure and flow of funds as well. Defense counsels have been complaining for some time about getting this information. Congress created the trusts to limit the liability from asbestos and make the legal actions run smoothly. But the trusts have become an entity unto themselves. Some believe that the lack of transparency in the trust's operations is not the only problem. It is possible that ethical issues generated by the unprecedented control that a small number of law firms exercise over the creation of asbestos bankruptcy trusts and the procedures for making claims against the trusts could also be problematic.

The issue attracted the notice of Capitol Hill lawmakers last year. U.S. Rep. Lamar Smith (R-Tx) requested in April 2010 that the Government Accountability Office (GAO) look into transparency of the trusts. As of September 2011 the report was reported to be published soon. Rep. Smith's request cited the problem that claimants are making multiple requests from different trusts and suing for damages in the tort system. He said that the trusts were not operating in the spirit in which they were created. More than 8,500 U.S. companies, which represent 90 percent of American industries, have been sued for asbestos-related claims. Some of these companies never produced or sold asbestos.

EPA Fugitives

The EPA launched a fugitives website in December of 2008. On September 13, 2011 one of the women on the "most wanted" list was sentenced to 87 months in prison followed by three years of supervised release. Additionally, U.S. District Judge Nathaniel M. Gorton ordered her to pay more than $1.2 million in restitution to the Internal Revenue Service and $369,015 to AIM Mutual Insurance Company. She was the fifth environmental criminal captured since the website was launched. Albania Deleon, 41, formerly of Andover, Mass., was the owner of the country's largest asbestos abatement training school. She fled the United States after being convicted in November 2008 of multiple offenses, including the sale of training certificates to thousands of illegal aliens who had not taken the mandatory training course. Deleon then placed these individuals in temporary employment positions as certified asbestos abatement workers in public buildings throughout Massachusetts and New England. Following a three-week trial, she was convicted of encouraging illegal aliens to reside in the United States; making false statements about matters within the jurisdiction of the EPA; procuring false payroll tax returns; and mail fraud.

From 2001 to 2006, Deleon owned and operated Environmental Compliance Training (ECT), a certified asbestos training school located in Methuen, Mass. ECT offered training courses on a weekly basis. However, many of the recipients of the certificates never took the required course. With Deleon's knowledge and approval, ECT's office employees issued course completion certificates to thousands of individuals who did not take the course. These individuals filed the certificates with the Massachusetts Division of Occupational Safety in order to be authorized to work in the asbestos removal industry. Many of the recipients were illegal aliens who wished to skip the four-day course so that they would not forego a week's pay. The EPA stated, "Since the company's training course records were subject to inspection, Deleon sought to cover up ECT's practice of issuing certificates to untrained applicants by having the applicants sign final examination answer sheets that already had been completed and graded, which she maintained in ECT's files. Based on the evidence at trial and information supplied by the Division of Occupation Safety, ECT issued training certificates to over 2,000 untrained individuals."[2] The EPA's position is that no level of exposure to asbestos is safe, so removal by untrained workers, performed without the necessary safeguards, threatens the health of those workers and the public, the announcement stated. "Today's sentence marks the final chapter in bringing Albania Deleon to justice, said Cynthia Giles, assistant administrator for EPA's Office of Enforcement and Compliance Assurance. Committing environmental crimes to make a profit that put workers and our communities at risk carry serious consequences."[3]

Toxic Waste Sites

The problem of toxic waste sites first came to national attention with the discovery of a contaminated area in the abandoned Love Canal near Niagara Falls, New York. The federal

---

[2] http://yosemite.epa.gov/opa/admpress.nsf/d0cf6618525a9efb85257359003fb69d/f6b4697eba0a90d78525790a00738b86!OpenDocument
[3] Ibid.

response was passage of the *Comprehensive Environmental Response, Compensation, and Liability Act of 1980 (CERCLA).* It set up a fund totaling $8.5 billion, known as *Superfund,* to evaluate and clean up inactive and abandoned sites throughout the United States.

A toxic waste site is an area identified by the EPA as containing a concentration of hazardous materials. About 1,290 such sites are known of in the country. Thirty of these sites are in Texas, with nearly half (fourteen) located in the Houston area. Although toxic waste sites are no bigger problems than areas polluted by other contaminants, they have attracted popular attention by being very visible. The catch phrase "the polluter pays" has been widely accepted as the way to handle this problem. Unfortunately, it has not worked quite this way because often the major polluter is out of business.

By placing liability for cleanup of these sites on anyone who has used the land, regardless of fault, the Superfund Act has created enormous litigation expenses and very little remedial action. Of the approximately $26 billion spent on toxic waste, the private sector has paid about $5 billion in litigation and the government, another $4 billion. Indeed, a toxic waste site known as the Brio site, just south of Houston, has created an active business for damaged claimants that nearly replaced efforts to clean up the real problem.

Extent of Liability

CERCLA places strict, joint and several liabilities for cleanup costs on all responsible parties. *Strict* means liable regardless of fault, and *joint and several* means the parties are both singularly and jointly liable for all cleanup costs. This is true whether the party involved had anything to do with creating the problem. No minimum amount of contamination is required to create liability for cleanup.

Although only about 250 of some 1,290 designated Superfund waste sites have been cleaned up, a rough estimate of average cost per site thus far has been $25 million. There is no limit on the liability that can be incurred, except for damage to natural resources, which is limited to $50 million.

Liability to the government may not be allocated; however, responsible parties may seek an allocation of costs among themselves. One result has been that much of the money spent on toxic waste problems has been directed to litigation centered primarily on insurance companies' denial of liability.

Hazardous Materials Covered by CERCLA

CERCLA does not include all substances that can be classified as dangerous to a person's health. Thus, liability for cleanup may be more specifically allocated by other laws for nonCERCLA-covered substances. CERCLA defines a hazardous substance as one specifically listed as poisonous by the EPA, comprising about 750 materials at present, in addition to those so designated by any other law.

There are a number of exclusions from the definition of CERCLA's hazardous substances, including petroleum and derivatives thereof, unless expressly listed as a hazardous substance by other statutes. Also excluded are natural gas, natural gas liquids, and synthetic natural gas usable for fuel. Furthermore, the exclusion includes mining wastes, cement kiln dust, and wastes generated from the combustion of coal or other fossil fuels.

Innocent Landowner Defense

An innocent landowner defense against liability for toxic waste cleanup may be sustained in the case of damages caused by a third party, not an employee and not under any contractual relationship with the defendant, *providing* the defendant did not know and had no reason to know that the facility had been used for the disposal of hazardous substances prior to the time the facility was acquired by the defendant.

Environmental Due Diligence Assessment

The purpose of a due diligence assessment is to analyze, evaluate, and manage a potential environmental risk. The method used is (1) to research the historical uses of the subject property, (2) to identify the presence and extent of environmental contamination, and (3) to determine the most feasible method of managing the environmental risk if hazardous substances are found.

Two key elements to making these assessments are not addressed in the Superfund Act. One is that there are no standards to determine what measure of contamination triggers liability for cleanup. Groups involved in the real estate industry have been seeking better clarification. One result has been a set of standards recently developed privately by the American Society for Testing of Materials (ASTM). The other important element not addressed in the act is that there are no legally identified credentials for persons making environmental assessments. Educational programs leading to professional designations that will better identify qualified people are offered through schools in Texas.

As dictated by CERCLA, the environmental assessment should be conducted in phases. A *Phase I Assessment* involves a limited inquiry into how the land has been used *prior* to conveyance of title, focusing on readily available sources of data and culminating in an inspection of the site.

If the assessment reveals actual or potential environmental problems, a *Phase II Assessment* is required. Phase II targets those areas believed to be contaminated and include the collection and chemical analysis of soil samples, surface and groundwater samples, and other relevant investigations and analyses. A *Phase III Assessment* involves defining the extent of soil and groundwater contamination and implementing the most appropriate cleanup activities.

Recovery of Brownfield Areas

Urban land that has become contaminated over the years often lies idle because of the cost and possible liability involved with its cleanup and restoration to good economic use.

Brownfield is the EPA's term for contaminated areas with the potential for reuse. The EPA estimates there are 450,000 brownfields nationwide. An example of restoration and a return to tax-paying value to the community is the construction of Minute Maid Park in downtown Houston.

Federal agencies have been working with the private sector to help redevelopment of brownfield sites. These agencies include the EPA, the Federal Housing Finance Board, and HUD. The private sector has been slow to become involved due to the availability of greenfields, concerns with liability, the time and cost of cleanup, and a reluctance to invest in older urban areas. Since 1995, the EPA has loosened some of its regulatory oversight. Although developers could technically be held liable for past contamination, nonlitigation agreements between Washington and some states encourage the cleanup of sites with lesser contamination.

The Federal Home Loan Bank system, a government-sponsored enterprise, is now involved in helping to finance redevelopment of city ground use. The FHLB's *Community Investment Cash Advance Program* encourages partnerships between the FHLB and public and private entities to reduce the financing costs for targeted projects. Last year the FHLB made $790 million available in term financing for brownfield redevelopment.

HUD programs, such as Community Development Block grants, Section 108, and the Brownfield Economic Development Initiative, could help stimulate economic development by leveraging private investment and making brownfield projects feasible.

An example of a successful cleanup in operation is in Dallas, Texas. The work is being promoted as the Victory Project by Ross Perot, Jr., CEO of Hillwood Development and son of the former presidential hopeful. The location is a 72-acre former city dump with an aging power plant and a row of abandoned grain silos. The mile-long site was purchased for $12 million, involving 25 parcels of land with virtually no records of possible contaminants. By 2001, the American Airlines Center had been completed, and the 8 million square feet of apartments, offices, stores, and recreation facilities was awaiting further financing. The Victory Project will be a $1 billion development catering to road-weary Dallasites who want to live, work, and play downtown.

Tax Relief for Brownfield Cleanup

In January 2001, legislation was passed to extend the Taxpayer Relief Act of 1997. Owners of brownfield sites can expense their cleanup costs rather than capitalize them until January 1, 2004. Also, the criteria for an eligible site has been expanded to include contaminated areas certified by a state environmental agency.

TSCA Enforcement Environmental Results

Examples of improvements to the environment resulting from enforcement of the Toxic Substances Control Act (TSCA) are shown in the following cases, used as examples of enforcement achievements. Case names link to additional information when it is available.

Apartment Investment and Management Company (AIMCO)

The U.S. Environmental Protection Agency (EPA) and the Department of Housing and Urban Development (HUD) entered into the broadest lead disclosure settlement ever with one of the nation's largest property management firms, the Denver-based Apartment Investment and Management Co. (AIMCO). Residents living in more than 130,000 apartments in 47 states and Washington, D.C., will live in lead-safe units as a result of this landmark settlement.

"Protecting our nation's children from the dangers of lead-based paint is of paramount concern. Eliminating lead-based paint hazards in older low-income housing is essential if childhood lead poisoning is to be eradicated," said EPA Administrator Christie Whitman. "AIMCO is to be commended for its voluntary disclosure and other efforts to make its housing lead-safe. We urge other landlords to take their cue from this responsible action."

AIMCO allegedly failed to warn its tenants that their homes may contain lead-based paint hazards in violation of the Residential Lead-Based Paint Hazard Reduction Act. Under the settlement, AIMCO has agreed to test and clean up lead-based paint hazards in more than 130,000 apartments nationwide and pay a $129,580 penalty. The penalty and the number of units being tested and cleaned are the largest ever in a lead disclosure settlement.

Hewlett-Packard

A civil administrative complaint filed in 1998 against Hewlett-Packard (HP) charged that HP had violated Sections 5, 8, 12 and 13 of TSCA. HP paid $112,750 in fines for failure to submit a Pre-Manufacturing Notice (PMN) for a new chemical and committed to audit other HP facilities. The settlement stipulated the liability for each type of violation, and further limited the liability of the entire audit in the aggregate to $600,000. As a result of violations found in the audit in 2001, HP paid $600,000, bringing the total penalties paid to $712,750.

The Hewlett-Packard case brought attention to TSCA Section 12(b), under which companies must 1) notify EPA of its exports and 2) notify countries to which products are exported that the shipment complies with TSCA. Many of HP's Section 12(b) violations were not penalized due to language in the enforcement response policy. Therefore, the enforcement response policy was modified to enable future enforcement actions against these types of violations. The combination of the HP case and the enforcement policy amendment motivated the Chemical Manufacturer's Association to request a coordinated effort with EPA that resulted in over 10,000 voluntarily self-disclosed violations of Section 12(b). In addition, HP submitted nine reports constituting TSCA Section 8(e), "substantial risk of injury." Each of these reports would have been million dollar enforcement actions if not for the liability limits in the settlement.

Newell Recycling - Region 6

In 1995, EPA issued a complaint against Newell Recycling for improper disposal of PCB-contaminated soil that had been excavated and stockpiled during a 1985 disposal of capacitors. The Environmental Appeals Board (EAB) issued a Final Decision in 1999 upholding the Agency's ruling that Newell had improperly disposed of PCB-contaminated soil. A civil penalty of $1,345,000, less the settlement amount paid by Newell's Co-Respondent Oklahoma Metal Processing Company, Inc., d/b/a Houston Metal Processing Company, Inc., was assessed against Newell. The decision and penalty were appealed to the 5th Circuit in November 2000 where both were affirmed.

At issue in this case was the Federal five-year statute of limitations. Newell argued that the statute of limitations should run from 1985 when the first act of improper disposal occurred, and therefore enforcement action could not be taken. The Agency successfully argued that it should begin when the first act of proper disposal occurred in 1995. The Court held that an enforcement action could be initiated during the period of continuing violations and up to five years after the violations have ceased. This ruling is of significance to future enforcement proceedings.

Rogers Corporation - Region 1

EPA filed a Complaint against Rogers Corporation in September, 1994. The Complaint charged that Rogers violated the disposal requirements of the PCB regulations and TSCA Section 15 by allowing a release of heat transfer oil containing PCBs at regulated levels to remain in a concrete containment berm from June, 1993 to March, 1994. Rogers was found liable and a penalty of $281,400 was assessed. The decision was appealed to the U.S. Court of Appeals on November 8, 2001. The Court of Appeals remanded the case to the EAB for further proceedings.

Chicago Lead Paint Settlements - Region 5

The U.S. Department of Justice, the U.S. Environmental Protection Agency and the U.S. Department of Housing and Urban Development settled in cases against three landlords in Chicago for failure to warn their tenants that their homes may contain lead-based paint hazards. The consent decrees in the Chicago include over $90,000 in civil penalties and agreements to test for and abate lead-based paint in over 10,000 apartments across the country. The settlements involved violations of the disclosure requirements of the Lead Hazard Reduction Act by multifamily apartment owners and management companies. The settlements were the result of a joint initiative by DOJ, EPA and HUD, as well as city and state health officials.

The United States Department of Justice filed complaints and lodged consent decrees on behalf of EPA and HUD with three companies in Chicago: Wolin Levin, Inc., East Lake Management & Development Corporation and Oak Park Real Estate, Inc., et al.. The State of Illinois joined in the action against Oak Park Real Estate, and the City of Chicago, Cook County and the State of Illinois joined in the actions against Wolin Levin and East Lake. Together, over 10,350 units in Chicago and suburban Chicago are subject to the terms of these three consent decrees. Under the consent decrees lodged in the U.S. District Court in the Northern District of Illinois, the defendants agreed to test for lead-based paint in their properties and abate any lead-based paint that is found. The companies are also required to pay $90,000 in penalties to the U.S. Treasury; in addition, Wolin Levin agreed to pay $100,000 to the City of Chicago Department of Health lead abatement program as a Child Health Improvement Project and East Lake agreed to give $77,000 to certain community-based health centers to provide free blood lead testing for children living in Chicago and South Chicago.

Frankland P. Babonis - Region 3

In April, 2001, Frankland P. Babonis was sentenced in the U. S. District Court for the Eastern District of Virginia, Alexandria, for felony violations in connection with Babonis' sale of false asbestos and lead training certificates, including false statements and mail fraud. Babonis's company, F&M Environmental Technology, Inc., was also sentenced for violations of 18 U.S.C. Section 1001 & 2 in conjunction with the sales.

The Court imposed on Babonis fifteen months incarceration in the Federal Penitentiary on each of the two counts, to run concurrent. Each count carries a three-year supervised probationary period, to run concurrent, a $ 4,000 fine, and a $100 special assessment.

In sentencing F&M, Ellis imposed a $30,000 fine, a $400 special assessment and two years of supervised probation. In addition, Ellis ordered that F&M not engage in any environmental training for a period of two years.

Collins Mechanical, Inc. and MedStar Health - Region 3

In June, 2001, Region 3 issued a Final Order against three different parties for violations of federal asbestos requirements. The violations occurred at the Boiler Plant of the Washington Hospital Center in Washington, D.C. and involved the improper handling of asbestos-containing material in October 1999. Respondents in the complaint, issued in September, 2000 were Collins Mechanical, Inc. (mechanical contractor), the Washington Hospital Center, and the Hospital Center's corporate parent, MedStar Health, Inc. Under the terms of the settlement, total civil penalties of $39,160 will be paid (CAA - $28,160, TSCA - $11,000), $29,160 by the Washington Hospital Center and $10,000 by Collins Mechanical, Inc.

Enterprise Investment Company - Region 3

In May, 2001, Region 3 filed a global settlement agreement with the Regional Hearing Clerk settling three cases involving a number of violations of the TSCA Lead Paint Disclosure Rule by Enterprise Investment Company. With respect to at least three leases involving two targeted housing units in York, Pennsylvania, the Respondent failed to comply with requirements of the Disclosure Rule. As part of the global settlement of all three cases, Respondent agreed to pay a penalty of $22,000, based in part on financial information submitted by the company, and to ensure future compliance with the Disclosure Rule.

Nordic Synthesis - Region 4

In June, 2001, Region 4 issued a CAFO against Nordic Synthesis, Inc. Nordic Synthesis, Inc., a chemical importer and distributor, is a Delaware corporation with a facility in Charleston, South Carolina. The company was found to have violated Section 8 of TSCA, by reporting false/misleading/incorrect information on the 1998 Inventory Update Report for two imported chemical substances. The company agreed to pay a civil penalty of $33,660.

UCB Chemicals Corporation - Region 4

In June, 2001, Region 4 filed a CAFO against UCB Chemicals Corporation. UCB Chemicals Corporation is a manufacturer, importer and exporter of chemical substances, with headquarters in Smryna, Georgia. The company violated Section 5(a) of TSCA in its failure to properly and timely submit the required notice of commencement for two nonexempt commercial shipments of imported chemical substances. The corporation agreed to pay a civil penalty of $6,824.

University of California - Region 9

In April, 2001, Region 9 filed a CAFO settling its case against the Regents of the University of California for violations of TSCA and the PCB regulations at UC's campuses in Los Angeles and San Diego, California.

The Region issued a civil complaint to UC on September 19, 2000 for failure to register the PCB transformers at both campuses with EPA's National Program Chemicals Division, Office of Pollution Prevention and Toxics on or before December 28, 1998 as required by the regulations. Under the terms of the CAFO, UC agreed to pay a civil penalty of $9,350 and perform a SEP involving removal and replacement of three PCB transformers from the two campuses.[4]

Texas Innocent Owner/Operator Program (IOP)

The Texas IOP, created by House Bill 2776 of the 75th Legislature, provides a certificate to an innocent owner or operator if their property is contaminated as a result of a release or migration of contaminants from a source or sources not located on the property, and they did not cause or contribute to the source or sources of contamination. Like the Texas Voluntary Cleanup Program (VCP), the IOP can be used as a redevelopment tool or as a tool to add value to a contaminated property by providing an Innocent Owner/Operator Certificate (IOC). However, unlike the VCP release of liability, IOCs are not transferable to future owners/operators. Future innocent owners or operators are eligible to enter the IOP and may receive an IOC only after they become an owner or operator of the site.

---

[4] http://www.epa.gov/compliance/civil/tsca/tscaenfenvresults.html

Becoming Eligible for Immunity - To become eligible for immunity, the innocent owner or operator must grant reasonable access to the property for future investigation or remediation, agree on necessary restrictions to protect human health and the environment, if appropriate, and demonstrate that:

- the property has become contaminated because of a release or migration of contaminants from a source or sources not located on or at the property;
- he or she has not caused or contributed to the source or sources of the contamination;
- he or she did not acquire the property from the person that caused the release; or if the property was purchased from the owner of the source property after September 1, 1997, the effective date of the IOP law, the applicant must demonstrate he did not know or have reason to know of the contamination at the time the property was acquired.
- As per the IOP law, it will be necessary for IOP parties to submit:
  - an application;
  - a fee of $1,000 to cover the TCEQ's review cost. (Any portion of the application fee not incurred or obligated in the review of the application shall be refunded.); and
  - a Site Investigation Report (SIR) that describes the contaminated area of concern.

Upon completion of a SIR that demonstrates that the above criteria have been met, then the owner/operator is eligible to receive an IOC from the TCEQ. Parties may terminate their participation in the IOP at any time by written notice to the program.

The state laws that are the foundation of the IOP program are summarized in the Health and Safety Code 361.751-361.754. The state rules that guide decision making in the IOP program are summarized in the Innocent Owner/Operator Program Rules 30 TAC 333.31-333.43.

Through December 2009, the IOP had received 649 applications representing undeveloped property, office/warehouses, supermarket/retail, commercial development and private residences. Of these sites, 454 have received IOCs.[5]

Supplemental Environmental Projects (SEP)

SEPs are environmentally beneficial projects that a respondent agrees to undertake in settlement of an enforcement action but which the respondent is not otherwise legally required to perform, unless the project is a Compliance SEP performed by a local government. Dollars directed to TCEQ-approved environmental projects may be used to offset assessed penalties in enforcement actions. Through a SEP, a respondent in an enforcement matter can choose to invest penalty dollars in improving the environment, rather than paying into the Texas General Revenue Fund.

---

[5] http://www.tceq.texas.gov/remediation/iop/iop.html

What is a SEP? - A SEP is a project that prevents pollution, reduces the amount of pollution reaching the environment, enhances the quality of the environment, or contributes to public awareness of environmental matters. A respondent in an enforcement action may negotiate an agreement to perform a SEP in return for an offset of the administrative penalty. The proposal to include a particular SEP in an agreed order will be presented to the Commission or Executive Director for consideration and final approval. Potential SEPs include such diverse projects as cleanups of abandoned tire sites or illegal dump sites, community collections of household hazardous waste, and pollution prevention projects that exceed regulatory requirements. SEPs that have a direct benefit allow a respondent to offset one dollar of its penalty for every dollar spent on the SEP.

In certain circumstances, a local government respondent may be able to perform a SEP to correct the violations or to remediate environmental harm caused by the violations ("Compliance SEP"). For more information on Compliance SEPs, see the SEP Information section of the SEP website.

Key features of the March 2009 guidance (TCEQ publication GI-352) are:

- **Compliance history.** Repeat violators are less appropriate candidates, as are those who are not in compliance with previous agency orders.
- **Resolution of the violation.** A SEP is appropriate where violations have been or are being corrected, the resulting pollution is cleaned up, and the violator has taken steps to ensure that the problem will not happen again.
- **Deterrence objectives.** As a result of enforcement, violators and other regulated entities should be deterred from future noncompliance with environmental laws and regulations. Therefore, the negotiation of an SEP should not compromise deterrence, which is the main objective in the enforcement process.
- **Other factors as circumstances may require.** (1) The ED may consider the violator's good-faith participation in the settlement of the action and the degree of culpability of the violator for the violations at issue, in addition to other factors. (2) Whether the project meets state and regional environmental priorities. (3) Whether the project is in the same media as the alleged violation. (4) Whether the project is in or near the community where the alleged violation occurred. (5) That the project not be an on-site project that benefits the alleged violator, unless the respondent is a Local Government that is eligible to perform a Compliance SEP.
- **Pre-Approved SEPs.** In 2005, the Commission approved the use of Pre-Approved SEPs, which allow a respondent to contribute to a project on the Commission's list of approved third-party SEPs in lieu of payment of an administrative penalty. Pre-approved SEPs are simple, convenient, and a quick way for a respondent to avoid paying a penalty to the State.

The SEP program was developed as an approach to resolving enforcement actions and improving environmental quality. For respondents who wish to contribute directly to the environmental improvement of their communities, the SEP policy provides an alternative to payment of the full amount of an administrative penalty.

For more information, please contact SEP Central by phone at 512/239-2223 or by e-mail at sephelp@tceq.texas.gov.[6]

Wetlands Protection

In the past, swampy, marshy, or water-saturated soils were considered a source of sickness, a breeding place for disease-bearing mosquitoes. Farmers were encouraged to drain or fill such areas. In addition, large areas of wetlands were eliminated for federal flood control projects, canal building, and mosquito control projects. Then, too late in many cases, scientists learned that wetlands could help control flooding, filter out pollution, clean drinking water, and provide habitat for fish and other wildlife. Environmentalists were quick to expand the new intelligence with rather far-reaching and perhaps unintended results.

Wetlands may be natural or manmade. Decorative lakes or water hazards on golf courses, for example, may become protected wetlands. *Wetlands* is not a scientific term, and because of a lack of clear definition, each agency involved has its own definition. If an area that involves a wetland is disturbed before discovering it is so defined, the result can be enforcement action, including the assessment of administrative, civil, and/or criminal penalties.

Regulations did not prohibit *drainage* of a wetland area, but disallowed the dumping of fill material. That seemed to be a loophole, and in 1993, the administration prohibited drainage, as the excavation work of drainage allowed fill material to be dumped in the wetlands. In late 1996, the change in rules was disallowed, restoring drainage as a legal procedure.

Wetlands Definition

As defined by the Corps, wetlands are "areas inundated or saturated by surface or groundwater at a frequency and duration sufficient to support, and that under normal circumstances do support, a prevalence of vegetation typically adapted for life in saturated soil conditions." The definition is broad and leaves many landowners with less than a clear understanding of its consequences.

If cattails are growing in a landowner's swampland, that area is most likely wetlands. However, many areas may or may not qualify depending on how one interprets such words as *normal circumstances and prevalence of vegetation*. Because the Corps and the EPA exercise authority over wetlands, in 1987, the two agencies combined to produce the Federal *Wetlands Determination Manual*, which explains the technical criteria in greater detail. However, the manual does not distinguish between natural and manmade wetlands. Thus, a wet area in a cornfield created by a farmer's irrigation ditch would be classified the same as an ancient cypress swamp in the Florida Everglades.

---

[6] http://www.tceq.texas.gov/legal/sep/info.html

So the only way to be certain whether an area comes under the wetlands definition is to request the Corps to make an inspection and issue its own determination. Each of the twenty-six Corps district offices throughout the country is authorized to make these determinations, which are final unless a landowner brings suit in federal court to overturn them. There is no right to administrative appeal. Texas has two Corps district offices, one in Galveston and one in Fort Worth.

The federal Department of Agriculture enters into the proper usage of such land when it is designated as agricultural land.

Wetlands Mitigation Banking

If a wetlands area must be filled to complete a development project, it is possible to obtain the necessary Corps permit by restoring or creating another wetlands area—usually on a ratio of 1.5 acres of new wetland for every acre of developed wetland—on or near the project site. To obtain a permit for such work, the developers must agree to flood the area; plant trees, grass, and other vegetation; and guarantee to maintain the new wetland in perpetuity. This method leaves many developers facing a big obstacle.

Fortunately, another method may be available. Entrepreneurs are developing large reserves, or banks, comprising 500 acres or more of functioning wetlands in areas that were previously farmed. Costs to develop this new wetlands bank run about $10,000 per acre. The sponsor offers the acres that may be needed for sale, and the developer can use the land as a credit to fulfill the Corps' requirements. Developers can buy the acreage needed, but they do not take title to the land. The sponsor continues to maintain the new wetlands bank.

This method, known as *mitigation banking*, is gaining recognition, as it offers opportunities for commercial real estate developers to go forward with projects that involve existing wetlands areas and for entrepreneurs to work with developing the wetlands bank for sale at a profit.

Wetlands Case Studies

Environmental Suit Settled in Wisconsin

Mill Valley Corporation is an operator of a non-metallic mining business with its principal operation at the Village of Lannon in Wisconsin, as well as quarry operations at several locations throughout the state. The company allegedly didn't have the correct plans regarding stormwater pollution prevention plans at its state facilities at Jackson, Lannon and Sussex. Wisconsin Attorney General J.B. Van Hollen announced that his office has filed a civil complaint and a civil judgment against the corporation for allegedly violating state environmental laws.

Van Hollen alleges that discharges at the Lannon quarry harshly impacted one acre of wetland and four acres of primary environmental corridor land connected to the wetlands.

The suit also alleges similar and additional violations at the Richfield quarry. In a January, 2011 settlement, Mill Valley Corporation has agreed to pay $200,000 in forfeitures, statutory surcharges and costs immediately upon execution of the judgment. Additionally, the company will implement all of the activities required by its accepted stormwater pollution prevention plan. It has also agreed to purchase 1.5 acres of wetland bank credit as consideration for the damage to the onsite wetland.

Massachusetts Wetlands Suit Settled

On August 25, 2011, Massachusetts Attorney General Martha Coakley announced a settlement with the highway maintenance company of Burlington, Mass., that allegedly dumped solid waste illegally. Gillis Brothers Inc. allegedly filled wetlands and dumped solid waste material that it removed from state highway catch basins, violating the Solid Waste and False Claims Act. Under the terms of the settlement, Gillis will restore the damaged wetlands, pay $37,500 in civil penalties, and contribute $12,500 to the Mystic River Watershed Association for the construction of a rain garden at the Beebe School in Malden, Mass. Coakley commented that anyone contracting with state or local government for services must comply with the terms of the contract, especially provisions that are included for the protection of the public health and environment. According to the complaint, Gillis entered into a contract with the Massachusetts Highway Department to clean catch basins at various locations. The contract required the disposal of the catch basin cleanings in accordance with the policies, regulations and guidance of the Massachusetts Department of Environmental Protection and to notify the MHD of the location of the approved dumpsites. Despite the explicit requirements in the contract that the material be disposed of in accordance with state environmental laws, Gillis allegedly disposed of the cleanings at its property in Burlington and at private property in Pittsfield, Mass. The $37,500 in civil penalties includes a $10,000 penalty for the alleged violation of the False Claims Act by improperly disposing of the catch basin cleanings despite the terms of the contract with MHD. It also includes a $12,500 penalty for the alleged violation of the Wetlands Protection Act and the Solid Waste Disposal Act and a $15,000 penalty that will be waived provided the defendant complies with all terms of the judgment.

Enforcement

The Corps and the EPA share enforcement powers for violations of the wetlands program. Under a Memorandum of Agreement between the two agencies executed in January 1989, the Corps handles enforcement actions involving violations of Corps-issued permits and for unpermitted discharges. The EPA is the lead agency only in unpermitted discharge cases that involve repeat violators and flagrant violations.

Enforcement action can also be instigated by citizen groups who sue the regulatory agencies for improper issuance of a permit or the alleged violator for illegal actions. However, these groups are not entitled to compensation for damages they may have suffered, but they can seek compliance and the imposition of civil penalties. Citizen groups can also recover litigation costs if the court thinks the award is appropriate.

Endangered Species Protection

Landowners have recently become more aware of the fact that the Endangered Species Act of 1973 (16 U.S.C.A. Section 1531 et. seq.) can have a profound impact on the value of their land. One reason for the delay in recognizing its importance is that since the initial act was passed, it has been substantially expanded by bureaucratic regulations. The 1973 act was intended to protect endangered species on federal land and passed Congress by a vote of 92-0 in the Senate and 355-4 in the House. In spite of the overwhelming initial support, the act quickly caused serious consternation when it threatened to shut down construction of the Tellico Dam in Tennessee to protect the snail darter. Since then, regulations have focused on controlling land usage, including private land, which may contain an endangered species' habitat, almost without regard to the actual presence of such species.

Implementation and regulation of the act was assigned to the U.S. Fish and Wildlife Service under the Department of the Interior.

Kinds of Endangered Species

The popular concept of what comprises an endangered species (such as bald eagles, elk, bears, and certain fish and plant life) has been expanded to include 1,177 species on the threatened or endangered lists. The list includes such little-known species as the giant kangaroo rat, the Tooth Cave pseudoscorpion, and the furbish lousewort. Regulations prohibit the modification of habitats for any of these.

When Congress passed the initial Endangered Species Act, it mandated that a protected endangered species be determined by the "best scientific and commercial data available." Nevertheless, no standards were set, and the responsible agencies now make their own determinations without peer review. They specifically require that economic consequences shall not be considered. A challenge is being made to require consideration of economic consequences to EPA rules.

Taking Is Prohibited

The act prohibits the "taking" of endangered species as listed by the federal government. In this context, taking means the killing of any listed plant, animal, fish, or insect. Also, U.S. Fish and Wildlife Service regulations prohibit any *harm* or *harassment* of an endangered species, including modifying, damaging, or destroying the habitat even though the species may not be present. A recent court ruling held that an unintentional catching of an endangered species of salmon was an allowable incidental taking, even though fishing for salmon was a purposeful activity on the part of the fisheries involved. Plaintiffs in this case challenged the failure of the U.S. Department of Commerce and other federal agencies to respond to the "taking" of three species of salmon listed as endangered. Plaintiffs contended that the fisheries should be barred from harvesting all salmon because they could not distinguish between listed and unlisted species. Defendants argued that the "taking" of an endangered species is incidental to the permitted activity. The court held that Congress could not have intended to penalize the fisheries by wholly denying them the ability to fish for salmon because they cannot distinguish between listed and unlisted species before they are caught. *Pacific NW Generating Coop. v. Brown*, 25 F3d 1443 (9th Cir., 1994).

Although the regulatory definition of a taking is broad, it is not clearly defined by case law. An underlying question is this: Can such prohibitions of land usage entitle the landowner to undertake an inverse condemnation suit against the government entities involved? The 5th Amendment to the U.S. Constitution clearly states "…nor shall private property be taken for public use without just compensation." Earlier opinion interpreted this clause as meaning compensation is due only when title to property is taken under eminent domain. The difficult-to-define gray area that has since arisen concerns the partial taking of property that leaves the landowner with title but with only limited usage.

Incidental Take Permit

A developer or landowner who wants to build on land that is home to a threatened or endangered species must apply for an incidental take permit. The process can be lengthy and complex. The application for an incidental take permit must be accompanied by a habitat conservation plan (HCP). The purpose of the plan is to ensure that any incidental take and its effects are minimized. Developing such a plan can take from 8 to 24 months.

Backlog of Listing Requests

[The following is an excerpt from an article by Todd Woody published in the New York Times on April 20, 2011:]

The federal *Fish and Wildlife Service* is in emergency triage mode as it struggles with an avalanche of petitions and lawsuits over the endangered species list, the chief tool for protecting plants and animals facing extinction in the United States. Over the last four years, a few environmental groups have requested that more than 1,230 species be listed, compared with the previous 12 years in which annual requests averaged only 20 species.

Some environmental groups argue that vastly expanded listings are needed as evidence mounts that the world is entering an era of mass extinctions related to destruction of habitat, climate and other changes. Such threats require a focus on entire ecosystems, they say, rather than individual species.

"The many requests for species petitions has inundated the listing program's domestic species listing capabilities," the service wrote in its 2012 budget request. Already it faces a backlog of 254 species, including the yellow-billed loon, Gunnison's prairie dog and the North American wolverine. It says their protection is warranted but precluded by a lack of resources.

Two environmental groups, the *Center for Biological Diversity* and *WildEarth Guardians*, have filed 90 percent of the listings petitions since 2007 and maintain that a bioblitz, as it is often called, is the best strategy for forcing the service to be more assertive in its wildlife protection mission.

In its 2012 budget request, the service estimated that in 2011 it will be able to make final listing decisions on only 4 percent of warranted petitions within one year as required by law, down from 12 percent in 2010.

Since Congress passed the Endangered Species Act 37 years ago, some 1,370 species have been listed, the last being the southern rockhopper penguin. Last month, the agency asked Congress to impose a cap on the amount of money the agency can spend on processing listing petitions, both to control its workload and as a defense against lawsuits. "We would essentially use that as our defense for not doing more," Mr. Frazer, the agency's assistant director for endangered species, testified, "so that we can balance among the various duties that we have."

Underground Storage Tanks (USTs)

The Resources Conservation and Recovery Act of 1976 (RCRA) has been amended so as to require the EPA to develop a comprehensive program to prevent, detect, and correct releases from Underground Storage Tanks (USTs). Under the EPA definition, a UST is any tank that has 10 percent or more of its volume below ground and contains either petroleum or hazardous substances. The EPA estimates that 2 million USTs are covered by the regulations and that 95 percent of those are used to store petroleum and its products.

Certain tanks are excluded from the definition, including farm or residential tanks of 1,100 gallons or less storing fuel for noncommercial purposes, heating oil tanks holding oil for consumption on the premises, septic tanks, wastewater collection systems, and storage tanks located in an enclosed underground area (basement). Although excluded by the EPA, these types of tanks may be covered by state or local laws.

UST owners must provide certain safety precautions, including corrosion protection, leak detection by monthly monitoring or inventory control, and tank-tightness testing, in addition to spill and overflow devices. Compliance has been phased in over 5 years and now applies to all USTs.

USTs installed after December 1988 must have all requirements in place upon installation. Qualified contractors must install new tanks according to code, and tank owners must provide the EPA with certification of proper installation. The same is true for tank removal.

There are reporting requirements for containment of leaks and spills; also, various records must be kept to evidence a tank owner's ongoing compliance with the regulations. Since October 1990, owners and operators of USTs must demonstrate responsibility for corrective actions and be able to compensate for injury or property damage from $500,000 to $4 million, depending on the number of tanks owned. If a landowner finds an underground tank on the property, he must find out what it contains and what condition it is in. Some abandoned tanks have been filled with sand, gravel, or other inert material. If the tank contains a liquid, the landowner needs to find out what the liquid is so it can be properly disposed of and whether the tank has leaked or is leaking. A professional may need to perform a tank-tightness test. If a hazardous substance is involved, a report to the EPA may be necessary.

Landlords whose tenants have tanks, mortgagees whose borrowers have tanks, and purchasers of property on which tanks are located must make sure they are in compliance with the regulations. Familiarity with these regulations will enable a real estate agent to provide competent, professional suggestions in transactions involving USTs.

Electromagnetic Forces

Most environmental concerns are real and should be considered when dealing with land and what may be built on it. Yet there is no doubt that some people profit from environmental scares. Whether electromagnetic force is a scare tactic or a real concern has yet to be determined. Nevertheless, because it could be a consideration in buying property or evaluating some, electromagnetic force is a subject the agent needs to know about.

Electromagnetic fields (EMFs) fit nicely into scare tactics. They are silent and invisible, and few nonscientists know what they are or where they come from. Yet they exist anywhere electrons zip through transmission lines, in the innards of appliances, and in electric blankets, making them nearly impossible to avoid.

Over the years, various studies have linked electromagnetic fields to cancer. In 1979, epidemiologists found that children living near high-current power lines in Denver got leukemia at 1.5 times the expected rate. However, these studies are hobbled because it is nearly impossible to monitor actual EMFs continuously inside thousands of houses. So a stand-in for EMF exposure is used. The stand-in is called a wire-code rating and reflects a home's distance from a power line and the size of wires close by. When researchers actually measure EMFs, they find that fields are no higher in homes with leukemia cases than in homes without.

Thus far, there has been no clear relationship between the strength of an EMF and the incidence of leukemia. In November 1996, the National Research Council, after 3 years of examining more than 500 studies, issued its report. Quoting from the report, "The current body of evidence does not show that exposure to these fields presents a human health hazard." There is one possible exception—everyday levels of EMFs do suppress a cell's production of melatonin. This hormone slows the growth of breast cells on their way to becoming cancerous.

Mold

Mold exists everywhere all of the time. Usually, it does not bother anyone. However, at times, mold can be a problem, particularly for people who are unusually sensitive to it.

Some people experience respiratory problems when they are exposed to mold, and they can become very ill. Certain molds, in particular the "black mold," seem to make people ill. Even though mold exists everywhere, it thrives in dark, moist areas, such as dirty heating ducts. A roof that has leaked, no matter how slowly, for a long time can create moisture and encourage mold growth. Combine mold with a particularly sensitive person, and a lawsuit may result.

As a result, real estate practitioners and inspectors need to understand the mold issue. The presence of mold or mold-causing conditions, such as previous water damage, should be disclosed by sellers—especially when a homeowner knows about an ongoing mold problem that may not be apparent from a basic inspection. When to disclose is a fact-specific legal issue, but mold disclosure will probably not be uncommon in the near future.

Landlords also need to be vigilant about the mold issue. A chronic leaky roof, leaky water pipes, bathroom moisture, or a poorly maintained ventilation system may be an invitation to a lawsuit. If science establishes a causal relationship between the presence of mold and human illness, legal exposure will rise.

Landlords must take reasonable means to avoid harmful mold growth. Indoor air quality experts are available to provide assistance. If mold repairs are needed, an experienced mold remediation company should be contacted. Certain protocols should be followed, and real estate practitioners will want to ensure that they can prove that the job was done correctly.

Carbon Monoxide

Carbon monoxide (CO) is an odorless, colorless gas produced by the combustion of fuels such as natural gas, oil, and propane in devices such as furnaces, water heaters, and stoves. These items are normally designed to vent the CO to the outside, but harmful interior levels of CO can result from incomplete combustion of fuel, improper installation, or blockages, leaks, or cracks in the venting systems. Homeowners can take action against potential CO poisoning by following the steps given below:

- Have all fuel-burning appliances professionally inspected yearly, preferably before the start of the cold-weather season when heaters and furnaces are first used.
- These appliances include gas stoves and ovens, furnaces and heaters, water heaters, generators, and clothes dryers.
- All such devices should be properly installed and vented to the outside whenever possible.
- If repairs are necessary, be sure they are performed by a qualified technician.
- Always use the proper fuel specified for the device.
- Have flues and chimneys for fuel-burning fireplaces or wood stoves inspected regularly for cracks, leaks, and blockages that may allow a buildup of CO to occur.
- Never use gas stoves or ovens to heat the home, even temporarily.
- Do not start or idle a vehicle in a garage, even with the outer garage door open.
- For additional protection, purchase a CO detector (either battery operated or plug-in) and follow the manufacturer's instructions for proper location and installation.
- Learn what to do should the CO alarm activate.

If anyone in the home experiences symptoms such as fatigue, dizziness, blurred vision, nausea, or confusion, everyone should leave immediately and seek medical attention. If no symptoms are felt, open doors and windows immediately and shut off all fuel-burning devices that may be potential sources of CO.

Chim Chimney, Chim Chimney

In October, 2011, New Jersey Attorney General Paula Dow and the state Division of Consumer Affairs announced a lawsuit against a chimney cleaning and repair company. The company allegedly used high-pressure deceptive tactics to mislead consumers into paying thousands of dollars for repair services that they did not need and performed shoddy work that created a danger of carbon monoxide leaks into the homes. The lawsuit alleges that the company and its owner violated New Jersey's Consumer Fraud Act, Contractors' Registration Act, Regulations Governing Home Improvement Practices and Regulations Governing Contractor Regulations. According to the complaint, the company engaged in aggressive sales tactics in the state including unsolicited phone calls and door-to-door solicitations, sales pitches that offered services ranging from $39 to $60 followed by alarming claims that the consumers' chimneys were in very bad condition and created an imminent danger unless consumers paid for repairs costing thousands of dollars. Workers allegedly showed consumers bricks or cell phone pictures of damaged chimneys, falsely claiming that the brick and the picture came from the consumer's chimney. Based on these representations, consumers allegedly agreed to purchase chimney parts and repairs ranging from $1,800 to $4,800. The state's complaint notes that Princeton Township issued a notice of violation and notice of penalty against the company arising from its performance of work without a permit. Due to the company's alleged failure to respond to the notices, penalties of $74,000 have accrued. The state is asking the court to revoke the company's registration as a home improvement contractor in New Jersey and to appoint a receiver, at the defendants' expense, to assume control over the defendants' assets and to sell or convey assets for the restoration of affected consumers.

EPA's Bad Science to Blame for State's Latest Challenge[7]

The state of Texas is again being forced to take legal action against the federal EPA, this time to stop enforcement of the new Cross-State Air Pollution Rule (CSAPR). EPA apologists continue to demonstrate a lack of basic understanding of the rule and a dangerous, misguided belief that CSAPR should be accepted without the scrutiny of law, science, and common sense.

When the EPA puts forward a regulation that is not based on facts, doesn't follow its own rules and will have significant adverse impacts to this state, Texas has the right and the obligation to its citizens to pursue legal remedies. Texas must protect Texans from the real, immediate harm this rule will inflict. Blame EPA's insistence on using bad science and flawed legal arguments for Texas' need to stand up and challenge EPA's actions yet again.

---

[7] http://www.tceq.texas.gov/news/releases/10-11ShawOpinion10-4

Let's be very clear about the facts. The last-minute inclusion of Texas in the sulfur dioxide portion of the rule is based on modeling that says an Illinois monitor, located across the street from a steel mill, shows a theoretical reading that is slightly above attainment. Actual data from 2009 forward shows that this monitor is meeting the federal air quality standards today. And even if the feds relied on their own computer simulated modeling predictions, that monitor would be in attainment in 2014 without any reductions from CSAPR. So does Texas' tenuous link to this monitor justify the state's inclusion in CSAPR? No.

The EPA stridently insists the law doesn't go into effect until March 2013, and this gives companies plenty of time to comply. This is patently wrong, so let's clear the air on this misrepresentation as well. Fines, and even criminal penalties for noncompliance, will be based on how plants operate starting January 2012. March 2013 is merely the due date for the paperwork that demonstrates compliance. And since installing equipment to achieve compliance can take years, companies will have to depend on "credits" being available for purchase at a reasonable, predictable cost... an enormous gamble to take in the real world.

The EPA continues to throw out theoretical numbers showing impressive health effects from these initiatives, but federal legislators are growing increasingly short-tempered over the EPA's refusal to provide the data and studies to back these projections.

And while the EPA and its defenders cast doubts that these rules will really cost jobs and impact the state's supply of electricity, both the PUC and ERCOT have testified repeatedly that the power grid will be negatively impacted by CSAPR. Luminant was forced to make a business decision to comply with this rule, leading the company to announce that it will need to lay off 500 employees and shut down two of its units. Other companies are facing similar business decisions and their impacts will be felt throughout Texas.

The State of Texas cannot ignore the flaws of this rule. It would be irresponsible to simply accept that there are Texans who will lose air conditioning during the hottest hours of the hottest months next summer because an EPA computer model shows an air monitor in Illinois may exceed the standard.

While individuals can reach different conclusions based upon the same set of facts, defenders of the EPA should seriously consider the consequences of blindly endorsing bad law just because it comes out of Washington, D.C.

Texas Commission on Environmental Quality (TCEQ)

The TCEQ is the State's primary and comprehensive environmental regulatory agency. Its mission is to protect our State's precious human and natural resources consistent with sustainable economic development. The agency regulates approximately 460,000 public and private facilities and/or individuals in Texas that affect, or have the potential to significantly affect, the environment. The goal of the agency is clean air, clean water, and the safe management of waste.

TCEQ Penalties

In January of 2006, The Texas Commission on Environmental Quality (TCEQ) approved penalties totaling $503,051 against 69 regulated entities for violations of state environmental regulations.

The TCEQ's three commissioners approved agreed orders in the following enforcement categories: thirteen air quality; one municipal solid waste; one Edwards Aquifer; one industrial hazardous waste; five industrial waste discharge; three licensed irrigator; one multi-media; ten municipal waste discharge; fifteen petroleum storage tank; fifteen public water system; and two water quality. The commissioners also approved; one public water system default order; one industrial hazardous waste default order; and one water quality default order.

Included in the total fine figure is a penalty of $123,608 against Cemex, Inc., in Ector County for air violations. The agreed order resulted from eight violations found during investigations in 2004, and include exceeding permit emissions limits; failure to submit and submit timely various reports and compliance certifications; failure to notify TCEQ of emission events; failure to comply with opacity limits; failure to operate consistently with plant plans; failure to properly operate emissions equipment; and failure to comply with monitoring requirements. As a condition of the agreed order, Cemex will contribute $61,804 of the fine for a Supplemental Environmental Project to fund an education and recycling/disposal program by Keep Odessa Beautiful, Inc.

Agenda items from all commission meetings and work session agendas can be viewed on the TCEQ Web site.

TCEQ Annual Report

During the 75th Legislative Session, House Bills 1133 and 1367 added a new section (Section 5.126) to the Texas Water Code. Section 5.126 requires the TCEQ to prepare an electronic enforcement report each year by December 1. The report is required to show actions for each type of regulatory program. The report is to contain statistical indicators including the number of investigations, number of notices of violation issued, number of enforcement actions, type of enforcement actions, amount of penalties assessed, deferred, or collected; and any other information the Commission determines is relevant. The report must include a comparison with TCEQ's enforcement actions for each of the preceding five fiscal years. This report, the fourteenth of its kind, includes information from fiscal years 2005-2010.

The 77th Legislative Session added requirements which expanded the comparison requirement in the original section by adding a comparative analysis of data evaluating the performance, over time, of the Commission and of entities regulated by the Commission. The Legislature also added a requirement in TEX. HEALTH AND SAFETY CODE §382.0215 to assess emissions events, including actions taken by the Commission in response to the emissions events. Emissions events are unplanned or unanticipated occurrences of emissions (contaminants released into the air), emissions from unscheduled maintenance, startup, or shutdown activities that release air contaminants.

The 2010 report can be accessed by going to: http://www.tceq.texas.gov/enforcement/ reports/AER/annenfreport.html

This enforcement report contains statistical indicators and a comparative analysis for the following enforcement related activities:

- number of investigations and complaints by program and region;
- number of notices of violation issued by program and region;
- number and type of enforcement actions and lists of each action denoting the regulated entity name and location by county and region;
- amount of penalties assessed, deferred, and required to be paid to General Revenue;
- supplemental environmental project costs, offsets, and descriptions;
- number and percentage of enforcement actions issued to persons who previously have committed the same or similar violations;
- number and percentage of enforcement orders issued to entities that have been the subject of a previous enforcement order;
- classification of violations as major, moderate, or minor;
- most frequently cited rules/statutes in enforcement actions;
- emissions events; and
- other information which the Commission deems relevant, including information on the results of enforcement actions (i.e., environmental benefit, pollutant reductions, etc.).

TCEQ Free Email Updates

If you would like to receive free emails from TCEQ on subjects of their choice you can sign up on their website at https://public.govdelivery.com/accounts/TXTCEQ/subscriber/new?. You will only receive updates on items you choose and it is easy to change subscriptions or unsubscribe at any time.

It is also possible to use social media accounts with Google, Facebook or Yahoo.

The following are some of the categories that can be subscribed to:

- Job Openings at the Agency
- Regulatory Announcements for Small Businesses and Local Governments
- Schedule of Public Hearings for Proposed Rules Commission Meetings and Actions
- TCEQ Monthly Enforcement Reports (in PDF)
- Supplemental Environmental Projects
- TCEQ Publications and Online Resources
- Air Quality
- Water Quality
- Air Permitting and Compliance

- Advisory Groups - Air Permitting
- Laboratory Accreditation
- Business and Local Government Advisory Groups to the TCEQ
- Cleanups and Remediation
- Exchange Network: RENEW
- Available Raw Materials You Might Need
- Someone Interested in Purchasing or Reusing Your Waste
- Waste Management
- Water Supply
- Environmental Flows Program
- Radioactive Materials
- Low Level Radioactive Waste (LLRW)
- TCEQ Conferences, Seminars, Workshops

Environmental Websites

For additional research on the numerous environmental issues, please consult the following websites:

Radon Sites and Links of Interest:

Gardner, Marilyn, "Easy on the Eyes and the Environment," *The Christian Science Monitor*, March 3, 2004. Accessed on August 2, 2005, from
http://www.csmonitor.com/2004/0303/p11s01-lihc.html

A Citizen's Guide to Radon
http://www.epa.gov/radon/pubs/citguide.html

Buyer's and Seller's Guide to Radon
http://www.epa.gov/radon/pubs/hmbyguid.html

Table of Action Levels for Radon
http://www.co.jefferson.co.us/health/health_T111_R42.htm#epa

EPA radon page
www.epa.gov/iaq/radon

National Environmental Health Association, radon page, http://radongas.org/
Colorado Department of Public Health and Environment, radon page, www.cdphe.state.co.us/hm/rad/radon/index.htm

Other Resources

- Jefferson County Environmental Health Services: 303-271-5700
- Western Regional Radon Training Center: 1-800-513-8332
- Colorado Radon Hot Line: 1-800-846-3986

Lead Sites and Links of Interest:

EPA—Protect Your Family from Lead in Your Home
http://www.epa.gov/lead/pubs/ leadpdfe.pdf

Finding a Qualified Lead Professional for Your Home
http://www.epa.gov/lead/pubs/broch 32e.pdf

Testing Your Home for Lead
http://www.epa.gov/lead/pubs/leadtest.pdf

Reducing Lead Hazards When Remodeling Your Home
http://www.epa.gov/lead/pubs/ rrpamph.pdf

Water Quality Sites and Links of Interest:
Drinking Water and Health—What You Need to Know!
http://www.epa.gov/safewater/ dwh/dw-health.pdf

Water System Council
http://www.wellcarehotline.org/

WellOwner.org
http://www.wellowner.org/

EPA—Drinking Water From Household Wells
fhttp://www.epa.gov/safewater/private wells/

All About Your Water—Domestic Well Analysis
https://www.ecobroker.com/userdef/PDFs/example_well_water_results_letter.pdf

Mold Sites and Links of Interest:
A Brief Guide to Mold, Moisture, and Your Home
http://www.epa.gov/mold/pdfs/mold guide.pdf

Asbestos Sites and Links of Interest:

EPA—Asbestos in Your Home
http://www.epa.gov/asbestos/pubs/ashome.html

EPA—Asbestos Containing Materials
http://www.epa.gov/Region06/6pd/asbestos/asbmatl.htm

Indoor Air Quality Sites and Links of Interest:
EPA—An Introduction to Indoor Air Quality (IAQ)
http://www.epa.gov/iaq/ia-intro.html

EPA—Indoor Air Quality in Large Buildings
http://www.epa.gov/iaq/largebldgs/index.html

EPA—Inside IAQ
http://www.epa.gov/appcdwww/iemb/insideiaq/fw98.pdf

EPA—The Inside Story: A Guide to Indoor Air Quality
http://www.epa.gov/iaq/pubs/ insidest.html

Policy Assessment for the Review of the Carbon Monoxide National Ambient Air Quality
Standards
http://www.epa.gov/ttn/naaqs/standards/co/data/20101022copafinal.pdf

Report of the Interagency Task Force on Carbon Capture and Storage
http://www.epa.gov/climatechange/downloads/CCS-Task-Force-Report-2010.pdf

National Programs to Assess IEQ Effects of Building Materials and Products
http://www.epa.gov/iaq/pdfs/hal_levin_paper.pdf

Solutions to the Indoor Air Quality Problem – World Health Organization
http://www.who.int/indoorair/publications/iabriefing3.pdf

Toxic Waste Sites and Links of Interest:

EPA—Environmental Indicators Initiative
http://www.ecobroker.com/userdef/PDFs/EPABetterProtectedLand.pdf

EPA—National Priorities List Sites in the United States
http://www.epa.gov/superfund/ sites/npl/npl.htm

EPA—Search Your Community
http://www.epa.gov/epahome/commsearch.htm

EPA Targeted Brownfields Assessments—The Basics
http://www.epa.gov/swerosps/bf/ facts/tba_0403.pdf

Brownfields
https://www.ecobroker.com/misc/articleview.aspx?ArticleID=37

National Priorities List in Texas
http://www.epa.gov/superfund/sites/npl/tx.htm

Brio Site
http://cfpub.epa.gov/supercpad/cursites/csitinfo.cfm?id=0602601

Green Buildings and Health Sites and Links of Interest:

Benefits of Owning a Built Green Home
http://www.builtgreen.org/homebuyers/benefits.htm

Environmental Features and Benefits
http://www.builtgreen.org/homebuilders/environment.htm

About ENERGY STAR New Homes
http://www.energystar.gov/index.cfm?c=new_homes.hm_earn_star

Tight Construction Reduced Air Infiltration
http://www.energystar.gov/index.cfm?c=new_homes_features.hm_f_reduced_air_infiltration

Residential Energy Services Network
http://www.natresnet.org/

Green Building Basic Information
http://www.epa.gov/greenbuilding/pubs/about.htm

More information on Energy Star products:
http://www.energystar.gov/products

Miscellaneous Environmental Websites

More information on Winter Tips:
http://www.epa.gov/epahome/hi-winter.htm

More ways to Reduce Holiday Wastes:
http://www.epa.gov/epawaste/wycd/funfacts/winter.htm

Consumer Product Safety Commission:
http://www.cpsc.gov/

Food and Drug Administration:
http://www.fda.gov/

Federal Insecticide, Fungicide and Rodenticide Act:
http://www.epa.gov/regulations/laws/index.html

Regional EPA Office:
http://www.epa.gov/epahome/regions.htm

Appendix
Documents and Forms

PROMULGATED BY THE TEXAS REAL ESTATE COMMISSION (TREC)

5-2-2011

NOTICE OF BUYER'S TERMINATION OF CONTRACT

CONCERNING THE CONTRACT FOR THE SALE OF THE PROPERTY AT

_____

(Street Address and City)

BETWEEN THE UNDERSIGNED BUYER AND_____

_____ (SELLER)

Buyer notifies Seller that the contract is terminated pursuant to the following:

❑(1) the unrestricted right of Buyer to terminate the contract under Paragraph 23 of the contract.

❑(2) Buyer cannot obtain Credit Approval in accordance with the Third Party Financing Addendum for Credit Approval to the contract.

❑(3) the Property does not satisfy the lenders' underwriting requirements for the loan under Paragraph 4A(1) of the contract.

❑(4) Buyer elects to terminate under Paragraph A of the Addendum for Property Subject to Mandatory Membership in a Property Owners' Association.

❑(5) Buyer elects to terminate under Paragraph 7B(2) of the contract relating to the Seller's Disclosure Notice.

❑(6) Other (identify the paragraph number of contract or the addendum): _____

_____

_____

_____

_____

NOTE: Release of the earnest money is governed by the terms of the contract.

_____   _____
Buyer   Date   Buyer   Date

This form has been approved by the Texas Real Estate Commission for use with similarly approved or promulgated contract forms. Such approval relates to this form only. TREC forms are intended for use only by trained real estate licensees. No representation is made as to the legal validity or adequacy of any provision in any specific transactions. It is not suitable for complex transactions. Texas Real Estate Commission, P.O. Box 12188, Austin, TX 78711-2188, (512) 459-6544 (http://www.trec.state.tx.us) TREC No. 38-3. This form replaces TREC No. 38-2.

TREC No.38-3

Reprinted by permission of Texas Real Estate Commission.

TEXAS ASSOCIATION OF REALTORS®

INTERMEDIARY RELATIONSHIP NOTICE

USE OF THIS FORM BY PERSONS WHO ARE NOT MEMBERS OF THE TEXAS ASSOCIATION OF REALTORS® IS NOT AUTHORIZED.
©Texas Association of REALTORS®, Inc. 2004

To: _____ (Seller or Landlord)

    and _____ (Prospect)

From: _____ (Broker's Firm)

Re: _____ (Property)

Date: _____

A. Under this notice, "owner" means the seller or landlord of the Property and "prospect" means the above-named prospective buyer or tenant for the Property.

B. Broker's firm represents the owner under a listing agreement and also represents the prospect under a buyer/tenant representation agreement.

C. In the written listing agreement and the written buyer/tenant representation agreement, both the owner and the prospect previously authorized Broker to act as an intermediary if a prospect who Broker represents desires to buy or lease a property that is listed by the Broker. When the prospect makes an offer to purchase or lease the Property, Broker will act in accordance with the authorizations granted in the listing agreement and in the buyer/tenant representation agreement.

D. Broker ❑ will ❑ will not appoint licensed associates to communicate with, carry out instructions of, and provide opinions and advice during negotiations to each party. If Broker makes such appointments, Broker appoints:

_____ to the owner; and

_____ to the prospect.

E. By acknowledging receipt of this notice, the undersigned parties reaffirm their consent for broker to act as an intermediary.

F. Additional Information: *(Disclose material information related to Broker's relationship to the parties, such as personal relationships or prior or contemplated business relationships.)*

The undersigned acknowledge receipt of this notice

Seller or Landlord	Date	Prospect	Date

Seller or Landlord	Date	Prospect	Date

(TAR-1409) 1-7-04   Page 1 of 1

Reprinted by permission of Texas Association of REALTORS®

8-01-2011

PROMULGATED BY THE TEXAS REAL ESTATE COMMISSION (TREC)

ONE TO FOUR FAMILY RESIDENTIAL CONTRACT (RESALE)

NOTICE: Not For Use For Condominium Transactions

1. PARTIES: The parties to this contract are _____(Seller) and _____(Buyer). Seller agrees to sell and convey to Buyer and Buyer agrees to buy from Seller the Property defined below.

2. PROPERTY:

  A. LAND: Lot _____ Block_____, _____ Addition, City of _____ , County of _____ , Texas, known as _____ (address/zip code), or as described on attached exhibit.

  B. IMPROVEMENTS: The house, garage and all other fixtures and improvements attached to the above-described real property, including without limitation, the following **permanently installed and built-in items,** if any: all equipment and appliances, valances, screens, shutters, awnings, wall-to-wall carpeting, mirrors, ceiling fans, attic fans, mail boxes, television antennas and satellite dish system and equipment, mounts and brackets for televisions and speakers, heating and air-conditioning units, security and fire detection equipment, wiring, plumbing and lighting fixtures, chandeliers, water softener system, kitchen equipment, garage door openers, cleaning equipment, shrubbery, landscaping, outdoor cooking equipment, and all other property owned by Seller and attached to the above described real property.

  C. ACCESSORIES: The following described related accessories, if any: window air conditioning units, stove, fireplace screens, curtains and rods, blinds, window shades, draperies and rods, door keys, mailbox keys, above ground pool, swimming pool equipment and maintenance accessories, artificial fireplace logs, and controls for: (i) satellite dish systems, (ii) garage doors, (iii) entry gates, and (iv) other improvements and accessories.

  D. EXCLUSIONS: The following improvements and accessories will be retained by Seller and must be removed prior to delivery of possession:_____ _____.

The land, improvements and accessories are collectively referred to as the "Property".

3. SALES PRICE:

  A. Cash portion of Sales Price payable by Buyer at closing ....$_____

  B. Sum of all financing described below (excluding any loan funding fee or mortgage insurance premium) ....$_____

  C. Sales Price (Sum of A and B) ....$_____

4. FINANCING: The portion of Sales Price not payable in cash will be paid as follows: (Check applicable boxes below)

  ❑ A. THIRD PARTY FINANCING: One or more third party mortgage loans in the total amount of $_____ (excluding any loan funding fee or mortgage insurance premium).

    (1) Property Approval: If the Property does not satisfy the lenders' underwriting requirements for the loan(s) (including, but not limited to appraisal, insurability and lender required repairs), Buyer may terminate this contract by giving notice to Seller prior to closing and the earnest money will be refunded to Buyer.

    (2) Credit Approval: (Check one box only)

      ❑ (a) This contract is subject to Buyer being approved for the financing described in the attached Third Party Financing Addendum for Credit Approval.

      ❑ (b) This contract is not subject to Buyer being approved for financing and does not involve FHA or VA financing.

  ❑ B. ASSUMPTION: The assumption of the unpaid principal balance of one or more promissory notes described in the attached TREC Loan Assumption Addendum.

  ❑ C. SELLER   FINANCING: A promissory note from Buyer to Seller of $_____, secured by vendor's and deed of trust liens, and containing the terms and conditions described in the attached TREC Seller Financing Addendum. If an owner policy of title insurance is furnished, Buyer shall furnish Seller with a mortgagee policy of title insurance.

Initialed for identification by Buyer_____ _____ and Seller _____ _____   TREC NO. 20-10

Contract Concerning _____ Page 2 of 9   8-01-2011
(Address of Property)

5. EARNEST MONEY: Upon execution of this contract by all parties, Buyer shall deposit $_____ as earnest money with _____, as escrow agent, at _____ (address). Buyer shall deposit additional earnest money of $_____ with escrow agent within _____ days after the effective date of this contract. If Buyer fails to deposit the earnest money as required by this contract, Buyer will be in default.

6. TITLE POLICY AND SURVEY:
  A. TITLE POLICY: Seller shall furnish to Buyer at ❑ Seller's ❑ Buyer's expense an owner policy of title insurance (Title Policy) issued by _____ (Title Company) in the amount of the Sales Price, dated at or after closing, insuring Buyer against loss under the provisions of the Title Policy, subject to the promulgated exclusions (including existing building and zoning ordinances) and the following exceptions:
    (1) Restrictive covenants common to the platted subdivision in which the Property is located.
    (2) The standard printed exception for standby fees, taxes and assessments.
    (3) Liens created as part of the financing described in Paragraph 4.
    (4) Utility easements created by the dedication deed or plat of the subdivision in which the Property is located.
    (5) Reservations or exceptions otherwise permitted by this contract or as may be approved by Buyer in writing.
    (6) The standard printed exception as to marital rights.
    (7) The standard printed exception as to waters, tidelands, beaches, streams, and related matters.
    (8) The standard printed exception as to discrepancies, conflicts, shortages in area or boundary lines, encroachments or protrusions, or overlapping improvements. Buyer, at Buyer's expense, may have the exception amended to read, "shortages in area".
  B. COMMITMENT: Within 20 days after the Title Company receives a copy of this contract, Seller shall furnish to Buyer a commitment for title insurance (Commitment) and, at Buyer's expense, legible copies of restrictive covenants and documents evidencing exceptions in the Commitment (Exception Documents) other than the standard printed exceptions. Seller authorizes the Title Company to deliver the Commitment and Exception Documents to Buyer at Buyer's address shown in Paragraph 21. If the Commitment and Exception Documents are not delivered to Buyer within the specified time, the time for delivery will be automatically extended up to 15 days or the Closing Date, whichever is earlier.
  C. SURVEY: The survey must be made by a registered professional land surveyor acceptable to the Title Company and Buyer's lender(s). (Check one box only)
    ❑(1) Within _____ days after the effective date of this contract, Seller shall furnish to Buyer and Title Company Seller's existing survey of the Property and a Residential Real Property Affidavit promulgated by the Texas Department of Insurance (T-47 Affidavit). **If Seller fails to furnish the existing survey or affidavit within the time prescribed, Buyer shall obtain a new survey at Seller's expense no later than 3 days prior to Closing Date.** If the existing survey or affidavit is not acceptable to Title Company or Buyer's lender(s), Buyer shall obtain a new survey at ❑Seller's ❑Buyer's expense no later than 3 days prior to Closing Date.
    ❑(2) Within _____ days after the effective date of this contract, Buyer shall obtain a new survey at Buyer's expense. Buyer is deemed to receive the survey on the date of actual receipt or the date specified in this paragraph, whichever is earlier.
    ❑(3) Within _____ days after the effective date of this contract, Seller, at Seller's expense shall furnish a new survey to Buyer.
  D. OBJECTIONS: Buyer may object in writing to defects, exceptions, or encumbrances to title: disclosed on the survey other than items 6A(1) through (7) above; disclosed in the Commitment other than items 6A(1) through (8) above; or which prohibit the following use or activity: _____
_____
_____.
    Buyer must object the earlier of (i) the Closing Date or (ii) _____ days after Buyer receives the

Initialed for identification by Buyer_____ _____ and Seller _____ _____   TREC NO. 20-10

Contract Concerning _____ Page 3 of 9   8-01-2011
(Address of Property)

Commitment, Exception Documents, and the survey. Buyer's failure to object within the time allowed will constitute a waiver of Buyer's right to object; except that the requirements in Schedule C of the Commitment are not waived. Provided Seller is not obligated to incur any expense, Seller shall cure the timely objections of Buyer or any third party lender within 15 days after Seller receives the objections and the Closing Date will be extended as necessary. If objections are not cured within such 15 day period, this contract will terminate and the earnest money will be refunded to Buyer unless Buyer waives the objections.

E. **TITLE NOTICES:**

(1) ABSTRACT OR TITLE POLICY: Broker advises Buyer to have an abstract of title covering the Property examined by an attorney of Buyer's selection, or Buyer should be furnished with or obtain a Title Policy. If a Title Policy is furnished, the Commitment should be promptly reviewed by an attorney of Buyer's choice due to the time limitations on Buyer's right to object.

(2) PROPERTY OWNERS ASSOCIATION(S) MANDATORY MEMBERSHIP: The Property ☐is ☐is not subject to mandatory membership in a property owners association(s). If the Property is subject to mandatory membership in a property owners association(s), Seller notifies Buyer under §5.012, Texas Property Code, that, as a purchaser of property in the residential community identified in Paragraph 2A in which the Property is located, you are obligated to be a member of the property owners association(s). Restrictive covenants governing the use and occupancy of the Property and a dedicatory instrument governing the establishment, maintenance, and operation of this residential community have been or will be recorded in the Real Property Records of the county in which the Property is located. Copies of the restrictive covenants and dedicatory instrument may be obtained from the county clerk. You are obligated to pay assessments to the property owners association(s). The amount of the assessments is subject to change. Your failure to pay the assessments could result in a lien on and the foreclosure of the Property. **If Buyer is concerned about these matters, the TREC promulgated Addendum for Property Subject to Mandatory Membership in a Property Owners Association should be used for each association.**

(3) STATUTORY TAX DISTRICTS: If the Property is situated in a utility or other statutorily created district providing water, sewer, drainage, or flood control facilities and services, Chapter 49, Texas Water Code, requires Seller to deliver and Buyer to sign the statutory notice relating to the tax rate, bonded indebtedness, or standby fee of the district prior to final execution of this contract.

(4) TIDE WATERS: If the Property abuts the tidally influenced waters of the state, §33.135, Texas Natural Resources Code, requires a notice regarding coastal area property to be included in the contract. An addendum containing the notice promulgated by TREC or required by the parties must be used.

(5) ANNEXATION: If the Property is located outside the limits of a municipality, Seller notifies Buyer under §5.011, Texas Property Code, that the Property may now or later be included in the extraterritorial jurisdiction of a municipality and may now or later be subject to annexation by the municipality. Each municipality maintains a map that depicts its boundaries and extraterritorial jurisdiction. To determine if the Property is located within a municipality's extraterritorial jurisdiction or is likely to be located within a municipality's extraterritorial jurisdiction, contact all municipalities located in the general proximity of the Property for further information.

(6) PROPERTY LOCATED IN A CERTIFICATED SERVICE AREA OF A UTILITY SERVICE PROVIDER: Notice required by §13.257, Water Code: The real property, described in Paragraph 2, that you are about to purchase may be located in a certificated water or sewer service area, which is authorized by law to provide water or sewer service to the properties in the certificated area. If your property is located in a certificated area there may be special costs or charges that you will be required to pay before you can receive water or sewer service. There may be a period required to construct lines or other facilities necessary to provide water or sewer service to your property. You are advised to determine if the property is in a certificated area and contact the utility service provider to determine the cost that you will be required to pay and the period, if any, that is

Initialed for identification by Buyer_____ _____ and Seller _____ _____   TREC NO. 20-10

required to provide water or sewer service to your property. The undersigned Buyer hereby acknowledges receipt of the foregoing notice at or before the execution of a binding contract for the purchase of the real property described in Paragraph 2 or at closing of purchase of the real property.

(7) PUBLIC IMPROVEMENT DISTRICTS: If the Property is in a public improvement district, §5.014, Property Code, requires Seller to notify Buyer as follows: As a purchaser of this parcel of real property you are obligated to pay an assessment to a municipality or county for an improvement project undertaken by a public improvement district under Chapter 372, Local Government Code. The assessment may be due annually or in periodic installments. More information concerning the amount of the assessment and the due dates of that assessment may be obtained from the municipality or county levying the assessment. The amount of the assessments is subject to change. Your failure to pay the assessments could result in a lien on and the foreclosure of your property.

7. PROPERTY CONDITION:

A. ACCESS, INSPECTIONS AND UTILITIES: Seller shall permit Buyer and Buyer's agents access to the Property at reasonable times. Buyer may have the Property inspected by inspectors selected by Buyer and licensed by TREC or otherwise permitted by law to make inspections. Seller at Seller's expense shall turn on existing utilities for inspections.

B. SELLER'S DISCLOSURE NOTICE PURSUANT TO §5.008, TEXAS PROPERTY CODE (Notice): (Check one box only)
- ❑ (1) Buyer has received the Notice.
- ❑ (2) Buyer has not received the Notice. Within _____ days after the effective date of this contract, Seller shall deliver the Notice to Buyer. If Buyer does not receive the Notice, Buyer may terminate this contract at any time prior to the closing and the earnest money will be refunded to Buyer. If Seller delivers the Notice, Buyer may terminate this contract for any reason within 7 days after Buyer receives the Notice or prior to the closing, whichever first occurs, and the earnest money will be refunded to Buyer.
- ❑ (3)The Seller is not required to furnish the notice under the Texas Property Code.

C. SELLER'S DISCLOSURE OF LEAD-BASED PAINT AND LEAD-BASED PAINT HAZARDS is required by Federal law for a residential dwelling constructed prior to 1978.

D. ACCEPTANCE OF PROPERTY CONDITION: (Check one box only)
- ❑ (1) Buyer accepts the Property in its present condition.
- ❑ (2) Buyer accepts the Property in its present condition provided Seller, at Seller's expense, shall complete the following specific repairs and treatments: _____ _____.(Do not insert general phrases, such as "subject to inspections" that do not identify specific repairs.)

NOTICE TO BUYER AND SELLER: Buyer's agreement to accept the Property in its present condition under Paragraph 7D(1) or (2) does not preclude Buyer from inspecting the Property under Paragraph 7A, from negotiating repairs or treatments in a subsequent amendment, or from terminating this contract during the Option Period, if any.

E. LENDER REQUIRED REPAIRS AND TREATMENTS: Unless otherwise agreed in writing, neither party is obligated to pay for lender required repairs, which includes treatment for wood destroying insects. If the parties do not agree to pay for the lender required repairs or treatments, this contract will terminate and the earnest money will be refunded to Buyer. If the cost of lender required repairs and treatments exceeds 5% of the Sales Price, Buyer may terminate this contract and the earnest money will be refunded to Buyer.

F. COMPLETION OF REPAIRS AND TREATMENTS: Unless otherwise agreed in writing, Seller shall complete all agreed repairs and treatments prior to the Closing Date. All required permits must be obtained, and repairs and treatments must be performed by persons who are licensed or otherwise authorized by law to provide such repairs or treatments. At Buyer's election, any transferable warranties received by Seller with respect to the repairs and treatments will be transferred to Buyer at Buyer's expense. If Seller fails to complete any agreed repairs and treatments prior to the Closing Date, Buyer may do so and receive reimbursement from Seller at closing. The Closing Date will be extended up to 15 days, if necessary, to complete repairs and treatments.

G. ENVIRONMENTAL MATTERS: Buyer is advised that the presence of wetlands, toxic substances, including asbestos and wastes or other environmental hazards, or the presence of a threatened or endangered species or its habitat may affect Buyer's intended use of the Property. If Buyer is concerned about these matters, an addendum promulgated by TREC or required by the parties should be used.

Initialed for identification by Buyer_____ _____ and Seller _____ _____   TREC NO. 20-10

H. RESIDENTIAL SERVICE CONTRACTS: Buyer may purchase a residential service contract from a residential service company licensed by TREC. If Buyer purchases a residential service contract, Seller shall reimburse Buyer at closing for the cost of the residential service contract in an amount not exceeding $_____. Buyer should review any residential service contract for the scope of coverage, exclusions and limitations. **The purchase of a residential service contract is optional. Similar coverage may be purchased from various companies authorized to do business in Texas.**

8. **BROKERS' FEES:** All obligations of the parties for payment of brokers' fees are contained in separate written agreements.

9. **CLOSING:**

A. The closing of the sale will be on or before _____, 20_____, or within 7 days after objections made under Paragraph 6D have been cured or waived, whichever date is later (Closing Date). If either party fails to close the sale by the Closing Date, the non-defaulting party may exercise the remedies contained in Paragraph 15.

B. At closing:

(1) Seller shall execute and deliver a general warranty deed conveying title to the Property to Buyer and showing no additional exceptions to those permitted in Paragraph 6 and furnish tax statements or certificates showing no delinquent taxes on the Property.

(2) Buyer shall pay the Sales Price in good funds acceptable to the escrow agent.

(3) Seller and Buyer shall execute and deliver any notices, statements, certificates, affidavits, releases, loan documents and other documents reasonably required for the closing of the sale and the issuance of the Title Policy.

(4) There will be no liens, assessments, or security interests against the Property which will not be satisfied out of the sales proceeds unless securing the payment of any loans assumed by Buyer and assumed loans will not be in default.

(5) If the Property is subject to a lease, Seller shall (i) deliver to Buyer the lease(s) and the move-in condition form signed by the tenant, if any, and (ii) transfer security deposits (as defined under §92.102, Property Code) if any, to Buyer. In such an event, Buyer shall deliver to the tenant a signed statement acknowledging that the Buyer has received the security deposit and is responsible for the return of the security deposit, and specifying the exact dollar amount of the security deposit.

10. **POSSESSION:** Seller shall deliver to Buyer possession of the Property in its present or required condition, ordinary wear and tear excepted: ❑upon closing and funding ❑according to a temporary residential lease promulgated by TREC or other written lease required by the parties. Any possession by Buyer prior to closing or by Seller after closing which is not authorized by a written lease will establish a tenancy at sufferance relationship between the parties. **Consult your insurance agent prior to change of ownership and possession because insurance coverage may be limited or terminated. The absence of a written lease or appropriate insurance coverage may expose the parties to economic loss.**

11. **SPECIAL PROVISIONS:** (Insert only factual statements and business details applicable to the sale. TREC rules prohibit licensees from adding factual statements or business details for which a contract addendum, lease or other form has been promulgated by TREC for mandatory use.)

Initialed for identification by Buyer_____ _____ and Seller _____ _____   TREC NO. 20-10

Contract Concerning _____ Page 6 of 9   8-01-2011
(Address of Property)

12. SETTLEMENT AND OTHER EXPENSES:
    A. The following expenses must be paid at or prior to closing:
       (1) Expenses payable by Seller (Seller's Expenses):
          (a) Releases of existing liens, including prepayment penalties and recording fees; release of Seller's loan liability; tax statements or certificates; preparation of deed; one-half of escrow fee; and other expenses payable by Seller under this contract.
          (b) Seller shall also pay an amount not to exceed $ _____ to be applied in the following order: Buyer's Expenses which Buyer is prohibited from paying by FHA, VA, Texas Veterans Land Board or other governmental loan programs, and then to other Buyer's Expenses as allowed by the lender.
       (2) Expenses payable by Buyer (Buyer's Expenses): Appraisal fees; loan application fees; adjusted origination charges; credit reports; preparation of loan documents; interest on the notes from date of disbursement to one month prior to dates of first monthly payments; recording fees; copies of easements and restrictions; loan title policy with endorsements required by lender; loan-related inspection fees; photos; amortization schedules; one-half of escrow fee; all prepaid items, including required premiums for flood and hazard insurance, reserve deposits for insurance, ad valorem taxes and special governmental assessments; final compliance inspection; courier fee; repair inspection; underwriting fee; wire transfer fee; expenses incident to any loan; Private Mortgage Insurance Premium (PMI), VA Loan Funding Fee, or FHA Mortgage Insurance Premium (MIP) as required by the lender; and other expenses payable by Buyer under this contract.
    B. If any expense exceeds an amount expressly stated in this contract for such expense to be paid by a party, that party may terminate this contract unless the other party agrees to pay such excess. Buyer may not pay charges and fees expressly prohibited by FHA, VA, Texas Veterans Land Board or other governmental loan program regulations.

13. PRORATIONS: Taxes for the current year, interest, maintenance fees, assessments, dues and rents will be prorated through the Closing Date. The tax proration may be calculated taking into consideration any change in exemptions that will affect the current year's taxes. If taxes for the current year vary from the amount prorated at closing, the parties shall adjust the prorations when tax statements for the current year are available. If taxes are not paid at or prior to closing, Buyer shall pay taxes for the current year.

14. CASUALTY LOSS: If any part of the Property is damaged or destroyed by fire or other casualty after the effective date of this contract, Seller shall restore the Property to its previous condition as soon as reasonably possible, but in any event by the Closing Date. If Seller fails to do so due to factors beyond Seller's control, Buyer may (a) terminate this contract and the earnest money will be refunded to Buyer (b) extend the time for performance up to 15 days and the Closing Date will be extended as necessary or (c) accept the Property in its damaged condition with an assignment of insurance proceeds and receive credit from Seller at closing in the amount of the deductible under the insurance policy. Seller's obligations under this paragraph are independent of any other obligations of Seller under this contract.

15. DEFAULT: If Buyer fails to comply with this contract, Buyer will be in default, and Seller may (a) enforce specific performance, seek such other relief as may be provided by law, or both, or (b) terminate this contract and receive the earnest money as liquidated damages, thereby releasing both parties from this contract. If, due to factors beyond Seller's control, Seller fails within the time allowed to make any non-casualty repairs or deliver the Commitment, or survey, if required of Seller, Buyer may (a) extend the time for performance up to 15 days and the Closing Date will be extended as necessary or (b) terminate this contract as the sole remedy and receive the earnest money. If Seller fails to comply with this contract for any other reason, Seller will be in default and Buyer may (a) enforce specific performance, seek such other relief as may be provided by law, or both, or (b) terminate this contract and receive the earnest money, thereby releasing both parties from this contract.

16. MEDIATION: It is the policy of the State of Texas to encourage resolution of disputes through alternative dispute resolution procedures such as mediation. Any dispute between Seller and Buyer related to this contract which is not resolved through informal discussion ☐will ☐will not be submitted to a mutually acceptable mediation service or provider. The parties to the mediation shall bear the mediation costs equally. This paragraph does not preclude a party from seeking equitable relief from a court of competent jurisdiction.

17. ATTORNEY'S FEES: A Buyer, Seller, Listing Broker, Other Broker, or escrow agent who prevails in any legal proceeding related to this contract is entitled to recover reasonable attorney's fees and all costs of such proceeding.

Initialed for identification by Buyer_____ _____ and Seller _____ _____   TREC NO. 20-10

Contract Concerning _____ Page 7 of 9   8-01-2011
(Address of Property)

18. ESCROW:
    A. ESCROW: The escrow agent is not (i) a party to this contract and does not have liability for the performance or nonperformance of any party to this contract, (ii) liable for interest on the earnest money and (iii) liable for the loss of any earnest money caused by the failure of any financial institution in which the earnest money has been deposited unless the financial institution is acting as escrow agent.
    B. EXPENSES: At closing, the earnest money must be applied first to any cash down payment, then to Buyer's Expenses and any excess refunded to Buyer. If no closing occurs, escrow agent may: (i) require a written release of liability of the escrow agent from all parties, (ii) require payment of unpaid expenses incurred on behalf of a party, and (iii) only deduct from the earnest money the amount of unpaid expenses incurred on behalf of the party receiving the earnest money.
    C. DEMAND: Upon termination of this contract, either party or the escrow agent may send a release of earnest money to each party and the parties shall execute counterparts of the release and deliver same to the escrow agent. If either party fails to execute the release, either party may make a written demand to the escrow agent for the earnest money. If only one party makes written demand for the earnest money, escrow agent shall promptly provide a copy of the demand to the other party. If escrow agent does not receive written objection to the demand from the other party within 15 days, escrow agent may disburse the earnest money to the party making demand reduced by the amount of unpaid expenses incurred on behalf of the party receiving the earnest money and escrow agent may pay the same to the creditors. If escrow agent complies with the provisions of this paragraph, each party hereby releases escrow agent from all adverse claims related to the disbursal of the earnest money.
    D. DAMAGES: Any party who wrongfully fails or refuses to sign a release acceptable to the escrow agent within 7 days of receipt of the request will be liable to the other party for liquidated damages in an amount equal to the sum of: (i) three times the amount of the earnest money; (ii) the earnest money; (iii) reasonable attorney's fees; and (iv) all costs of suit.
    E. NOTICES: Escrow agent's notices will be effective when sent in compliance with Paragraph 21. Notice of objection to the demand will be deemed effective upon receipt by escrow agent.

19. REPRESENTATIONS: All covenants, representations and warranties in this contract survive closing. If any representation of Seller in this contract is untrue on the Closing Date, Seller will be in default. Unless expressly prohibited by written agreement, Seller may continue to show the Property and receive, negotiate and accept back up offers.

20. FEDERAL TAX REQUIREMENTS: If Seller is a "foreign person," as defined by applicable law, or if Seller fails to deliver an affidavit to Buyer that Seller is not a "foreign person," then Buyer shall withhold from the sales proceeds an amount sufficient to comply with applicable tax law and deliver the same to the Internal Revenue Service together with appropriate tax forms. Internal Revenue Service regulations require filing written reports if currency in excess of specified amounts is received in the transaction.

21. NOTICES: All notices from one party to the other must be in writing and are effective when mailed to, hand-delivered at, or transmitted by facsimile or electronic transmission as follows:

To Buyer at: _____   **To Seller at:** _____

_____   _____

_____   _____

_____   _____

Telephone: (____) _____   Telephone: (____) _____

Facsimile: (____) _____   Facsimile: (____) _____

E-mail: _____   E-mail: _____

Initialed for identification by Buyer_____ _____ and Seller _____ _____   TREC NO. 20-10

Contract Concerning _____ Page 8 of 9   8-01-2011
(Address of Property)

22. AGREEMENT OF PARTIES: This contract contains the entire agreement of the parties and cannot be changed except by their written agreement. Addenda which are a part of this contract are (Check all applicable boxes):

☐ Third Party Financing Addendum for Credit Approval

☐ Seller Financing Addendum

☐ Addendum for Property Subject to Mandatory Membership in a Property Owners Association

☐ Buyer's Temporary Residential Lease

☐ Loan Assumption Addendum

☐ Addendum for Sale of Other Property by Buyer

☐ Addendum for Reservation of Oil, Gas and Other Minerals

☐ Addendum for "Back-Up" Contract

☐ Addendum for Coastal Area Property

☐ Environmental Assessment, Threatened or Endangered Species and Wetlands Addendum

☐ Seller's Temporary Residential Lease

☐ Short Sale Addendum

☐ Addendum for Property Located Seaward of the Gulf Intracoastal Waterway

☐ Addendum for Seller's Disclosure of Information on Lead-based Paint and Lead-based Paint Hazards as Required by Federal Law

☐ Other (list): _____

23. TERMINATION OPTION: For nominal consideration, the receipt of which is hereby acknowledged by Seller, and Buyer's agreement to pay Seller $_____ (Option Fee) within 2 days after the effective date of this contract, Seller grants Buyer the unrestricted right to terminate this contract by giving notice of termination to Seller within _____ days after the effective date of this contract (Option Period). If no dollar amount is stated as the Option Fee or if Buyer fails to pay the Option Fee to Seller within the time prescribed, this paragraph will not be a part of this contract and Buyer shall not have the unrestricted right to terminate this contract. If Buyer gives notice of termination within the time prescribed, the Option Fee will not be refunded; however, any earnest money will be refunded to Buyer. The Option Fee ☐ will ☐ will not be credited to the Sales Price at closing. **Time is of the essence for this paragraph and strict compliance with the time for performance is required.**

24. CONSULT AN ATTORNEY: TREC rules prohibit real estate licensees from giving legal advice. READ THIS CONTRACT CAREFULLY. If you do not understand the effect of this contract, consult an attorney BEFORE signing.

Buyer's
Attorney is: _____

Telephone: (____)_____

Facsimile: (____)_____

E-mail: _____

Seller's
Attorney is: _____

Telephone: (____)_____

Facsimile: (____)_____

E-mail: _____

EXECUTED the _____ day of _____, 20_____ (EFFECTIVE DATE).
(BROKER: FILL IN THE DATE OF FINAL ACCEPTANCE.)

_____
Buyer

_____
Buyer

_____
Seller

_____
Seller

The form of this contract has been approved by the Texas Real Estate Commission. TREC forms are intended for use only by trained real estate licensees. No representation is made as to the legal validity or adequacy of any provision in any specific transactions. It is not intended for complex transactions. Texas Real Estate Commission, P.O. Box 12188, Austin, TX 78711-2188, (512) 936-3000 (http://www.trec.texas.gov) TREC NO. 20-10. This form replaces TREC NO. 20-8.

TREC NO. 20-10

Contract Concerning _____	Page 9 of 9 8-01-2011
(Address of Property)	

BROKER INFORMATION

Other Broker Firm _____ License No. _____

represents ☐ Buyer only as Buyer's agent
☐ Seller as Listing Broker's subagent

Licensed Supervisor of Associate ___ Telephone ___

Associate ___ Telephone ___

Other Broker's Address ___ Facsimile ___

City ___ State ___ Zip ___

Associate Email Address ___

Listing Broker Firm _____ License No. _____

represents ☐ Seller and Buyer as an intermediary
☐ Seller only as Seller's agent

Licensed Supervisor of Associate ___ Telephone ___

Listing Associate ___ Telephone ___

Listing Broker's Office Address ___ Facsimile ___

City ___ State ___ Zip ___

Listing Associate's Email Address ___

Selling Associate ___ Telephone ___

Selling Associate's Office Address ___ Facsimile ___

City ___ State ___ Zip ___

Selling Associate's Email Address ___

Listing Broker has agreed to pay Other Broker _____ of the total sales price when the Listing Broker's fee is received. Escrow agent is authorized and directed to pay other Broker from Listing Broker's fee at closing.

OPTION FEE RECEIPT

Receipt of $_____ (Option Fee) in the form of _____ is acknowledged.

Seller or Listing Broker _____ Date _____

CONTRACT AND EARNEST MONEY RECEIPT

Receipt of ☐ Contract and ☐ $_____ Earnest Money in the form of _____ is acknowledged.
Escrow Agent: _____ Date: _____

By: _____

Email Address _____

Address _____ Telephone (___) _____

City ___ State ___ Zip ___ Facsimile: (___) _____

TREC NO. 20-10

Reprinted by permission of Texas Real Estate Commission.

PROMULGATED BY THE TEXAS REAL ESTATE COMMISSION (TREC)   11-29-2010

ADDENDUM FOR PROPERTY SUBJECT TO MANDATORY MEMBERSHIP IN A PROPERTY OWNERS ASSOCIATION
(NOT FOR USE WITH CONDOMINIUMS)
ADDENDUM TO CONTRACT CONCERNING THE PROPERTY AT

_____

(Street Address and City)

_____

(Name of Property Owners Association)

A. SUBDIVISION INFORMATION: "Subdivision Information" means: (i) the restrictions applying to the subdivision, (ii) the bylaws and rules of the Property Owners Association (Association), and (iii) a resale certificate, all of which comply with Section 207.003 of the Texas Property Code.

(Check only one box):

☐ 1. Within _____ days after the effective date of the contract, Seller shall, at Seller's expense, deliver the Subdivision Information to Buyer. If Buyer does not receive the Subdivision Information, Buyer may terminate the contract at any time prior to closing and the earnest money will be refunded to Buyer. If Seller delivers the Subdivision Information, Buyer may terminate the contract for any reason within 7 days after Buyer receives the Subdivision Information or prior to closing, whichever first occurs, and the earnest money will be refunded to Buyer.

☐ 2. Buyer has received and approved the Subdivision Information before signing the contract. Buyer ☐ does ☐ does not require an updated resale certificate. If Buyer requires an updated resale certificate, Seller, at Buyer's expense, shall deliver it to Buyer within 10 days after receiving payment for the updated resale certificate from Buyer. Buyer may terminate this contract and the earnest money will be refunded to Buyer if Seller fails to deliver the updated resale certificate within the time required.

☐ 3. Buyer does not require delivery of the Subdivision Information.

If Seller becomes aware of any material changes in the Subdivision Information, Seller shall promptly give notice to Buyer.

Buyer may terminate the contract prior to closing by giving written notice to Seller if: (i) any of the Subdivision Information provided was not true; or (ii) any material adverse change in the Subdivision Information occurs prior to closing, and the earnest money will be refunded to Buyer.

B. FEES: Except as provided by Paragraph C, Buyer shall pay any and all Association fees or other charges resulting from the transfer of the Property not to exceed $_____ and Seller shall pay any excess.

C. DEPOSITS FOR RESERVES: Buyer shall pay any deposits for reserves required at closing by the Association.

NOTICE TO BUYER REGARDING REPAIRS BY THE ASSOCIATION: The Association may have the sole responsibility to make certain repairs to the Property. If you are concerned about the condition of any part of the Property which the Association is required to repair, you should not sign the contract unless you are satisfied that the Association will make the desired repairs.

_____   _____
Buyer   Seller

_____   _____
Buyer   Seller

The form of this addendum has been approved by the Texas Real Estate Commission for use only with similarly approved or promulgated forms of contracts. Such approval relates to this contract form only. TREC forms are intended for use only by trained real estate licensees. No representation is made as to the legal validity or adequacy of any provision in any specific transactions. It is not intended for complex transactions. Texas Real Estate Commission, P.O. Box 12188, Austin, TX 78711-2188, (512) 459-6544 (http://www.trec.state.tx.us) TREC No. 36-6. This form replaces TREC No. 36-5.

TREC NO. 36-6

Reprinted by permission of Texas Real Estate Commission.

PROMULGATED BY THE TEXAS REAL ESTATE COMMISSION (TREC)   02-13-06

AMENDMENT
TO CONTRACT CONCERNING THE PROPERTY AT

_____
(Street Address and City)

Seller and Buyer amend the contract as follows: (check each applicable box)

☐(1) The Sales Price in Paragraph 3 of the contract is:
   A. Cash portion of Sales Price payable by Buyer at closing ....$_____
   B. Sum of financing described in the contract...$_____
   C. Sales Price (Sum of A and B) ....$_____

☐(2) In addition to any repairs and treatments otherwise required by the contract, Seller, at Seller's expense, shall complete the following repairs and treatments:

☐(3) The date in Paragraph 9 of the contract is changed to _____, 20_____.

☐(4) The amount in Paragraph 12A(1)(b) of the contract is changed to $_____.

☐(5) The cost of lender required repairs and treatment, as itemized on the attached list, will be paid as follows: $_____ by Seller; $_____ by Buyer.

☐(6) Buyer has paid Seller an additional Option Fee of $_____ for an extension of the unrestricted right to terminate the contract on or before _____, 20_____. This additional Option Fee ☐ will ☐ will not be credited to the Sales Price.

☐(7) Buyer waives the unrestricted right to terminate the contract for which the Option Fee was paid.

☐(8) The date for Buyer to give written notice to Seller that Buyer cannot obtain Financing Approval as set forth in the Third Party Financing Condition Addendum is changed to _____, 20_____.

☐(9) **Other Modifications**: (Insert only factual statements and business details applicable to this sale.)

EXECUTED the _____day of _____, 20_____ . (BROKER: FILL IN THE DATE OF FINAL ACCEPTANCE.)

_____   _____
Buyer   Seller

_____   _____
Buyer   Seller

This form has been approved by the Texas Real Estate Commission for use with similarly approved or promulgated contract forms. Such approval relates to this form only. TREC forms are intended for use only by trained real estate licensees. No representation is made as to the legal validity or adequacy of any provision in any specific transactions. It is not intended for complex transactions. Texas Real Estate Commission, P.O. Box 12188, Austin, TX 78711-2188, 1-800-250-8732 or (512) 459-6544 (http://www.trec.state.tx.us) TREC No. 39-6. This form replaces TREC No. 39-5.

TREC NO. 39-6

Reprinted by permission of Texas Real Estate Commission.

11-29-2010

PROMULGATED BY THE TEXAS REAL ESTATE COMMISSION (TREC)

THIRD PARTY FINANCING ADDENDUM FOR CREDIT APPROVAL

TO CONTRACT CONCERNING THE PROPERTY AT

_____

(Street Address and City)

Buyer shall apply promptly for all financing described below and make every reasonable effort to obtain credit approval for the financing (Credit Approval). Buyer shall furnish all information and documents required by lender for Credit Approval. Credit Approval will be deemed to have been obtained when (1) the terms of the loan(s) described below are available and (2) lender determines that Buyer has satisfied all of lender's requirements related to Buyer's assets, income and credit history. If Buyer cannot obtain Credit Approval, Buyer may give written notice to Seller within _____ days after the effective date of this contract and this contract will terminate and the earnest money will be refunded to Buyer. **If Buyer does not give such notice within the time required, this contract will no longer be subject to Credit Approval. Time is of the essence for this paragraph and strict compliance with the time for performance is required.**

NOTE: Credit Approval does not include approval of lender's underwriting requirements for the Property, as specified in Paragraph 4.A.(1) of the contract.

Each note must be secured by vendor's and deed of trust liens.

CHECK APPLICABLE BOXES:

❑ A. CONVENTIONAL FINANCING:
    ❑ (1) A first mortgage loan in the principal amount of $ _____ (excluding any financed PMI premium), due in full in _____ year(s), with interest not to exceed _____% per annum for the first _____year(s) of the loan with Adjusted Origination Charges as shown on Buyer's Good Faith Estimate for the loan not to exceed _____ % of the loan.
    ❑ (2) A second mortgage loan in the principal amount of $_____(excluding any financed PMI premium), due in full in _____year(s), with interest not to exceed _____% per annum for the first _____year(s) of the loan with Adjusted Origination Charges as shown on Buyer's Good Faith Estimate for the loan not to exceed _____ % of the loan.
❑ B. TEXAS VETERANS LOAN: A loan(s) from the Texas Veterans Land Board of $_____ for a period in the total amount of _____years at the interest rate established by the Texas Veterans Land Board.
❑ C. FHA INSURED FINANCING: A Section _____ FHA insured loan of not less than $_____ (excluding any financed MIP), amortizable monthly for not less than _____years, with interest not to exceed _____% per annum for the first _____year(s) of the loan with Adjusted Origination Charges as shown on Buyer's Good Faith Estimate for the loan not to exceed _____ % of the loan. As required by HUD-FHA, if FHA valuation is unknown, "_It is expressly agreed that, notwithstanding any other provision of this contract, the purchaser (Buyer) shall not be obligated to complete the purchase of the Property described herein or to incur any penalty by forfeiture of earnest money deposits or otherwise unless the purchaser (Buyer) has been given in accordance with HUD/FHA or VA requirements a written statement issued by the Federal Housing Commissioner, Department of Veterans Affairs, or a Direct Endorsement Lender setting forth the appraised value of the Property of not less than $_____. The purchaser (Buyer) shall have the privilege and option of proceeding with consummation of the contract without regard to the_

Initialed for identification by Buyer_____ _____ and Seller_____ _____

TREC NO. 40-4

Third Party Financing Condition Addendum Concerning   Page 2 of 2 11-29-2010

_____
(Address of Property)

amount of the appraised valuation. The appraised valuation is arrived at to determine the maximum mortgage the Department of Housing and Urban Development will insure. HUD does not warrant the value or the condition of the Property. The purchaser (Buyer) should satisfy himself/herself that the price and the condition of the Property are acceptable."

☐ D. VA GUARANTEED FINANCING: A VA guaranteed loan of not less than $_____ (excluding any financed Funding Fee), amortizable monthly for not less than_____years, with interest not to exceed_____% per annum for the first _____year(s) of the loan with Adjusted Origination Charges as shown on Buyer's Good Faith Estimate for the loan not to exceed _____% of the loan.

VA NOTICE TO BUYER: "It is expressly agreed that, notwithstanding any other provisions of this contract, the Buyer shall not incur any penalty by forfeiture of earnest money or otherwise or be obligated to complete the purchase of the Property described herein, if the contract purchase price or cost exceeds the reasonable value of the Property established by the Department of Veterans Affairs. The Buyer shall, however, have the privilege and option of proceeding with the consummation of this contract without regard to the amount of the reasonable value established by the Department of Veterans Affairs."

If Buyer elects to complete the purchase at an amount in excess of the reasonable value established by VA, Buyer shall pay such excess amount in cash from a source which Buyer agrees to disclose to the VA and which Buyer represents will not be from borrowed funds except as approved by VA. If VA reasonable value of the Property is less than the Sales Price, Seller may reduce the Sales Price to an amount equal to the VA reasonable value and the sale will be closed at the lower Sales Price with proportionate adjustments to the down payment and the loan amount.

Buyer hereby authorizes any lender to furnish to the Seller or Buyer or their representatives information relating only to the status of Credit Approval of Buyer.

_____   _____
Buyer   Seller

_____   _____
Buyer   Seller

This form has been approved by the Texas Real Estate Commission for use with similarly approved or promulgated contract forms. Such approval relates to this form only. TREC forms are intended for use only by trained real estate licensees. No representation is made as to the legal validity or adequacy of any provision in any specific transactions. It is not intended for complex transactions. Texas Real Estate Commission, P.O. Box 12188, Austin, TX 78711-2188, (512) 459-6544 (http://www.trec.state.tx.us) TREC No. 40-4. This form replaces TREC No. 40-3.

TREC NO. 40-4

Reprinted by permission of Texas Real Estate Commission.

PROMULGATED BY THE TEXAS REAL ESTATE COMMISSION (TREC)   12-15-08

ADDENDUM FOR RESERVATION OF OIL, GAS, AND OTHER MINERALS

ADDENDUM TO CONTRACT CONCERNING THE PROPERTY AT

_____
(Street Address and City)

_____

NOTICE: For use only if Seller reserves all or a portion of the Mineral Estate.

A. "Mineral Estate" means all oil, gas, and other minerals in or under the Property, any royalty under any existing or future lease covering any part of the Property, surface rights (including rights of ingress and egress), production and drilling rights, lease payments, and all related benefits.

B. The Mineral Estate owned by Seller, if any, will be conveyed unless reserved as follows (check one box only):

❑ (1) Seller reserves all of the Mineral Estate owned by Seller.

❑ (2) Seller reserves an undivided _____ % interest in the Mineral Estate owned by Seller. *NOTE: If Seller does not own all of the Mineral Estate, Seller reserves only this percentage of Seller's interest.*

C. Seller ❑ waives ❑ does not waive Seller's surface rights (including rights of ingress and egress). *NOTE: Any waiver of surface rights by Seller does not affect any surface rights that may be held by others.*

D. If B(2) applies, Seller shall, on or before the Closing Date, provide Buyer contact information known to Seller for any existing lessee.

If either party is concerned about the legal rights or impact of the above provisions, that party is advised to consult an attorney BEFORE signing.

TREC rules prohibit real estate licensees from giving legal advice.

_____   _____
Buyer   Seller

_____   _____
Buyer   Seller

The form of this addendum has been approved by the Texas Real Estate Commission for use only with similarly approved or promulgated forms of contracts. Such approval relates to this contract form only. TREC forms are intended for use only by trained real estate licensees. No representation is made as to the legal validity or adequacy of any provision in any specific transactions. It is not intended for complex transactions. Texas Real Estate Commission, P.O. Box 12188, Austin, TX 78711-2188, 1-800-250-8732 or (512) 459-6544 (http://www.trec.state.tx.us) TREC No. 44-0.

TREC NO. 44-0

Reprinted by permission of Texas Real Estate Commission.

PROMULGATED BY THE TEXAS REAL ESTATE COMMISSION (TREC)

12-15-08

SHORT SALE ADDENDUM

ADDENDUM TO CONTRACT CONCERNING THE PROPERTY AT

_____

(Street Address and City)

A. This contract involves a "short sale" of the Property. As used in this Addendum, "short sale" means that:

  (1) Seller's net proceeds at closing will be insufficient to pay the balance of Seller's mortgage loan; and

  (2) Seller requires:

    (a) the consent of the lienholder to sell the Property pursuant to this contract; and

    (b) the lienholder's agreement to:

      (i) accept Seller's net proceeds in full satisfaction of Seller's liability under the mortgage loan; and

      (ii) provide Seller an executed release of lien against the Property in a recordable format.

B. As used in this Addendum, "Seller's net proceeds" means the Sales Price less Seller's Expenses under Paragraph 12 of the contract and Seller's obligation to pay any brokerage fees.

C. The contract to which this Addendum is attached is binding upon execution by the parties and the earnest money and the Option Fee must be paid as provided in the contract. The contract is contingent on the satisfaction of Seller's requirements under Paragraph A(2) of this Addendum (Lienholder's Consent and Agreement). Seller shall apply promptly for and make every reasonable effort to obtain Lienholder's Consent and Agreement, and shall furnish all information and documents required by the lienholder. Except as provided by this Addendum, neither party is required to perform under the contract while it is contingent upon obtaining Lienholder's Consent and Agreement.

D. If Seller does not notify Buyer that Seller has obtained Lienholder's Consent and Agreement on or before _____, this contract terminates and the earnest money will be refunded to Buyer. Seller must notify Buyer immediately if Lienholder's Consent and Agreement is obtained. For purposes of performance, the effective date of the contract changes to the date Seller provides Buyer notice of the Lienholder's Consent and Agreement (Amended Effective Date).

E. This contract will terminate and the earnest money will be refunded to Buyer if the Lienholder refuses or withdraws its Consent and Agreement prior to closing and funding. Seller shall promptly notify Buyer of any lienholder's refusal to provide or withdrawal of a Lienholder's Consent and Agreement.

F. If Buyer has the unrestricted right to terminate this contract, the time for giving notice of termination begins on the effective date of the contract, continues after the Amended Effective Date and ends upon the expiration of Buyer's unrestricted right to terminate the contract under Paragraph 23.

G. For the purposes of this Addendum, time is of the essence. Strict compliance with the times for performance stated in this Addendum is required.

H. Seller authorizes any lienholder to furnish to Buyer or Buyer's representatives information relating to the status of the request for a Lienholder's Consent and Agreement.

I. If there is more than one lienholder or loan secured by the Property, this Addendum applies to each lienholder.

Buyer _____   Seller _____

Buyer _____   Seller _____

The form of this addendum has been approved by the Texas Real Estate Commission for use only with similarly approved or promulgated forms of contracts. Such approval relates to this contract form only. TREC forms are intended for use only by trained real estate licensees. No representation is made as to the legal validity or adequacy of any provision in any specific transactions. It is not intended for complex transactions. Texas Real Estate Commission, P.O. Box 12188, Austin, TX 78711-2188, 1-800-250-8732 or (512) 459-6544 (http://www.trec.state.tx.us) TREC No. 45-0.

TREC NO. 45-0

Reprinted by permission of Texas Real Estate Commission.

Index